Uganda Handbook

Mike Hodd
Angela Roche

Many travellers visit Uganda for two reasons – the gorillas and whitewater rafting. Neither is particularly cheap, with gorilla permits costing US$500 per person (with a proposed increase to US$750) and whitewater rafting costing around US$125 per person. Both, however, are unforgettable experiences.

The capital, Kampala, is a handsome city, set among seven hills, with a range of comfortable hotels, al fresco eating places, lively nightlife and a fine public garden.

There is not a huge amount to see in the towns outside of Kampala. Typically they will have a modest colonial centre, bustling markets and historical and cultural interest provided by the burial grounds of the kings.

Otherwise, the main attractions include game-viewing in Uganda's parks, particularly chimpanzees and monkeys as well as the gorillas; birdwatching and butterfly-viewing; trekking and climbing in the Rwenzoris and Mount Elgon; fishing, cruising and canoeing on the many lakes; and spectacular scenery on the route to Kisoro in the southwest. It is a compact country with good road links.

This page Giant lobelias at Lac de la Lune in the Rwenzori Mountains.
Previous page Uganda contains more than half the world's 820 endangered mountain gorillas.

SUDAN

Modole
(3020m)

Moyo
Koboko
Yumbe
Kitgum
Albert Nile
Kalongo
Arua
Rhino
Camp
Gulu

Goli
Pakwach
Victoria Nile
Lira

DR CONGO
7 〰 Murchison Falls
National Park
Kaberamaido
Budongo
Forest Reserve
Karuma
Wildlife
Reserve
Lake
Kwania
Lake
Albert
6 ♦
Hoima
Ziwa Rhino
Sanctuary
Nakasongola
Lake Kyogo

Semliki
National
Park
Toro-Semliki
Wildlife
Reserve
Kiboga
Luwero
Kamuli
Kaliro
Victoria Nile
Fort
Portal
Kibale
Mubende
Mityana
Kayunga
Bombo
Iganga
Rwenzori
National
Park
Kibale
National Park
KAMPALA
4
Jinja
8 ♦
Lake
George
Mpigi
2
Entebbe
Ngogwe
Kinoni
1
3
Equato
Lake
Edward
Queen Elizabeth
National Park
Masaka
Buggala I
Lyantonde
Bukasa I
Bushenyi
Kalisizo
Ssese
Islands
Kyotera
9
Lake Mburo
National Park
Lake Victoria
11
Bwindi Forest
Impenetrable
National Park
TANZANIA
10 ♦
Lake
Bunyonyi
12 ♦
Mgahinga
Gorilla
National
Park
RWANDA

4

Highlights

See colour maps back of book

1 Kampala
See the internationally acclaimed Ndere Dance Troupe's dazzling performance. ▸▸ page 66

2 Uganda Wildlife Education Centre
Sleep in a zoo, lulled by the sound of roaring lions' and other Ugandan wildlife. ▸▸ page 74

3 Ngamba Island, Lake Victoria
Visit the island for a close-up encounter with chimpanzees. Observe them as they feed or take them for a jungle walk. ▸▸ page 74

4 Bujagali Falls
For adrenaline junkies, Bujagali offers a 44-m-high bungee jump, rafting on Grade V rapids or jet-boating on the Nile. ▸▸ page 91

5 Kidepo National Park
Meet Bulbul, a large male elephant, while he inspects the bandas and grounds of Apoka Safari Lodge. ▸▸ pages 115 & 118

6 Ziwa Rhino Sanctuary
The sanctuary enables close inspection of these mega-faunas, the core of the planned re-introduction of rhino to Uganda. ▸▸ page 126

7 Murchison Falls National Park
Take a safari in a high-speed swamp boat through Lake Albert, north towards Sudan. ▸▸ page 131

8 Rwenzori Mountains
Trek to Margherita Peak at 5109 m, matching the achievement of 78-year-old Canadian Beryl Parks. ▸▸ pages 163 & 165

9 Lake Mburo National Park
Take a safari around the park by quad bike, on horseback or on foot. ▸▸ page 207

10 Lake Bunyonyi
Explore this peaceful island-studded lake by canoe, staying in a solar-powered geodome. ▸▸ page 218

11 Bwindi Impenetrable Forest National Park
Visit the rare mountain gorillas in their misty, forested hideaway, clambering up ridges that peak at over 2600 m. ▸▸ page 221 & 223

12 Mgahinga Gorilla National Park
Trek the rare, beautiful golden monkey, only found in the Virunga Mountains. ▸▸ page 230

A canoe glides peacefully across the glorious Lake Bunyonyi.

Pupils on the way to school, in the area of Kisoro, near the Rwandan border.

Contents

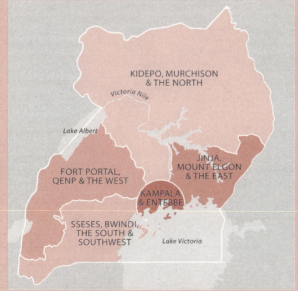

KIDEPO, MURCHISON & THE NORTH

Victoria Nile

Lake Albert

FORT PORTAL, QENP & THE WEST

JINJA, MOUNT ELGON & THE EAST

KAMPALA & ENTEBBE

SSESES, BWINDI, THE SOUTH & SOUTHWEST

Lake Victoria

Contents

Footprint features

Essentials

Planning your trip

Where to go

The minimum time to spend in Uganda is a week but a fortnight will enable visitors to enjoy most of Uganda's attractions. Its main draws are tracking the mountain gorillas, birdwatching, primate watching (with the world's highest concentration are in Kibale Forest), or the exciting whitewater activities on the Nile. These can be combined with visits to the national parks to see Uganda's diverse mammal population. It is a compact country with good road links between its main attractions.

Kampala and around

In an attractive setting on seven hills, the capital is a most handsome and friendly city and has a range of comfortable hotels, exciting nightlife and one of the finest public gardens in Africa. The interesting Uganda Museum is in the outskirts. Westwards is Mengo where the Kabaka's palace and Bugandan Parliament are found. Northeast is Makerere, Africa's oldest university. Beyond the city are the remains of the Kasubi Tombs, burial place of the Kabakas, the Kings of Buganda, a World Heritage Site, burnt down in March 2010 but being rebuilt. Nearby is Kabalagala, renowned for restaurants, bars and nightclubs. Munyonyo is a popular spot beside Lake Victoria, 13 km from central Kampala, along with nearby Mulungu Beach. Entebbe on the shore of Lake Victoria is also worth seeing, with its colonial buildings, botanical gardens and chimpanzee sanctuary on Ngamba Island.

Bwindi Impenetrable Forest and Mgahinga Gorilla National Park

Uganda offers the chance of tracking the endangered mountain gorillas in their spectacular volcanic montane setting, densely covered by tropical rainforests. Of the estimated 820 mountain gorillas remaining, about half are located in Uganda's far southwest in Bwindi Impenetrable Forest and Mgahinga Gorilla National Park. Visiting gorillas can vary greatly in price, depending on your accommodation and transport choices. Tracking them can be difficult given the terrain inhabited, scrambling up and down steep ravines, but coming face to face with these gentle giants is an unforgettable experience.

Queen Elizabeth, Kibale Forest, Lake Mburo and Murchison Falls national parks

These three are the best parks for game viewing. All the major wildlife attractions can be seen and there are no great crowds of visitors, and you can feel that you have the parks pretty much to yourself. Queen Elizabeth National Park (QENP) has 95 mammal species including the elusive tree-climbing lions in the southern sector. Nearby Lake Bunyonyi offers peaceful canoeing in glorious surroundings. Kibale Forest National Park has 13 species of primates, the world's greatest concentration.

Murchison Falls National Park

Located in northwest Uganda, Murchison Falls National Park has a wide diversity of vegetation and wildlife habitats. The Nile transects the park, transformed as it funnels through a 7-m cleft in the Rift Valley Escarpment into a spuming pool, 43 m below. Launch trips to the base of the falls give excellent views of hippos, giant Nile crocodiles and mammals drinking at the water's edge.

Packing for Uganda

Most travellers tend to take too much. Laundry services are generally cheap and speedy.

A travel pack, a hybrid backpack/suitcase (rather than a rigid suitcase) covers most eventualities and survives the rigours of a variety of modes of travel well. Bundle wrapping your clothes around a core object greatly reduces creasing and the volume of your clothes. Trekkers will need a sturdier backpack. A lock for your luggage is strongly advised as there are cases of pilfering by airport baggage handlers. Take valuable items such as cameras and radios as hand luggage on flights. Pack secure, screw-top bottles and double wrap shampoo or other liquids, as baggage holds are not always pressurized, and as the air in a bottle expands it can force out the liquid.

Select wrinkle-free clothes to avoid ironing. Modern microfibres, high-quality nylon or washable silk are quick drying compared to cotton or denim. Layering mix and match clothing enables comfort at varying temperatures. Bring a fleece, thermal vest or woollen clothing for the evenings. Take a hat, ideally wide brimmed to reduce sunburn risk, and protect your eyes from the sunlight. Bring comfortable shoes with socks as feet may swell in hot weather, and a pair of sandals.

The source of the Nile

Jinja and nearby Bujagali are the centre of one of Uganda's biggest tourist attractions. The source of the Nile offers thrilling whitewater rides through the upper cataracts, and other adventure activities such as bungee jumping, jet-boating and kayaking. There are also more sedate activities like fishing for giant perch or birdwatching. You can explore the local area on horseback, mountain bike or quad bike.

Mountains

The snow-capped Rwenzori Mountains, the highest range in Africa, run along the border with DR Congo. There is exceptional trekking on the lower slopes and some challenging peaks of over 5100 m for mountaineers. Or climb Mount Elgon, a heavily forested ancient volcano with peaks of over 4000 m, straddling the Kenyan border. Giant lobelia and other montane flora thrive and are quite like anything else you'll see in the country. Afterwards, you can relax by the magnificent Sipi Falls, on Mount Elgon's slopes.

Ssese Islands

Located on Lake Victoria just southwest of Kampala, these idyllic, unspoilt islands have sandy beaches and are an ideal place to relax.

When to go

Uganda, which straddles the equator, has a warm climate all year round with minor temperature fluctuations. More significant is the rainfall pattern when planning a trip. The heavy rainy season is March to May, and there are lighter rains in November and December. Generally there is some sunshine each day, even in the rainy seasons. From a practical point of view, it is probably best to try to avoid March-May, as the murram roads can become bogged (with lorries having to be dug out) and so journey times are extended. Gorilla tracking can become difficult as the jungle trails are very steep and it is hard to keep your footing on the slippery slopes. During heavy downpours climbing, trekking and camping on Rwenzori Mountains and Mount Elgon all increase in difficulty.

Many hotels have different high and low season rates, with the latter being significantly cheaper; it is always worth bartering. Fare prices rise on public transport at peak holiday times like Christmas and Easter. When the new national park fee structure is implemented a visit to track the gorillas will cost US$750 in high season (June-September and December-March) compared with US$500 in low season (October-November and April-May). See also box, page 26.

What to do

Birdwatching
For its size Uganda has Africa's greatest birdlife variety with over 1000 species recorded, including the rare shoebill stork. Around 100 species are unique to Uganda and some claim that you will be able to spot over 300 species in a day. Birders can join specialist tours visiting multiple sites lasting 1-2 weeks. If well prepared it is possible to see 450-500 species in 2-3 weeks. The prime birding sites are found in the western rainforests including Bwindi Impenetrable Forest National Park, Semliki National Park, Budongo Forest, Kibale Forest National Park and the Rwenzori Mountains. Even Entebbe's Botanical Gardens has several easily identifiable species. There are birdwatching trips by canoe down the Nile at Jinja.

Canoeing and whitewater rafting
Whether it's a casual 30-min paddle or a fully fledged expedition, a canoe trip on one of Uganda's rivers is great fun. For wildlife enthusiasts, gliding down the river in a canoe is an excellent way of getting a close look at birds and game without frightening them away. Lake Bunyonyi in the far southwest near Kabale offers peaceful canoeing trips between its many islands.

The source of the Nile at Jinja offers thrilling rides through the Upper Nile's cataracts and Grade V rapids.

Climbing, trekking and mountaineering
The snow-capped Rwenzoris offer some exceptional trips to both trekkers and mountaineers. Mount Elgon, a heavily forested ancient volcano straddling the Kenyan border, offers climbing excursions.

Fishing
Permits are required for sport fishing. Lake Victoria is home to the giant Nile perch, the world's largest game freshwater fish that can weigh over 100 kg. The main method of sport fishing is trolling with lures. Tilapia weighing up to 15 kg have been caught using bait. However, Lake Victoria has been overfished so alternative sites may offer better fishing. Fly fishing is available in **Sipi River Lodge**, see page 107. There is excellent fishing available at **Arra Fishing Lodge**, near Adjumani, T077-237 4560 (mob), www.nileperch.org. Several companies offer sport fishing including **Ugandan Safaris**, T0414-232657, www.ugandansafari.com. The **South African Travel Agency**, Uyaphi, www.uyaphi.com/uganda, offer a combination of fishing in Lake Victoria and at Murchison Falls. UWA have allocated a concession to develop the Gwara Fishing Concession at Karuma Wildlife Reserve.

Game viewing and safaris
The best national parks for game viewing are Lake Mburo, Queen Elizabeth, Kibale Forest and Murchison Falls. Compared to Kenya and Tanzania the amount of wildlife can be disappointing, but the horrendous visitor numbers there are avoided, and patient game-tracking can be rewarding. In Lake Mburo you can view wildlife on

foot, quad bike or horseback. The unique Katonga Wildlife Reserve can be explored by canoe. The remote Kidepo Valley National Park is arid savannah, with a great variety of mammals, easily viewed as they migrate south to access the water in the Narus Valley during the long dry season from Dec to late Mar. See also National parks and safaris, page 25.

Gorilla and chimpanzee tracking

Of the estimated 820 mountain gorillas remaining, about half are located in Uganda either at Bwindi Impenetrable Forest or Mgahinga Gorilla national parks. The scenery in this far southwestern area is mountainous and spectacular. A number of gorilla groups are now accustomed to close contact with humans. Chimpanzees can be seen in their forest habitat at Kibale, Budongo, Kasyoha Kitomi, and Kyambura River Gorge.

Getting there

Air

Uganda's international airport is at Entebbe, 37 km from the capital, Kampala, see page 46. It is an efficient, modern airport. You will probably be asked for a yellow fever vaccination certificate (see page 32) on arrival and given the confirmed outbreak in northern Uganda in November 2010 you will definitely require one on departure.

Alternatively, an economical way to access Uganda is to buy a cheap flight to Nairobi and then to travel overland or take a local connecting flight with Kenya Airways. Deals are often available at Kampala travel agents and these can sometimes be much better value than those on offer in Nairobi.

From Europe
Direct flights are only available from three cities in Europe: London (**British Airways**), Amsterdam (**AirFrance** and **KLM**) and Brussels (**Brussels Airlines**). Flight time from London is eight to nine hours and there are five departures a week.

From North America
There are no direct flights from North America to Uganda. Americans have to change planes in Europe or Dubai (**Emirates**).

From Africa
The only direct flights between Uganda and other African countries are: Addis Ababa (**Ethiopian Airlines**), Cairo (**Egypt Air**), Nairobi (**Kenya Airways**), Kigali (**Rwandair**) and Johannesburg (**South African Airways**).

Discount flight agents

UK and Ireland
Flightbookers, T0871-2235000, www.ebookers.com.
Flight Centre, T0844-8008660, www.flightcentre.co.uk.

STA Travel, T0871-2300040, www.statravel.co.uk.
Trailfinders, T0845-0585858, www.trailfinders.com.
Travelbag, T0871-7034698, www.travelbag.co.uk.

North America
Air Brokers International, T800-8833273, www.airbrokers.com.
STA Travel, T800-7814040, www.statravel.com.
Travel Cuts, T866-2469762 (Canada), www.travelcuts.com.

Australia and New Zealand
Flight Centre, T133-133 (Australia), www.flightcentre.com.au.
Skylink Travel, T02-9223 4277, www.skylink.com.au.
STA Travel, T134-782 (Australia), www.statravel.com.au, or T0800-474400 (New Zealand), www.statravel.co.nz.
Travel.com.au, T1300-130483, www.travel.com.au.

Rail

In 1997 the passenger rail service in Uganda was discontinued. There has only been a freight service since then and there are no plans to restart the passenger train service.

Road → *See also Getting around, page 19.*

Private vehicle
If you are driving into Uganda you must be registered in your home country and have registration plates, log book and third-party insurance. It is useful to have a *carnet de passage en douanes* from your home motoring organization (in the UK, contact the **RAC**). If you have no carnet you will need to buy a Temporary Import Licence (TIP) at immigration. A 30-day licence will cost between US$20 (for a 2000 kg vehicle) and US$100 (10,000 kg), payable in Ugandan shillings. Make sure you get a receipt, which is later stamped by the customs official. Do not give anybody your original documentation apart from the official sitting at the desk.

The interface between customs, immigration and police to clear vehicles through the border crossings is poor. There is much to-ing and fro-ing between several huts and departments to complete the process, including a ridiculous requirement to obtain a gate pass from the police (often just a scrap of paper torn from a notebook with the policeman's signature on it) to give to the man lifting the barrier.

At the Kenyan border expect to be swamped by people offering their services as border clearing agents. They are quite unnecessary as you can work through the process yourself. It can take between 30 minutes and two hours to get through the Ugandan bureaucracy at the border. If you are driving your own vehicle entering Tanzania you will require a letter from the government in Kampala confirming that the vehicle you are using is yours and not for sale. It is advisable to cross the border early in the morning and at the beginning of the week, as travelling after midweek may necessitate bribes for the official's weekend entertainment requirements. Most border crossings open from 0800-1700 but allow sufficient time for the bureaucracy.

Public transport
Kenya and Tanzania There are regular long-distance bus services between Uganda and her neighbouring countries, to Nairobi in Kenya (12-15 hours) and Dar es Salaam in Tanzania (28-35 hours). The bus from Kampala to Dar es Salaam takes up to 35 hours; actual road travel time is Kampala to Nairobi, 13 hours; Nairobi to Arusha six hours; Arusha to Dar es Salaam eight hours. Ideally, wherever possible avoid night-time driving, as road traffic accidents are more common, with a very high mortality rate.

Border crossings

Uganda–Kenya
Busia, the main road crossing, see page 98.
Malaba, see page 97.
Suam, see page 104.

Uganda–Tanzania
Kikagati, 61 km south of Mbarara crossing the Kagere River, is rarely used except by locals.
Mutukula, the main road crossing, see page 198.

Uganda–Rwanda
Gatuna/Katuna, open 24 hours, is the main road crossing, see page 218.
Kafunzo/Kakitumba is rarely used except by locals.
Kisoro–Kyanika/Cyanika Officials here sometimes request a 'letter of invitation' to enter Rwanda depending on your nationality. This apparently can be a letter from your hotel, which is possibly just an income-generating scam. See page 229.

Uganda–Sudan and Uganda–DR Congo
At the time of going to press, the FCO and US State Department had issued travel warnings against travel to the areas of DR Congo bordering Uganda and southern Sudan, so use of these border crossings is currently not recommended.

Rwanda See Transport, page 69, for long-distance bus services between Kampala and Kigali. There are frequent daily minibuses between Kabale in Uganda and the Katuna border post, the trip taking an hour (see page 218). There are frequent minibuses to Kigali from Katuna until mid-afternoon and they take about two hours. Check locally. The other crossing is from Kisoro in Uganda to Ruhengeri in Rwanda via Kyanika (see page 229). This route is less busy. **Note** Rwanda is one hour ahead of Uganda and they drive on the right-hand side of the road. US citizens do not need a visa to enter Rwanda.

DR Congo At the time of going to press, the FCO and US State Department advise against all travel to eastern and northeastern DR Congo due to insecurity and lawlessness. Should conditions improve the most reliable crossing is Kisoro to Rutshuru. Take a minibus from Kisoro (see page 226) to the border, about 10 km, and on the DR Congo side a motor-taxi (motorbike) to Rutshuru.

Alternatively, go from Kasese (see page 169) to Beni via Kasindi. There is infrequent public transport along this route. Some minibuses from Kasese go to the border at Kasindi. The leg from Kasindi to Beni can be awkward. There are some minibuses, but a motor-taxi (motorbike) is probably the best possibility. There are small hotels on both the Uganda and DR Congo sides of the border in case you are stuck there late at night. Finally, it is possible to cross the border from Kasese to Rutshuru, the border post being at Ishasha (see page 159). There are infrequent minibuses on this route and hitching is possible. The crossing to the north of Lake Albert at Arua (see page 124), although theoretically possible, is extremely difficult to access and security is uncertain.

Sudan At the time of going to press, the FCO and US State Department advise against all travel to southern Sudan due to risk of terrorism and political unrest linked to the referendum on self-determination. Should the situation improve, it is possible to travel by minibus to and from Juba to Gulu, via crossings at Moyo and Nimule to the west and east of the Nile respectively.

Overland trucks

Overland trucks safaris offer an opportunity to explore many of Uganda's places of interest by road in a compact group. It's a great adventure, traversing the country and making friends whilst camping under equatorial skies. The standard two-week trip is likely to include whitewater rafting adventures at Bujagali, tracking the gorillas, visiting the tree-climbing lions at Ishasha, hiking through Kyambura Gorge to see the chimpanzees, walking through the foothills of the Rwenzori Mountains, seeing the spectacular Murchison Falls and taking a river cruise below them, tracking the habituated rhinos at Ziwa Rhino Sanctuary before returning to Jinja and the source of the Nile where an extra day can be spent volunteering on a community project.

The following companies offer a Ugandan experience: **Exodus** (www.exodus.co.uk), **Explore** (www.explore.co.uk), **Kumuka** (www.kumuka.com) and **Overland Africa** (www.overland africa.com). However, many other companies combine their trips with Kenyan, Tanzanian or Rwandan itineraries.

Getting around

Air

Eagle Air (T0414-344292, www.flyeagleuganda.com) offer scheduled internal flights to northern Ugandan towns including Gulu, Kitgum, Kidepo, Adjumani, Arua and Moyo and special diversions on request to Kotido, Pakuba and Nebbi.

It is also possible to charter light aircraft with **Eagle Air** and **Kampala Aeroclub** (T077-270 6107 (mob), www.flyuganda.com) to fly to airstrips around the country. These are located in Moroto, North Soroti, Lira, Kasese and Ishasha. There are also airfields near the national parks of Murchison Falls, Kidepo Valley, Queen Elizabeth, Mount Elgon, the Bwindi Impenetrable Forest and Mgahinga. Toro-Semliki Wildlife Reserve also has one. However, bear in mind that these charter flights are prohibitively expensive and are mostly used by a few wealthy visitors who book them via a tour operator before arrival in Uganda.

Lake

Boats

Steamers, ferries and small cargo boats sail between ports on the shore of Lake Victoria and the Ssese Islands. There is no lake ferry service leaving from Port Bell at present.

Road

There are good roads on the main routes and travel is comfortable and swift if the road is sealed. Care is needed though as accidents are waiting to happen, with overloaded charcoal lorries often tangling with speeding *matatus*. Further hazards are bicycles carrying *matoke* (green bananas) to market; each one usually has three 'stems' and it is clearly back-breaking work to push them uphill. Each district is obliged to keep the verges clean, free from rubbish and the grass cut. This is done even in the most isolated of places and the result creates an excellent impression. Away from the main roads, the roads are constructed from murram (laterite). This is generally well maintained although there are some notorious stretches where travel is very slow, bumpy and pretty uncomfortable. In the dry season dust is a big problem, while in the wet lorries often get bogged down and, as the roads are usually only single tracked, this can cause real problems.

Boda-bodas

These have a very poor safety record. In small towns 'taxi' mopeds known as *boda-bodas* and bicycles are common. These can be useful for travel where public transport is scarce, for example, Entebbe/Kasenyi (for Ssese Islands) or Sanga/Lake Mburu National Park. Only pick up *boda-bodas* from a 'stage', where they hang out for custom, so that you are seen boarding by others. *Boda-boda* drivers are generally honest, but a few are responsible for much crime. Agree the price with the driver before boarding the bike. If you are not sure, ask a local or friend what you should pay. If the driver seems drunk or very young, find another one. Accidents are horrific. If you want a *boda-boda* to slow down say '*mpola mpola*' ('slowly slowly'). Don't ride during a storm or downpour, as sudden gusts of wind are a major cause of accidents.

Buses and matatus (minibuses)

These are a cheap way to travel, costing roughly US$0.02 per kilometre. Most buses and *matatus* wait until they are full before departure. That can take a long time on Sundays and holidays. Buses are cheaper than *matatus* but less regular. However, a few bus companies adhere strictly to listed departure times, so avoid being late. Post office buses are generally safely driven and well maintained (see below). On *matatus* or buses the very centre of the vehicle is the safest place to sit. Avoid the front seats. One piece of baggage is allowed at no additional charge. Inform the conductor which 'stage' (destination) you require. Fares are paid before arrival.

Matatus are minibuses or converted pickup trucks, cars or station wagons carrying passengers, distinguished by their white colour with blue stripes. They are privately owned, and operate the main routes, only leaving the terminus when full. *Matatus* are notorious for fast and dangerous, but they are better than those in Kenya. Nissans with individual (rather than bench) seats are frequently used. They are the cheapest way of travelling around and between towns. You are unlikely to get your own seat and may share the space with domestic livestock. The *matatu* parks appear chaotic and there is no system of route numbering, but the *matatus* all have regular stations in the park. Keep an eye on your belongings and keep any valuables out of sight, particularly in the evenings. Most *matatus* stop running at about 2200; any that run later usually charge more.

Minibuses are fine for short journeys. Shared taxis, usually carrying four to six people, are more comfortable and safer for a longer journey. Agree a price beforehand as drivers often overcharge tourists. Costs are roughly US$0.04 per kilometre.

Car

Car hire There is a wide choice of tariffs and some extra charges you might not expect (for example 'up country driving'). Prices are often quoted in US dollars, but have to be paid in local currency, converted at a rate determined by the local operative. Drivers are an asset in case of a breakdown, but some can be obstructive. Self-drive saloons cost US$50-60 per day, plus US$0.40-US$0.50 per kilometre per day over 100 km, plus tax (15%). A Toyota Landcruiser, including driver, is US$150 per day, plus US$0.60 per kilometre after 100 km per day, including fuel. Take great care when hiring vehicles as they are not always well maintained.

Driving This is on the left side of the road and official speed limits are 50 kph in built up areas and 80 kph on open roads, widely ignored but occasionally monitored by police checks. Breaking speed limits can result in a fine, imprisonment or both. Driving after dark is inadvisable outside the main towns, except on the road between Kampala and Entebbe International Airport, for road safety and personal security reasons. Always keep vehicle doors locked and the windows closed.

Travelling on the roads in Uganda can be hazardous, particularly outside the main cities. In wet weather unsealed roads quickly deteriorate into a quagmire and a 4WD is preferable. Driving standards are very low, vehicles are often poorly maintained and the accident rate is high. Hazards include: other road users' reckless driving, often without lights, with overloaded, poorly secured loads; large potholes; broken down vehicles blocking the road; high speed bumps; cyclists, children and livestock meandering across the roads; and bicycles transporting several stands of bananas obstructing your passage. The Jinja–Kampala and the Kampala–Masaka roads are particular accident blackspots. Piles of leaves laid on the road a few metres apart are a warning of a broken down vehicle ahead.

Traffic accidents attract large crowds. If serious injury has occurred Ugandans consider it inadvisable to leave their car, as mob anger often leads to violent retaliation. Drive to the nearest police station to report the accident. There are few medical facilities outside Kampala.

In February 2011 a travel warning was issued by the FCO and US State Department to avoid overland travel to and within several northeastern Ugandan districts including Kotido, Nakpiripiriti, Moroto and Katakwi, due to banditry and armed interclan conflicts.

Overseas nationals are permitted to drive in Uganda on their local driving licence for a period of up to three months, after which a Ugandan driving licence should be obtained through the Uganda Revenue Authority. Alternatively, international driving licences are acceptable in lieu of a Ugandan licence. By law, all vehicle occupants must wear a seat belt at all times and a driving licence or a photocopy and passport must available for inspection.

Always bring spare fuel in a jerry can, oil, water and emergency engine sealants. In addition ensure you have a first aid kit, sufficient drinking water and adequate funds, as not all petrol stations accept credit cards or have an ATM.

Finally from the Uganda theory test handbook, with thanks to Joe Powell: 'if you hear the siren or see blue flashing lights of the state motorcade approaching draw your vehicle to the extreme left ... Do not try to overtake or join the motorcade'.

Hitchhiking

In the Western sense hitchhiking (standing beside the road and requesting a free ride) is not an option. However, truck drivers and many private motorists will often carry you if you pay, and if you are stuck where there is no public transport you should not hesitate to approach likely vehicles on this basis.

Post Bus

The Post Bus (T0414-236436, T077-235 7427 mob) is well driven with some luggage space and runs to a fixed timetable. It leaves Kampala central post office Monday-Saturday at 0800. The service runs to Masaka, Masindi, Gulu via Karuma, Jinja, Mbale, Tororo, Hoima, Mbarara, Kabale and Soroti. It no longer serves Arua and Fort Portal. For fares, see Transport, page 69.

Taxis

These are generally available in large towns known as 'special hire'. It's always advisable to agree the fare before departure.

Rail

There has been no passenger rail service in Uganda since 1997. The network is now used only for freight transportation.

Maps

The better maps are Macmillan's 1:350,000 *Uganda Traveller's Map*, Reise 1:600,000 *World Mapping Project* and Nelles 1:700,000 *Uganda Map*. An excellent source of maps is **Stanfords** ① *12-14 Long Acre, London WC2E 9LP, T0207-836 1321, www.stanfords.co.uk.*

Sleeping

Where to stay

Hotels

The most luxurious hotels used by business travellers and upmarket tourists have prices set in dollars. However, devaluation of the Ugandan currency has made most other accommodation, particularly that used by ordinary Ugandans, good value. There is plenty of budget accommodation at less than US$10 a night, and reasonably comfortable lodgings can be had from US$20 to US$30. It is always worth while trying to negotiate a discounted rate at most hotels apart from at peak periods like Christmas and New Year. If business is quiet the hotels may offer a discount of 10-25%.

Various rates may be listed: full board, half board, B&B or room only. If you opt for half board there is a cap on how much you can spend on a meal at many of the hotels. Should you exceed this amount – for example, by having an extra beer or soda – you will be charged at the full board rate. This is rarely explained in advance and causes ill-feeling when it comes to settling your bill.

However, if you underspend your meal allowance (by missing a meal) you do not receive a refund. If on a tight budget one way to avoid unexpected extra charges is to book either room only or B&B and buy your meals and beverages à la carte.

Campsites

See also National park and safari accommodation, below. Toilet facilities on campsites can be primitive, with the 'long drop', a basic hole in a concrete slab, being very common.

Sleeping price codes

LL	over US$200	**C**	US$31-45
L	US$151-200	**D**	US$21-30
AL	US$101-150	**E**	US$12-20
A	US$66-100	**F**	US$7-11
B	US$46-65	**G**	under US$7

Unless otherwise stated, prices refer to the cost of a double room including tax.

Most camps are guarded but despite this you should ensure that valuables are not left unattended. Be careful about leaving items outside your tent. Many campsites have troupes of baboons nearby, which can be a nuisance. Wild camping is rarely done in Uganda.

National park and safari accommodation
There are campsites in most national parks. Most of the accommodation is in a luxury tented camp, which is very atmospheric. Tents usually have a central dining area. Each tent will have a thatched roof to keep it cool inside, proper beds, a veranda and they will often have a small bathroom at the back. The staff will fill up a header tank with hot water for a shower. But at the same time you will have the feeling of being in the heart of Africa and at night you will hear animals surprisingly close by.

The best lodges are expensive, at around US$150 for a double room with full board. One of their charms is that they often have no electricity and you will be entertained as the guest of the owner or manager. Meals are taken around a large table with other guests and are usually very simple (with no choice) but are delicious. Make sure that you inform them of any special dietary requirements (including if you are a vegetarian) when you check in. Avoid drinking wine at these establishments; it is very expensive.

Accommodation in the parks is good value if you camp or stay in the park *bandas*, simply constructed cabins or huts, often with a thatched roof, and sometimes made of more permanent materials like stone or concrete. Some have an attached long-drop toilet, otherwise there is a communal toilet and shower block. Campsites are often most attractively sited, perhaps in the elbow of a river course, but always have plenty of shade. Birds are plentiful and several hours can be whiled away birdwatching. See also box, page 26, for park fees.

Insects
Be prepared for mosquitoes in particular, and other insects. Sleep under a net treated with insecticide wherever mosquitoes are a problem; smear exposed skin with insect repellent; use an electric heat-pad insecticide tablet vapourizer at night; and buy a can of insecticide to spray your hotel room.

Eating price codes

🍴🍴🍴 over US$12   🍴🍴 US$6-12   🍴 under US$6

Prices refer to the cost of a main course with either a soft drink, a glass of wine or a beer.

Eating

Food
Simple meals are good value, but the range and variety of food is limited. The food in the larger hotels is often a buffet. There is usually a choice of chicken, fish (tilapia is very good) and steak (which is often goat). Breakfast is usually quite large and you will be asked how you like your eggs. Spanish omelettes are very popular in this respect. Most hotels and lodges will prepare a packed lunch if you are travelling. Packed breakfasts (for an early morning game drive) can be interesting! Local food includes *posho* (known as *ugali* in other parts of East Africa), which is maize ground and boiled to form a stiff dough, and *matoke*, which is boiled plantains. Indian additions to the menu include chapatti and *pilau*, rice and meat together with a vegetable curry.

Eating out
Kampala has excellent restaurants and there is a wide variety of cuisine on offer. When you eat in a local Ugandan restaurant their daily menu is pre-prepared and you can choose from food like *matoke*, rice, meat and beans. If you want a dish that is not listed on the menu, like chips, expect a very long wait. In smaller towns there may be Indian and Chinese restaurants as well as local food, although small cafés usually only serve local food. Meals are reasonably priced, with only the large hotels being expensive. Street food is good value, but of variable quality.

Drink
Uganda produces several soft drinks and beers that are quite acceptable and good value compared with the imported alternatives. There are two main breweries, Bell and Nile (based in Jinja), both of which produce a range of lagers that are sold in 500 ml bottles. Bell also produces a draught beer that is readily available in Kampala. Nile is more widely distributed up country with their Club brand being especially popular and which has won several brewing prizes internationally. Imported wines, spirits and beers are widely available but very expensive.

Avoid buying the cheapest brand of bottled water in supermarkets as, although it may be clean, it often doesn't taste so. When going on safari check whether water is provided beforehand and if it isn't, make sure you take sufficient supplies.

Entertainment

In Kampala and larger towns, discos are very much the order of the day especially on Friday and Saturday nights. In theory the style of music varies from night to night – house one night and African the next. In practice it tends to merge. It is extremely loud and goes on until dawn. No hotels in the centre of Kampala are immune. Out of the towns, there is virtually no nightlife. Occasionally the manager of a lodge will arrange for a local dance group to put on an entertainment. The best advice is to listen and watch for an hour or so and then gracefully depart for bed. This will not cause offence and the dancers and drummers will continue to perform for the staff.

Festivals and events

Public holidays

Uganda recognizes both Christian and Muslim holidays in addition to fixed public holidays. Government offices, post offices, banks and forex bureau will be closed but many shops are open. Prices for hotel accommodation and on the slightly less frequent public transport network often escalate over holiday periods, as many Ugandans travel to their regions of origin.

January
1 Jan New Year's Day
26 Jan NRM Day

March/April
(variable) Good Friday
(variable) Easter Monday

May
1 May International Labour Day

June
3 Jun Uganda Martyrs' Day
9 Jun National Heroes Day

October
9 Oct Independence Day

December
25 Dec Christmas Day
26 Dec Boxing Day
(variable) **Idd-el-Fitr**
(variable) **Iddi Adhuha**

Shopping

Outside Kampala, the lodges in the national parks usually have a handicrafts shop, but the best option is to head for the handicraft shops in Kampala (see page 67). If you want something authentically Ugandan, look out for the attractive woven pots and mats. These can also be found on the road to Mbarara at the equator and Kinoni. Drums can also be bought on this road at Mpigi. Some bargaining is possible.

National parks and safaris

One of the main reasons for going to Uganda is the wonderful wildlife. Seeing the animals on safari can be a most rewarding experience at any time of year. However, for the vast majority of travellers it is something to be prepared for, as it will almost certainly involve a

Uganda national parks & game reserves

◆	**National parks & game reserves**	11	Rwenzori Mountains NP	20	Mgahinga Gorilla NP
1	Kidepo Valley NP	12	Toro-Semliki Wildlife Reserve	21	Mabira Forest Reserve
2	Ajai GR	13	Kibale Forest NP	22	Mpanga Forest Reserve
3	Achwa Lolim GR	14	Katonga Wildlife Reserve	23	Kabwoya Wildlife Reserve
4	Matheniko GR	15	Queen Elizabeth NP	24	Bugungu Wildlife Reserve
5	Murchison Falls NP	16	Kyambura River Gorge	25	Karuma Wildlife Reserve
6	Bokora Corridor GR	17	Ssese Islands	26	Kasyoha-Kitomi Wildlife Reserve
7	Pian Upe GR	18	Lake Mburo NP		
8	Budongo Forest Reserve	19	Bwindi Impenetrable NP		
9	Mount Elgon NP				
10	Semliki NP				

National park fees

Category A covers Murchison Falls, Queen Elizabeth, Kibale, Bwindi Impenetrable and Mgahinga Gorilla national parks.

Category B covers all other Uganda Wildlife Authority (UWA) protected areas.

Prices are per person unless stated otherwise.

Park entry fees
Entrance per 24 hours. Under 5s are free.
Category A
Adult US$30
Child 5-15 years US$15
Category B
Adult US$20
Child 5-15 years US$10

Accommodation

Single	Double	Triple	Extra person
Category A: en suite			
20,000/-	30,000/-	40,000/-	10,000/-
Category B: basic/traditional			
10,000/-	15,000/-	20,000/-	5,000/-

Note Prices are in Ugandan shillings unless otherwise stated. Advanced booking requires a 50% non-refundable advance payment.

Camping with own tent per person per night US$10

Vehicle entry fees
Only for Murchison, Queen Elizabeth, Kidepo, Lake Mburo national parks and all wildlife reserves.

Motorcycles	US$30
Minibuses, cars and pickups	US$50
Rescue fees	US$10

Gorilla tracking
Bwindi Impenetrable National Park*
US$500 plus park entry fee advance booking
Mgahinga Gorilla National Park*
US$500

Chimpanzee tracking
Kyambura Gorge	US$50

Primate walk
Kibale National Park	US$90
Toro-Semliki	US$30

degree of discomfort and long journeys. The roads in Uganda can be very exhausting. The unsealed roads are bumpy and dusty, and it will be hot. It is also important to remember that despite the expert knowledge of the drivers, they cannot guarantee that you will see any animals. When they do spot one of the rarer animals – a leopard perhaps – their pleasure is almost as enjoyable as seeing the animal. To get the best from your safari, approach it with humour, look after the driver (a disgruntled driver will quickly ruin your safari), and do your best to get on with, and be considerate to, your fellow travellers.

Booking safaris
Safaris can be booked either at home or in Uganda; if you go for the latter you may find substantial discounts. If booking in Uganda avoid companies offering cheap deals on the street; they will almost always turn out to be a disaster and may appear cheap because they do not include national park entrance fees.

Safaris do not run on every day of the week. Trips are often timed to end on a Thursday night. So a six-day safari will start on a Saturday, a four-day one on a Monday. In the low season you may also find that these will be combined. If you are on a four-day safari you

Chimpanzee habituation experience
1 day US$220
2 days US$400
3 days US$550

Golden monkey tracking
Mgahinga Gorilla National Park US$50
Launch cruise/boat trip US$15
Queen Elizabeth National Park (2 hours)
Minimum charge per cruise US$150
Murchison Falls National Park (3 hours)
Minimum charge per cruise US$150
Lake Mburo National Park (2 hours)
US$40 per trip

Guided nature walk
All protected areas

	Half day	Full day
	(up to 4 hours)	(over 4 hours)
Adult	US$10	US$15
Child 5-15 years	US$2.50	US$3

Mountaineering*
Rwenzori Mountains National Park
RMS fees US$780 plus food costs US$140/
cook US$70/extra porters US$70
Mount Elgon National Park
US$50, US$50 per extra day

Virunga volcano climb
Mgahinga Gorilla National Park US$50

Sport fishing
Murchison Falls, day permit US$50

Note All fees are currently under revision. Increases are expected to be implemented shortly, with a high and low season cost variation.

Examples of the proposed new fees are US$35 per 24 hours for park visitation fees, compared with the current US$30 per 24 hours; US$750 per day for gorilla tracking in high season June–September and December–March fee, compared with the current US$500; and US$150 chimpanzee tracking in Kibale, currently US$90.

Uncertainty over fees reflects the fact that if Uganda raises its fees unilaterally, Rwanda and DR Congo will undercut it on gorilla tracking, which is the most lucrative component of their tourist income. Revised fees were supposed to be implemented in 2010, but had not been by the time this book went to press.
Includes park visitation fee

can expect to join another party. This can be awkward as the 'six-dayers' will already have formed into a cohesive group.

Food and drink
Standards at lodges and tented sites are the same as at normal hotels. Camping safaris usually have a cook. Food is wholesome and surprisingly varied. Companies will cater for vegetarians. Tea and coffee are available all day. Insects are a fact of life and despite valiant attempts by the cook it is virtually impossible to avoid flies (as well as moths at night) alighting on plates and uncovered food. Despite this, hygiene standards are high.

Game drives
There are usually two game drives daily. The morning drive sets off at about 0700 and lasts until midday. The afternoon drive starts at about 1600 and lasts until the park closes (roughly 1830-1900). In addition you may have an early morning drive that will mean getting up well before dawn at about 0500. If you have arrived at the park by public transport, the warden and guides can arrange drives for a moderate charge in the park vehicles.

Specialized safaris and tours

Most safaris and tours focus on wildlife but other possible activities include walking and trekking, birdwatching, canoeing, cycling, mountain climbing and fishing. Truck safaris demand a little more fortitude and adventurous spirit. The compensation is usually the camaraderie and life-long friendships that result from what is invariably a real adventure, going to more remote places. See also Tour operators, page 40.

Tipping

How much to tip the driver on safari is tricky. It is best to enquire from the company when booking. As a rough guide you should allow US$5-7 per adult per night (half this for a child). Try and come to an agreement with other group members and put the tip into a communal kitty. Remember that Ugandan wages are low and there can be long lay-offs during the low season. If you are on a camping safari and have a cook, give all the money to the driver to sort out the split.

Transport

It is worth emphasizing that most parks are some way from departure points. The added problem with Uganda is that various species are spread out around different parks, which means that you will almost certainly need to visit more than one park to see all the animals. Much time is spent travelling, around four to six hours in the vehicle each day getting to the next destination. This leaves only a limited time in the park itself. On a more upmarket safari the vehicle will almost certainly be of the minivan variety for eight people. Leg room can be very restricted. They will have a viewing point through the roof and sometimes a sunshade. In practice this means that only one or two people can view out through the roof at any one time; the sight-lines of the others may be impeded by legs.

Camping safari companies tend to use converted 10-tonne lorries. Although very basic, they are surprisingly comfortable, being well sprung, with good leg room and large windows which fully open. Views of the animals on both sides of the truck are therefore good. They can be a little cramped if there is a full party of about 20 people.

What to take

Room is restricted in both minivans and lorries. You will be asked to limit the amount you bring with you. There is very little point in taking too much clothing; expect to get dirty, particularly during the dry season when dust can be a problem. Try to have a clean set of clothes to change into at night when it can also get quite cold. Comfortable, loose clothing and sensible footwear is best. Bear in mind that you may well travel through a variety of climates; it can be very cool at the top of the slopes at Bwindi but very hot and humid at Entebbe. It is worth having warm clothing to hand in your transport as well as plenty of mineral water. Few safari companies provide drinking water and it is important to buy enough bottles to last your trip before you set off. It is surprising how much you get through and restocking is difficult.

Other important items are binoculars, preferably one pair per member of your party and a camera with a telephoto lens as you will not get close enough to the animals without one. Bring spare memory cards for digital cameras or sufficient film.

The Wildlife section in this handbook will enable you to identify many animals. However, you may wish to take a more detailed field guide. The Collins series is particularly recommended. The drivers are usually a mine of information. Take a notebook and pen as it is good fun to write down the number of species of animals and birds that you have spotted; anything over 100 is thought to be pretty good.

Responsible travel

Bargaining

Without tourism, preserving the glorious attractions of this region would not be possible. People in East Africa are very poor, and the need to keep body and soul together in the immediate future takes priority over everything. Bargaining over the cost of items is the norm, and overcharging tourists a little is commonplace. However, bear in mind the huge difference in income and living standards between tourists and poor Ugandans before haggling too enthusiastically. If shopping in a market check the prices on other stalls. Transport charges are often inflated for tourists; ask before you start the journey.

Clothing

As in much of Africa, it is considered a courtesy and a mark of respect to dress neatly and smartly. If you have an appointment with a senior government official or member of the business community, men should wear a collar and tie and women should be conservatively dressed with a medium length skirt that covers the knee. The importance of exchanging formal greetings prior to talking business cannot be over-emphasized.

Conduct

Always greet people by asking how they are before asking for directions or a service. This enormously improves the quality of the exchange you will have. It is considered pretty rude not to show respect in this way, unless there is an emergency. Shouting and swearing is viewed with great disdain. If you raise your voice when addressing someone, it shows disrespect to them, and will probably draw a curious crowd. Implying that someone is stupid, even in jest, is a deadly insult. The same is literally true of calling someone a thief; people have been lynched because of off-hand accusations. If someone is providing a personal service, such as a *boda-boda* driver, a waitress or a shopkeeper, it is considered polite to address them by their name, and it can win you great discounts. A few words of Luganda are invaluable.

Most visitors are well aware of the need to act courteously, behave unobtrusively, dress modestly and ask before photographing or filming. Do not take photos of military, official or diplomatic sites, including Owen Falls Dam at the source of the Nile near Jinja. Avoid littering, polluting and destroying the environment, and conserve water.

It may come as a surprise that a considerable number of Ugandans are Muslim. This is a result of Idi Amin's policies in the 1960s when he tried to outlaw Christianity. Most towns have mosques and Muslim schools. If entering a religious site (including the tombs of the kings), you will be asked to remove your shoes. Eating places run by Muslims will usually not serve alcohol.

Prohibitions

Be careful about accepting any wildlife object from villagers and guides. They should be left where found. Your bags may be searched when you leave Entebbe airport and, if you are found with any bones, this can be awkward and may lead to some form of fine. There is an extensive list of endangered species prepared by the United Nation Environmental Programme and the Wildlife Conservation Monitoring Centre (UNEP-WCMC) under the Convention on Trade in Endangered Species (CITES), see www.cites.org. Any souvenir

How big is your footprint?

The point of a holiday is, of course, to have a good time, but if it's relatively guilt-free as well, that's even better. Perfect ecotourism would ensure a good living for local inhabitants, while not detracting from their traditional lifestyles, encroaching on their customs or spoiling their environment. Perfect ecotourism probably doesn't exist, but everyone can play their part. Here are a few points worth bearing in mind:

- Think about where your money goes and be fair and realistic about how cheaply you travel. Try to put money into local people's hands; drink local beer or fruit juice rather than imported brands and stay in locally owned accommodation wherever possible.
- Haggle with humour and appropriately. Remember that you want a fair price, not the lowest one.
- Think about what happens to your rubbish. Take biodegradable products and a water bottle filter. Be sensitive to limited resources like water, fuel and electricity.
- Help preserve local wildlife and habitats by respecting rules and regulations, such as sticking to footpaths and not buying products made from endangered plants or animals.
- Don't treat people as part of the landscape; they may not want their picture taken. Ask first and respect their wishes.
- Learn the local language and be mindful of local customs and norms. It can enhance your travel experience and you'll earn respect and be more readily welcomed by local people.
- And finally, use your guidebook as a starting point, not the only source of information. Talk to local people, then discover your own adventure.

made from an endangered species is prohibited. Insist on a receipt that displays the address of the seller and this will help if you run into problems at the airport when you leave – and help the authorities enforce the regulations. Rare antique objects cannot generally be taken out of Uganda, but most curios purchased in regular souvenir shops will not fall into this category. Again, ask for a receipt with an address on it.

Ugandan culture is socially conservative. Homosexuality is illegal with draconian penalties. Drug abuse is similarly unacceptable, incurring severe punishment (see page 32).

Essentials A-Z

Accidents and emergencies

Police: 999. **Fire**: 112. Local people are unfailingly helpful in the event of an accident, directing you to the nearest hospital, or sending a taxi or motor-bike if an ambulance is needs to be called.

For emergencies, or trouble with the law, contact your consular representative, see page 70.

Children

Ugandans are very tolerant of children. Local children are friendly but shy, very well behaved and respectful. Large hotels and restaurants with gardens will usually have a children's play area. Children get significant discounts for national park entry; under 5s are free (see box, page 26). Animals and safaris are very exciting for them, especially when they catch their first glimpse of an elephant or lion. However, small children may get bored driving around a hot game park or national park all day if there is no animal activity. If you travel in a group, think about the long hours inside the vehicle sharing little room with other people. Noisy and bickering children can annoy your travel mates and scare the animals away.

Outside the main towns you will need to take everything with you. Particular attention needs to be given to the risks of malaria, dysentery, sunburn and heat exhaustion (see Health, page 32). There is plenty to interest children in the wildlife parks and on the shores of Lake Victoria. Long dusty road journeys can be a trial, but can be enlivened by wildlife spotting. Audio books will keep children amused for long periods.

Customs and duty free

The following items are allowed to be imported duty free: cigarettes and tobacco 500 g or 400 cigarettes; wines and spirits 1 litre; toilet water and perfume 0.5 litre (perfume 0.25 litre max). For details prohibitions, including export restrictions according to the CITES convention, see page 29.

Disabled travellers

There are few facilities for disabled people in Uganda. Wheelchairs are very difficult to accommodate on public road transport, and you will normally need a private hire. However, people will do their best to help, and being disabled should not deter you from visiting Uganda. Some hotels such as the Sheraton in Kampala (see page 60) and Paraa Lodge in Murchison Falls National Park (see page 136) cater for disabled travellers in wheelchairs. Entebbe International Airport has wheelchairs. The Uganda Tourist Board (www.visituganda. com) will be able to advise further.

Useful contacts include: **RADAR**, 12 City Forum, 250 City Rd, London EC1V 8AF, T020-7250 3222, www.radar.org.uk. **SATH**, 347 Fifth Ave, Suite 605, New York 10016, T0212-447 7284. **Disability World**, T01383-823420, **Holiday Care**, T01293-774535, and **Travelability**, T0870-2416127, www. accessibletravel.co.uk, are specialist travel agents who can advise and help arrange holidays for disabled travellers.

Electricity

220/240 volts AC at 50 Hz (cycles). You will encounter a variety of sockets, particularly in the older hotels, and a multi-socket adaptor is advisable. Newer sockets are square 3-pin plugs, but older round 3-pin large or small sockets are still found in unmodernized hotels. A 2-way step-down transformer will be needed if your electronic device supports only 110-120 volt electricity. North American electricity is generated at 60 Hz (cycles). Most international 220-240 volt electricity is generated at 50 Hz (cycles). These cycles' difference may slow the motor in the North American appliance, causing malfunction in clocks. Power surges cause problems for laptop users without a surge protection plug. Most hotels and businesses use back-up generators during the frequent power cuts. Shavers usually have 2 round-pin sockets.

Embassies and consulates

For a list of Ugandan embassies abroad, see http://embassy.goabroad.com/embassies-of/Uganda.

Gay and lesbian travellers

Homosexuality is illegal in Uganda and extreme discretion is advocated. However, there is a general toleration by ordinary people of discreet behaviour. Gay clubs and bars are conspicuous by their absence. If you wish to get updated information try a gay website such as www.mask.org.za for news or www.gay2afrika.com for travel arrangements.

Health

Before you go

Ideally, you should see your GP/practice nurse or travel clinic at least 6 weeks before your departure for general advice on travel risks, malaria and recommended vaccinations. Your local pharmacist can also be a good source of advice. Make sure you have comprehensive medical insurance including full medical repatriation, with additional cover for extreme sports if appropriate, get a dental check (especially if you are going to be away for more than a

month), know your own blood group and if you suffer from a long-term condition such as diabetes or epilepsy make sure someone knows or that you have a Medic Alert bracelet/necklace with this information on it.

Vaccinations

First of all confirm that your primary courses and boosters are up to date (usually hepatitis A, typhoid, poliomyelitis and tetanus). Vaccines commonly recommended for travel in Uganda are yellow fever, diphtheria, hepatitis A and B, cholera, typhoid, meningococcal meningitis and rabies, especially if staying for long periods in remote areas. Meningococcal meningitis rates increase during the dry seasons. There was a laboratory-confirmed outbreak of yellow fever, see below, in northern Uganda in Nov 2010, the first since the 1970s. Travellers to Uganda will need to produce a Certificate of Vaccination before travelling onwards to other countries. The final decision on vaccinations should be based on a consultation with your GP or travel clinic. Also, advice can change so check again for future visits.

Infectious and water-borne diseases are prevalent. Some protection is offered by vaccinations but many common problems like malaria, bilharzia (schistosomiasis), gastro-intestinal disturbances or sunburn, require avoidance measures; see relevant sections below. There are English-speaking doctors in Kampala and some of the larger towns with experience in tropical diseases.

A-Z of health risks
Altitude sickness

Uganda has 2 areas of high altitude: the Rwenzori Mountains with peaks over 5100 m and Mount Elgon at 4321 m. Acute mountain sickness can occur over 3000 m, with severe headache, insomnia, exhaustion, dizziness, nausea and vomiting. Gradual ascent, small meals and alcohol and cigarette avoidance reduces the risk. Acute pulmonary oedema is a more rare condition, affecting mountaineers who ascend rapidly. It may begin with acute mountain sickness but develops rapidly to severe breathlessness, noisy breathing, blue lips and frothing at the mouth. If affected, a rapid descent is imperative, oxygen is given and hospital care sought.

Watch out for sunburn at high altitude where the rays increase in intensity, when the use of sun block preparations based on zinc oxide or titanium oxide should be applied thickly to especially sensitive areas like lips and nose.

Bilharzia

Also known as schistosomiasis, bilharzia is common in Uganda especially around the Ssese Islands. It's caused by parasitic flatworms or flukes, caught by wading or bathing in infested waters, including fresh water lakes, slow-moving rivers or irrigation systems. The fluke spends part of its life cycle inside freshwater snails, where they multiply and are released as cercariae (flukes) into the water. The cercariae penetrate human skin and migrate via the blood stream to the liver, lungs, bowels and bladder. There is no vaccine available, so prevention is the key. Avoid wading or swimming in rivers, lakes, and irrigation systems. Only swim in chlorinated pools. Treatment is by a single dose of Praziquantel that kills the flukes and is effective.

Bites and stings

Many tropical diseases are spread by, rather than caused by insects. These include bacteria, viruses, and protozoans, when the micro-organism causes the disease and the insect (the vector) is responsible for transmitting the condition.

Mosquitoes are the vectors for malaria, yellow fever, dengue, West Nile fever and filariasis. Sandflies are the vectors of leishmaniasis and tsetse flies are the vectors for sleeping sickness (human African trypanosomiasis). All are endemic in Uganda. Typhus fever is spread by fleas,

ticks and lice and plague is spread by fleas; both are endemic worldwide. Bite avoidance is the most important protection measure. A combination of 0.5% Permethrin on clothing and bedding and 20% DEET repellent on skin is the most effective insect repellent combination. Take care around eyes and with spectacles as DEET dissolves plastic. Sleep off the ground, use insecticide-impregnated mosquito nets and burn 'mosquito' (pyrethroid) coils before going to bed. Spray thin clothing with Permethrin 0.5% as most insects can bite through fine fabrics. Cover up your limbs at dawn and dusk paying attention to cuff areas of the wrists, ankles and neck, apply insect repellents on exposed skin and wear trousers tucked into socks and sturdy footwear if walking in the bush. Mosquitoes bite at any time of day but most bites occur during the evening. Permethrin impregnated insect repellent clothing, available from specialist outlets, are ideal for children. Remedies like eating garlic or vitamin B, or using ultrasonic devices are ineffective. If bitten or stung, itching may be relieved by cool baths, antihistamine tablets, or mild corticosteroid creams but do not use if infected. Treat infected bites with a local antiseptic or antibiotic cream such as Cetrimide.

In some parts of Africa the **jigger flea** commonly burrows its way into people's feet causing a painful itchy swelling which finally bursts in a rather disgusting fashion. Avoid these by wearing sandals and if they do become established have someone experienced winkle them out with a sterile needle.

Leishmaniasis transmitted by sand flies causes a non-healing skin ulcer, widespread in Uganda especially around Lake Victoria and the Ssese Islands. The severity of the disease reflects the numbers of parasites.

Foreign visitors are very rarely bitten by **snakes**. Most snake species are non-venomous and venomous snakes often inflict a 'dry bite' where no venom is injected. Visitors are unlikely to be able to differentiate between a venomous or harmless snake species. If bitten reassure the victim and keep them still; keep the bite below the level of the heart; clean the surrounding skin with an antiseptic wipe; remove watches and jewellery from the affected area or limb; immobilise the affected limb with a splint and apply a pressure bandage; get the victim to hospital as soon as possible. Do not apply a tourniquet, suck or cut open the bite wound. A suction device may be used to extract venom. Snake bite avoidance measures include not walking barefoot in vegetation, climbing foliage covered rocks and trees or swimming in murky waters. After dark use a torch and tap the ground in front of you with a walking stick if unable to see your feet. Avoid snakes and do not provoke them.

Bites from **scorpions** are very painful but rarely dangerous to adults. Seek medical advice if a young child is bitten. Do not immerse the bite in cold water as this increases the pain. If camping, shake out boots and shoes, and check the back of backpacks to dislodge scorpions or spiders before putting them on. The underside of toilet seats should also be checked before sitting down.

Diarrhoeal diseases

Diarrhoea can be caused by viruses such as hepatitis A, E coli, cholera, salmonella, shigella and typhoid; or protozoa, such as amoebas and giardia. The diarrhoea may come on suddenly or rather slowly. It may or may not be accompanied by vomiting or by severe abdominal pain and the passage of blood or mucus when it is called dysentery. Common causes of transmission of gastro-intestinal diseases are by the faecal-oral route - in other words ingestion of contaminated food, drinking water or ice. Swimming in dilute effluent is another cause, and sea or river water is more likely to be contaminated by sewage than swimming pools.

The symptoms of **cholera** are passing profuse watery diarrhoea 1-5 days after infection which can lead to rapid dehydration. It may be accompanied by vomiting. Treatment is re-hydration with a sugar/salt fluid mixture. Tetracycline can shorten the disease process.

Diarrhoea treatment principles are rest, fluid and salt replacement, antibiotics such as Ciprofloxacin for the bacterial types and special diagnostic tests and medical treatment for the amoeba and giardia infections. Any kind of diarrhoea, whether with vomiting or not, responds well to the replacement of water and salts, taken as frequent small sips, of a re-hydration solution. Oral re-hydration is a life-saving technique and is especially important for use with children. There are proprietary preparations consisting of sachets of powder which you dissolve in boiled water (Dioralyte/Rehydrate) or you can make your own by adding half a teaspoonful of salt (3.5 g) and 4 tbsp of sugar (40 g) to 1 litre of boiled water.

If you can closely time the onset of the diarrhoea ('acute') then it is probably due to a virus or a bacterium and/or the onset of dysentery. The treatment in addition to re-hydration is Ciprofloxacin 500 mg every 12 hrs. If diarrhoea comes on slowly or intermittently ('sub-acute') then it is more likely to be protozoal, caused by an amoeba or giardia. Chronic prolonged diarrhoea is notoriously resistant to amateur attempts at treatment and warrants proper diagnostic tests. Most towns with reasonable sized hospitals have laboratories for stool samples. These cases are best treated by a doctor, as is any outbreak of diarrhoea continuing for more than three days. Sometimes blood is passed in amoebic dysentery, which requires medical help.

If you're getting severe stomach cramps, the following drugs may help but are not very useful in the management of acute diarrhoea: Loperamide (Imodium) and Diphenoxylate with Atropine (Lomotil). They should not be given to children.

The standard advice to prevent problems is to avoid shellfish, unwashed fruit and vegetables, salads, eggs and undercooked meat, especially if they have been left out exposed to flies. Stick to fresh food that has been cooked from raw just before eating and make sure you peel fruit yourself. Wash and dry your hands before eating; wet wipes are useful for this. See also Water below.

Hepatitis A and B and AIDS

Hepatitis A virus is contracted by eating contaminated food. Hepatitis B can be transmitted in saliva and semen, tattoos and body piercings, shared needles or direct contact with infected blood via blood transfusion or if in a traffic accident. A vaccine exists against both conditions but no vaccine guarantees 100% protection. AIDS is widespread in Africa and heterosexual spread is the most common source. The main risk to travellers is from alcohol-fuelled casual sex, heterosexual or homosexual. The same precautions should be taken as when encountering any sexually transmitted disease.

Malaria

Malaria is endemic in Uganda, more common in the rainy seasons. Malaria precautions are essential. Check with your doctor or nurse about suitable anti-malarial tablets. If travelling to remote areas, a course of emergency 'standby' treatment should be carried. Although malaria drug regimes vary between countries, there is consensus that all visitors to Uganda should take a course of anti-malarial medication. The drugs of choice are the Atovaquone 250mg/Proguanil 100mg combination called Malarone x 1 tablet daily; Mefloquine 250 mg (Larium) weekly; and Doxycycline 100mg daily. Bite avoidance is also essential; see Bites and stings above. Start taking these drugs 2 days to 2½ weeks prior to travel and for 1-4 weeks after your return as advised. People living in malarial zones acquire a level of resistance but this protection is lost after 6 months

living in non-malarial zones, so returnees need to take the same precautions as visitors. It is important to complete the course of anti-malarial drugs when leaving the tropics. If you get any flu-like symptoms either during your stay or for 3 months after leaving a malarial zone, seek medical advice, and have your blood tested for malaria.

Malaria begins with a flu-like illness, headache, fever and lethargy. Do not ignore vague, early symptoms but seek medical attention as it can cause death within 24 hrs. For more details see www.malariahotspots.co.uk. Certain people are at higher risk of succumbing to malaria and need to be forewarned. These include under 5s, pregnant women, the immuno-compromised or those who have had their spleen removed.

Rabies

This is transmitted by mammals like dogs, cats, foxes, jackals and bats. Avoid contact with them and be aware that an unusually tame wild animal may have rabies. Aggressive behaviour or apparent neurological symptoms are other indicators. If bitten or licked scrub the area with soap and water and seek hospital treatment immediately, especially if unvaccinated.

Sun

The sun is very strong in Uganda compared to Europe; if you are fair skinned you will quickly burn. Do not be fooled into thinking the sun cannot harm you when there is a fog; the UV rays will still penetrate the mist. In the longer term, over-exposure can lead to skin cancer and premature skin aging. The best advice is simply to avoid exposure, wearing a hat and staying out of the sun if possible, particularly between late morning and early afternoon. Apply a higher-factor sunscreen (at least SPF15) to the skin and also make sure it screens against UVB.

A further danger in hot climates is heat exhaustion or more seriously heat stroke. Heat stroke can be avoided by good hydration, which means drinking water past the point of simply quenching thirst. Also when first exposed to tropical heat take time to acclimatize by avoiding strenuous activity in the middle of the day. If you cannot avoid heavy exercise it is a good idea to increase salt intake.

Trypanosomiasis (sleeping sickness)

This is essentially a brain infection causing drowsiness, transmitted by a large, greyish-brown tenacious insect, the size of a honey bee, the tsetse fly, not always repelled by DEET but very susceptible to Pyrethroid fly spray and Permethrin. It can bite through lightweight clothes and is attracted to moving vehicles. The main risk is in game parks where these aggressive flies are common. Symptoms include headaches, fever, weakness and aching muscles. If unrecognized and untreated it may progress to encephalitis or meningitis.

Viral haemorrhagic fevers

Lassa fever, Marburg disease and Ebola virus are classified as viral haemorrhagic fevers. There are confirmed intermittent outbreaks in Uganda, most recently in 2008. Early signs include fever, headache, severe muscle pain progressing to bleeding disorders. All have a high mortality rate.

Water

Tap water is unreliable throughout East Africa. Bottled water is usually safe, although unauthorized re-filling from the tap and hammering on a new cap is commonplace. Choose carbonated bottled drinking water or sodas if there is a choice. Ice for drinks is best avoided.

Boiling water for 10 mins will kill all enteric bacteria, viruses and protozoa. The absolute minimum boiling period should be one minute. Allow an extra minute boiling time for every 1000 m above sea level. The most effective agent is 2% tincture of iodine. Add 5 drops per litre. Cover and allow the water to stand for 15 hrs to

kill Cryptosporidium. Chlorine is another chemical used to purify water, but is less effective than iodine. Cloudy water should be filtered before boiling or chemical disinfection. There are a number of filters on the market with varying prices and levels of effectiveness. The most effective are the reverse-osmosis filters that will protect against bacteria, viruses and protozoa. Newer options include Ultraviolet Water Sterilisers that kill most common pathogens.

Yellow fever

The areas surrounding Gulu and Kitgum have had an outbreak of yellow fever with 174 confirmed cases and 45 deaths. Yellow fever is a viral haemorrhagic disease, causing kidney failure and death if untreated, first noted in Nov 2010 and laboratory-confirmed in Dec 2010. These were the first confirmed cases since 1972. A mass-immunization programme is planned when the 2.5 million vaccine supplies are ready. It was possibly re-introduced as a result of people eating bush meat as monkeys can also contract it. Yellow fever is transmitted by the female aedes aegypti mosquito, which is only active during the daytime. See also Vaccinations, above.

Books

Dawood, R (ed) *Travellers' Health: How to Stay Healthy Abroad*, Oxford University Press, 2002. We recommend this book especially for intrepid travellers heading to remote places.
Lankester, T *Travellers' Good Health Guide*, 3rd edition, Sheldon Press, 2006.

Further information

www.cdc.gov US government site with comprehensive travel health and disease outbreak information.
www.fitfortravel.nhs.uk Travel health information for people travelling abroad from the UK with links to travel vaccinations and disease prevention.

www.malariahotspots.co.uk An outstanding resource with information about malaria risks, identification and preventative measures.

www.traveldoctor.co.uk Offers an excellent interactive travel advice service and a free travel doctor manual to download.

www.who.int World Health Organization, updates of disease outbreaks.

Insurance

Insurance companies have tightened up considerably over recent years and it is now almost impossible to make a successful claim if you have not followed their procedures correctly. The problem is that these often involve dealing with Uganda's bureaucracy that can lead to some inconvenience at best and long delays at worst. There is no substitute for suitable precautions against petty crime. The level of insurance chosen is often dictated by the level of medical insurance that you require. Also make sure you obtain sports extensions if you are going to go rafting, climbing, etc. Most policies do not cover very high levels of baggage/cash. Don't forget to check whether you can claim on your household insurance. These often have worldwide all-risks extensions. Most policies exclude manual work while away although working in bars or restaurants is usually allowed. All losses must be reported to the police and/or hotel authorities within 24 hrs of discovery and a written report obtained.

Internet

Internet cafés are widely available in Kampala and all the main towns. Connection rates vary but you should expect to pay about US$0.60-1 for a 30-min connection. A big hotel will often have an internet connection in its business centre; it will be fast, but expensive, at up to US$10 per 30 mins. Most medium-size hotels will have a connection and you can usually arrange to use it. There are a few Wi-Fi hotspots in the luxury hotels, Kampala Backpackers and Entebbe airport, but it is not widespread. Satellite internet links are available in locations like Buhoma, in Bwindi Impenetrable Forest National Park.

Language

The official language is English, and it is widely spoken, although for most Ugandans it is their second language. However, as there are well over 50 local dialects it does provide a unifying language. Swahili is also spoken, but not as widely as in Kenya and Tanzania. Many Ugandans also speak Luganda.

Media

Newspapers

The main newspaper is *New Vision* (www.newvision.co.ug), published in English. Although it is government owned it has considerable editorial freedom but has no advertising. It has good events listings. Its rival, *The Monitor* (www.monitor.co.ug), is independent, has advertising and is widely available in Kampala as well as up country. Both papers have some coverage of international news and sport. Most Ugandans seem to buy both papers.

Radio

Radio broadcasts are mainly in English, but some are in Swahili and Luganda. The **BBC World Service** is broadcast to Uganda, and can be received on a short waveband radio, check the website for frequencies (www.bbc.co.uk/worldservice). **Radio Uganda's Red Channel** (98 FM) is a government-owned English-speaking station with good coverage. **CBS FM** (88.8 and 89.2 FM) had its service resumed in Oct 2010 after a year-long government-enforced closure. **Radio Simba** (97.3 FM) is a popular, commercial Kampala-based Lugandan station.

Television

There is a TV service run by the government and broadcasts for about 6 hrs every evening, mostly in English. Satellite is widely available and is usually DSTV (Digital Satellite Television), South African satellite TV, with over 100 channels of film, music, sport and light entertainment. The most popular are the sports channels. A number of hotels and bars have widescreen TV for watching big sporting events.

Money

Currency → *US$1 = USh 2356, £1 = USh 3767, 1 Euro = USh 3185 (Mar 2011).*
Most transactions are carried out with Ugandan shilling notes although there are some coins in use. Notes come in dominations of 1000, 5000, 10,000 and 20,000. When changing money you will normally be given high denomination notes. These can be difficult to change so make sure that you have an adequate supply of 1000 and 5000 shilling notes. Coins are 50, 100, 200, and 500 shillings. The Ugandan shilling floats against other currencies, and the exchange rate can be expected to depreciate steadily as prices have been rising faster in Uganda than in the rest of the world.

US dollars are the best form of cash to carry, although euros are also widely accepted. It is helpful to have some US currency in small denomination notes to avoid changing too much at an unfavourable rate, and for last-minute transactions when leaving. However, it is difficult to exchange or spend bills of denominations of less than US$20. The best exchange rates are offered on larger denominations like US$50 or US$100 notes. US dollar bills issued before 2000 are universally refused, with some banks reluctant to change notes pre-dating 2006. Dollar bills with the slightest mark or tear will be rejected, even if they pass the 'electronic counterfeit detectors' that are

in use everywhere. The rates can be up to 5-10% better in Kampala.

There are no restrictions on the amounts of any currencies that can be brought into or taken out of the country. Large sums may need to be declared. Consult the Ugandan Central Bank website www.bou.or.ug.

Banks

Money can be exchanged in banks or in the foreign exchange bureaux that are widespread. The bureaux tend to offer better rates than the banks and to stay open longer hours but commission rates are steep. Money can be changed in the larger hotels 24 hrs a day (although often restricted to their guests). It is possible to get money out at ATMs on most credit cards at Barclays and Stanbic banks, but charges may be imposed. Other banks' ATMs usually only accept local cards. Several banks act as agents for Western Union. Bank opening hours are usually Mon-Fri 0800-1700 and Sat 0800-1300.

Credit cards and TCs

Credit cards are accepted by the large hotels, airlines, main car hire firms, tour operators and travel agents, but an additional levy of 3-5% will be charged. American Express is the most widely accepted card, while Visa, Diners and MasterCard are also taken by some establishments.

It can be difficult to change TCs away from Kampala. A charge of 1-1.5% is levied for changing TCs and banks often demand to see the proof of purchase receipt, which travellers are advised to keep separately as no claim for refund will be processed without it. Stanbic Bank offers the most widespread service for TC exchanges in the larger towns.

Cost of travelling

Budget travellers can stay in backpacker accommodation, travel and eat for US$20 a day. To eat well and travel in reasonable comfort allow US$50-60 per person a day.

However, if you are going on a safari with an upmarket travel company you can at least double this figure. In addition you will pay US$150-200 for a car and driver. Do not forget to allow for national park fees, rafting and gorilla- and chimp-tracking permits. These could easily amount to US$1000 per person if you go to a few parks.

Opening hours

Banks Mon-Fri 0800-1700 and Sat 0800-1300. **Business and offices** Mon- Fri 0800-1300 and 1400-1700. **Post offices** Mon-Fri 0830-1700. **Shops** Mon-Fri 0800-1800.

Post

Services are reliable and airmail letters take about 10 days to Europe, US$1.10 up to 20 g. Postcards and letters cost US$0.50 when sent within Uganda. There is a poste restante service in Kampala (Poste Restante, GPO, Kampala Rd, Kampala). Most post offices offer a fax service, costing US$2 per page outgoing overseas, US$0.50 for an incoming fax.

Safety

Overall, Uganda is very safe, with far less petty crime than is found in Kenya. Every bank, shop, store, restaurant, hotel and even the hospital has armed guards, which may alarm you at first, but you quickly get used to the sight of guns. The general rule, when walking at night is don't exhibit anything valuable and keep wallets and purses out of sight. It is rare for tourists to be attacked. The most common crimes are pickpocketing, purse-snatching and thefts from vehicles, and most thefts happen in crowded markets and bus stations. Unaccompanied women are at particular risk of assault. Opening zippers on rucksacks of unwary travellers is common. Do not accept any food or drink from strangers as it may be drugged and

used to facilitate a robbery. It is wise to take taxis at night and avoid dark or deserted areas. Be careful about your belongings in crowded areas. Before travelling, check out www.fco.gov.uk for the UK's latest official travelling advice or http://travel.state.gov/travel/cis_pa_tw/cis/cis_1051.html for the American equivalent.

National parks

It's not only crime that may affect your safety; you must also take safety precautions when visiting national parks. If camping, it is not advisable to leave your tent or *banda* during the night. Wild animals wander around the camps freely during the hours of darkness, which is especially true of organized campsites where local animals have got so used to humans that they've lost much of their inherent fear. Exercise care during the day too; remember that wild animals can be dangerous.

Smoking

In Mar 2004, smoking was banned in public places, including workplaces, restaurants and bars. There is some doubt as to how strictly the ban is being implemented. An extension to private homes is said to be under consideration.

Student travellers

There are generally no discounts for students (apart from international air travel). Student rates advertised for museums and parks will usually only apply to local residents.

Tax

VAT is levied at 18%, but only on larger business with permanent premises, such as hotels. Small traders are outside the VAT net. Departure tax is included in the airline ticket price. A local hotel tax was introduced in 2008 – it varies by local government area..

Telephone → *Country code: 256.*

International calls can be made from the GPO office on Kampala Rd in Kampala. Phone cards are required, offered by Uganda Telecom and private companies. Newly privatized services are also available using pre-paid phone cards. Some, like MTN, offer half-price international calls at the weekends. Phone cards can also be used in public phone boxes.

Mobile phone use is widespread and is widely supplanting landlines especially outside Kampala. A recent operator tariff war has made rates very competitive. Overseas visitors are able to use their phones within Uganda provided they have arranged roaming with their service providers at home. Not only are outgoing calls (both local and international) expensive, beware of high charges for receiving calls under these arrangements. A better value alternative is to buy a cheap phone and SIM card for Ugandan use, costing about US$25. SIM cards are cheap and pay-as-you-go top-up cards are widely available. Before travelling see www.cellular. co.za/africa-cellguide.htm, a useful South African resource. Celtel are marginally cheaper but MTN have better coverage. An 07 prefix indicates a mobile phone number. Access to Uganda Telecome 071, Celtel network 075, MTN network 077 and 078.

Time

GMT + 3 hrs.

Tipping

It is customary to give waiters and porters a small tip. More of a problem is what to do about national park guides, as you may have 6 or 7 people accompanying you when you go gorilla tracking. The best guide is to remember that many will earn no more than USh 40,000 per month. Tips can therefore be quite small, maybe USh1000 per person, and should be given to the head guide who will distribute them. See also National parks and safaris, page 28, for tipping on safari.

Tour operators

See also Overland trucks, page 18, for companies offering overland trips.

UK
Adrift, T01488-71152, www.adrift.co.uk. Specialist adventure holidays.
Africa Travel Centre, 3rd floor, New Premier House, 150 Southampton Row, London WC1B 5AL, T0845-450 1520 (holidays), T0845-450 5701 (flights), www.africatravel.co.uk.
The Travelling Naturalist, T01305-267994, www.naturalist.co.uk. Wildlife and birdwatching holidays.
Tribes Travel, T01728-685971, www.tribes.co.uk. Award-winning independent travel agency.

Tourist information

Contact **Tourism Uganda**, 42 Windsor Cres, Kololo, Kampala PO Box 7211, Kampala, T0414-342 196/7, www.visituganda.com. The **Uganda Wildlife Authority** (UWA), 7 Kira Rd, Kamwokya, T0414-355 000, www. ugandawildlife.org, open 0900-1700, has information on national parks and reserves, including accommodation, activities and transport information. See *Travel Africa* (www.travelafricamag.com), published quarterly, which is a comprehensive source of information for all travellers in Africa. Ugandan embassies overseas are also helpful; see Embassies and consulates, page 32. The **Backpackers Hostel and Campsite** or **Red Chilli Hideaway** are excellent sources of reliable up-to-date information about Uganda; see pages 61 and 62. **Mountain Clubs of Uganda**, T077-284 3367, email idc@imul.com, is a useful source of information on mountaineering activities, such as rock climbing, hill walking, and ice climbing.

Useful websites

www.fco.gov.uk UK's Foreign Office site, for the 'official' advice on latest political situations.

www.go2africa.com Full accommodation and safari booking service for Africa, with useful practical information.

www.monitor.co.ug Online version of the national daily *Monitor* newpaper, see page 37.

www.newvision.co.ug Online version of the *New Vision* newpaper, see page 37.

www.overlandafrica.com A variety of overland tours offered throughout Africa.

www.traveluganda.co.ug Uganda Travel Planner has detailed travel and accommodation listings for all budgets.

www.uganda.co.ug A site with news and cultural overviews of the country.

www.ugandawildlife.org Website of the UWA, which manages the national parks and reserves.

www.visituganda.com Official site of the Ugandan tourist board.

www.web-dubois.fas.harvard.edu/ DuBois/baobab/baobab.html The Baobab Project is one of the largest academic studies of African art.

Visas and immigration

Note All these regulations change frequently. All visitors must be in possession of a passport valid for 1 year beyond the entry date, a visa, evidence of yellow fever vaccination, and a polio vaccination for under 5s. Visas are available at Entebbe airport, or may be obtained from Ugandan embassies and consulates overseas. The current fee for a 3-month visa from the date of entry is US$50. In case of cancellation the visa fee is non-refundable. Be aware that a 3-month visa does not determine how long you may remain in Uganda. The Ugandan immigration officer at the point of entry will decide that, normally a period of 1-3 months as a tourist.

Multi-entry visas are only available from Ugandan embassies and consulates overseas. If visiting Rwanda to track gorillas be aware that visitors with single-entry visas will be required to purchase another US$50 visa on re-entry to Uganda. Visa fees at borders are frequently payable in US$ cash only. Carry extra passport-sized photographs. Proof of sufficient funds or an onward ticket are occasionally requested at land borders.

Visitors from the following organizations and countries do not require a visa: Common Market for Eastern & Southern Africa (COMESA), East African Community (EAC) and the following countries: Antigua, Bahamas, Barbados, Belize, Cyprus, Fiji, Gambia, Grenada, Jamaica, Lesotho, Malta, Sierra Leone, Singapore, Solomon Islands, St Vincent, The Grenadines, Tonga and Vanuatu.

Visa extensions can be applied for before the visa expires at the **Ugandan Ministry of Internal Affairs**, 75 Jinja Rd, Kampala, T0414-231059. Visitors who overstay their visa face fines of US$30 per day, plus the risk of detention. See also www.mia.go.ug/page.php?1=immig_ services&&2=immigration%20Services.

Volunteering and NGO opportunities have to be arranged before arrival in Uganda. The appropriate visa costing US$250 per annum will need to be organized via a Ugandan embassy or consulate overseas, along with a copy of the NGO certificate, letter of appointment, qualifications record and criminal record check. Information is available from www. vso.org.uk and www.peacecorps.gov. For shorter stays try www.responsibletravel.com and www.traveltree.co.uk.

Weights and measures

Metric.

Women travellers

Normal caution is required. In particular, dress modestly, be wary of unsolicited male company, move around in a group where possible, avoid sunbathing alone and take taxis at night.

Working and volunteering

There are no virtually no opportunities for travellers to obtain casual paid employment in Uganda. Most foreign workers are employed through embassies, development or volunteer agencies or through foreign companies. For the most part these people will have been recruited in their countries of origin.

Once the domain of students and young backpackers, volunteering abroad has become popular with more 'mainstream' visitors, who combine voluntary work with a sightseeing holiday. Set this up before you travel. Useful websites are: www. volunteerafrica.org and www.wildnetafrica. co.za. See also Visas and immigration, above.

There is a vast amount of foreign aid being ploughed into Uganda and with it there are opportunities to work within the country as an expat. Several companies are offering 'gap year' projects but casual work is hard to get. **Nile River Explorers** are working closely with the local community to paint and help with the maintenance of projects. They have an arrangement with several overland companies that overlanders will do a day or 2 of voluntary work. It's good fun and rewarding. Email Sharon Webb on sharon@softpowereducation.com if you are interested. You can also help the local community with **Soft Power** (http://softpowereducation.com), working on projects such as renovating an orphanage and painting primary schools.

Contents

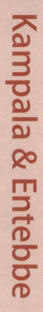

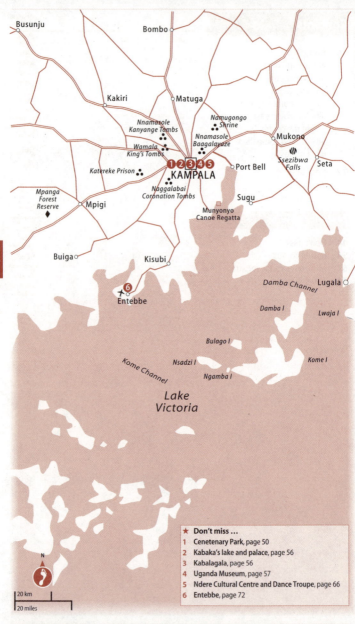

Busunju

Bombo

Kakiri

Matuga

Namugongo
Shrine

Nnamasole
Kanyange Tombs

Nnamasole
Baagalayaze

Mukono

Wamala
King's Tombs

1 2 3 4 5
KAMPALA

Port Bell

Ssezibwa
Falls

Seta

Katereke Prison

Naggalabai
Coronation Tombs

Sugu

Mpanga
Forest
Reserve

Mpigi

Munyonyo
Canoe Regatta

Buiga

Kisubi

Lugala

Damba Channel

6
Entebbe

Damba I

Lwaja I

Bulago I

Kome I

Kome Channel

Nsadzi I

Ngamba I

Lake
Victoria

N

20 km

20 miles

★ **Don't miss ...**
1 Cenetenary Park, page 50
2 Kabaka's lake and palace, page 56
3 Kabalagala, page 56
4 Uganda Museum, page 57
5 Ndere Cultural Centre and Dance Troupe, page 66
6 Entebbe, page 72

The capital of Uganda, Kampala, with its seven hills, is a surprisingly modern city. Over the last few years the centre has been transformed and is now dominated by skyscrapers. These have interrupted the views, although the three religions, Catholic, Protestant and Muslim, with their cathedrals, churches and mosques perched on separate hills, still keep a wary eye on each other.

Kampala is a friendly city and you can wander around and not worry about being hassled, which is a very pleasant change from other East African capital cities. It is small enough to explore without taking a city tour. In the last few years security has improved dramatically so that the nightlife is lively again and very loud especially at weekends.

Entebbe is situated on the shores of Lake Victoria, about 37 km from Kampala, and until 1962 was the administrative capital of the country. Very quiet compared to Kampala, it's a rather pretty town, built on lots of small hills that slope down to the shores, with almost constant views of the lake. The Entebbe–Kampala road bustles with activity.

Kampala

→ *Altitude: 1230 m. Phone code: 0414. Colour map 2, B5.*

The city centre is largely made up of government buildings and is neatly bisected by the Kampala–Jinja road. Uphill, all is calm with pleasant colonial-style buildings and pretty streets lined with jacaranda trees and flamboyants. Most of the buildings, if not government offices or embassies, have been turned into apartments. Downhill all is frenetic with a huge street market surrounding the chaotic matatu station and Nakivubo Stadium. The city has always been known for its greenery, although in recent times much of this has been lost. But even today, with many of the valleys built over, the impression is still an extremely pleasant one: a mixture of blue sky, green open spaces and red roofs.

Ins and outs

Getting there

It is about 40 km from the airport at Entebbe, see page 72. A taxi to Kampala is US$30, although new arrivals can get overcharged. A cheaper option is to take a taxi (quoted at US$6.50 at the airport desk, but if you go out to the parking area you can negotiate a cheaper rate) to Entebbe, and from there frequent *matatus* (minibuses) go to Kampala, one hour, US$1.25. There are also plenty of *matatus* shuttling between Entebbe and Kampala, though getting from the airport to Entebbe is not so easy. The bigger hotels offer an airport shuttle service. If arriving by bus from Nairobi, you'll enter along the Jinja Road and will need to take a *matatu* to get to the backpackers' hostels, 2-3 km from the centre. ▸▸ *See also Transport, page 69.*

Getting around

Unless you are staying outside the city centre you probably will not need to use public transport much as the city centre is compact and most places are within easy walking distance. However, a number of hotels and restaurants, and some sights such as the Uganda Museum, cathedrals, palace and Kisubi tombs, are away from the centre. Public transport runs from 0500 to midnight. There are taxi ranks around the centre and *matatus* patrol the streets. The taxi and *matatu* park are near the Nakivubo Stadium below Kampala Road; just keep heading downhill. A convenient and cheap way of travelling about town is to use a 'motor-taxi', motorbikes known as *boda-bodas*, which are available from stages on Kampala Road.

Safety

Be especially vigilant at night. You can walk in most of the centre of Kampala safely, but exercise caution in back streets. Kabalagala is even safer, but can get rowdy, particularly around places like Punchline and Cherie. When walking at night, conceal wallets, purses and anything valuable. Do not accept any food or drink from strangers as it may be drugged and used to facilitate a robbery.

Tourist offices

Tourism Uganda ① *42 Windsor Cres, Kololo, T0414-342196, www.visituganda.com,* have very helpful staff. The **Uganda Wildlife Authority (UWA)** ① *main office, 7 Kira Rd, between the British High Commission and the Uganda Museum, Kamwokya, T0414-355000, www.*

ugandawildlife.org, *Mon-Fri 0800-1300 and 1400-1700, Sat 0900-1300*, controls all Uganda's national parks and game reserves. Arrange to pay for and collect permits to see the gorillas in Bwindi and Mgahinga and book *banda* accommodation in the national parks and game reserves. The **Kampala Backpackers Hostel and Campsite** (see page 61) and **Red Chilli Hideaway** (see page 62) are also excellent sources of up-to-date information. **Buganda Tourism Centre** (see page 55) is a great resource about Bugandan affairs.

Background

Early days

The name Kampala came from the Bantu word *mpala* meaning a type of antelope, which, it is said, the Buganda chiefs used to keep on a hill near Mengo Palace. The name 'Hill of the Mpala' was given specifically to the hill on which Captain Fredrick Lord Lugard, a British administrator, established his fort in December 1890. At the fort, also an administrative post, Lugard hoisted the Imperial British East African Company flag in 1890, which in 1893 was replaced by the Union Jack. The Fort at Kampala Hill, as it became known (now Old Kampala Hill), attracted several hundred people and a small township developed.

Traders erected shops at the base of the hill, and by 1900 the confines of the fort had become too small for administrative purposes and it was decided that the colonial offices and government residences that were in Kampala (at this time most offices were at Entebbe) should be moved to Nakesero Hill. The shops and other commercial premises followed.

Kampala grew and the town spread, like Rome, over the surrounding seven hills. These historical hills are Rubaga, Namirembe (Mengo), Makerere, Kololo, Kibuli, Kampala (Old Kampala) and Mulago. On top of three of these hills, Rubaga, Namirembe and Kibuli, places of worship were built: Catholic, Protestant and Muslim respectively.

Modern Kampala

In 1906 Kampala was declared a township, and the railway joining it with the coast reached Kampala in 1931. In 1949 it was raised to municipality status, in 1962 it became a city and, in October of the same year, it was declared the capital. The city has continued to grow and now covers 23 hills over an area of nearly 200 sq km.

Like the rest of Uganda, Kampala suffered enormously in the post-Independence upheavals. Prior to these years Kampala had developed into a green city; it was spacious and well laid out and had evolved into the cultural and educational centre of Eastern Africa. During the Amin period the most dramatic changes to Kampala came with the expulsion of the Asian community. By the early to mid-1980s there were many business premises and blocks of flats that had not been touched for over a decade and had become very dilapidated. Many of these are in fact Asian properties that have since been returned to their original owners as part of the government's attempts to attract investment to the country. Other buildings have also been renovated and the roads repaired, and Kampala is gradually smartening itself up and looks like a modern capital with a number of imaginatively designed skyscrapers dominating the skyline.

Visitors to Kampala often comment on the greenness of the city and its number of trees, many of them inhabited by marabou storks. Many of these trees have been lost in the last few years. This is due to the city's massive building boom since 1986 that has used locally made bricks baked in wood-fuelled furnaces. As you drive into Kampala you may see these furnaces dotted over the countryside, trying to keep up with the tremendous demand for bricks, and in the process decimating Kampala's trees.

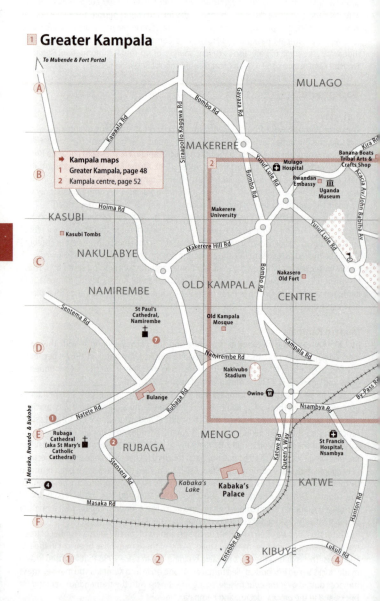

Greater Kampala

Kampala maps
1 Greater Kampala, page 48
2 Kampala centre, page 52

Labels on map:

To Mubende & Fort Portal

MULAGO

MAKERERE

Kawaala Rd

Bombo Rd

Gayaza Rd

Ssiraagolo Rd

Yusuf Lule Rd

Mulago Hospital

Banana Boats Tribal Arts & Crafts Shop

Kira Rd

Acacia Av/John Babiiha Av

Rwandan Embassy

Uganda Museum

Hoima Rd

KASUBI

Kasubi Tombs

Makerere University

NAKULABYE

Makerere Hill Rd

Bombo Rd

NAMIREMBE

OLD KAMPALA

CENTRE

Nakasero Old Fort

Sentema Rd

St Paul's Cathedral, Namirembe

Old Kampala Mosque

Kampala Rd

Namirembe Rd

Nakivubo Stadium

By-Pass Rd

Natete Rd

Bulange

Rubaga Rd

Owino

Nsambya Rd

To Masaka, Rwanda & Bukoba

Rubaga Cathedral (aka St Mary's Catholic Cathedral)

RUBAGA

MENGO

Katwe Rd

Queen's Way

St Francis Hospital, Nsambya

Stensera Rd

Kabaka's Lake

Kabaka's Palace

KATWE

Masaka Rd

Entebbe Rd

KIBUYE

Lukuli Rd

Hanton Rd

To Kabira Club, Ndere Cultural centre,
Bahai Temple & Ujuzi Art Studios

Bukoto Rd

MAGURA

N

200 metres
200 yards

Afriart
Gallery

KATALE

Lugogo By-Pass/Rotary Av

KOLOLO

Upper Kololo Terr

Indoor
Sports
Stadium

Tennis
Courts

Lugogo
Mall

New
Port
Bell Rd

To Jinja, Mount Elgon & Kenya

Volleyball
Astro Football
Ground

Lugogo
Cricket
Oval

Rugby
Grounds

Kampala Rd

Spring Rd

Old Port Bell Rd

To Bugolobi & Port Bell

Elgin St

Namuwongo Rd

Kibuli
Mosque

BUGOLOBI

KIBULI

Mbogo Rd

Zinwe Rd

International
Hospital

Ggaba
Rd

American
Embassy

Nsambya Rd

Kisugi
Church
Rd

Barmabat Rd

Tank Hill Rd

Tank Hill Rd

To Muyenga Club

KABALAGALA

Ggaba Rd

Gogonya Rd

To ⑦⑫ & in Munyonyo
③⑤⑨⑬⑳㉑㉓㉔

Kisugi
Church
Rd

Mbogo Rd

Tank Hill Rd

Tank Hill
Parade

KABALAGALA

Ggaba Rd

City centre

Exploring on foot

The city centre is located about 7 km to the north of Port Bell on the shores of Lake Victoria. A pleasant way to spend a day would be to walk around central Kampala. Start at the Parliament building and go east along Parliament Avenue to the National Theatre and African Craft Village behind it. Walk back along De Winton Road and turn left down Siad Barre Avenue (watch out for the elephant fountain at the bottom). Turn west on to Jinja Road until you see the Railway Station. Jinja Road now turns into Kampala Road; both have lots of shops, restaurants and places to have a cooling drink and something to eat. There is a great view of the Kibuli mosque looking back down Jinja Road, with its three green and white minarets. Turn north up Colville Street and west again along Kimanthi Avenue at Christ the King Church. You will then see the Sheraton Gardens at the end of this road. Walk round them along Speke Road (going underneath a bridge), and turn right up Ternan Avenue. You can make a detour here along Victoria Avenue to the Nommo Gallery, then stop at the Sheraton Hotel for a drink in the gardens. Turn right out of the Sheraton to see the Kampala Club. As the Speke Gate is now permanently closed, continue on Ternan Avenue until it becomes Kintu Road and curves round to the south, past the Kampala Serena Hotel, and becomes Siad Barre Avenue. Go straight over the roundabout to arrive back at the National Theatre. Otherwise, go left (east) on Nile Avenue. The first left takes you on to Hannington Road and the Tulifanya Gallery. If you keep going straight you will end up at the golf course and the Garden City Complex. If you cannot face the modern shopping mall experience, then proceed right down the incline to the large junction. Go left onto Jinja Road and keep your eyes open for the entrance into Centenary Park.

Centenary Park

This leafy space is a relief after a long day on the dusty streets and is family friendly, with lots of security and a colourful children's playground. The park was recently transformed from a mugger's hangout to an open-air bar/restaurant complex.

Parliament buildings

The complex is located on Parliament Avenue (the road that has undergone the most name changes in Kampala; it has been Obote Avenue twice and this is the third time it has been Parliament Avenue) and is the seat of the Uganda government. It is lined with lovely umbrella trees. The archway at the entrance is the symbol of Uganda's Independence (declared on 9 October 1962) and here are often perched what must be one of the world's most sinister birds: the marabou stork. The archway has now been completely renovated. On the metal gates at the entrance are the emblems of the original districts of Uganda. Inside, at the entrance to the main Chambers (which is far as visitors can go), there are engravings representing the different modes of life in all the districts. The white building with the clocktower further up the hill is the Kampala City Council building. A pleasant garden separates the two.

National Theatre

Located on De Winton Road at the junction of Siad Barre Avenue, the theatre took three years to build and was opened in 1959 by the then Governor Sir Frederick Crawford. It is a curious building and is faced with a whole series of interconnected concrete circles. Check the noticeboard for dance, drama and music performances outside. See also page 66.

Railway station

South of centre, the solid, colonial-style railway station was completed in 1928. The final stretch of line, west to Kasese, was opened in 1956, and the ceremonial copper fish-plates and bolts are on display. Today, with no passenger trains running, the building is rather sad looking.

Nommo Gallery

ⓘ *4 Victoria Ave, next to State Lodge, T0414-234475. Mon-Fri 0900-1700, Sat and Sun 0900-1500. Free.*

This small building, once a private house set in spacious grounds, houses Uganda's national art gallery, where artwork by local artists and those from other parts of East Africa are displayed. Exhibitions are advertised in the local press. There is a shop attached with both artworks and crafts for sale. A small restaurant inside serves snacks.

Sheraton Gardens

These used to be known as the Jubilee Gardens but are now kept – in superb condition – by the **Sheraton Hotel** (see page 60). They originally commemorated George V's jubilee and there is a bust of the king in the gardens. Speke Gate is now permanently closed. However, visitors can relax and have a drink in the gardens or have a delicious breakfast buffet in the Victoria Dining Room. Entry security to the hotel is now tight.

Just outside the gardens, opposite the **Imperial Hotel** at the top of Speke Road, is an impressive statue of a mother and child. Sculpted by Gregory Maloba, *Independence* depicts a mother with bandages around her legs and waist lifting a child with arms held aloft.

Sikh and Hindu temples and market area

In the town centre close to the *matatu* park are two temples: one Hindu and one Sikh. One was used as a school for some years but has now been returned to its original use. Just to the north of them lies **Nakasero Market**. There are some fine examples of old colonial stores with spacious balconies. They are rather neglected now, with peeling paint and rusting roofs. A little further west, the area around the taxi park and bus station and Nakivubo Stadium is known as **Owino Market**. Most of the pavements in the streets surrounding it are covered in all manner of goods. It's an absolute hive of activity as shoppers race to catch their *matatus* clutching their purchases.

West of the centre

Kampala Old Fort

ⓘ *Matia Mulumba Rd, close to the Old Kampala Hospital.*

Captain Lugard built a fort on Old Kampala Hill in 1890. The building served as the colonial administrative centre until 1905. A small block house on a hill west of the present day centre of Kampala was demolished in 2002 and a replica built nearby, behind Old Kampala Mosque (see below), just to the east of the original fort. The replica is all that remains of the fort. The original building was not dismantled systematically to enable reuse of the materials, so the replica has different brickwork. The area around the fort, encircled by Old Kampala Road, Old Kampala and was where many of the Asian population lived before expulsion by Amin. Old Kampala contains many fine colonial European and Asian buildings.

Old Kampala Mosque, also called the National Mosque, is located nearby. The construction began during the 1970s when Idi Amin was in power, and was completed in 2007 with generous financial support from Libya.

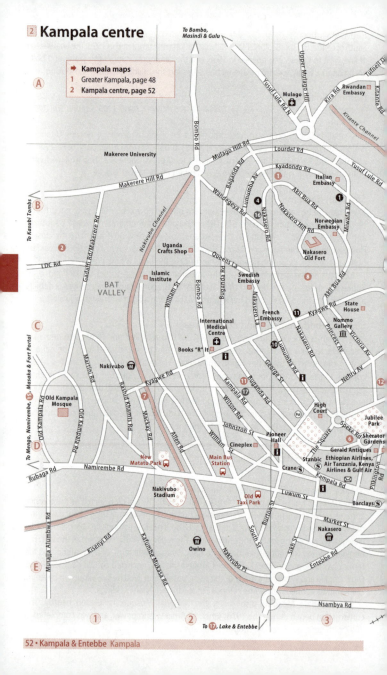

➡ **Kampala maps**
1 Greater Kampala, page 48
2 Kampala centre, page 52

To Bombo,
Masindi & Gulu

Upper Mulago Hill

Kira Rd

Rwandan
Embassy

Kitante Channel

Kitante Rd

Tufnell Dr

Yusuf Lule Rd N

Mulago

Mulago Hill Rd

Lourdel Rd

Yusuf Lule Rd

Makerere University

Makerere Hill Rd

Kyadondo Rd

Italian
Embassy

Baganda Rd

Lumumba Av

Wandegeya Rd

Akii Bua Rd

Nakasero Hill Rd

Norwegian
Embassy

Mwanga Rd

To Kasubi Tombs

Gadaffi Rd/Makerere Rd

Nakivubo Channel

Uganda
Crafts Shop

Queens La

Nakasero
Old Fort

LDC Rd

BAT
VALLEY

William St

Islamic
Institute

Bombo Rd

Baganda Rd

Nakasero La

Swedish
Embassy

French
Embassy

Kyagwe Rd

State
House

Nommo
Gallery

Princess Av

Victoria Av

Nehru Av

International
Medical
Centre

Nakasero Rd

Lumumba Rd

George St

Books "R" It

Nakivubo

Kyagwe Rd

Martin Rd

Bashir Khamis Rd

MacKay Rd

Allen Rd

Kampala Rd

Buganda Rd

Wilson Rd

Johnston St

William St

Pioneer
Hall

Cineplex

The Square

High
Court

Pol

Speke Rd

Jubilee
Park

Sheraton
Gardens

Gerald Antiques

Old Kampala
Mosque

Old Kampala Rd

To Mengo, Namirembe, Masaka & Fort Portal

New
Matatu Park

Namirembe Rd

Stanbic

Ethiopian Airlines,
Air Tanzania, Kenya
Airlines & Gulf Air

Crane

Kampala Rd

Pilkington Rd

Main Bus
Station

Rubaga Rd

Nakivubo
Stadium

Old
Taxi Park

Luwum St

Market St
Nakasero

Barclays

Musajja Alumbwa Rd

Kisenyi Rd

Katumbe Mukasa Rd

Owino

Nakivubo Pl

Bombo Rd

South St

Sikhs St

Entebbe Rd

Nsambya Rd

To Lake & Entebbe

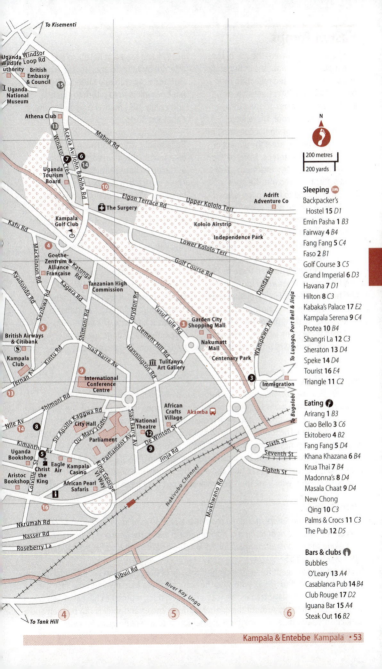

Sleeping

Backpacker's
  Hostel **15** *D1*
Emin Pasha **1** *B3*
Fairway **4** *B4*
Fang Fang **5** *C4*
Faso **2** *B1*
Golf Course **3** *C5*
Grand Imperial **6** *D3*
Havana **7** *D1*
Hilton **8** *C3*
Kabaka's Palace **17** *E2*
Kampala Serena **9** *C4*
Protea **10** *B4*
Shangri La **12** *C3*
Sheraton **13** *D4*
Speke **14** *D4*
Tourist **16** *E4*
Triangle **11** *C2*

Eating

Arirang **1** *B3*
Ciao Bello **3** *C6*
Ekitobero **4** *B2*
Fang Fang **5** *D4*
Khana Khazana **6** *B4*
Krua Thai **7** *B4*
Madonna's **8** *D4*
Masala Chaat **9** *D4*
New Chong
  Qing **10** *C3*
Palms & Crocs **11** *C3*
The Pub **12** *D5*

Bars & clubs

Bubbles
  O'Leary **13** *A4*
Casablanca Pub **14** *B4*
Club Rouge **17** *D2*
Iguana Bar **15** *A4*
Steak Out **16** *B2*

Kasubi Tombs

The Kasubi Tombs were the site of the burial place of the Kabakas of Buganda and were constructed reflecting the typical Ganda architectural style of a large circular house, topped by a domed, thatched roof. There were several buildings of similar construction in the surrounding area, the largest of which housed the tombs. Many of the artefacts of the kings, including spears, drums, furniture and a stuffed pet leopard, reputed to have been owned by Muteesa I, were on display. The site contained the tombs of Muteesa I (1856-1884), Mwanga II (1884-1897), Sir Daudi Chwa (1897-1939), and Edward Muteesa II (1939-1966). Mwanga II was exiled to the Seychelles in 1899; he died there in 1903 and his body was returned to Uganda and buried at Kasubi in 1910. Muteesa II was removed from his position soon after Independence during the Obote I regime and died three years later in 1969 in London. His body was returned to Uganda in 1971 and buried at Kasubi in an attempt by Amin to appease the Baganda. During Museveni's rule Muteesa II's son has been allowed to return to Uganda and in July 1993 he was crowned as the Kabaka at Budo.

There was a two-doored house, Bujjabukula, which you passed through as you enter the main enclosure, as well as the drum house Ndoga-Obukaba. There were also a number of smaller buildings of similar design around the outside, within the inner enclosure, which were for the royal wives. Originally there was an outer fence that enclosed the whole of the area, which held over 500 houses, over 6 km in length.

The largest building, which was the tomb house, was called Muzibu-Azaala-Mpanga. It was a large thatched round house reflecting traditional Ganda architecture. The thatch was supported by 50 rings, each made by a different Bugandan clan.

Kasubi Tombs

ⓘ *About 3 km west from the centre on Nabulagala Hill, off the Kampala–Hoima Rd.*
In March 2010 the main buildings of the Kasubi Tombs, burial place of the Bugandan Kabakas or kings, caught fire and were reduced to ashes. Many artefacts were destroyed in the conflagration. The tombs were listed as a World Heritage Site and in late 2010 UNESCO approved emergency funds to support their restoration at an estimated cost of US$1 million. The restoration work has a proposed completion date of 2012. For a description of the tombs prior to the fire, see box, above. In the interim it is possible to visit the Wamala Tombs, see below, which are built in similar style but have been poorly maintained.

Wamala Tombs

ⓘ *13 km along the Kampala–Hoima road near Mpigi, 30 mins' drive northwest of Kampala. After 6.8 km take the right turning to Nansana Town and at the Nansana Trading Centre turn right along the rough murram road for 1.5 km. The hilltop tomb is visible from the environs. Open 0900-1700. US$1.*
Set on a hilltop in beautiful surroundings is the site of the palace and sacred burial ground of Kabaka Suuna II (d 1856), who was the son of Kabaka Kamanya and the first Kabaka to receive the Arab slave traders. He was a despotic ruler, reputed to have had 148 wives and over 200 children. Around the central platform spears and shields can be seen and a bark-cloth screen hides the mythical eternal forest to where he went for everlasting life.

Although larger and similar in design to the Kasubi Tombs, there are no inner or outer enclosures. The main tomb is in disrepair with a broken down thatched roof that reputedly supports a large bat colony. Nearby is the Tomb of Nnamasole Kanyange, Kabaka Suuna's mother, who was buried on an adjacent hilltop.

Namirembe Cathedral
ⓘ *Sun 0700 English service, 1030 Lugandan service.*
This brick-red Anglican Cathedral, also known as St Paul's Cathedral, has an impressive dome and is visible from much of Kampala. It's located at the top of Namirembe Hill (Mengo) offering spectacular views. Namirembe means 'mother of peace'.

The original church built in 1890 was made of bamboo poles, grass thatch and reed work by local craftsmen. It was relocated shortly afterwards as it was built in a swampy area. The second church was also short-lived. Built in 1891 the roof blew off in a thunderstorm the following year. The third church seating 4000 people was built between 1894 and 1895 with traditional African materials but dismantled due to termite infestation in 1900. A replacement building was begun in 1901 and completed in 1904. This was made of earth-baked bricks and thatch, but the roof was destroyed by lightning just six years later. The fifth building was constructed between 1915 and 1919 with the tiled roof that can be seen today. Particularly interesting is the graveyard where Sir Albert Ruskin Cook, who was the first to diagnose sleeping sickness in East Africa and established Mengo Hospital, and his wife Lady Katherine, who started midwifery training in Uganda, are buried. Also here are the remains of Bishop Hannington, who was murdered in 1885 (see box, page 98).

The cathedral has beautiful stained glass windows, and an interesting history, including a small piece of St Paul's Cathedral in London and a piece of the Berlin Wall cemented into the wall near the altar. A guide is available. The congregation is called to the service by the beating of drums and by bells, audible if staying at **Namirembe Guesthouse** (see page 61).

Bulange
ⓘ *US$10 guided tours of Bulange, Mengo, lake and palace (tours do not enter the palace itself, but the estate and surrounding area). Tickets to tour the building are on sale next door at the Buganda Tourism Centre, see below.*
This complex off the Natete Road, passed on the way to Rubaga Cathedral, houses the Bugandan Parliament (Lukiko) and hosts the Kingdom's administration. One of the conditions of the king's return in 1993 was that his role would be purely ceremonial and cultural, without any political function. The Bulange is an imposing building with two small spires and a large central one. There is a large statue of King Ronald Muwenda Mutebi II. Most of the land around this building belongs to the king.

The **Buganda Tourism Centre** ⓘ *Kabaka and Kisingiri roads, T0414-421166, open 0900-1700*, is located just before the Kabaka's palace. You can organize trips for the Kabaka's Trail (see page 59) from here and they are helpful with tourist information. They sell souvenirs adorned with royal regalia. There are giant tortoises in the grounds. You will probably be told that the oldest is 450 years old whilst the youngest is a mere stripling of 300.

Further down the road in a blue building is **Libateroi church**. The Supreme Court moved from here to 10 Upper Kololo Terrace in 2010.

Rubaga Cathedral of the Sacred Heart
Rather confusingly a number of signs refer to this building as Lubaga Cathedral, also known as St Mary's Catholic Cathedral, built by the White Fathers between 1914 and

1925. Restored in preparation for the visit of Pope John Paul II to Uganda on 9 February 1993, the garden next to the cathedral commemorates the papal visit. It is a huge building with sculptures of the heads of prominent Catholics above the main door. There is an illuminated cross outside and you look across to a fenced area that belongs to the Kabaka. Inside the cathedral are the remains of the first African Catholic Bishop and the first African Archbishop of Kampala Diocese, Joseph Kiwanuka. Archives on the lives of the 22 Catholic martyrs, killed in the 1880s, are kept here. There are two sets of steeple bells, one for everyday usage and the other solely reserved to proclaim the death of a pope.

Mengo and Kabaka's lake and palace

A Lugandan word for grinding stones, Mengo is an inner western district of Kampala just over 1 km from Kampala Old Fort. Mengo Hospital, the first in the city, was built in 1897 by Sir Albert Cook, a British medical missionary who is buried nearby at Namirembe Cathedral (see page 55).

Also found here is the Kabaka's lake and palace. Located close to the Kabaka's capital the lake was constructed from about 1885 to 1888 by Kabaka Mwanga. The original plan was to link it up with Lake Victoria but this was not to be, as Mwanga was deposed. The lake got into a fairly terrible state and became stagnant. The Kabaka-to-be reopened the lake in 1993 and unveiled a statue to Mwanga. The lake is a pleasant scenic stretch, formed by damming two streams from the north, with two small islands in the centre. It's possible to walk round most of the lake shore. The lake attracts a wide variety of birds including an estimated 5000 cattle egrets (*Bubulcus ibis*), sighted at a single roost in April 2010.

The hilltop palace at Mengo, just west of Kampala, has been returned to the Kabaka. The palace was once the pride of Buganda, with its high walls, beautiful gardens and lake. It contains a handsome building with a cupola in Classical style, and it faces across the valley north toward the Bulange building. Within the palace complex of many buildings is the Kabaka's official residence called Twekobe Palace on Lubiri hill, shelled by Amin on Obote's orders in 1966 when Kabaka Edward Mutesa was exiled, and afterwards used by Amin's soldiers for their appalling deeds during their terror reign. Amin built underground torture and execution chambers here, and wall writings describe some of the horrors enacted. These cells are not officially open to visitors. The soldiers moved out in 1993 when restoration work began, helped in 1995 when Museveni initiated his policy to restore cultural institutions. The palace complex and Bulange are connected by a straight road, and halfway along there is a roundabout bisected by a road, reserved solely for the use of the Kabaka, as legend dictates that the king must only travel along a straight road to ensure there is no obstacle in the Kabaka'a spirits' way. A group of Ugandan royalists prepared the palace for the return of the Kabaka. By tradition the king is forbidden to enter the palace until he has been anointed by witch doctors, soothsayers and healers. At the main gate is a fireplace called Kyoto Ggombolola, where a fire is kept alight at all times, only extinguished when the king dies.

Kabalagala

Kabalagala derives its name from a locally made pancake, made of sweet bananas, cassava flour and spiced with peppers. It is a lively area, 2 km south east of central Kampala at the junction of Ggaba Road, Nsambya Estate Road and Tank Hill Road. It has a large number of restaurants and bars and attracts many tourists and residents. The American Embassy is located nearby on the Ggaba Road.

North and east of the centre

Nakasero Old Fort

About 1.5 km from the centre, Nakasero Hill is dominated by the old Ugandan Television building, soon to be the new Kampala Hilton. The Old Fort lies just behind it and overlooks the Kitante Valley where the golf course has been built. It is of brick construction, with rifle slits. It now houses police offices, and access is restricted.

Uganda Museum

ⓘ *5-7 Kira Rd, T0414-232707, mumod@mtti.go.ug. Mon-Sat 1000-1800, Sun and public holidays 1500-1900. US$1.50, camera US$2.50, video camera US$10. The library is manned by volunteers 3 days a week, days vary according to volunteer availability and are posted on the library. US$1.50 (you do not pay museum entry if only accessing library).*

Founded in 1908 on the site of the Old Fort on Old Kampala Hill, the Uganda Museum moved to the present site out of the town centre in 1954. Most of the displays have been renovated and the rest are in the process of being restored. Many of the items were looted between 1970 and 1986 and efforts are being made to return the museum to its former standard. In late 2010 plans were announced to demolish the Uganda Museum, replace it with a 60-storey tower block, two floors of which would be allocated to the museum, the remainder earmarked for government offices. However, these plans have been delayed indefinitely amidst significant protest.

Displays include a number of artefacts from archaeological sites from around the country, with exhibitions of Stone and Iron Age finds, and fossil materials from the Albertine Rift Region. The Ethnographic section has models of dwellings, settlements and hunting scenes, wood carvings, metalwork, leather craft, pottery, traditional weaponry and a large and impressive canoe. The museum is also home to a collection of musical instruments including many drums, which visitors are allowed to play. Occasionally the museum holds live traditional music in the afternoon. The first printing press used in Uganda, a movable variety, is on display. It was imported by Reverend Alexander Mackay, an Anglican Church missionary, and used to print catechism lessons and the Bible in Uganda.

The museum is home to the Uganda Society, the Historic Building Society, and the Uganda Food and Drink Society. The books of the East African Wildlife Society are stored here as well as the Uganda Society's library, housed in one of the museum's rooms. This is a collection of approximately 3000 books, maps, photographs and periodicals, including a complete collection of *The Uganda Journal* published since 1934, covering historical, scientific and cultural topics.

You can carry on past the museum along Kira Road. The pleasant drive down John Babiiha Avenue (previously Acacia Avenue) takes you to the golf course. There are a number of restaurants in this area, known as **Kololo**.

Bahá'í Temple

ⓘ *Off Gayaza Rd, 4 km out of Kampala on Kikaya Hill. Open daily for prayers 0830-1730.*

The Bahá'í Temple, also known as the Uganda House of Worship, was built between 1958 and 1962 and is the only temple of the Bahai religion in Africa. The nine-sided temple has bright coloured windows of amber, green and blue, topped by a large dome. Founded by Baha'u'llah (1817-1892) in Iran in 1844, followers of the Bahá'í religion believe that every religious manifestation forms a successive chapter in the revelation of God and all the world's major religions form a progressive process by which God reveals His will to humanity. People of all faiths are therefore welcome to visit this temple for prayer and meditation at any time. A wonderful view of the temple can be seen from the end of Kira Road in Kampala, just beyond the Uganda Museum to the left. From the temple itself there are excellent views of Kampala and the surrounding countryside.

Makerere University
① *Daily 1000-1700.*
This is the oldest university in East Africa and for many years had a fine international reputation. However, it suffered greatly in the 1970-1980s and is now struggling to return to its former high standards. Despite the rather shabby look at present, the original impressive appearance is unmistakable. The main campus contains the administrative buildings, the academic faculties, the library, seven halls of residence, the guesthouse and staff residences, as well as recreational facilities including the Student Guild and a pool.

Within the Faculty of Fine Art there is a gallery that hosts exhibitions of students' works. The building dates from 1923, and there is a permanent display of sculptures. In a room on the ground floor is an interesting collection of British Victorian industrial machinery, including a Victorian art printing press bearing the Royal Arms, with handsome cast iron feet and the maker's name: Payne & Sons, Otley, Yorkshire, England.

Kibuli Mosque
① *Prayers are held here 5 times a day. Guided tours can be arranged for a donation.*
On Kibuli Hill is the oldest mosque in Kampala. This land was given to Muslim settlers in mid-19th century when a mosque was built but later fell into disrepair. The foundation stone for the current building was laid by Prince Aly Khan in 1941 and he returned 10 years later for the opening ceremony. There are spectacular views of Kampala from the minaret.

Muyenga
Muyenga Hill, at 1306 m, is one of Kampala's highest points, 2.5 km from the centre. An affluent inner Kampala suburb, east of Kabalagala (see page 56), it's often called Tank Hill after the water reservoirs on the summit of Muyenga Hill. The International Hospital is located here, along with a few expensive restaurants.

Bugolobi
A leafy suburb, Bugolobi lies 4 km due east of central Kampala. **Red Chilli Hideaway**, the excellent backpackers' hostel, see page 62, is located here.

Around Kampala

In addition to the places described below, pleasant day trips, either in your own vehicle or by public transport, can be made to Entebbe (see page 72), Mabira Forest Reserve (see page 82), Jinja (see page 84) and the Mpanga Forest Reserve (see page 194).

Namugongo Shrine
① *12 km from Kampala off the Jinja road.*
The Namugongo Martyrs' Shrine is the site where 22 Ugandan Christian converts were burnt to death on the orders of Kabaka Mwanga in 1886. On the visit of Pope Paul VI to Uganda in 1969, the victims were canonized and since then the shrine has been an important site for Ugandan Christians. On the site there are two churches: one built by the

Roman Catholic Church, and the other by the Church of Uganda. The steel structure, built in traditional style, has artistic work on its interiors depicting scenes from this episode and, in the centre, preserved in glass, are some of the remains of one of the martyrs, Kaloli-Lwanga. Nearby is an artificial lake. There is a public holiday every year on 3 June in remembrance of the martyrs.

Kabaka's Trail

ⓘ *All sites are within easy reach of Kampala. For booking details contact the Buganda Tourism Centre (see page 55) or Tourism Uganda (see page 46). The price varies according to numbers, season, time and exact route.*

This eco-tourism initiative, started in 2002, introduces travellers to Uganda's rich cultural heritage by taking them around a circuit, taking one to three days, that encompasses the most important sites of the Bugandan Kabakas (kings). Traditional dance, music and craft-making activities are demonstrated as well as storytelling. The Kabaka's Trail has been developed as part of the Heritage Trails Project and the income generated goes to local communities. Plans are afoot to develop other Heritage Trails.

The sites visited include the following. The **Naggalabi Buddo Coronation site** is 19 km from Kampala along the Masaka Road. Take the left turn on the sharp bend that leads to King's College Buddo and Naggalabi Buddo is just after the college. The site is where previous Kabakas have been enthroned for the past 700 years and the current Kabaka was crowned in 1993. It's advisable to check with Buganda Tourism Centre (see page 55) or a local guide before going.

Katereke Prison, a *komera* or prison ditch, 14 km from Kampala and 3 km off the Kampala–Masaka road, is where Kabaka Kalema imprisoned and starved to death rival claimants to the throne as well as other opponents during the 1888-1889 succession struggles. There is an older prison ditch in Kyebando opposite the Baha'i Temple, built by Queen Muganzilwaza, mother of Mutesa I in 1856 for the same purpose. The **Wamala Tombs**, see page 54, is a shrine built for the powerful and despotic Kakaba Suuna II in 1856. The **Ssezibwa Falls**, an area of outstanding beauty, are located northeast of Kampala and were a spiritual site associated with traditional healing rites, with many local shrines, and were also a royal retreat. **Nnamasole Baagalayaze Tombs** are where Kabaka Mwanga's mother was laid to rest and the cultural centre offers traditional performances, storytelling and the chance to see local crafts being made.

Munyonyo

An upmarket residential neighbourhood, Munyonyo lies 13 km southeast of Kampala, 30 minutes' drive away on Lake Victoria's Murchison Bay. Its beaches attract many weekend visitors from the city. The famous annual canoe race, overseen by the Kabaka and his ministers from a small, rusty pavilion in the car park, is held here (see box, page 67). **Mulungu Beach** is a relatively unknown but lovely spot, frequented only by locals and the odd expat. There are many bars. To get there, go 200 m past **Speke Resort** on Munyonyo Road, take a left down the dirt road at the T-junction and the beach is at the end of this road, about 1 km. The only food available is fried tilapia and chips. It gets very busy at weekends, with a regular crowd of Ugandan bikers showing off their 'chrome horses'.

⊙ Kampala listings

Hotel prices

LL over US$200 **L** US$151-200 **AL** US$101-150
A US$66-100 **B** US$46-65 **C** U$31-45
D US$21-30 **E** US$12-20 **F** US$7-11
G under US$7

Restaurant prices

🍴🍴🍴 over US$12 🍴🍴 US$6-12 🍴 under US$6
See pages 21-23 for further information.

🛌 Sleeping

Several new hotels were built in Kampala for the Commonwealth Heads of Government meeting in 2007, attended by Queen Elizabeth II. The **Hilton Hotel Kampala** is a 24-storey development on Nakasero Hill on a 5.7-ha site. It's behind schedule but is due to open shortly.

City centre *p50, map p52*

LL Emin Pasha Hotel, 27 Akii Bua Rd, Nakasero, T0414-236977, www.eminpasha. com. Boutique hotel 10 km north of the city centre with 20 tastefully decorated a/c rooms and suites and 1 apartment, all with internet. Converted from a gracious 1930s colonial house with wide verandas in 0.8 ha of rambling, mature gardens with a pool. The **Fez Restaurant and Wine Bar** (🍴🍴🍴) offers inside or outside dining with excellent food, service and a good selection of wine. Spa and small conference and business centre facilities. Highly recommended.

LL Kampala Serena Hotel, Kintu Rd, T0414-309000, www.serenahotels.com. Built on the site of the notorious **Nile Hotel** on Nakasero Hill, where Amin's secret service thugs were based. Opened in 2006, the US$30 million upgrade was funded by the Aga Khan. It has a slick, modern atmosphere compared to its competitors. Although its gardens are no match for the **Sheraton** and its architecture isn't as picturesque as the **Grand Imperial**, it does have excellent facilities. The large pool, roof terrace for private functions,

Moorish-themed spa, bandstand, helipad, banqueting and conference facilities are all 5-star standard and prices. Recommended.
LL Sheraton Kampala Hotel, Ternan Ave, T0414-420000, www.sheraton.com/kampala. Upgraded in 2005, 222 a/c rooms and suites set within 4 ha of Sheraton Gardens (see page 51), beautifully maintained by the hotel. Pool, squash, tennis, health club and conference and banqueting facilities. Good coffee bar and free Wi-Fi in the lobby. All rooms have DSTV, internet and balconies. The **African Paradise** restaurant offers international cuisine. Breakfast buffet on the first floor, with lovely views of the gardens and city, open to non-residents. The **Equator Bar** has a wide selection of cocktails.
LL-L Golf Course Hotel, 64-88 Yusuf Lule Rd, T0414-563500, www.golfcoursehotel. com. Situated beside the Uganda Golf Club and the Garden City Shopping Mall overlooking the west side of the city, this luxurious hotel offers a choice of 3 rooftop 'executive pyramids', deluxe suites or 115 a/c rooms. Revolving restaurant with panoramic city views. Use of the golf club is included plus there's a pool, gym, internet, helipad and conference and banqueting facilities.
LL-L Protea Hotel Kampala, 4 Upper Kololo Terrace, Kololo, T0414-550000, www. proteahotels.com/kampala. Among the best for modern luxury, part of the efficient South African hotel chain, with 59 a/c rooms and 11 suites with free Wi-Fi, restaurant and bar, gym, airport transfer and conference facilities. The front-facing rooms offer wonderful views of Kololo.
LL-AL Grand Imperial Hotel, 6 Nile Ave, T0414-311048, www.imperialhotels.co.ug. Pleasant conversion of a colonial building, 103 a/c rooms and suites, very central, 3 restaurants, 4 bars, ballroom, pool, saunas, jacuzzis, steam and spa baths, massage, shopping mall, satellite TV and business centre and conference facilities. Outgoing international telephone charges are exorbitant.

LL-AL Speke Hotel, 7-9 Nile Ave, T0414-259221-4, www.spekehotel.com. Built in the 1920s, this popular hotel is the oldest in town. 50 a/c rooms, some with balconies. Attractive decor with striking murals and portraits of John Manning Speke. Rooms at the rear are the quietest. Recommended.

L-AL Hotel Triangle, 16 Buganda Rd, T0414-231747, www.hoteltriangle.co.ug. New 4-star hotel opposite the African Crafts Centre, well positioned and relatively quiet for the centre. Large, well-lit rooms with DSTV and a/c. Pool, steam bath and sauna. Slightly lacking character, but welcoming service and a spacious, calm interior.

AL Shangri La Hotel, formerly Shanghai Hotel, 8-10 Ternan Ave, T0414-250366, www.shangri-la.co.ug. Positioned behind the **Sheraton** in the grounds of the Kampala Club. Restaurant, pool, gym, badminton and tennis. Rooms have DSTV.

AL-A Fairway, 1-2 Kafu Rd, T0414-259571, www.fairwayhotel.co.ug. Opposite the golf course, this is a pleasant hotel, one of the more friendly in Kampala, set in attractive grounds. 110 rooms and suites, most with balconies. There's a pool, a health club, 2 restaurants, a bar and a business and conference centre. Free airport shuttle bus.

AL-A Fang Fang Hotel, 9 Sezibwa Rd, T0414-233115, reservations@fangfang.co.ug. Central, comfortable old-style hotel.

A-C Havana Hotel, 28 Mackay Rd, T0414-343532, gkkhavanahotel@yahoo.co.in. Entering from the chaos of the nearby taxi park, this is a surprising haven of tranquillity. All rooms have a/c. Deluxe and executive rooms have DSTV and lake views from the upper floors. A good restaurant offers Indian, African and international dishes and there's a sports bar, pool, children's park and attractive gardens. Friendly staff, good security and safe parking. Business centre with internet. Airport shuttle service.

B Tourist, 9 Market St, T0414-251471/2, www.touristhotel.net. Centrally located, spacious and good value for money. Close to the taxi stands.

C Faso Hotel, 512 Makerere Hill Rd, opposite the Law Development Centre, Wandegeya, T0414-532151, T077-269 6634 (mob), fasohotels@yahoo.com. Basic, quiet and secluded. Unpretentious restaurant and bar open all day. Good value. Long-term rates available.

Mengo p56, map p48

B Hotel Barbados International, 4 Rubaga Rd, West Mengo, T077-283 6569 (mob), www.hotelbarbadosinternational.com. Modern, good value hotel. Relatively quiet but easy access to the town centre. The health club offers massage and sauna.

B Namirembe Guest House, 1085 Willis Rd, T0414-273778, www.namirembe-guesthouse.com. Close to Mengo hospital, high on Namirembe Hill, just below the cathedral, with a fine view. Run by Church of Uganda. The restaurant serves quality local food, and pizzas and burgers on Tue night. Small gift/crafts shop, beauty salon and internet.

D-G Kampala Backpackers Hostel and Campsite, Natete Rd, on Kikandwa Hill just past Mengo, 2 km from the centre, T0414-274767, T077-243 0587 (mob), www.backpackers.co.ug. Grass-thatched *bandas*, camping US$5pp, dorm US$6-8pp. Bar, restaurant (0730-2130) or you can cook your own food. Good noticeboard with lots of travel information/advice. Wi-Fi and email facilities. Can get noisy and crowded with overlanders' trucks. Laundry facilities and hot showers. Pool 250 m away. Nile rafting can be arranged with New Zealand company **Adrift**, 1-day trip US$125 including lunch, pick-up in Kampala or Jinja. Many other trips and safaris can be arranged including climbing the Rwenzoris. New satellite backpacker camp planned in Murchison Falls National Park, due to open in 2011. To get here, take a *matatu* for Natete from the *matatu* station opposite Nakivubo Stadium in the city centre, US$0.50

Kabalagala p56, map p48

L Le Petit Village, 1273 Ggaba Rd, T0312-265530, www.lepetitvillage.net. Belgian-owned thatched roof boutique hotel, with 12 a/c rooms or suites next to the US Embassy. Free Wi-Fi and minibar.

A-C Hotel Diplomate, Tank Hill, Muyenga, T0414-267655, diplomatekampala@hotmail.com. Peaceful, away from the city noise with some of best views in Kampala. Difficult to reach without your own transport. Bar, restaurant and a small business centre. Price includes breakfast. Quirky hotel, look out for the stuffed lion.

Bugolobi p58, map p48

B-G Red Chilli Hideaway Hostel and Campsite, 17 Gangaram Ave, off Old Port Bell Rd, Mbuya, T0414-223903, T077-250 9150 (mob), www.redchillihideaway.com. In lovely surroundings with good security. Camping US$4pp, 40 dorm beds US$6 and self-catering cottages. Very clean, with a good atmosphere. Barbecue on Sun, Fri night Happy Hour. Bar, good restaurant (0730-2130) serving large portions at reasonable prices. Satellite TV, video, internet facilities, pool table, book swap, hot showers, Western toilets, laundry facilities (handwash or machine). Access from town by *matatu* going towards Bugolobi, Luzira or Port Bell. Get off opposite Silver Springs Hotel and follow signpost to the left. Take the second left turn, approximate distance is 500 m. Trips organized to their sister branch in Murchison Falls National Park at the very reasonable rate of US$240 for 3 days.

Munyonyo p59, map p48

The following 3 hotels are all highly recommended.

LL-AL Speke Resort Munyonyo, T0414-227111, www.spekeresort.com. Lovely location, 20-30 mins' drive from the centre. Large, comfortable rooms in cottages, en suite apartments or studios with balconies, DSTV and internet. Conference and leisure facilities include equestrian centre and Olympic-size pool. Extraordinarily lavish breakfast buffet. Antique hansom cab in the forecourt is occasionally used to transport elderly dignitaries to the many international conferences held here. Excellent value for money.

L Lagoon Resort, T077-578 7291 (mob), www.lagoonresort.com. The nearest offshore resort to Kampala, a 25-min boat ride from Munyonyo. Described as "the nicest place in East Africa, very idyllic and wild," by a satisfied guest. Activities include jet and waterskiing, kayaking, sport fishing, biking, birdwatching, sunset boat cruise or swimming. The glass-fronted restaurant has lake views. Pre-booking essential as it has only 6 *bandas* in 4 ha.

AL Cassia Lodge, Buziga Hill, T075-577 7002 (mob), www.cassislodge.com. 20 safari-style a/c rooms with balconies offering stunning views, the best of all the Kampala hotels, of both Lake Victoria and Kampala. The excellent restaurant, with inside and outside patio dining, and bar have Wi-Fi. Pool and a business and conference centre.

Eating

City centre p50, map p52

There is also Japanese and Cuban cuisine (**Kyoto Club** and **Ache Havana**). For the most open garden seating and seriously good goat, head for the **Barbecue Lounge**. Most establishments turn up the music volume after dark.

¶¶ Arirang Restaurant, 15 Kyedro Rd, Nakasero, next to the Indian Embassy, T0414-346717. Korean menu of beef, pork, poultry and vegetarian dishes, a range of soups, salads and excellent seafood. Recommended.

¶¶ Fang Fang Restaurant Roof Terrace, 1 Colville St, T0414-344806. Popular Chinese restaurant serving a wide range of dishes. A large indoor dining hall or veranda for open-air dining, bar and dancing.

Khana Khazana Restaurant, 20 Acacia Ave, Kololo, T0414-233049, T072-247 9896 (mob), khana@khanakhazana.co.ug. Authentic Indian vegetarian and non vegetarian food. It has a lovely outdoor setting.

Krua Thai, Windsor Cres, Kololo, T0712-777433. Closed Sun. Delicious, fresh, delicately spiced Thai food.

New Chong Qing Restaurant, Simbomanyo House, 2 Lumumba Ave, behind Central Police Station, T0414-253336, T077-235 3313 (mob). Serves good Chinese food in a pleasant setting.

Palms & Crocs, 13 Nakasero Rd, next to South African Embassy, T071-284 4944 (mob). Serves game meat, mostly crocodile.

Ciao Bello, Centenary Park, Jinja Rd, T078-223 2123 (mob). Truly Italian in every sense of the word. The pizzas here are authentic, and there's good antipasti. They also do barbecues. Home delivery available.

Ekitobero Restaurant, Nakasero Rd, near Kyagwe Rd. Unpretentious, authentic Ugandan cuisine with efficient table service indoors or in the peaceful gardens. There's also a separate bar for post-prandial drinks and a digestive game of pool. They cope well with large parties of diners. Highly recommended.

Madonna's Restaurant, 9 Colville St, T071-283 3076 (mob). Local and continental food, with good service.

Masala Chaat House, 3b De Winton Rd, opposite the Crafts Market and National Theatre, T0414-255707. Very good value, quality Indian food. The *uttapams* and *dosas* (rice pancakes) are recommended. Excellent choice for vegetarians.

The Pub, De Winton Rd. A small sports bar opposite the National Theatre's rear entrance by the Crafts Market. The dining room is hidden away at the back. Interesting primarily for its restaurant that serves outstanding *ekigere*, cow hoof cooked in an aromatic sauce, although their chicken stew is good too. Noisy and crowded during football matches.

Kabalagala *p56, map p48*

Le Chateau Restaurant, 1273 Ggaba Rd, next to **Petit Village** hotel, T0414-510404. Serves fine, rich Gallic food, with interesting touches, like large Ugandan snails, lovingly prepared by the Belgian owner. Excellent wine list. Save room for the waffles.

Café Ciao Ciao, Tank Hill Parade shopping centre. Offers quality local food, some of the best ice creams in town, and a real Italian espresso to round off the meal.

Ethiopian Village, Tank Hill Rd, near the turning from Kabalagala to Kibule, T0414-510378, T077-262 3440 (mob). Sit either in terrace seating or in small, unlit traditional *bandas*, hence 'the village'. They serve excellent Ethiopian food and wonderful coffee, accompanied by a smoking brazier of incense. There is a plaque commemorating the bomb attacks that claimed scores of lives in the restaurant during the 2010 World Cup Final.

Fasika, Ggaba Rd, at Kabalagala junction, T077-230 2716 (mob). This is undoubtedly one of the most serene venues in Kabalagala, with shaded garden seating. They serve excellent coffee and on busy nights you might see the famous bean-roasting ritual performed by a waitress in traditional dress. There are Ethiopian shops and a café down the alley behind **Fasika** for a more cut-price and less formal alternative.

Hakuna Matata, Ggaba Rd, 100-m walk from Tank Hill Rd, T077-243 5542 (mob). One of the best pork joints in town, with plenty of seats in a dimly-lit terrace.

My Chuchi, Tank Hill Rd, close to **Capital Pub**, T078-346 9122 (mob). This is a favourite spot amongst expats. Oscar, the long-time Swiss manager and a local character, has never changed the menu of straightforward, weighty meals, with a vaguely European orientation. Gets busy when the football's on.

Muyenga *p58, maps p48 and p52*

Beijing Restaurant, corner Tank Hill Rd and Zimwe Rd, opposite **Fuego Cocktail**. Decent Chinese food with indoor and garden seating. From the quaintly decorated interior there are splendid views up towards leafy Muyenga hill. Friendly Chinese management. Children's playground.

Café Roma, 689 Tank Hill Rd, T077-220 0086 (mob). This quiet garden restaurant serves pizza and pasta. Decent wines and friendly, relaxed service.

Fuego Cocktail Restaurant & Bar, Zimwe Rd, T070-459 0634 (mob). Go all the way up the hill from Kabalagala and go left at the crossroads, away from Tank Hill Parade. Lovely garden setting with wooden furniture. Pizzas from an authentic stone oven, plus Continental and Eritrean cuisine. Tranquil atmosphere popular with Eritreans and expats.

Other areas
Bukoto
Cayenne Restaurant, 12-13 Kira Rd, by the **Kabira Country Club**, Bukoto, T079-269 2692 (mob). Relaxed atmosphere and unusual Moroccan decor, with clay floor and low sofas. Poolside table service popular with expats.

Kansanga
Kansanga is a suburb in southeast Kampala 3.5 km from the centre, west of the Ggaba Rd, and about a third of the way along the road to Munyonyo.

Go Greek, Ggaba Rd, in Soja just after Kansanga. Juicy gyros and a range of other Greek specialities from the grill. Lovely management, vast thatched roof and excellent Greek music.

Petit Bistro, about 200 m after Kansanga market, Ggaba Rd, opposite **Barclay's Bank**. French oriented, with superlative steaks.

Samurai Restaurant, Ggaba Rd, Bunga, T070-270 0007 (mob), T078-261 6845, chefprado@yahoo.com. Located on the right-hand side just after Okapi Gardens. The large painted Japanese flower on the gate welcomes you into a haven of

tranquillity. Seating is arranged around the mini-ornamental garden, or you can go inside for the authentic kneeling-round-the-table experience. Saki costs US$10 a jug. The food is properly prepared and so takes a while to arrive.

Bars and clubs

City centre *p50, map p52*
Bubbles O'Leary, 19 John Babika Ave, Kololo, T0312-263815. If you're missing Irish pubs then head here for a pint of Guinness and some pop music. The ultimate expat hangout, with rarely an Ugandan in sight.

Casablanca Pub, 26 John Babika Ave, Kololo, T078-274 8840, thespace2008@yahoo.com. Open, spacious compound with terraced seating plus small cottages for extra privacy. Very relaxed by day and a small club with Ethiopian and African pop by night. Shisha pipes are an attraction, as are the reasonably priced Ethiopian and Continental dishes.

Iguana Bar, 8 Bukoto St, Kamwokya. The stylish crowd come for the interesting music, which varies every night. Attractive wooden building with grass-thatched roof. Restaurant serves decent African and Continental (mostly French) cuisine. Popular with expats and wealthier Ugandans.

Rouge, 2 Kampala Rd, T077-478 9782 (mob). Classic 70s-style swanky nightclub, with mirrored walls, low lighting, comfortable lounge seating, attracting an upmarket crowd. It has a reputation for premiering new superstar talent.

Steak Out, 50 Lumumba Ave, Nakasero, T0414-680296, T071-529 0068 (mob). Nightclub and restaurant with the eating area separated from the dance floor. Reasonable steaks and African food but mostly known for its musical attractions, reggae Wed night, rock on Thu, funky Fri and anything goes weekends. Very popular with students.

Kabalagala *p56, map p48*

Capital Pub, Tank Hill Rd. Celebrated pub/disco. At the back there is a relatively quiet sports room with 3 pool tables and a giant TV screen for football. The main room is open air, with a raised thatched roof. The dance floor is packed from 2300 almost every night. The music varies from heavy Ugandan dance hall to Cliff Richard, often mixed together.

Cherie Royale, Tank Hill Rd, T077-664 9698. Kabalagala popular bar and music venue. Hosts Dr Jose Chameleone, one of Uganda's most famous recording artists, every Tue. Gets very noisy and crowded on gig nights and during football matches, which are shown on a giant screen, but is otherwise quiet. Owned by the *abakama* (king) of Tooro's family, one of Uganda's traditional rulers.

Da Posh Bar, Muyenga Rd. New to Kabalagala and marketing itself as the most chic venue in the area. Kitsch red decor and over-attentive service. Comfortable sofas.

Family Restaurant & Guesthouse, Tank Hill Rd, halfway up the main drag of Kabalagala, nearly opposite the MTN service centre (a prominent yellow building). The food is forgettable and the lodgings unattractive, but the café atmosphere, with cosy terraced seating tucked under small trees and bushes, makes a visit worthwhile.

Flamin' Chicken, Ggaba Rd, 50 m from Kabalagala towards Kansanga/Munyonyo, T070-110 5858 (mob). Relaxed open-air bar with a view of the busy thoroughfare. Friendly Iranian management and authentic shisha pipes.

Molober, aka **Lalibela**, Tank Hill Rd, directly opposite **Pearl Microfinance Bank**. Located upstairs above a small clothes boutique, it can be hard to locate the staircase leading up to this small Eritrean bar. It has an excellent view of the bustling street life from its narrow balcony. The management plays good Ethiopian music at a tolerable volume and the regulars are friendly.

Vision Congo, Tank Hill Rd, T0414-267363. Famous Congolese disco-pub. Located in the heart of Kabalagala, opposite MTN shop. Kitsch mirrored entrance reminiscent of Kinshasa in its heyday. There are 2 sections inside: pub with gambling machines and disco dance floor. Club music with occasional live bands, ask inside for forthcoming gigs.

Bugolobi *p58, map p48*

Club Silk, 15-17 First St, industrial area, off Kampala Rd not far from Centenary Park, T0414-250907. Probably the most successful nightclub in Uganda and thanks to UB40 a franchise has opened in London. A massive, gloomy factory conversion, which gets seriously busy at weekends. World-class DJs play a variety of music all night.

Munyonyo *p59, map p48*

Camooflage, Munyonyo Rd, just before **Speke Resort**. Fri-Sun night. Outdoor bar and children's playground run by an ex-mercenary. Paintballing Wed-Fri, book in advance at the venue. Good family fun at weekends, with lots of space for kids to run around while the parents drink at the bar. Excellent reggae night on the last Fri of each month, from the legendary Blood Brothers Band, famed for over a decade.

La Boheme, Munyonyo Rd (leading to **Speke Resort**), 2 mins' drive from Ggaba Rd, T077-624 5327 (mob). A popular bar that offers tasty freshly grilled goat. Overlooking the main road from its 1st-floor perch, this classy bar/restaurant is like a giant, open-air living room. Recline in the expansive sofas and let the jazzy tunes waft over you.

Miki's Pub & Restaurant, Cape Rd, T077-264 4212 (mob). Primarily a bar but famed for its ambience and barbecued pork. Recommended, especially if you're staying in east Kampala.

Slider's, Ggaba Rd, opposite Bunga market, just before Engen petrol station, T078-5173 1163 (mob). This eccentric expat favourite has enjoyed varying fortunes, once being one of the most popular live music venues in Kampala. It has delightful terraced seating (with a giant chess set), a dim indoor bar with pool table and a large hall at the back, which is used for film screenings, theatre, dance performances and, most importantly, live music. It's now a little quiet, but there are plans to convert it into a cultural centre for Ugandan film and music.

⊕ Entertainment

The informative free bimonthly publication *The Eye* lists what's on in Kampala. It is widely available. See the *New Vision* for where local bands are playing.

Casinos
Kampala Casino, 3 Kimathi Ave, T0414-343628.

Cinemas
Cineplex, 3rd floor, Garden City Shopping Mall, Yusuf Lule Rd, T0312-261415, www.cineplexuganda.com.

Cricket
Lugogo Sports Complex, Jinja Rd, T077-272 8255 (mob). Exceptional location in a natural amphitheatre that was originally a quarry. Holds regular cricket games on Sundays between local clubs. Europeans, Indians and Africans all participate.

Cultural centres
Alliance Française, 6 Mackinnon Rd, Nakasero, T0414-344490. Offers films, art exhibitions and literary readings. Along with the Ugandan-German Cultural Society (see below), it makes sterling efforts to promote Ugandan folk and jazz music.
British Council, 4 Windsor Loop, Kira Rd, T0414-560800, www.britishcouncil.org. Excellent facilities, with films, concerts and talks, a library and all UK newspapers.
Ugandan-German Cultural Society (Goethe Institute), 6 Mackinnon Rd, Nakasero, T0414-533410, www.goethe.de/kampala. Promotes German culture through

similar cultural activities as the Alliance Française, which is at the same address.

Dance
Ndere Cultural Centre, Ntinda, junction of Northern Bypass and Kisaasi-Kira Rd, T0414-288222, T077-220 0104 (mob), www.ndere.com. An internationally renowned dance troupe in a modern auditorium perform every Sun evening 1800-2130, US$4.50. Highly recommended for all ages.

Football
Nakivubo War Memorial Stadium, 7 Namirembe Rd near the taxi park. Football is the most popular sport in Uganda. As well as international matches for the Africa Cup, there are also league matches at this stadium. Supporters are extremely loyal. Even if you're not a great football fan, you'll find the occasion fun.

Theatre
National Theatre, De Winton Rd, at the junction of Siad Barre Ave, T0414-344490. Box office Mon-Fri 0830-1230 and 1400-1645, Sat 0830-1200, also open 30 mins before each performance. The British Council shows films once a month, and the Alliance Française conducts French classes. Occasionally there are visiting musicians from around the world; see the main daily paper, *New Vision*, and posters around town.

✷ Festivals and events

Early Jan Canoe race at Munyonyo, on Lake Victoria (see box, opposite). Check the exact date with Buganda Tourism Centre (see page 55).
Jul/Sep Goat Race at Munyonyo, *Speke Resort*. Dates vary.

O Shopping

Antiques
Gerald Antiques, Colline House, 4 Pilkington Rd, T077-245 1169 (mob).

Muntyonyo canoe regatta

Munyonyo is a small landing site on Lake Victoria. In 1871 Kabaka Muteesa I fell in love with Munyonyo and a hunting lodge was built for him where he could indulge in some of his favourite pastimes: canoeing on the lake and hunting for hippos. Muteesa's grandson Kabaka Daudi Chwa was the first of the Kabakas to hold an organized canoe race and the tradition was passed down the generations. In 1986, when peace began to return to Uganda, a group of Baganda royalists got together and organized a canoe race to mark the centenary of the Uganda martyrs. A year later the event was repeated for Prince Ronnie Mutebi. Since then it has been an annual event.

There's a festive mood on the day of the races as thousands of Baganda arrive for a day out. The men are dressed up in the traditional white *kanzus*, the women in brightly coloured *basutis*, many wearing hats to show which clan they support. There are a number of races. In the first the teams race to the nearby island and back. The major race of the day is the longest and follows a course around the nearby island. During much of the race the teams are out of sight and dancers and musicians entertain the crowds. It is also possible, for a small fee, to go for a trip in one of the motor canoes that follow the racing canoes during the contest. On the day of the regatta it's easy to get public transport.

Tiny shop with an interesting collection of old coins, notes and postage stamps from different parts of Africa. Also has old African books, masks, photographs, sculptures and other quirky bygones.

Art galleries
Afriart Gallery, 57 Kenneth Dale Dr, off Kira Rd, Kamwokya, T071-245 5555 (mob), www.afriartgallery.org. Relocated from Lugogo Centre, Daudi Karungi's gallery hosts an unusual selection of work by Ugandan artists. Check for hidden gems from previous exhibitions tucked away in the storerooms.
Tulifanya Gallery, 28 Hannington Rd, opposite Crested Towers, T0414-254183, tulifanya@utonline.co.ug. This small but charming art gallery is run by Maria Fischer. It features African artists. There's a pleasant café in the gardens.

Bookshops
Aristoc, 19 Kampala Rd, T0414-253122. The best bookshop in Kampala. Sells a useful city map, *A-Z Kampala*. Also has a branch in Garden City Mall, on the 2nd floor.

Handicrafts
African Crafts Village, behind the National Theatre. Mon-Sat 0900-1700, Sun 1000-1600. A compound of small shops and kiosks built in a semicircle, selling batiks, prints, carved folding chairs, wooden sculptures, bark-cloth, jewellery and antique masks, all reasonably priced and bargaining is possible especially if trade is slow.
Banana Boat Crafts. There are 3 franchises: **African Crafts & Interiors**, Lugogo Mall, T0414-222363, www.bananaboat.co.ug, open daily; **Craft and Gift Shop**, Garden City Shopping Mall, T0414-252190, open daily; **Tribal Arts and Crafts**, 23 Cooper Rd, Kisementi, T0414-232885, Mon-Sat. Each shop has a slightly different emphasis, with the first outlet aimed at the local middle class and the 2 latter outlets selling mainly interesting tourist goods hand-picked from the markets or commissioned from popular workshops.
Uganda Crafts, 32 Bombo Rd, T077-267 3435 (mob). The largest craft shop in Uganda with a range of products from all over East Africa made by disabled people. Prices are fixed and the quality is good.

Ujuzi Art Studios, Kisasi Rd (60 m before the turning to Kisu/Kabiri International School, adjacent to Bukoto Market), Bukoto, www.pauloakiiki.com. Mon-Sat 0800-1900, Sun 1200-1900. Small gallery with unusual fine art collection, including abstract paintings and wooden sculptures, by the talented Paulo Akiiki.

Malls

Garden City Shopping Mall, Yusuf Lule Rd. This modern shopping mall has an excellent bookstore, **Aristoc**, see page 67, some interesting souvenir and clothes shops, a large electronics store, a cinema, several decent cafés and **Ranchers** steakhouse. Garden City is always filled with wealthy Ugandans and eccentric expats. Look out for the Afro-kitsch concrete statues in the car park, courtesy of Okapi Gallery (Kansanga). **Nakumatt Oasis Mall**, next to **Garden City**, Yusuf Lule Rd. A little more enclosed. However, it has some high-class handicrafts shops, with an unusual, pricey selection of original products.

Tank Hill Parade, on the top of Tank Hill. A useful spot, with a well-stocked Italian supermarket, a cafeteria, a **Barclays** bank, and a travel agent and IT shop on the upper level. The supermarket has good range of Mediterranean cheeses and cold cuts, as well as organic vegetables. Café Ciao Ciao's, see page 63, is also very good.

Markets

Owino Market, Kisenyi, was one of East Africa's largest street markets with 500,000 stalls, before it was destroyed by fire in Feb 2009, but reconstruction is well underway. **Nakasero Market**, town centre. The best and largest fruit and vegetable market in central Kampala. The prices are slightly high as it caters mainly for expats. **Nakivubo Place**, by the Nakivubo Stadium. A huge and bustling market, plus a secondary overspill market established 10 years ago in the car park of Nakivubo stadium known as the Nakivubo Parkyard

Market, sells everything from food, spices, pots and pans to sheets, bags and clothes. Be prepared to bargain. There is also a large second-hand clothes section where you may find cheap designer clothes. Any repairs or alterations can be done for you while you wait. The market stays open until 2300, with stalls lit by small kerosene lamps.

▲▲ Activities and tours

For a comprehensive listing of sports facilities (including gyms), see www.ugandatourism.org/sports.

Climbing, trekking and walking
Mountain Club of Uganda, at Athina Club, Windsor Ave, T077-284 3367 (mob), idc@imul.com. Climbers and walkers meet on the second Thu of the month at 1730. **Nature Uganda**, T0414-540719, www.natureuganda.org. Organize monthly nature walks. Meet at 0700 at the Makerere Faculty of Science car park. No charge.

Golf
Kampala Golf Club, Kitante Rd, opposite Fairway Hotel, T0414-236848, ugagolf@africaonline.co.ug. Visitors can play for US$30 a round.

Running
Hash House Harriers, T0712-859402, www.kampalahhh.tripod.com. Meet every Mon at 1800 and 1st Sat of the month.

Sailing
Victoria Nyanza Sailing Club, Kaazi, 16 km south of Kampala, T077-237 8791 (mob), www.sailuganda.com. Sailing on Sun. Dinghies and lasers available for hire.

Squash
Kampala Club, Ternan Ave, T0414-230577. Daily membership.

Swimming
Available at most large hotels at a daily fee.

Tennis

Lugogo Sports Complex, see page 66.

Tour operators

Adrift, 14 York Terrace, Kololo, T0312-237438, T077-223 7483 (mob), http://adrift.ug. Specialists in whitewater rafting, bungee jumping, jet boating and river surfing.

Afri Tours and Travel, Fairway Hotel, 1 Kafu Rd, T0414-233596, T077-623 3596 (mob), www.afritourstravel.com. Specialize in safari planning, hotel and lodge bookings.

African Pearl Safaris, 2nd floor, Station House, 3 Kampala Rd, T0414-233566, www.africanpearlsafaris.com. Well-established firm offering trips to the gorillas, parks and other parts of Uganda.

Let's Go/BCD Travel, 1st floor, Garden City Shopping Centre, Yusuf Lule Rd, T0414-346667, www.bcdtravel.co.ug. Long-established company offering safaris.

Pearl of Africa Tours & Travel, Oasis (Nakumatt) Mall, 88-94 Yusuf Lule Rd, T0414-340533, T077-240 3614 (mob), www.pearlofafricatours.com. Offers wide range of tours.

Rwenzori Trekking Services, T077-411 4499 (Kampala), T077-611 4442 (Kilembe in the Rwenzoris), www.rwenzoritrekking.com. Reliable trips of various duration and difficulty.

Ugandan Safari Company, T0414-251182, www.safariuganda.com. Run **Apoka Lodge**, see page 118, and **Semliki Lodge**, see page 181, as well as tailor-made safaris.

Volcanoes Safaris, 27 Lumumba Ave, T0414-346464, T0312-263823, www.volcanoessafaris.com. Gorilla safari specialists.

Wild Frontiers, T0414-321479, www.wildfrontiers.co.ug. Arrange wildlife safaris, Murchison Falls boat cruises, fishing safaris, visits to Ngamba Island and run lodges in Queen Elizabeth National Park and Bwindi.

Whitewater rafting

See under Jinja (page 90).

⊖ Transport

Air

The main international airport is at Entebbe (see page 46). Airlines using Entebbe including **British Airways**, **Brussels Airlines**, **Emirates**, **Kenya Airways**, **Air France/KLM**, **Ethiopian Airways**, **Egypt Air**, **Rwandair** and **South Africa Airways**. Domestic airlines **Eagle Air** offers scheduled flights to northern Uganda as well as regional charter flights. **Kampala Aeroclub**, based at Kajjansi airfield between Kampala and Entebbe, also operates a charter service.

Airline offices Air Uganda, 14 Parliament Ave, T0412-165555, www.air-uganda.com. **British Airways**, 4 Ternan Ave, Nakasero, T0414-257414, www.britishairways.com. **Eagle Air**, Adam House, 11 Portal Ave, T0414-344292, www.flyeagleuganda.com. **Egypt Air**, 11 Grand Imperial Arcade, Speke Rd, T0414-233960, www.egyptair.com. **Emirates**, FCN Building, Kimathi Ave, T0414-349941, www.emirates.com. **Ethiopian Airlines**, United Assurance Building, Kimathi Ave, T0414-345577, www.ethiopianairlines.com. **Kampala Aeroclub**, T077-270 6107 (mob), www.flyuganda.com. **Kenya Airways**, United Assurance Building, Kimathi Ave, T0312-236000, www.kenya-airways.com. **KLM**, Jubilee Insurance Building, 3rd floor, 14 Parliament Ave, T0414-338001, www.klm.com. **SN Brussels**, Rwenzori House, 1 Lumumba Ave, T0414-234200, www.brusselsairlines.com.

Bus

Buses are cheaper than *matatus* (minibuses) but less regular, with fewer routes and are extremely crowded. They have the advantage of going across town so on some routes you do not have to change. They stop around City Square and are usually marked by their destination. The buses don't leave until they are full.

The **Post Bus**, T0414-236436, T077-235 7427 (mob), is well driven with some luggage space and runs to a fixed timetable.

The stops to load and unload mail don't add much to the journey time. It leaves Kampala central post office Mon-Sat at 0800 to **Masaka** US$2.65, **Masindi** US$4.00, **Gulu** via **Karuma** route US$7.85, **Mbale** route US$5.25 via **Tororo** US$4.50, **Hoima** route US$5.25 via **Masindi** US$4.50, **Kabale** route US$7.85 via **Mbarara** US$5.25, **Soroti** via **Jinja** and **Mbale** US$5.25. It no longer goes to Arua and Fort Portal.

Most people travel to **Kenya** by road. The journey to Nairobi takes 12-15 hrs and fares range from US$15 to US$25. Buscar and **Gateway** have a poor safety record. Akamba, 28 De Winton Rd, T0414-250412, www.akambabus.com, has a Royal service departing daily at 0700, which is the most comfortable; the Executive departs daily at 0700, 1400, 1500 and 1600. **Kampala Coach**, Jinja Rd, opposite Shell, T075-555 3377 (mob), www.kampalacoach.com, also operate a Kenyan service. **Tanzania**: Gateway bus leaves at around 1100 for the border town of Mutukula, en route to Bukoba, Tanzania. **Tawfiq Buses**, T077-240 7914 (mob), offer an alternative service leaving 10 Mackay Rd daily at 1500, US$12.

Jaguar, T0414-251855, and **Kampala Coach**, T075-555 3377 (mob), www. kampalacoach.com, operate services to Kigali, **Rwanda**, 8-9 hrs, US$12. There is a 1 hr time difference between Uganda and Rwanda.

Car hire

Europcar, 1-11 Nsambya Rd, T0414-237211. Mon-Fri 0800-1800, Sat 0800-1400.

Take care with hire cars and mopeds, as vehicle maintenance can be very poor. See also page 19

Ferries

There is no ferry service leaving from Port Bell at present.

Matatus

Matatus operate the main routes, only leaving the terminus when full. They are

the cheapest way of travelling between the centre and the suburbs; the fare to most places in town is US$0.30. To **Entebbe**, US$1. There are 2 *matatu* taxi parks: the new one is opposite the stadium in Namirembe Rd and the old one is in Ben Kiwanuka St, 400 m away, with the bus station in between. The busier old park serves towns in eastern Uganda. The new taxi park serves western and northern destinations. Buses for Entebbe leave from both parks.

Taxis

If you have a lot of luggage or miss the last *matatu* you can get a 'private hire'; this may be a *matatu* or a taxi. You'll have to bargain; from Kampala city centre to one of the suburbs is about US$10.

⊙ Directory

Banks

Many foreign exchange bureaux offer a quick service Mon-Fri and Sat morning. Rates vary by only a few shillings. Money may also be changed at banks, but it takes longer. Changing TCs can be a problem at some banks; try **Stanbic** and **Barclays** first. A charge of 1-1.5% is levied for changing TCs and banks often want to see the original sale receipt for the cheques.

Embassies and consulates

Australia, Zambia and Zimbabwe handle diplomatic affairs for Uganda from their Nairobi embassies or high commissions. **Austria**, 3 Portal Ave, T0312-235104, www.entwicklung.at. **Belgium**, 1 Lumumba Ave, T0414-349559, www.diplomatie.be-kampala. **British High Commission**, 4 Windsor Loop, Kira Rd, T0312-312000, http://ukinuganda.fco.gov.uk/en. **Canada**, 14 Parliament Ave, T0414-258141, kampala@canadaconsulate.ca. **DR Congo**, 20 Philip Rd, Kololo, T0312-343100. **Denmark**, 3 Lumumba Ave, T0312-263211, www.ambkampala.um.dk. **Ethiopia**, 3L Kitante Close, Kitante, T0414-348340, ethiokam@

utonline.co.ug. **EU**, 15th floor, Crested Towers, 17-23 Hannington Rd, T0414-701000, www.deluga.ec.europa.eu. **France**, 16 Lumumba Ave, T0414-304500, www.ambafrance.ug.org. **Germany**, 15 Philip Rd, T0414-501111, www.kampala.diplo.de. **Ireland**, 25 Yusuf Lule Rd, T0417-713000, www.embassyofireland.ug. **Italy**, 11 Lourdel Rd, T0414-250450, www.ambkampala.esteri.it. **Japan**, 8 Kyadondo Rd, T0414-349542/3, jembassy@jembassy.or.ug. **Kenya**, 41 Nakasero Rd, T0414258235, kenhicom@africaonline.co.ug. **Netherlands**, 2 Nakasero Rd, Rwenzori Courts, 4th floor, T0414-2311861, www.netherlandsembassyuganda.org. **Norway**, 18b Akii-Bua Rd, Nakasero, T0417-112000, www.norway.go.ug. **Rwanda**, 2 Nakayima Rd, Kitante, T0414-344045, ambakampala@minisset.gov.rw. **South Africa**, 15A Nakasero Rd, Nakasero, T0414-343543, kampala.sahc@foreign.gov.za. **Spain**, 27 Baskerville Ave, Kololo, T0414-342372. **Sweden**, 24 Lumumba Ave, Nakasero, T0417-700800, ambassaden.kampala@foreign.ministry.se. **Switzerland**, 1-27 Nasser Lane, Kololo, T0414-347282, swissconsulateug@roko.co.ug.

Internet
Email and internet facilities are widely available at competitive rates.

Medical services
There are several hospitals but the quality of care varies. **International Hospital Kampala (IHK)**, St Barnabas Rd (off Tank Hill Rd), Namuwongo, southeast of city centre, T0312-200400, www.img.co.ug. Has a good reputation. **International Medical Center (IMC)**, KPC Building, Bombo Rd, T0413-41291, T031-234 1291, www.img.co.ug. **St Francis Hospital**, Hospital Rd, Nsambya, T0414-267012. Commonly known as Nsambya Hospital, this place offers an excellent and cheaper service. It is managed as a not-for-profit by the Little Sisters of St Francis, with a busy private service and a well-run private wing. Go directly to the private wing. Like most hospitals there can be long waiting times to be seen. **The Surgery**, John Babika Ave (formerly Acacia Ave), T0414-256003 (Mon-Sat 0800-1800), emergencies 24 hrs T075-275 6003 (mob), www.thesurgeryuganda.org. A central medical and travel clinic run by Dr Stockley, a GP from the UK. **Dentist**: Dr Paul Aliker, 14 Bukoto St, T0414-531259.

Entebbe

→ *Phone code: 0414. Colour map 2, B4.*

Prior to Independence Entebbe was the colonial administrative capital of Uganda, 37 km from Kampala. It's a rather pretty town on hilly terrain along the northwestern shoreline of Lake Victoria, virtually on the equator. The pace of life is less frenetic than Kampala. State House, the official residence of the president, is situated here. Although most visitors just past through it on their way from the airport, Entebbe has several worthwhile sights, including the well-laid out Botanical Gardens and the Uganda Wildlife Education Centre (UWEC). Both are of great interest to birdwatchers with a diverse array of over 250 forest and shorebirds. On Ngamba Island, 23 m offshore, visitors can observe orphaned chimpanzees living in a heavily forested sanctuary.

Sights

The Kampala to Entebbe road has become a popular area for middle-class Ugandans to set up home. Consequently, travel to and from the capital can be very busy indeed. On the drive down to Entebbe you will pass a signpost for the **Kajansi Fish Farm**, which used to be home to a number of huge crocodiles. It attracts large numbers of water birds.

Entebbe is the home of Uganda's international airport and became infamous in 1976 when an Air France plane from Israel was hijacked and forced to land there. The Jewish passengers were held hostage as demands were made for the release of prisoners held in Israeli jails. All but one of the prisoners were rescued when Israeli paratroopers stormed the airport building.

At the turn of the 19th century the colonialists built their administrative centre at Entebbe and some government offices are still located here. One relic from former times is the **cannon** in the square in front of the Entebbe Club, captured from the Germans during the First World War. It bears the maker's number, name and date: 103, Krupp of Essen, 1917. The gun now sits on a plinth and is surrounded by fountains (not always working). Standing alongside the gun are the statues of two modern camouflaged soldiers peering through binoculars across Lake Victoria.

Colonial Entebbe

Walking along the criss-cross of lanes between the main road and the lake shore there are a number of beautiful old buildings to be seen. Most of these were built when Entebbe was the capital of the Uganda Protectorate.

Botanical Gardens

ⓘ *Just north of the centre, along the lakeshore, T0414-320638. Daily 0900-1800. US$1, plus US$1 for a camera (if declared) and US$1 for a vehicle. The gardens are located along Berkeley Rd, that runs roughly parallel to, but east of the Kampala–Entebbe and Portal roads. If travelling by* matatu *get off at the junction of Kampala–Entebbe Rd with Apolo Sq (by the Gately Inn Entebbe hotel.) Turn east along Apolo Sq for 500 m until you reach Berkeley Lane that runs alongside the Surveys and Mapping office. Turn left and after 50 m you reach Berkeley Rd. The entrance is opposite.*

Covering 16 ha with a 1.5-km stretch of lakeshore, the gardens were established in the early 20th century by the Protectorate government, and the first curator was a Mr Whyte. This was originally a natural forest and the gardens were used as a research ground for the introduction of various exotic fruits and ornamental plants to Uganda. There are species in the gardens from all over the world, including cocoa trees, and rubber plants, which were introduced to see how well they would thrive in Uganda's climate and soils. The gardens' claim to fame is that the first Johnny Weismuller *Tarzan* film was shot here.

Some trees have died a natural death and have not been replaced. Many others still have their metal labels on them, and there is a small patch of virgin forest down close to the lake shore. Walking through this, you will experience lots of different noises and smells, and it's worth remembering that large areas of Uganda were once forested like this

Entebbe

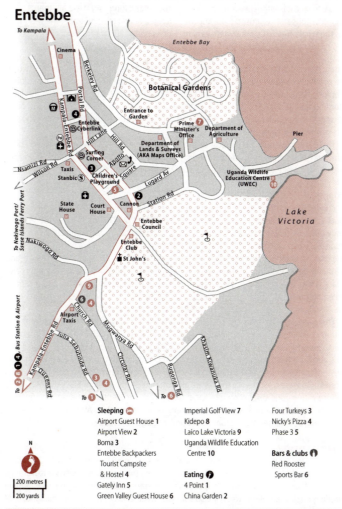

Sleeping 🛏

Airport Guest House **1**
Airport View **2**
Boma **3**
Entebbe Backpackers
 Tourist Campsite
 & Hostel **4**
Gately Inn **5**
Green Valley Guest House **6**

Imperial Golf View **7**
Kidepo **8**
Laico Lake Victoria **9**
Uganda Wildlife Education
 Centre **10**

Eating 🍴

4 Point **1**
China Garden **2**

Four Turkeys **3**
Nicky's Pizza **4**
Phase 3 **5**

Bars & clubs 🍸

Red Rooster
 Sports Bar **6**

Shoebill storks

You won't get very far in Uganda without seeing a picture of a shoebill stork. It's the size of a heron and its plumage is an anonymous battleship gray. But it's most memorable feature is its enormous bill in the shape of a shoe, albeit one with a hook. In fact, it is rather like a cobbler's blank in appearance. It used to be known as the whale-headed stork and it's easy to see why. It's quite rare; the best places to see it are Murchison Falls and Toro-Semliki Wildlife Reserve.

It hunts by standing motionless in papyrus swamp waiting for its prey, which can be anything from baby crocs to water snakes and lung fish. These are then lunged at and crushed under the weight of its body.

patch. Watch out for the dragon spiders (so named because they catch dragonflies), which are pretty big and weave enormous webs. There is a troupe of black and white colobus monkeys here, as well as green vervet that can be seen playing on the grass in the early morning and at dusk. For people spending longer in Uganda, there is a very good plant nursery. It is a popular picnic and swimming spot at weekends and holidays; usually with lots of noise and, sadly, litter.

There is a small café and picnic area by the lake. Some tourists have complained about informal guides appearing and demanding high rates for tours of the gardens: if you are approached make sure you negotiate a price before engaging their services.

Uganda Wildlife Education Centre (UWEC)

ⓘ *Lugard Ave, just past the Imperial Botanical Beach Hotel, off the main Kampala–Entebbe road, 1.5 km from central Entebbe, T0414-322169, T077-269 1439 (mob), www.uweczoo.org. Daily 0900-1830, last admission 1730. US$10. Take a* matatu *to the Botanical Beach Hotel stage and either walk or take a* boda boda *to the centre.*

The zoo at Entebbe was originally established in 1952 as an animal orphanage and gradually developed into a zoo by the 1960s with non-indigenous species like tigers and bears. It was redeveloped in 1994 as a conservation and education centre, and a captive breeding centre for endangered animals. The master plan was designed by experts from the New York Zoological Society. It is still widely referred to locally as the zoo.

There are regular talks by keepers throughout the day. The centre replicates the country's ecological zones in miniature, such as savannah, wetlands and tropical forest. It's worth visiting just to support the efforts of the staff. There is a pair of shoebill storks (see box, above), a few lions, as well as hyenas, waterbucks, impalas, giant forest hogs, ostrich, crested cranes and several varieties of monkeys. In November 2001 a pair of southern white rhino were relocated to the centre and, more recently, a pair of black rhinos. There's an interesting zone displaying medicinal plants with excellent explanatory plaques and a 1-km forest trail, where you can see monkeys and butterflies. Also here is a lakeside restaurant, an internet café, accommodation (see page 76) and a craft shop.

Ngamba Island

ⓘ *Run by the Chimpanzee Sanctuary and Wildlife Conservation Trust (CSWCT), 24 Lugard Ave, Entebbe, T0414-320662, http://ngambaisland.com. There are no budget visits to Ngamba Island. Half-day visits by a 50-min speedboat ride start at US$90pp, subject to minimum numbers on board. Full-day visits by a 90-min ride (weather dependent) on a traditional boat* *from US$72pp. Book via the CSWCT, see above. The lake crossing is rough if weather conditions are windy (more common in June and July) when a change of clothes may be necessary. Visits include an overview of the project and observing the supplementary feeding of the chimps from the visitor platform. It's worth bringing a pair of binoculars for the birdlife. Sun protection is strongly advised; insect repellent, sandals, a sweater and a torch (if staying overnight) are also recommended.*

About 23 km southeast of Entebbe lies Ngamba Island, west of Kome Island in Lake Victoria. A chimpanzee sanctuary was established here in 1998 by the CSWCT, formed from the Jane Goodall Institute, Born Free Foundation, Uganda Wildlife Education Centre Trust, International Fund for Animal Welfare and the Zoological Parks Board of New South Wales, Australia. Ngamba Island is approximately 45 ha in size, covered with tropical rainforest, containing over 50 species of plants used by the chimpanzees and providing an ideal habitat for them.

Originally 19 chimpanzees were relocated here from Isinga Island, Queen Elizabeth National Park, and the Uganda Wildlife Education Centre, Entebbe. Their numbers have risen to 40 animals as orphaned chimpanzees, mainly rescued from smugglers or illegal dealers, have been resettled here following a period in quarantine. Orphaned or captured chimpanzees cannot be released back into the wild as they are likely to be rejected, injured or killed by other chimpanzees. Ngamba Island offers them a sanctuary that closely resembles life in the wild and an alternative for visitors to view the chimpanzees in their forest habitats in western Uganda. Numbers are equally divided between males and females, and the chimpanzees have the freedom of the island, which they share with water monitor lizards, hippos, otters and a large variety of birds including fish eagles and kingfishers. The adult females are given a contraceptive implant, inhibiting reproduction but not other social interaction.

Ngamba Island has permanent staff caring for the animals, helping to integrate new arrivals to the group. A viewing platform enables visitors to see the chimpanzees being given supplementary feeds twice daily at 1100 and 1430 as the forest provides insufficient food for these primate numbers. Another sanctuary on nearby Nsadzi Island is planned to relieve the overcrowding and some of the chimpanzees will be relocated there to form a new social group.

Uganda Reptile Village

ⓘ *Abaita-Ababiri, 2 km north of Entebbe on the Kampala–Entebbe highway, T078-234 9583 or T075-625 0102 (both mob), www.reptiles.ug. Daily 0800-1800. Free to foreign visitors, but donation appreciated. Take the 1st right turning immediately after the Petro City fuel station; Reptile Village is signposted 4 km from the main road.*

Home to the largest collection of poisonous snakes in the country, 14 species in all, including cobras, vipers, mambas, boom slang, twig and vine snakes. It has an education and conservation brief and is planning to set up an anti-venom bank as anti-venom is currently imported from Europe. Non-venomous snakes are also on display: the python, house snake and green tree snake. In addition there are tortoises, chameleons and monitor lizards.

Kigungu Landing

Located about 5 km off the Airport Road is the place where the first Catholic Missionaries to Uganda, Reverend Father Simon Lourdel and Brother Amans of the Society of White Fathers, landed on 17 February 1879. There is a small brick church marking the spot, a memorial plaque and painted statues commemorating these venerable missionaries.

Entebbe listings

For Sleeping and Eating price codes and other relevant information, see Essentials pages 21-23.

Sleeping

The **Uganda Safari Company** and **Wildplaces** are redeveloping the lodge on Bulago Island (T0414-251182, www. wildplacesafrica.com), 16 km from Entebbe and 7 km north of Ngamba Island. Their trademark is sumptuous accommodation. Activities offered will include sailing, fishing for Nile perch and tilapia, water sports, birdwatching and horse riding.

LL Laico Lake Victoria, Circular Rd, T0312-310100, www.laicohotels.com. Refurbished ex-government hotel in wonderful gardens with ancient trees and great lake views. Grand entrance, opulent decor and a 5-star atmosphere but not much character. 104 large, comfortable a/c rooms with DSTV. The restaurant serves international dishes. Pool, open to non-residents for US$3. Conference facilities.

LL Tented Camp Overnight Excursions, Ngamba Island Chimpanzee Sanctuary. 4 2-person safari tents on elevated platforms, prices are full board. Optional extras for overnight visitors, subject to pre-approval and proof of various innoculations. Forest walks US$400pp per walk, caregiver for the day US$200. Extended visits of 1-2 weeks from US$2000-3500. Income generated helps fund the project. Trips are arranged through **Wild Frontiers**, T0414-321479, T077-2502155 (mob), www. wildfrontiers.co.ug/ngambavisits.html.

LL-AL Gately Inn, 2 Portal Rd, T0414-321313, T077-755 5966 (mob), www. gatelyinn.com. Part of the Gately on Nile Jinja group, 9 luxurious, well-appointed en suite rooms in the main house, and cottages or annexe with an outdoor area, fans, nets, Wi-Fi and DSTV. Attentive staff. Free airport shuttle if requested when booking. Well-maintained gardens. The restaurant serves an international menu. An excellent gift shop sells crafts. Sited on the airport road near the concrete rhino at the intersection of the road to UWEC, with traffic noise.

AL Airport View Hotel, 34 Kiwafu Close, T0312-261751, T077-222 1881 (mob), airportviewhotel@googlemail.com. Located in Kitoro, an Entebbe suburb, 3 km from the airport. Modern, large en suite rooms, Wi-Fi, DSTV. Restaurant offers a varied menu. Pleasant bar. Very friendly and obliging staff. Free airport transfers. Accept major credit cards, US dollars, pounds sterling and euros.

AL The Boma Entebbe, 20A Julia Ssebutinde Rd, T0312-264810, T077-246 7929 (mob), www.boma.co.ug. Converted from a 1940s colonial home, this quiet, family-run hotel in lovely grounds offers excellent value. 9 en suite rooms with small veranda, Wi-Fi and pool. Restaurant offers home-made food, ice cream (recommended) and a well-stocked bar. Day rooms, luggage storage and airport pick-up service available. Highly recommended.

AL Imperial Golf View, 6 km from the airport, T0414-311400, www.imperialhotels. co.ug. 61 en suite rooms with DSTV, some with a/c. Restaurant with an international menu. It has great lake views, lovely gardens and is adjacent to the golf course. Conference facilities.

B Airport Guesthouse, 17 Mugula Rd, T0312-264810, www.gorillatours.com. 10 en suite comfortable rooms, set in beautiful gardens with patio, delicious food, good internet connections and pleasant, helpful staff. An excellent **Gorilla Tours** enterprise. Free airport transfers.

B-D Uganda Wildlife Education Centre (UWEC), see page 74. Fully furnished en suite cottages or *bandas* with cooking or campfire facilities can be rented within the UWEC zoo premises with complimentary nocturnal vocalizations from the lions and hyenas. Airport pick-up US$20. Income generated supports UWEC's work.

C Green Valley Guest House, 12 Mugwanya Rd, T0414-321212, T077-296 5200 (mob), info@greenvalleyentebbe.

com. Comfortable, quiet, converted colonial house with spacious rooms, some with private balconies, set in lush gardens. Restaurant. Free airport transfers if full board. US$30 transfer service to Kampala.

E-G Entebbe Backpackers, aka **Frank's Place**, 33-35 Church Rd, T0414-320432, T071-284 9973 (mob), www.entebbebackpackers.com. Long-established clean hostel situated just behind the **Laico Lake Victoria**. Range of accommodation, garden cottages with private bathrooms for 2-4, en suite double rooms with TV, dorms with communal bathrooms. Camping US$3pp with own tent or US$5pp with a **Backpacker's** tent, in a lovely garden under mango and guava trees heavy with fruit. The garden is a bit small so tents are closely pitched at busy periods. Restaurant (0800-2000) serves reasonably priced, basic à la carte menu, or you can use the kitchen. Lounge has DSTV. Fully stocked bar.

Eating

†††-† Phase 3 Restaurant, 6 Circular Rd, T0312-671345, T0414-598080. Branch of the popular **Phase 2** restaurant in Kampala. Continental and Indian food. One of the best places to eat. Large, well-organized restaurant with indoor and outdoor seating. Live music every Fri courtesy of an Italian musician called Angelo, popular with the middle classes.

† China Garden, 6 Lugard Ave near the Post Office on Apolo Sq, T078-218 0088 (mob). Offers good variety of Chinese dishes. Ambiance enhanced by decor, tableware and Chinese music. It stays open later than the competition.

† Entebbe Club, T077-255 5360 (mob). Very pleasant, with tables outside. This was the club for colonial officials. Mongolian buffet along with pizza, fish and meat options.

† Junior's Pork Joint, at Red Rooster Sports Bar, 3A Church Rd. Large garden with lots of outdoor seating. The atmosphere is fun and the music is not deafening. Wide-ranging

tasty grills: steaks, chicken and, of course, pork. Fresh lemon soda recommended.

† Nicky's Pizza, near the Shell petrol station on Kampala–Entebbe Rd. Authentic pizza oven, has indoor and outdoor seating. Relaxed atmosphere.

Bars and clubs

4 Point, Airport Rd, at the edge of town. Popular bar and restaurant serving simple fare (†). Large premises with grass-thatched roof, with indoor and outdoor terraced seating. Pool tables and a widescreen TV showing sports. Turns into a disco at night. Open till very late every night, going on till morning at weekends, with large crowds in the holiday season.

Four Turkeys, Kampala Rd. Very popular, lively venue offering Chinese and Continental food (†) from 1100 till late. Metamorphoses into a bar at night with loud music. Widescreen TV for sports broadcasts.

Shopping

Entebbe has a range of small shops including a supermarket and pharmacy as well as a spice and fruit market. On the road down to Entebbe there are a number of stalls selling everything from pottery, mats and baskets to a huge range of fruit and vegetables. Prices are not as cheap as you might expect as the sellers are obviously used to people buying on their way to and from the airport. The wares include brightly coloured woven baskets made by Nubian women. Generations of Nubians have lived close to Entebbe, but have maintained their cultural identity.

Maps

Department of Lands and Surveys, turn left opposite the playground and walk down the road. Good if you need maps, but a slow process. Sells 1:50,000 sheets for most of Uganda at US$4.50 each. This is also a good source of Kenyan maps, which are not always available in Nairobi for security reasons.

Activities and tours
Golf and cricket
Entebbe Club, T0414-322067. This was the
1st golf course in East Africa, built around
1900, still popular and in a glorious position.
Non-members can play a round for US$15
for 18 holes, bag hire US$13.50.

Cricket is played in the middle of the golf
course by the 18th hole. It's very pleasant
and spectators can watch from the Entebbe
Club. Other sports available include tennis
US$2.50, badminton, basketball, snooker
and ping pong.

Transport
Minibus to the *matatu* park in **Kampala**.
They go every few mins, 1 hr, US$1.25.

Directory
Banks Barclays Bank, Airport Rd, Kitoro,
opposite the Gapco petrol station. **Stanbic
Bank**, Kampala Rd. Exchanges TCs and cash.
Internet Entebbe Cyberlink, close to
the Chinese Restaurant. Open 0800-2130.
Surfing Corner, 100 m away opposite
Stanbic Bank. Open 0800-2200.

Contents

Jinja, Mount Elgon & the east

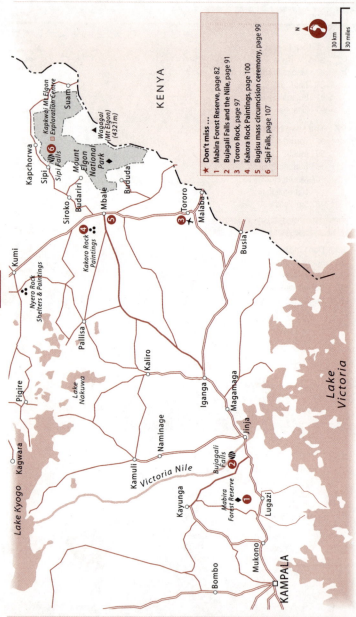

N

30 km
30 miles

★ **Don't miss ...**
1 Mabira Forest Reserve, page 82
2 Bujagali Falls and the Nile, page 91
3 Tororo Rock, page 97
4 Kakora Rock Paintings, page 100
5 Bugisu mass circumcision ceremony, page 99
6 Sipi Falls, page 107

KENYA

Kapkwai Mt Elgon
Exploration Centre

Kapchorwa

Sipi   Sipi Falls

6

Wagagai
(Mt Elgon)
(4321m)

Mount
Elgon
National
Park

Budariri

Siroko

Mbale

5

Bududa

Tororo

Malaba

3

Busia

BUSIA

Kumi

Kakora Rock
Paintings

4

Nyero Rock
Shelters & Paintings

Pallisa

Kaliro

Pigire

Lake
Nakuwa

Kagwara

Lake Kyoga

Kamuli

Naminage

Iganga

Magamaga

Jinja

Bujagali
Falls

2

Victoria Nile

Kayunga

Mabira
Forest Reserve

1

Lugazi

Lake
Victoria

Bombo

Mukono

KAMPALA

Compared to the west of Uganda, the east receives relatively few visitors apart from those passing through on their way to and from Kenya. The excellent road out of Kampala to Jinja, 82 km east, passes through Mabira Forest. Huge trees, darkening the sunlight, tower over the road before it emerges once more into the brightness of sugar cane fields.

Jinja is a very popular stopping point, however, as it offers some of the best whitewater rafting in Africa on the Victoria Nile. First, though, spend a little time in Jinja looking for the ripples of the Ripon Falls, the source of the Nile. You'll be surprised at how big the river already is. Jinja is also a good place to do a village walk and gain an insight into plants and crops.

Interest in climbing Mount Elgon from the Uganda side is once again increasing and many are taking the opportunity of exploring the caldera with its fascinating plant life. New trails have been developed enhancing the region. The Sipi Falls on the northern foothills of Mount Elgon are magnificent, and posters of them are seen all over Uganda. Exploring the foothills is an alternative activity for travellers who do not wish to climb the extinct volcano.

The eastern region has some of the most spectacular rock paintings in Uganda at Nyero near Kumi and at Kakora, close to Mbale. Other geological features of the region include Tororo's volcanic plug, 1800 m high, which can be scaled, a precariously balanced rock gong and nearby rock slide close to the Kakora rock paintings in Pallisa District and the impressive caves around Mount Elgon.

Mabira Forest Reserve and Jinja

Mabira Forest contains more than 300 varieties of trees and is home to several varieties of monkeys, over 300 mainly forest bird species. It's also famed for its clouds of glorious butterflies. Areas of primary and secondary forest can be explored on foot or by bicycle via an extensive trail network.

The fabled River Nile, Africa's longest river, begins its epic journey northwards at the attractive town of Jinja, Uganda's second city. Jinja suffered badly under the Amin regime but some fine Asian-influenced architecture dating from the colonial era survives. Nearby are the impressive Bujagali Falls, the centre for adventure sports including whitewater rafting, kayaking, jet-boating, bungee jumping or exploring the countryside on quad bikes. More sedate activities are available like horse riding, fishing, birdwatching, cycling or guided village walks.

Mabira Forest Reserve → *Colour map 2, B5.*

Ins and outs

Getting there Taxis and *matatus* are frequent in both Jinja and Kampala and run all day. To visit Mabira Forest from Kampala, take a *matatu* taxi from either the old or new taxi park, heading towards Jinja. Get off at Najjembe village, 55 km along the highway. If you are on Kampala Road, catch a *matatu* or taxi from the Caltex gas station near **Nando's**.

If you are coming from Jinja, take a taxi heading for Kampala from the taxi park by the market or by the Caltex on Main Street and get off at Najjembe, about 26 km out of Jinja. At Najjembe village, on the north side of the highway, follow the path by the 'Mabira Forest' sign for about 500 m to the forest centre where trained local staff can help you. To reach Griffin Falls get off at Lugazi and take a *boda-boda* through the sugar cane plantations to Wasswa village, US$1.50.

Fees The cost of a day permit to the forest for both walking and cycle trails is US$5 for foreign visitors. A guide costs an additional US$5 per person, although these fees will escalate if the new NFA tariffs are implemented.

Flora and fauna

Mabira, technically a moist semi-deciduous forest, covers 306 sq km and ranges in height from 1070 m to 1340 m. Much is secondary forest, having been heavily influenced by human activity until the late 1980s. There are more than 300 species of trees and shrubs recorded here. Several species occur in the forest outside their altitudinal range. Nine restricted species and one unique species (*Caesalpicia volkensii*) grow in the forest. The famous 'strangler fig', *Ficus nantalensis*, is widely present in the forest and is the source of the fibre for the bark-cloth that is traditional to central Uganda. Red-tailed monkeys are fairly common and seen more often than the elusive black and white colobus. There are more than 20 species of shrews and rodents.

The large moth fauna here is quite typical of a large forest on the Victoria Lake crescent. The forest is home to approximately 100 species of large moths, including seven range-restricted, three hawkmoth and four rare forest silkmoth species. Mabira has extremely rich butterfly fauna and supports species seldom found in Uganda, including several species with 'novel' distribution patterns and limited ranges. Despite the heavy historical influence of humans, the butterfly populations have shown marked resilience. Approximately 200 species have been recorded with more than 75% of them being forest-dependent.

The bird community at Mabira Forest is especially rich with rare and threatened species present and a lot of conservation work is being undertaken. There are over 300 species present in the forest, more than 50 of which can be viewed just from the picnic area. Almost half the species found in the forest are strictly forest-dependent. Many rare birds have been recorded at Mabira forest, including the blue swallow, the Papyrus gonolek and the Nahan francolin. Other species present and seldom seen elsewhere in Uganda are the tit hylia, purple-throated cuckoo shrike and the grey apalis. Mabira is especially valuable for its lowland species as well; for example, the whitebellied kingfisher and the blue-crested flycatcher.

Mabira Forest's future was recently under threat. In order to meet the increased sugar demand for bio-fuels a proposal, approved by President Museveni, was put forward in 2007 to hand over 7100 ha, more than a quarter of the forest, to the Mehta Group for sugar plantation. This plan was widely opposed by conservationists and a protest rally in Kampala in May 2007 resulted in at least three fatalities. This proposal was dropped later that year given the scale of the opposition.

Walking and biking trails

Walking and cycling trails are the main attraction at the forest centre. Both guided and self-guided walking trails wander through both primary and secondary forest teeming with butterflies, birds and monkeys. If you are out to see the monkeys, it's best to go in the morning or during the late afternoon when the heat of the day has passed. Mountain bike trails will take you through a wide variety of landscapes: through the local communities, sugar cane and tea plantations, past waterfalls and through the rainforest. The latter is a damp place, so protective clothing, long trousers, hiking boots, a fleece, mosquito repellent and drinking water are advisable.

Mabira Forest Reserve listings

For Sleeping and Eating price codes and other relevant information, see Essentials pages 21-23.

Sleeping

LL Mabira Forest Lodge, T041-425 8273, info@geolodgesafariafrica.com. Opened in 2007, this is an upmarket development, with 15 spacious cottages nestling in forest glades, a restaurant, a gym and 2 pools, one available for use by non-residents.

F Griffin Falls Campsite, near Wasswa Village, www.ecotoursuganda.com/griffinfalls. Located 10 km from the main road that runs through Lugazi, to the west of the forest. A community-run campsite that opened in 2009 offering a much quieter experience than the facilities at Najjembe,

where there is a constant traffic drone. A single *banda* costs US$4.50, double US$9, tent US$6.50 plus Mabira Forest entry permit US$5. Forest walks and cycling are on offer. The walk to Griffin Falls takes about 1 hr.

F Little Kingston da Global Village, Najjembe, T077-261 5618, www.littlekingston.com. A Belgian-Ugandan enterprise offering an alternative to the NFA **Mabira Forest Ecotourism Centre**, see below. 1 twin, 3 double rooms and a 4-bed dorm plus camping. The restaurant/bar favours reggae music. Mountain biking and forest walks can be organized. Tent rental US$7, bike rental US$14 daily.

F Mabira Forest Ecotourism Centre, near Najjembe Trading Centre, T071-248 7173. A community ecotourism centre established by the National Forestry Authority (NFA) in 1995. It offers simple facilities of *bandas* with outside toilets and washing facilities and a campsite. The visitor centre is a useful resource about local flora and fauna. Local women's crafts can be purchased and the Mabira Eco-Tourism Drama Group is happy to entertain. All guides are trained and knowledgeable. Single *bandas* are US$4.50, a double *banda* is US$9 and a family *banda* sleeping 4, US$13. Camping (own equipment) is US$5 pp plus Mabira Forest entry permit US$5.

Eating

The Ecotourism Centre at Najjembe, (see Sleeping) has picnicking facilities in traditional umbrella-thatched shelters available for free. Both local and more Western-style foods are available at good prices. A local cook can prepare food for visitors at reasonable rates; however, you must order well ahead of time. You can bring your own food and have it prepared for you while you relax. Or you can go up to the roadside market 500 m away for fried chicken, goat or beef. Cold sodas, beer and local food including chapatis and *gonja* are also available at the roadside. The price, quality and variety of fruits and vegetables are fantastic. This roadside market is considered the best along the Kampala–Jinja highway. Alternatively, try the restaurant at **Little Kingston da Global Village** (see Sleeping above). At Wasswa preparation of meals also needs to be pre-arranged with the campsite staff.

Jinja → *Phone code: 0434, Colour map 2, B5.*

Jinja would probably be a fairly nondescript town if it were not for its location. The town is perhaps best known for being the source of the Nile. Practically everything to do with the town is connected to the river: electricity production, brewing and now tourism being its main sources of income. It is at the head of Napoleon Gulf, on the northern end of Lake Victoria, and lies on the east bank of the Victoria Nile.

It suffered severely during the bad times but it is now a pretty and vibrant place. The shops in the main street are well maintained and, as you walk through the town, you will see the old colonial and Asian bungalows in their spacious gardens, many of which have been renovated. Some of the back streets remain fairly desolate. It is a sprawling town covering a wide area. The section popular with tourists is around Main Street, where there is a grid street pattern, home to most of the shops, cafés, restaurants, banks and internet cafés.

Ins and outs

Getting there The journey from Kampala to Jinja takes around two hours by bus or *matatu*. If you want to explore the area more independently, it is cheaper to hire a 4WD here than in Kampala. ▶ *See Transport, page 96.*

Source of the Nile

ⓘ *3 km from Jinja, US$2.50, no public transport so take a* boda-boda, *over the dam wall towards Kampala, along the Nalufenya Rd, then ask for directions from locals.*

The source of the Nile was originally designated at the site of the Ripon Falls. These were submerged during the construction of the Owen Falls Dam, although ripples can still be seen from the picnic area. It is lovely to sit on the lawn in the shade listening to the birds and watching the swirling river below. Many people consider this setting on the west bank to be much more atmospheric than the other side. The islets and rocks recorded by Speke

Jinja

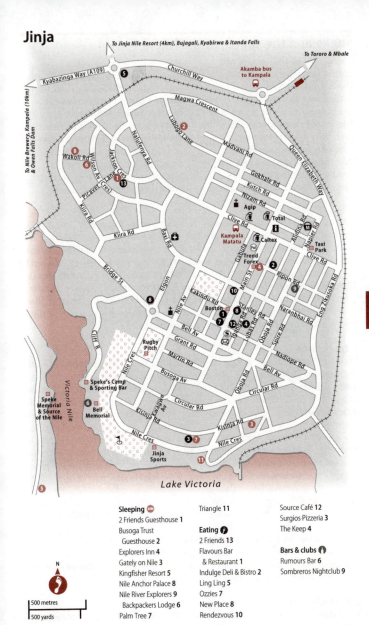

To Jinja Nile Resort (4km), Bujagali, Kyabirwa & Itanda Falls

To Tororo & Mbale

To Nile Brewery, Kampala (10km) & Owen Falls Dam

Kyabazinga Way (A109)

Churchill Way

Akamba bus to Kampala

Magwa Crescent

Lubogo Lane

Madvani Rd

Wakoli Rd

Jackson Cres

Naluferya Rd

Gokhale Rd

Kutch Rd

Nizam Rd

Wilson Av Lane

Picaver Cres

Kiira Rd

Kiira Rd

Baxi Rd

Bridge St

Elgon

Nile Av

Clive Rd

Agip

Total

Kampala Matatu

Caltex

Trend Forex

Gabula Rd

Main St

Ripon Rd

Clive Rd

Annirai Rd

Napier Rd

Taxi Park

Kakindu Rd

Boston

Stanley Rd

Naranbhai Rd

Ein Zikuloka Rd

Bell Av

Grant Rd

Lubas Rd

Oboja Rd

Iganga Rd

Nadiope Rd

Rugby Pitch

Martin Rd

Busoga Av

Bell Av

Oboja Rd

Circular Rd

Speke's Camp & Sporting Bar

Circular Rd

Kisinja Rd

Bell Memorial

Lwazoge Av

Kisinja Rd

Nile Cres

Nile Cres

Jinja Sports

Speke Memorial & Source of the Nile

Victoria Nile

Cliff R

Nile Cres

Lake Victoria

N

500 metres

500 yards

Sleeping

2 Friends Guesthouse 1
Busoga Trust
  Guesthouse 2
Explorers Inn 4
Gately on Nile 3
Kingfisher Resort 5
Nile Anchor Palace 8
Nile River Explorers 9
  Backpackers Lodge 6
Palm Tree 7

Triangle 11

Eating

2 Friends 13
Flavours Bar
  & Restaurant 1
Indulge Deli & Bistro 2
Ling Ling 5
Ozzies 7
New Place 8
Rendezvous 10

Source Café 12
Surgios Pizzeria 3
The Keep 4

Bars & clubs

Rumours Bar 6
Sombreros Nightclub 9

Speke and the source of the Nile

During his 1860-1863 journey with Captain James Grant from Zanzibar to Khartoum via the west shore of Lake Victoria, John Hanning Speke was the first European to see the source of the Nile, in 1862, from the other side of the inlet to the present picnic area.

He recorded the moment thus: "Most beautiful was the scene, nothing could surpass it! It was the very perfection of the kind of effect aimed at in a highly kept park; with a magnificent stream from 600 to 700 yds wide, dotted with islets and rocks, the former occupied by fishermens' huts, the latter by terns and crocodiles basking in the sun, flowing between fine high grassy banks, with rich trees and plantains in the background. The expedition had now performed its functions; old Father Nile without any doubt rises in the Victoria Nyanza."

(see box, above) also disappeared with the building of the Owen Falls Dam. A plaque mounted on a small rock marks the spot from which the Nile begins its 7000-km journey through Uganda, Sudan and Egypt. Known as the Speke Memorial, or more commonly called the Source of the Nile Plaque, it indicates the spot where Speke stood when he first sighted the source of the Nile, on 28 July 1862. He named it the Ripon Falls after Lord Ripon, the Viceroy of India and President of the Royal Geographical Society at the time.

On the eastern bank, easier to access from the town via Cliff Road, is the other 'Source of the Nile' venture. This costs US$4.50 to get in to an unappealing park with surly staff, vendors selling overpriced souvenirs, and a dilapidated bar.

Satya Narayan Temple
The Hindu Satya Narayan Temple close to Jinja contains shrines to Ambaji, Shankar Bhagwan, and Shitla Mata. The bronze bust of Mahatma Gandhi located in the outer compound was unveiled by the Indian Prime Minister Gujral, accompanied by President Museveni, in 1997. Gandhi Javanti is celebrated on 2 October, reflecting Gandhi's association with Jinja. Although Gandhi never visited Uganda some of his ashes were immersed in the Nile in 1948. When Amin expelled the people of Asian origin in 1972 only a handful of Hindus remained in Jinja. During their period of exile the temple's hall was used by local people for gatherings and dancing, and part of the temple was utilized for accommodation. However, the temple's shrines were not damaged. The temple and memorial bust are located close to the Source of the Nile Plaque.

Bell Memorial
ⓘ *US$4.50, walk or take a bicycle taxi from the centre, if walking, go along Bell Ave beyond the Sports Club and then turn left along Cliff Rd.*
On the Jinja side, on the east bank, stands the Bell Memorial. It's popular with Ugandans and is often swarming with secondary school children. In 1905, Sir Hesketh Bell was appointed the first Governor of Uganda Protectorate, and was responsible for developing the cotton industry and the elimination of sleeping sickness.

Owen Falls Dam
This dam was built in 1954 and supplies most of Uganda, and a good part of Kenya, with electricity. During the turmoil of the Amin period a group of dedicated engineers managed

to keep the generators going almost without interruption. The falls themselves were hidden during construction of the dam, but the dam and the new falls that it creates are impressive in themselves. The main road from Kampala crosses the dam, so try and get a seat on the appropriate side (left if you are heading east) in order to get a good view. Due to the dam's strategic and economic importance, you are not allowed to take photographs.

The once-magnificent **Ripon Falls Hotel** has now fallen into disrepair. The hotel overlooks the submerged Ripon Falls and was built in 1950 for a royal visit from Queen Elizabeth II to open the Owen Falls Dam in 1954.

Jinja listings

For Sleeping and Eating price codes and other relevant information, see Essentials pages 21-23.

Sleeping

LL-AL Gately on Nile, Nile Cres, 34b Kisinja Rd, T0434-122400, www.gatelyonnile.com. An exclusive B&B on the shores of Lake Victoria, opened in 2000 by an Australian, Merryde Loosemore. A beautiful refurbished old colonial house and 4 cottages set in 4 acres of stunning grounds. Restaurant serves excellent Continental, Mexican and Thai food, worth visiting even if staying elsewhere. DSTV, Wi-Fi, conference facilities. Bookings for local activities can be organized from here. There are 4 simpler (and cheaper) self-catering B&B rooms in the annexe.

AL Samuka Island, Lake Victoria, 40 mins by motorboat from Jinja. A 4-ha island that is a bird sanctuary, home to over 50 migratory and endemic bird species including the long-tailed cormorant and little egret. A new solar-powered upmarket resort is close to completion. The island is scheduled to reopen in 2011. Access to the island will be via boats leaving from the jetty close to **Rumours** bar.

AL-A 2 Friends Guesthouse, 5 Jackson Cres, T0783-160804, restaurant T077-298 4821, www.2friends.info. An Icelandic-Irish enterprise offering comfortable rooms either in the main house or by the poolside, DSTV, free Wi-Fi, pool enhanced by sculptures and a popular bar. Has an excellent restaurant of the same name in a lush garden setting offering a varied menu including Indian dishes. Deservedly popular. Safe parking.

A Hotel Triangle, 26 Nile Cres, T0434-122098/9, www.hoteltriangle.co.ug. Unappealing modern building with stunning views over the lake close to the submerged site of the Ripon Falls. Double rooms have private balconies. DSTV, 25 m pool (open to non-residents for a small fee), gym, pool table and laundry facilities. Free internet. The restaurant provides a running buffet for breakfast and dinner.

A Surjios Pizzeria & Guest House, formerly **Palm Tree Guest House**, 24 Kisinja Rd, T077-250 0400, www.surjios.com. A former presidential lodge, now a guesthouse with 11-rooms, 4 with balconies overlooking Lake Victoria. Good river and lake views from the patio. Quiet, clean, comfortable with polite, attentive staff, breakfast included, well-maintained gardens and a great pool. The restaurant serves excellent food. Safe parking.

A-B Kingfisher Safari Resort, T077-263 2063 (mob), www.kingfisher-uganda.net. Family hotel under German management past the source of the Nile with restaurant, an attractive pool (closed for cleaning on Mon). Thatched cottages in a garden setting. Quiet location on the west bank of the Nile, looking across the lake to Jinja. Well-maintained gardens ideal for birdwatching. Hot water supply unpredictable. Restaurant serves Continental and local dishes. Slow service. Camping facilities US$7pp. Accessed via the main A109 Kampala road, at the Owen Falls Dam take the turn eastwards by the Nile Brewery and follow this road for 5.5 km.

C Nile Anchor Palace, 4 Wakoli Pl, T071-260 0223, nileanchorpalace.com. Lovely old restored house in the southwest outskirts of Jinja, not far from **NRE** (see below). Spacious, clean, airy en suite rooms, friendly, courteous and helpful staff. Free Wi-Fi, safe parking. Excellent food.

D Explorer Inn, 23 Iganga Rd near junction with Ripon Rd, T077-716 4979. Close to **Indulge Deli**. Very central, lively location, single storey pink building with tiled roof, 8 en suite rooms with TV. Bar and a lounge.

D-F Nile River Explorers (NRE) Backpackers Lodge, Plot 41, Wilson Ave, T0434-120236, T077-296 0964 (mob), www.raftafrica.com. Double rooms, dorms US$7pp, camping US$5pp. Bar with cold beer, free tea and coffee all day, inexpensive meals, pool table, free Wi-Fi and email facilities, DSTV, hot showers, laundry facilities and Western toilets. Free Kampala–Jinja shuttle, must be pre-booked. Can help organize gorilla permits in Uganda and Rwanda and other bookings such as Ngamba (Chimp) Island, and vehicle hire. Credit cards, local and international currencies accepted. Highly recommended.

E Busogo Trust Guest House, 18 Lubogo Lane, T077-265 3306, www.busogatrust. co.uk. Late colonial house c1950 with 10 spacious rooms, veranda and terrace, popular with NGOs, a 10 min-walk from the town centre. It has 3 8-bed dorms or 7 en suite double rooms. Attractive garden with a barbecue. Laundry service, internet facilities, well-equipped kitchen and living room with DVD. Guests can accompany the NGOs to nearby villages to observe the water/sanitation provision and maintenance. Can arrange pick-ups from Entebbe Airport, US$57. All profits generated go to fund the NGO Busogo Trust, which installs boreholes for communities supplying clean safe water in 6 regions of Uganda, alongside an education programme about sanitation and the prevention of water-borne diseases. Guests get a 10% discount if rafting with

NRE Backpackers (see above), paying only US$110.

Camping
Within Jinja town the best option is **NRE Backpackers** (see above). However, the majority of camping facilities are based downriver at Bujagali (see page 93).

Eating
The more upmarket hotels all offer good standard menus. Main St has lots of local eating houses in the low price range; the best are **Rendezvous**, **Flavours**, **Boston** and **The New Place**. Local meals cost about US$2-3.

¶¶ 2Friends Restaurant, 5 Jackson Cres, T077-298 4821 (mob). Popular outdoor bar and restaurant in a lovely garden setting. The varied menu includes grills, fish, steaks, pizzas, Indian and local dishes.

¶¶ Gately on Nile Restaurant, Nile Cres, 34b Kisinja Rd, T077-246 9638 (mob). Serves excellent Continental, Mexican and Thai food in beautiful surroundings. The gardens overlook Lake Victoria. Efficient service.

¶ Indulge Delicatessen & Bistro, on corner of Iganga Rd and Ripon Rd, T078-264 8544 (mob). Mon, Wed-Sat 0900-1700, Sun 0900-1600. Offers a variety of well-presented cheeses, quiches, pies, sandwiches and salads and serves delicious coffee, ice creams, smoothies and milkshakes. Adventure booking office. Free Wi-Fi and **George's Book Exchange** (see below).

¶ Ling Ling, 30/32 Kyabazinga Way, Shell Ambercourt Station, T077-248 9616 (mob). Sister restaurant of the Kampala Chinese restaurant **Fang Fang**, sited in the forecourt of a petrol station, offers a range of dishes from different provinces. Situated outside the town centre, near the roundabout to Kampala. The restaurant is not particularly attractive, but the food is good.

¶ Surjios Pizzeria (previously **Palm Tree**), 24 Kisinja Rd, T077-250 0400 (mob). Open 1200-1430 and 1730-2130. Serves delicious pizzas freshly cooked in a wood-burning oven. Also Continental and Mexican food.

Flavours, 12 Main St, T077-626 3333 (mob), www.enjoyflavours.com. Tue-Sun 0830-2130. New coffee bar, restaurant and pub venue offers meals, snacks, coffee and smoothies, wine and beer. Wi-Fi and book exchange. Open-air movies on a big screen in the garden every Wed at 2000. Paintings and sculptures by local artists are displayed and are for sale.

The Keep Restaurant & Coffee Shop, 12 Iganga Rd. Open 0800-2200. Run by a pleasant American couple now resident in Uganda serving good espresso coffee, delicious milkshakes and a range of wholesome meals and snacks. Fast internet connection. Johnny runs Hackers for Charity, www.hfc-uganda.org, a charity offering IT training courses to provide locals with a source of sustainable income.

Ozzie's Café, Main St, opposite Source Café. Open until 1800, Fri and Sat until 2100. Lively venue offering Western dishes like burgers, pizzas, pasta, full English breakfast, milkshakes and cakes at reasonable prices. Popular with the many expats around Jinja. Service can be a problem though.

Source Café, 20 Main St, T0434-412 0911. Serves coffees, juices, homemade cakes and light meals in a pleasant environment. Also has a giftshop selling cards and batiks and internet facilities.

Bars and clubs

Rumours, accessed by a staircase to the left of the pathway going down to the east bank Source of the Nile, about 20 m upstream from the monuments, signs and boat cruise departure point. This is a popular bar/grill near the Nile source with a restaurant deck and a series of wooden walkways along the water's edge. Owned by an American who runs a Kenyan NGO. It's in a wonderful position to watch the sunset but is a bit of a hike from Main St.

Sombreros Night Club, 2A Spring Rd. Lays claim to be the only disco in town. Noisy, popular club offering a variety of music including R'n'B, reggae and ragga.

Shopping

Books

George's Book Exchange, in 3 local outlets: the main one at Explorers River Camp, Bujagali; 2 smaller outlets in town at Indulge Delicatessen and Flavours Coffee Shop. This is a non-profit enterprise fully funded by George, an expat Englishman resident in Jinja. George imports donated and charity shop books from the UK. The books are then exchanged with the swapper paying US$0.50 per book. All proceeds are donated to a local charity, Softpower Education, http://softpowereducation.com.

Markets

Jinja Market is a relaxed market which is worth a look, with occasional great clothing finds. More adventurous travellers may wish to try the fried grasshoppers and white ants.

Activities and tours

Fishing

Haven River Lodge, Kayunga Rd, about 20 km from Jinja, T070-290 5959, www.thehaven-uganda.com. Rods for hire.

Speke's Camp and Sports Bar, Source of the Nile, T0414-220906, T075-258 4171 (mob). US$25 per session.

Golf

Jinja Club. A 9-hole golf course, US$4.50 per round plus US$2.50 caddie fees. Golf club rental US$7.

Rugby

Impromptu games are held at the rugby pitch at weekends between Nile Cres and Nile Ave.

Swimming

The obvious choice for a swim would be the river. Avoid the lake due to risk of bilharzia, but anywhere with free-flowing water is safer. It's possible to swim at the Bujagali campsites (see page 93) in beautiful surroundings. There is a pool at Jinja Nile Resort (complete with pool bar) and at the

Jinja Club (where the water is a bit green!) as well as **Hotel Triangle**, **2Friends** and **Kingfisher Safari Resort**, costing between US$2.50-5.

Tennis and squash
Jinja Club. US$2.25 per session.

Tour operators
Advanced Tours & Travel Ltd, 28/30 Clive Rd, T0434-120457, T071-246 3474 (mob), www.advancedtours.ug. Organizes tours and car hire.

Tours
Nile Brewery tours, T0332-210009, office 0830-1700, closed Mon. Complimentary tours, including a free beer, run Tue-Fri according to demand. Pre-booking essential. It's an entertaining way to spend a day during the rainy season. Small souvenir shop. **Sunset Gin & Tonic Canoe Trips**, run by Kayak the Nile, see below. 2-hr trips on Lake Victoria.

Voluntary work
If you have the time, Jinja is a great place to do some voluntary work in a local primary school or orphanage. It is very popular with overlanders who camp at the **Nile River Explorers** camp. Volunteers give a day or more of their travels to visit the projects around Jinja and join in. The work is tailored to suit the capabilities of each volunteer. The project leader will designate a task for the day; anything from teaching nursery rhymes to laying a floor. US$15pp minimum voluntary contribution, all of which is invested into the project. Contact **Nile River Explorers (NRE) Backpackers Lodge**, page 88, and see http://softpowereducation.com.

Whitewater rafting
Equator Rafts, based at Speke Camp, is not recommended as it hasn't been verified by the safety body JASA (see page 95). It is likely to close in 2011-2012, given its proximity to Bujagali Falls, which is due to be submerged due to a hydroelectric scheme (see page 92). DVD footage of trips is available from all companies and makes an excellent memento.
Adrift, 14 York Terr, Kololo, Kampala, T031-223 7438, T077-223 7438 (mob), http://adrift.ug. Transport pick-up from the **Sheraton Hotel** and (Natate) **Backpackers Hostel**. No experience is necessary and they offer the option of paddling as a team or riding in an oar raft, with the guide rowing. 1- and 2-day trips down the Nile, starting from Bujagali Falls. Cost US$125 pp, includes transport from Kampala for 1 day's rafting and a barbecue. Nile High Bungee drops for US$80 or a combination of bungee jumping and rafting for US$195. Also a 30-min jet-boat ride on the Nile for US$75, or with rafting and bungee jumping for US$250.
Kayak the Nile (KTN), Explorers Campsite, Bujagali Falls, T077-288 0322 (mob), www.kayakthenile.com. In association with **NRE** (see page 88), KTN operates a kayak school tailored to individual clients as well as tandem kayaking.
Nalubale Rafting, 17 Kissinja Rd, T078-263 8938, www.nalubalerafting.com. Currently cheaper than its competitors, offering full-day rafting at US$100pp for grade 5 rapids, US$95 for grade 3 rapids. 2-day rafting all-inclusive costs US$199 and a taster 2-hr float trip, grade 1 and 2 costs US$30pp. Longer expedition of 8 days, US$1500.
Nile River Explorers (NRE), T0434-120236, T077-296 0964 (mob), nre@raftafrica.com. Based in Jinja, provides a free night's accommodation either at its **Backpackers Hostel** in Jinja or at the **Bujagali Explorers** campsite. Its package, at US$125 per day, has a rafting route, 30 km long including 12 rapids. Many consider that **NRE** runs a more personal day than **Adrift**; all guides and staff live locally and after the day's rafting will spend the evening with clients. The cost includes transport from Jinja to the river and back, a light lunch of fruit and sodas, and the day is rounded off with a

barbecue, beers and sodas. 2-day rafting trips are also available.

Transport
Bus
Jinja to **Kampala**, 2 hrs, US$3.50. Same journey time and fare by *matatu*. Jinja to **Busia** by *matatu* US$4. The taxi park in Jinja is located off Clive Rd, near the market.

An alternative route runs west of Mabira Forest from Kampala via Mukono, Kayunga, Nazigo and Kangalamira to Njeru by Jinja. Recommended if going to **Kalagala Falls**, **Naminya Village** or other west Nile activities. However, all the major activity companies offer a free shuttle service to and from either Jinja or Kampala to their bases if prebooked.

Car hire
This is relatively expensive at US$110-120 per day plus fuel. Given the condition of Ugandan roads few travellers opt to drive themselves. Check terms and conditions about a replacement vehicle in case of breakdown to avoid an expensive experience as many cars are rented on a daily basis whether the car is roadworthy or not. A 4WD with driver is available via **Walter Egger**, Wemtec Engineering, 14 Spire Rd, T077-221113 (mob), wemtec@source.co.ug, or from **Advanced Tours & Travel**, see page 90.

Directory
Banks Several banks in central Jinja offer foreign exchange services including **Barclays Bank**, 81 Main St, T0434-121266, or **Standard Charter Bank**, 2-4 Grant Rd, T0434-122661/2, who also have ATMs that accept most credit cards. **Forex** bureaux usually give better rates and quicker service than banks. **Internet** There are many internet cafés both in Jinja and at the various developments downriver. In central Jinja **Source Café**, **Indulge** and **The Keep Restaurant & Coffee Shop** offer reliable connections in a pleasant environment.

Bujagali Falls

Downstream from the Owen Falls Dam are the Bujagali Falls, a spectacular area with about 1 km of raging water. Local legend has it that a man called Mr Bujagali sometimes sits on the river on a bark-cloth mat. Even if you don't want to stay, Bujagali is worth a visit. For a small fee locals will offer to 'swim' over the falls whilst holding on to a jerry-can. This is a thoroughly stupid thing to do, and some have even drowned in the process, so it's not a good idea to encourage them by paying for this 'entertainment'.

Ins and outs
Getting there From Kampala, the falls can be reached by crossing the Owen Falls Dam (if you're coming from Kampala) and turning northwards at the Kyabazinga (Shell/Ling Ling) roundabout. From Jinja, the falls are 8 km (a two-hour walk); go straight on from Clive Rd, past the roundabout, and continue for a further 7 km. Watch out for speed bumps, children and cyclists and unlit vehicles. The sealed road changes to murram. Pass through Buwenda Trading Centre, across a small valley and as you climb out take a marked left-hand turn along the road to Bujagali. About 500 m along this road you will reach Chillington Gate.

Entry fees **Speke Camp** charges an entry fee of US$1.25. The other sites do not charge for entry.

The dam

Bujagali Falls will be submerged in 2011-2012, victim to the construction of a hydroelectric dam. On completion the river will be diverted through the western channel of the dam, so some of the current popular rapids will disappear. The well-established existing activities at Bujagali (see page 95) will continue after the dam opens, but rafting will start 3 km downstream and it is anticipated that additional sporting facilities will be developed on the newly formed lake. For example, **Nile River Explorers** plan to offer fishing, birdwatching and lunch and sunset cruises in a 50-person pontoon boat on the lake. There are other big rapids further downstream.

Building the dam has been contentious over the years, ranging from corruption claims to riding roughshod over the needs of the local people, with many property owners

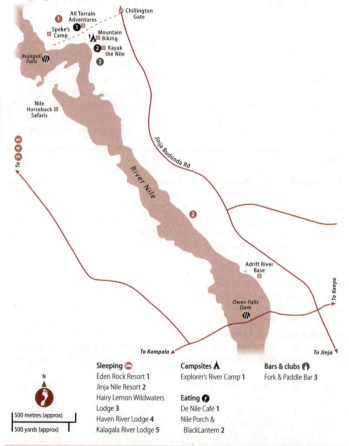

Bujagali Falls

Sleeping
Eden Rock Resort 1
Jinja Nile Resort 2
Hairy Lemon Wildwaters Lodge 3
Haven River Lodge 4
Kalagala River Lodge 5

Campsites
Explorer's River Camp 1

Eating
De Nile Café 1
Nile Porch & BlackLantern 2

Bars & clubs
Fork & Paddle Bar 3

N

500 metres (approx)
500 yards (approx)

still awaiting full compensation. Some infrastructure such as access roads have still to be completed. The positioning of high-voltage power lines and pylons along the west river valley are an eyesore, although as they have become discoloured and dusty they are beginning to blend into the background. Given its proximity to Kampala this area has become a popular weekend and second home resort.

◉ Bujagali Falls listings

For Sleeping and Eating price codes and other relevant information, see Essentials pages 21-23.

● Sleeping

Bujagali offers a range of accommodation from camping to an upmarket hotel.

East bank of the Nile *map p92*

There are 2 main centres on the eastern side; the first is **Adrift's Riverbase Camp** and **Jinja Nile Resort**, approximately 3 km and 4 km respectively from the Shell/Ling Ling roundabout north of Jinja. The second larger centre lies at Bujagali Falls 5 km further along the same road.

AL Jinja Nile Resort, 4 km from central Jinja up the Bujagali Rd, T0434-122190, T077-260 7385 (mob), www.madahotels.com. A large sprawling development with a pool and luxurious cottages with private balconies. Rooms facing the Nile cost an additional US$20 (try for a downriver outlook, otherwise the Owen Falls dam 1 km away spoils the view). Facilities include restaurants with fairly expensive buffets, 2 bars, a sauna, gym, tennis, squash, pool and 'chip & putt' golf. The pool and gardens and outside bar area are very pleasant and there are spectacular views across the river with its lush midstream islands, abundant with birdlife and monkeys. Popular conference venue.

B-G Adrift Riverbase, T031-223 7438, T077-223 7438 (mob), www.adrift.ug. Previously the **Nile High Camp**, although the bungee jump on location is still called the Nile High Bungee. Offers camping US$5pp, 41 dorm beds US$10pp, 8 safari tents or 3 wooden chalets. **Adrift** was the first company to raft the Nile and offers a variety of whitewater

rafting trips. The 44-m Nile High Bungee jump from a 12-m cantilevered tower on top of a 32-m cliff over the Nile with a rope attached to your ankles is for the intrepid or foolhardy depending on your viewpoint. There's also the option of being dipped headfirst into the Nile prior to the first bounce: US$80; bungee and raft US$195; or bungee, raft and jet boat US$250. A solo trip on the Wild Nile Jet boat costs US$75 or US$50 for under 12s. Well-organized popular venue. Booking advised. Has an all-day clifftop bar and restaurant.

D-F Explorers River Camp, T0434-120236, T077-242 2373 (mob), www.raftafrica.com. Run by **Nile River Explorers** (NRE). Wonderfully positioned overlooking the expanse of the river, with beautiful views, and a fantastic spot to watch the sun set or the varied tropical birdlife or monkeys. Previously called **Explorers Campsite**, it was renamed to prevent confusion about whether only camping was available as there is a range of accommodation options: A-frame *bandas* nestling on the terraces, dorms (US$7pp) or safari tents (US$5 pp), plus a well-stocked bar (**Fork & Paddle**, see Eating, below), **George's Book Exchange**, free internet with several computers in the reception area, international telephone facilities, laundry and good full-time security. Free Kampala–Jinja shuttle. Very popular, booking advised.

Camping

There are now several campsites at Bujagali. **A Nile Porch**, next door to **Explorers River Camp**, T078-232 1541, relax@nileporch.com sited. Run by NRE. Offers thatched-roof safari tents with river-facing verandas or cottages furnished with locally sourced furniture and fittings, pool and decorative ponds set in well-maintained gardens. Wi-Fi. Safari tents, family units (2 adults/3 children) or 5-person tents, under 2s free. Pre-booking advised at weekends.

E Speke's Camp. Not to be confused with **Speke's Camp and Sports Bar** at the Source of the Nile in Jinja, this place offers camping, *bandas* or dormitory *bandas* and is situated close to the water, just metres from Bujagali Falls. The tent sites by the river are lovely; however, all the other facilities are very run down and will cease to exist once the new lake is created in 2011. It costs US$1.25 to visit **Speke's Camp**.

West bank of the Nile *map p92*

LL Wildwaters Lodge, accessed from west Nile bank, 3 km down a murram road from Kangulumira, T031-323 7438, www.wild-uganda.com. New upmarket development opened by **Adrift's Riverbase Camp** in Oct 2010, located on 6.5 ha unspoilt midstream Muyanja island by Kalagala Falls. Raised wooden walkways link the lodges nestling in the rainforest and traverse the island. Activities include rafting, kayaking, jet boat, fishing, putting, guided walks, swimming, spa and massage. Several eateries serve international food. The majority of guests will arrive and depart by pre-arranged **Adrift** shuttle service either from Kampala or Jinja.

L-C The Haven River Lodge, about 20 km northwest of Jinja on the west bank of the Nile, 8 km downstream of Bujagali Falls, T070-290 5959, thehavenuganda@ yahoo.com. A peaceful lodge located on a bluff by the Overtime rapid amongst lots of bird and wildlife including fish eagles, monitor lizards and monkeys. German designed with rainwater harvesting and solar water heating. It has a range of accommodation from *bandas* with full board and more expensive luxury *bandas*. Honeymoon *banda* with king-size bed and large bath from where you can watch the river and wildlife. Camping US$12pp, full board US$40pp. Payment in cash only,

no cheques, credit or debit card facilities. Activities include fishing, rod hire available, birdwatching, sunset cruise and canoeing. DSTV, pool table and internet. A bar/restaurant (¶¶¶) offers a choice of excellent local or Western food. From Njeru travel 15 km towards Kayunga, then turn right at the sign and continue for another 3 km. Advanced booking required.

A-C Hairy Lemon Island resort, T077-282 8338 (mob). Journey time around 1 hr from Jinja. Turn right at Nile Brewery if heading for Kampala and follow road for 30 km through Kangulumira and Nazigo. Turn right at the Caltex service station along a murram road (signposted). Continue for 8 km, then turn right at 2nd signpost. After the 2nd set of speed bumps there is a track to the right (signposted). After a short distance park at the house with all the flowers, walk down the hill and summon the boatman by banging on the tyre rim. If returning to Kampala it is possible to take the route west of Mabira Forest via Nazigo, Katunga and Mukona. Solar-powered secluded island accessed by boat. Last departure time 1800. All supplies are ferried across therefore advanced booking is essential. The new owners in Jun 2010 have upgraded facilities with many positive changes. Clean and well run with friendly, competent staff. Offers kayaking, fishing and birdwatching. Well-stocked bar. Twin *bandas*, Jessie's Barn sleeps 4 in 2 bunk beds, Sugar Shack is a large private double *banda*, camping US$16pp, dorms US$22pp. All prices include 3 excellent meals a day.

Camping

AL Kalagala River Lodge, for access see **Wildwaters Lodge**, above. An **Adrift** (http://adrift.ug) development due to open in Jul 2011. Sited at a spectacular location by the Kalagala Falls, within sight of **Wildwaters Lodge**, about 25 km downstream from Owen Falls Dam and the key mitigation area for the Bujagali dam. Accommodation will be safari tents.

E-F Eden Rock Resorts, T0434-131476, T077-250 1222 (mob), www.edenrocknile. com. Has extensive camping grounds and a large thatched restaurant and lounge building. Camping (US$3pp), 2-person *bandas*, family *bandas* and dorms (US$6pp). Set back from the river in fenced grounds with lots of gardens. Quieter than NRE, popular with families. Breakfast US$5.

🍴 Eating

East bank of the Nile *map p92*
Beside Chillington Gate there are a number of stalls and *duki* (small shops) selling street snacks, as well as a range of household goods and souvenirs.

🍴 **The Black Lantern**, attached to the **Nile Porch**, T078-232 1541, relax@nileporch.com. Opens for breakfast, lunch or dinner. A la carte restaurant that is probably the best dining option in the Jinja environs. Wonderful location high above the Nile under a large thatched roof. Famous for its pork spare ribs but also offers Indian and Chinese and other Western dishes. Especially busy at weekends when pre-booking advised.

🍴 **DeNile Café**, at the **All Terrain Adventures** site by the main gate, T078-264 5034, denilecafé@gmail.com. All-day café with a large menu at budget prices. Breakfasts, lunches, snacks, coffee and great smoothies on offer. **All Terrain Adventures** have set up Africa Smart Rider (T077-286 9037 (mob), www.africasmartrider.com), an advanced motorcycle training facility at affordable prices with discounts for Ugandan citizens to help reduce the high rate of accidents.

🍴 **Fork & Paddle**, **Explorers River Camp** (see page 93). A lively bar with food, music and videos of the day's rafting adventures. Food on offer includes burgers, chips, baked potatoes, steak rolls, vegetarian meals and desserts. The well-stocked bar has a huge choice of drinks with guaranteed cold beers.

▲ Activities and tours

Over the past few years there has been massive development downstream on the Nile and Bujagali has become a major adventure centre. Jinja Adventures Safety Association (JASA) was set up in 2008 "to promote Jinja as the adventure activity capital of Africa, whilst ensuring that all JASA registered companies adhere to the highest international safety standards." Most of the companies and activities listed below meet with JASA standards.

On the western Nile bank several new facilities have also been developed, including **Nile Horseback Safaris**.

Horse riding
Nile Horseback Safaris, T077-410 1196 (mob), www.nilehorsebacksafaris.com. Located on the west bank of the Nile, the Kampala side, this new family-owned, antipodean enterprise offers options for all rider abilities, of short and longer treks including overnight ones, either sleeping at **The Haven River Lodge**, see page 94, or **Holland Park**, a self-catering cottage; bring your own food. Multi-day safaris are also available for experienced riders. There are guided pony rides for children aged 3-10 years: 20 mins US$9, 30 mins US$13.50. **Note** English-style saddles are used. Adult rides: 1 hr US$35, 3 hrs US$75, 6 days/5 nights from US$1825 (minimum 4 riders or pay a supplement). Helmets supplied. This lovely site has been somewhat blighted by the erection of pylons to feed the electricity to the national grid from the new dam. To get here, **Nile River Explorers**, see page 88, offer a shuttle service from Kampala for their joint clients. From Jinja cross the Owen Falls dam into Njeru, and turn right along the signposted sealed road to Kayunga. At Naminya Village turn right 1 km along an unmade road towards the Nile. Private taxis taking 4 passengers may cost up to US$45. A *boda-boda* takes about 20 mins, US$4.50. As it is a new venture it

may be advisable to print off the map from their website until the horseback safaris becomes more familiar to local taxi drivers.

Kayaking

Kayak the Nile, Bujagali Falls, T077-288 0322, www.kayakthenile.com. Located at and working in partnership with **Nile River Explorers**, see page 88, offer a daily 2-hr Gin and Tonic Lake Victoria Sunset trip in 2-person canoes, lifejackets supplied, US$50pp. Depart at 1600 from **NRE** campsite in Bujagali by *matatu*. Enjoy a G&T or a soft drink on the lake whilst watching the sunset. Booking essential. Longer guided kayaking trips of 2, 3 or 4 days down the Nile as far as Lake Kyoga are available. Supply own or rent a tent and sleeping bag. 7-day kayaking skills courses with accommodation on, US$1000. 3-hr Short Haul Explorer trip US$50, full-day kayak cruise US$125. Tandem kayaking is for inexperienced canoeists to experience Grade V rapids, US$140.

Mountain biking

Explorers Mountain Biking, T078-286 2088 (mob), www.raftafrica.com. Leisurely guided trips through the local villages in the Bujagali environs or longer. Bike hire US$25 per day, helmets provided. 2-hr Bujagali tour US$30, 2- to 4-hr tour to Bugembe Viewpoint US$45, including lunch, and 4-hr tour of Mabira Forest US$45, including lunch. More vigorous rides for fitter cyclists can be arranged through **Nile River Explorers**, see page 88.

Quad biking

An exciting venture involving rushing around on quad bikes through the lush countryside around Bujagali village. Tuition is given on mini quads on practice circuits before you graduate to the bigger bikes. Protective clothing, helmets, overalls, boots, gloves and eye protection supplied. A small donation is made to the local councils of the villages visited en route.

All Terrain Adventures, Bujagali opposite NRE campsite, T077-237 7185 (mob), www. atadventures.com. 1-4 hrs plus practice costs US$45-110, full day US$185 including lunch, twilight safari at 1700 including a traditional Ugandan banquet in Kyabirwa village, US$80.

Walking

A good way of learning more about rural life is to join a village walk. Knowledgeable villagers escort you around Bujagali and show agricultural production, building techniques and point out different plants and animals. The lifestyle and traditions of the villagers are all carefully explained. The walk finishes with a traditional meal. **Nile River Explorers** organize the walk. Allow at least 2-3 hrs. US$5pp includes local lunch.

⊖ Transport

Buses and *matatus* will take you to the Shell roundabout, where *boda-bodas* are readily available, US$1.50-2. Special hire taxis are preferable if it is wet and slippery or very dry and dusty and will cost 3-4 times as much as *boda-bodas*. Negotiate your price before departure. Most visitors use the pre-booked shuttle buses provided free of charge by the rafting and other adventure companies from either Kampala or Jinja.

The road to Kenya

From Jinja the road to Kenya continues first northeast and then swings east. A new 72.5-km section of this road from Jinja to Bugiri was opened in 2010, mostly funded by the European Union. About 20 km from Jinja the road goes through the small market town of Magamaga and then, after another 5 km or so, there is a road off to the right. Here is the little village of Buluba, where Bishop Hannington was murdered in 1885 (see box, page 98). After another 15 km, you will pass through the town of Iganga, the district headquarters.

Mount Elgon, an extinct shield volcano, with an enormous intact caldera, bestrides the Kenyan border. Mount Wagagai at 4321 m is the tallest peak, the fourth highest mountain in East Africa. It offers great trekking, cave exploration and varied montane flora. To the north are the magnificent 100-m-high Sipi Falls, an area famous for Bugisu Arabica coffee production. South of Mount Elgon lies the most commonly used road crossing to Kenya at Busia.

Iganga → *Phone code: 0434. Colour map 2, B6.*

This sleepy little town has wide streets bordered by shops and houses with broad verandas. Most people just pass through in transit and there are no tourist facilities at all. South of the town is Nenda Hill, a viewpoint for the surrounding plains. It contains the shrine of the Bazungu (white people) and is a 10- to 15-minute taxi ride from town. There are a few cheap B&Bs with basic facilities and only local street or small café food available.

Tororo → *Phone code: 0454. Colour map 1, C5.*

Situated in the far east of Uganda, Tororo is close to the border with Kenya but few people pass through on the way to and from the border crossing at **Malaba**, as most travellers use the border crossing at Busia. Tororo's major claim to fame is the rock named after it, which can be seen from miles around. Built during the colonial period in the late 1940s, the Tororo Cement Works made an important contribution to the development of Uganda as it took away the necessity of importing cement from Kenya. It functioned well until Amin's time. As everything in Uganda began to fall apart so did the cement works, its roof eventually collapsing under the weight of the cement dust. Now, however, the operation is up and running again. Another claim to fame is Tororo's very high frequency of spectacular thunderstorms.

The road to the border is fair, but has the usual pot-hole problems and you will pass through fairly typical Ugandan scenery: clusters of small huts surrounded by farmland, as well as areas of verdant bush and elephant grass with the occasional anthill. There are stretches of hills separated by marshy swamps. There are also many mango trees in this part of Uganda and during the season their fruit can be bought on the roadside. As you approach the border you can either continue straight on to Tororo for the Malaba crossing or more commonly take a right turning to Busia. From about this point you should be able to see the Tororo Rock sticking up in the distance. The Hindu temple is only open for services at 1800. Only a handful of Hindu families remain in Tororo and temple visitors are discouraged.

Tororo Rock, known locally as Morukatipe, is a forested volcanic plug that rises to about 1800 m above sea level. It is possible to climb and the views from the top are fantastic. There are steps and ladders to help you get to the summit, and the climb takes about an hour. Tours of the rock can be organized from the Rock Classic Hotel (see page 99). Contrary to some reports, Lake Victoria cannot be seen from the top of the rock.

Bishop Hannington

Coming from Kampala, a little beyond Jinja on the right, is Buluba, where Bishop Hannington, consecrated in 1884 as the first Bishop of the Diocese of Eastern Equatorial Africa, met his death. Hannington kept a detailed diary during his journeys and it is through this, and stories from the survivors, that we know what happened.

James Hannington had first visited East Africa in 1882 as the leader of a party of reinforcements for the Victoria Nyanza Mission in Uganda. He had suffered severely from dysentery and had been forced to return to Britain. However, after being made bishop, he planned his return to Africa. At this time the route into Uganda was from Zanzibar, through what is now Tanzania, to the south of Lake Victoria. In 1883 a new route was tried, through Kenya, via Busoga, to the north of the lake. This route through Masai country was more direct and climatic conditions were not as harsh.

Arriving on the East African coast in January 1885, Hannington planned to use the Masai route. On hearing this, the missionaries in Buganda informed him that the current political situation in Buganda was such that entering by the 'back door', through Busoga, was extremely dangerous. However, the warning arrived about two weeks after Hannington had set off.

Hannington's only real mistake was that he did not stick to his plans as set out in a letter to the missionaries in Buganda. He told them that he would go overland as far as Kavirondo on Lake Victoria, where the mission boat would meet him, and that he would enter Buganda by boat. This would mean he would avoid entering Uganda through Busoga, which was so sensitive. Mwanga, the son of King Mutesa I, had been told that those entering Buganda from the east (that is, Busoga) would destroy the Kingdom of Buganda and the missionaries in Buganda had assured Mwanga that the Bishop would not enter via that route. So when he did, it appeared as a calculated deceit.

On 21 October Hannington reached the headquarters of Luba, the chief of the area of Busoga. He was imprisoned and, on the orders of messengers from Buganda, speared to death and his porters massacred.

In March 1890 a boy who had been with Hannington arrived in the camp of Jackson, another missionary who was on his way to Uganda. The boy had with him a skull (its lower jaw bone missing), identified as belonging to Hannington by its gold teeth. He also had the soles of Hannington's boots, a hot water bottle and the lid of an Army and Navy canteen.

The remains eventually found their way to Kampala and on 31 December 1892 they were buried on Namirembe Hill.

Busia

Busia, together with its sister city of the same name in Kenya, is a hot, very dusty non-descript border town, with huge numbers of large trucks and even more motorcycles and bicycles crowding the long road through the town centre. A lively market in no man's land seeks to avoid import/export duties. If you need to stay there are a few basic hotels (F-G) and cheap eating places.

For Sleeping and Eating price codes and other relevant information, see Essentials pages 21-23.

Sleeping

C Rock Classic Hotel, 70 Osukulu Rd, T0454-445069, tororo@rockclassichotel.com. Set in gardens, behind the golf course, outside the centre. All rooms (doubles) are en suite. Prices include breakfast. DSTV and pool. Camping in grounds, secure parking. Good service. Internet service fluctuates. There's a snack bar and a restaurant.

E Crystal, 22 Bazaar St, T077-255 5174 (mob). This is the best central choice, with views of the Tororo Rock. Simple, clean, en suite rooms all have balconies with steel bars to deter intruders. It offers good value, with restaurant and bar facilities.

Eating

There are many cafés offering simple Western or local food.

Transport

Bus and taxi
Tororo is 217 km from Kampala, about 4 hrs by *matatu* that depart frequently. From the taxi park to **Mbale**, 1 hr, US$1.50. To **Busia** (40 mins), US$1.20. To **Jinja**, 2 hrs, US$3. To **Kampala**, 4 hrs, US$5.

Directory

Internet Tororo Computer Instituté, Bazaar St, next to Uganda Revenue office. Email facilities available.

Mbale → *Phone code: 0454. Colour map 1, C5.*

This town is in the foothills of Mount Elgon, giving it a pleasant climate. Mbale shows clearly the Asian influence on towns in Uganda; in particular, many of the buildings have the distinctive veranda that is seen all over East Africa. It is a pleasant, safe, bustling market town where tourists rarely hear taunts of '*muzungu*'.

During the colonial years eucalyptus plantations were planted all around Mbale as an anti-malarial mosquito measure. Over the past 25 years the trees have gradually been cut down and malaria, which was once eradicated from the area, has returned. There is a large Commonwealth War Graves Cemetery. Mbale is also the home of the Islamic University, founded in 1988 and one of only a few such institutions in Africa. It is a good base if planning to climb Mount Elgon.

Ins and outs

Tourist offices **Uganda Wildlife Authority (UWA)** ① *19-21 Masaba Rd, T0454-435035, menp@ugandawildlife.org, Mon-Fri 0800-1300 and 1400-1700, Sat 0900-1300*, is also called the Mount Elgon National Park Tourist Office, close to the **Mount Elgon** hotel, and provides information about climbing Mount Elgon. There are maps as well as up-to-date advice, and anyone planning to climb the mountain is advised to visit the office before travelling to Budadiri. However, information and booking can also be arranged at Budadiri and the Forest Exploration Centre at Kapkwai, both trailheads for climbing the mountain.

Wanale Ridge

Eleven kilometres southeast of Mbale is a large rock named Wanale Ridge or Cliffs, also known locally as Nkokonjeru, which means 'the white rock'. It is a 2320-m spur of Mount Elgon, and several waterfalls course down its rock face. Idi Amin once planned to build a huge international hotel and conference centre here. The building began with the construction of the road – almost a motorway – up to the top of the rock. That was as far as it got and the complex itself was never begun. There are wonderful views and it is sometimes possible to see the peregrine falcons, hawk eagles and rock kestrels that nest on the rock.

Kakora rock paintings

These paintings, about 20 km from Mbale, are to be found in the Pallisa district, behind the local schools. The paintings themselves, in red and white pigments, are not that impressive, and are being worn away by local children and by animals moving to graze. There are two sites with red paintings, including some concentric circles on the south and west sides of a rock pillar at the southern end of the hill. On the underside of a rock ledge there is a third example of rock art in white pigment, but the subject matter is unidentifiable. The paintings are thought to be the work of hunter-gatherers who lived in this region 2000 years ago. There is a spectacular ancient gong near the paintings that is balanced precariously some 10 m in the air, and a rockslide near by. The rock paintings are in an area of scrubland surrounded by plantations of sweet potato and cassava. There is no accommodation but the local people are happy to talk to visitors about the rock paintings.

Further north are the more spectacular **Nyero rock paintings** near the town of Kumi (see page 112). The site can be reached by travelling north from Mbale towards Kumi to the village of Nakaloke, then turning west to the village of Kabwangasi, from which there is a track to the paintings. Take a *matatu* from Mbale to Nakatoke, US$0.50, then a *boda-boda* to Kakoro, US$1.50. Alternatively, it's possible to drive all the way to the site in a 4WD.

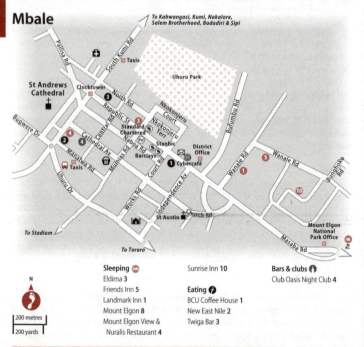

Mbale

To Kabwangasi, Kumi, Nakalore,
Salem Brotherhood, Budadiri & Sipi

Pallisa Rd
South Kumi Rd
Taxis
Uhuru Park
St Andrews Cathedral
Clocktower
North Rd
Republic St
Nkokonjeru Court
Bugwere Dr
Cathedral Av
Central Rd
Standard Chartered
Nkokonjeru Terr
Naboa Rd
Stanbic
District Office
Manafwa Rd
Mumias Rd
Barclays
Court Rd
Cybercafé
Taxis
Uhuru Dr
Independence Av
Works Rd
St Austin
Church Rd
To Stadium
To Tororo
Masaba Rd
Burumbu Rd
Wanale Rd
Wanale Rd
Bungokho Rd
Mount Elgon National Park Office
To 8

N

200 metres
200 yards

Sleeping
Eldima 3
Friends Inn 5
Landmark Inn 1
Mount Elgon 8
Mount Elgon View &
Nuralis Restaurant 4

Sunrise Inn 10

Eating
BCU Coffee House 1
New East Nile 2
Twiga Bar 3

Bars & clubs
Club Oasis Night Club 4

Mbale listings

For Sleeping and Eating price codes and other relevant information, see Essentials pages 21-23.

Sleeping

B Mount Elgon, 30 Masaba Rd, T0454-433612, T077-300 8903 (mob), infor@mountelgonhotel.com. 2 km out of town just past the National Park Offices. Renovated in 2006, this place has a grand colonial façade and commanding views of Wanale Ridge. Large and clean en suite rooms with nets and a/c or fans. Extensive gardens are being developed. Pool, DSTV, laundry service and secure parking. The restaurant has an Italian ambiance and serves good food, with a varied wine list. Excellent coffee in the bar.

C Sunrise Inn, 45 Nakhupa Rd, T077-249 4968, snrsinn@yahoo.com. Opened in 1996, this hotel is sited in a pleasant area in the Senior Quarters about 500 m past **Mount Elgon** hotel on the Masaba Rd, just over 2 km from the town centre, an easy 30-min walk or take a *boda-boda*. Lovely garden and good, clean, attractive accommodation with DSTV. Price includes breakfast. The restaurant (♥♥) serves excellent Western and local dishes, among the best in Mbale, is justly popular and needs to be booked well in advance. Camping available (**F**) in the grounds.

D-E Landmark Inn, Wanale Rd, T0454-433880, T077-728 3352 (mob). Charming Mangalore tiled, colonial house with a pillared terrace overlooking the lush, large mature garden in Mbale's 'Senior Quarters' favoured by Europeans during the colonial period. 3 spacious double en suite rooms, 2 with patio balconies. Booking advisable. Camping available in garden. The restaurant serves excellent Indian food.

E Friends Inn, 49 Wanale Rd, T0454-434434, T077-231 0445 (mob). Family guesthouse with en suite rooms, bar and extensive grounds/gardens. Price includes breakfast. Offers good views of Wanale Ridge.

E Hotel Eldima, 35 Republic St, T071-242 1686. Central location multi-storied hotel over a restaurant with 25 clean en suite rooms. Price includes breakfast. The restaurant serves mostly local food.

E Mount Elgon View Hotel, T077-244 5562. Centrally located above **Nuralis Restaurant**. Basic, clean en suite accommodation, with rooftop dining area and bar serving local, Indian, Chinese and Western food. Has a Forex, hot water, nets, fans and a laundry service. Extra charge for parking.

E Salem Guest House & Conference Centre Mbale, 12 km northwest of town on the road to Kolonyi, T077-250 5595, www.salem-mbale.com. **Salem Foundation** is a Christian NGO providing medical care and community support. It is partly funded by the SB in Germany but also raises funds through income-generating projects such as a conference centre, the guesthouses and sale of handicrafts. All profits made go towards the running of the health centre and children's home. Accommodation for up to 40 people in 1-, 2- or 3-bed rooms, mostly en suite or there are camping facilities. Fresh home-grown food is available. Can arrange hire of drivers and guides to Mt Elgon National Park, Sipi and Sisiyi Falls and Nyero Rock paintings. Highly recommended.

Eating

Food is available at the larger hotels, including the **Sunrise Inn**, see Sleeping above, which serves a good range of food at reasonable prices and has a lovely outdoor eating area.

♥♥ **Landmark Inn**, see Sleeping above. Serves outstanding Indian food in a garden setting.

♥♥ **Sunrise Inn Restaurant**. Good reputation.

♥ **Nuralis Restaurant**, on the ground floor of the same building as the **Elgon View Hotel** (but unrelated). A good place to eat in town, serving tasty local, Indian, Chinese and Western food at reasonable prices.

Bugisu circumcision

The Bugisu have a strong belief in their rites and the ceremony of circumcision is an important part of the life cycle. All men must undergo circumcision, and males who die before this has been done will be circumcised before they are buried, in order to complete their life on earth.

Circumcision takes place every other year and is performed on young men aged between 14 and 25. The circumcision season is said to be marked by the appearance of a strange bird whose singing marks the beginning of the preparations. The elders gather under the clan tree, which is said to be older than the memory of man itself. They then begin training the candidates for the rituals, which last three days.

On the first day the young man is smeared with sorghum paste all over the body. He wears the traditional dress of animal skins and a head dress, puts three heavy bangles on each leg and then visits his relatives, singing and dancing. The songs he sings are mainly praising his forefathers and the gods. Every so often he stops and leaps high in the air.

On the second day his hair is cut and he is allowed to bathe – the last opportunity before the ceremony proper begins. This symbolizes the death of the past and of what he has been, and a new beginning.

The white sorghum paste is again smeared on his body. The singing and dancing continues and this evening is one of great celebration amongst the people of the village.

On the morning of the circumcision the young man wakes at first light and is again smeared with sorghum paste. He then sets off to visit his maternal uncles, who give him gifts of cows or goats, which are part of the bride price paid by his father. Later in the day he is taken down to the river by the men who wash him thoroughly from the waist to the knees. He is then brought at a slow pace to the ground that is traditionally used for these ceremonies. On the ground is a Y-shaped stick, which he picks up and holds behind his head. The circumcision itself is over fairly quickly and a whistle is blown to announce that the candidate has been successful. Occasionally it happens that a man will try to run away, but this is looked upon as the epitome of disgrace and cowardice.

Traditionally, once a man has been circumcised he can sit in on tribal meetings and participate in decision making, and is also allowed to marry. Only once he has been through what is known as the pain of the knife can he be called a man, and it is said that, just like birth and death, it can only be done once in a lifetime.

Entertainment

The town is a bustling, lively place at night. **Club Oasis**, Cathedral Ave. Popular club.

Festivals and events

If you happen to be here during even-numbered years you may see some local festivities of the Imbalu people, as well as the mass circumcision ceremonies of the Bugisu and Sebei people (see box, above). The official 1st day of the circumcision season is on 1 Aug, when there is a celebration at the cultural centre just outside Mbale. There is a signposted turning to the east about 1 km south of Mbale on the Tororo–Mbale road. Everyone is welcome. The festivities reach a climax during Dec and involve singing, dancing, drumming and general merrymaking.

Shopping

There are small supermarkets close to the clocktower, as well as the market, where there is plenty of fresh produce.

Transport

Mbale is 272 km from Kampala, about 4 hrs or less via the tarmac road from Iganga on the Jinja–Tororo road. It is 1½ hrs from Busia on the Kenyan border.

Bus

There is a bus park just behind the taxi park (see map, page 100). To **Kampala**, 3½-4 hrs, US$5. The Post Bus goes to Kampala daily at 0800, 5½-6 hrs, US$5.25. The **Akamba** bus travels daily to **Nairobi**, from Bulambuli House, Mumias Rd, near the junction with Pallisa and Kumi Rd, at 1700, 11 hrs, US$25. Connections can be made in Nairobi for **Moshi**, **Arusha** and **Mombasa**. For **Dar es Salaam**, see under Kampala transport, page 69.

Matatus will drop you near the clocktower in Mbale in the town centre.

Car hire

Elgon Tours, 8 Manafwa Rd, opposite the taxi park, T0454-435018. Very helpful owner.

Taxi

There are 2 taxi parks in Mbale. The Kumi Rd taxis will take you out east to **Kumi** (1 hr, US$1.65), **Soroti** (2½ hrs, US$3), **Kapchorwa** (2 hrs, US$2.25) and **Budadiri** (45 mins, US$1.05). To **Sipi Falls**, 1½ hrs, US$1.80; the *matatu* can take a few hours to fill up so be prepared for a wait, the price varies according to the weather, from US$2 in fine conditions to US$3 when it's raining. Taxis from the Manafwa Rd park will take you to **Kampala** (4 hrs), **Jinja** (2 hrs), **Iganga** (2 hrs), **Tororo** (1 hr) and places south. Fares are around US$0.03 per km.

Directory

Banks Barclays Bank, 56 Kituntu Rd. ATM. Standard Chartered Bank, 37 Republic St. Changes currency (US$, Euro, and £) and TCs; ATM. **Stanbic Bank**, Republic St. Similar service. **Internet** Facilities are improving. Neema Café, 15 Republic St, and the Cybercafé, near the post office, both offer reasonable rates. Also in **Mount Elgon** hotel. **Telephone** International phone calls are quite straightforward.

Budadiri → *Colour map 1, C5.*

Budadiri, a small trading centre about 30 km from Mbale, is the site of the **Mount Elgon National Park Office** ⓘ *Mon-Fri 0800-1300 and 1400-1700, Sat 0900-1300*, where porters and guides can be arranged for climbers and walkers setting out on the main trail to the peak. The village of Budadiri can be reached by taking the road north and then taking the right-hand fork towards Siroka and Moroto after about 5 km, and then a right-turn after another 5 km, passing through the villages of Bulwalasi and Bugusege. There is an alternative route from the Mbale–Moroto road, which is to continue until you reach the right-hand turn just after Siroka. The latter route is a little longer, but the track is better. A *matatu* from the Kumi Road taxi park in Mbale costs US$1.50.

There was a major landslide in Budadiri, with a loss of over 300 lives, in March 2010, which has unsurprisingly had an adverse impact on tourist numbers visiting Mount Elgon.

For Sleeping and Eating price codes and other relevant information, see Essentials pages 21-23.

Sleeping
E Rose's Last Chance, T077-262 3206 (mob), lastchance.hotel@yahoo.com. The

simple but decent place to stay if you are making Budadiri a staging post for the climb up Mt Elgon. 7 rooms or camping. Breakfast included, meals and cold drinks available. Secure parking for a small fee.

Mount Elgon National Park

Located on the border of Uganda and Kenya near Mbale, Mount Elgon is an extinct volcano, believed to have had its last major eruption about 10 million years ago. It has gradual slopes up to the peaks on the crater rim, which means that even non-mountaineers can climb it. At 4321 m, Wagagai is the highest peak, and the fourth highest East African mountain. The foothills around the base of Mount Elgon, known to the locals as 'Masaba', is an excellent hiking area, very beautiful and virtually untouched by tourists. There are caves to visit as well as Sipi Falls.

Endemic flora includes the giant lobelia, giant heather and giant groundsel and wild flowers abound. Mammals include tree hyrax, bushpig and buffalo, blue monkey, baboon and black and white colobus monkeys. There are frequent sightings of casqued hornbill, the crowned eagle, Ross' touraco and the lammergeier. This area is well known for its high-quality Arabica coffee and you are likely to see coffee plantations. They are mostly small-scale farms using family labour.

Ins and outs
Information offices The **Mount Elgon Forest Exploration Centre**, on the lower slopes of Mount Elgon at 2057 m at Kapkwai, marks the boundary of Mount Elgon National Park. To get to the centre, it's a two-hour, 4-km guided walk across the undulating terrain from Sipi village. It's also possible to drive there from the village (approximately 12 km). Guided walk fees are US$10 for up to four hours. Trekking costs US$50 per day which includes fees for the park entry, camping and ranger guide/escort. The main office for bookings is in Mbale, T0454-435035, menp@ugandawildlife.org. The Mount Elgon National Park Office in Budadiri (see page 103) can arrange porters and guides for climbers. The Department of Lands and Surveys in Entebbe, see page 77, sells maps of the national park.

Foothills of Mount Elgon
There are essentially no tourist facilities outside Mbale, Sipi, the Forest Exploration Centre, Kapkwai and Budadiri, yet anyone who is reasonably adventurous can explore the foothills of Mount Elgon with the help of *matatus*. These serve surprisingly wide and apparently remote areas from Mbale, possibly due to the high population density in this region. However, travel in the area is inevitably fairly slow. It is advisable first to buy a map of Mount Elgon National Park from the Department of Lands and Surveys in Entebbe, see page 77. To get to a recommended starting area, travel along the road to the border village of **Suam**. The national park office advises that it takes about 45 minutes from Mbale to Budadiri, 1½ hours from Mbale to Sipi Falls (with another 30 minutes to the Forest Exploration Centre), and some two hours from Mbale to Kapkwata Visitor Centre, close to the border with Kenya.

It is also worthwhile exploring the area southeast of Mbale, leaving the tourist trail and heading towards places like **Busano**, a village in the shadow of Nkokonjeru, also called Wanale Ridge or Cliffs; **Bududa**, with good views of Mount Elgon from this area nestled amidst small hills; and **Bupoto/Buwabwala**, an attractive and remote area adjacent to a peak called Namisindwa, which, although it doesn't look it, is not much lower than Nkokonjeru. All these places are the final destinations of *matatus* from Mbale, which run several times daily, especially to Bududa. You'll have a memorable journey, not least because you are likely to find yourself cramped by another 20 or so people, plus a goat and chickens in a minibus built for 14.

There are no hotels in these areas but the people are very helpful and friendly – ask for permission to pitch a tent. If you get stuck they may put you up for the night if you ask. The major problem you are likely to encounter is the poor standard of English; try and find a school and talk to one of the teachers. You shouldn't go hungry though, as small local eating places are everywhere, usually serving tea, chapatti, *mandazi*, *posho* and beans. There are also tiny shops selling an amazing array of goods.

Climbing Mount Elgon

Encompassing the largest surface area of any extinct volcano in the world, Mount Elgon rises through a series of gradual slopes punctuated by steep cliffs to a height of 4321 m above sea level. Volcanic foothills, cliffs, caves, gorges and waterfalls combine with panoramic views across wide plains to create some of the most spectacular scenery in Uganda. Elgon's upper slopes are cloaked in tropical montane forest while above this lies a vast tract of Afro-Alpine moorland. This unique vegetation extends over the caldera, a collapsed crater covering over 40 sq km at the top of the mountain.

Facilities are better on the Ugandan side than the Kenyan, making this a viable alternative to tackling the mountain from the neighbouring country. The period to avoid is during the long rains, which are in April and May. The Mount Elgon National Park office in the village of Budadiri (see page 103) can arrange guides, porters, food, etc, for the climb and the village is the starting point of the Sasa Trail, the most popular of the three trails mentioned below.

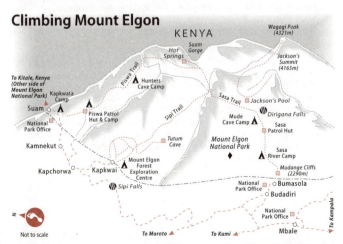

Climbing Mount Elgon

The **Sasa Trail** (four days), accessed from Budadiri, is quite steep in places with a climb of 1600 m on the first day. The **Sipi Trail** (seven days) starts at the Forest Exploration Centre, Kapkwai, 12 km by road or 4-km hike from Sipi. This route includes a visit to Tatum cave. The **Piswa Trail** (seven days) starts from Kapkwata, 30 km beyond Kapchorwa near Suam, and is longer but gentler. The Sasa-Piswa trails or Sasa-Sipi trails can be combined. However, if you are less ambitious there are many alternative walks, ranging from easy hikes to harder climbs.

Numagabwe Cave is within walking distance of Budadiri (see below). The Mount Elgon National Park Office in Budadiri (see page 103) or Mbale (see page 99) can give you maps and make suggestions to suit your requirements. The climb itself is straightforward and can be accomplished easily by non-mountaineers. The trail is steep in places but it is possible to reach the caldera and return to the roadhead within three days of setting off walking at a comfortable pace. With an extra two days you could also reach **Jackson's Summit** on the highest point, **Wagagai**, or visit the hot springs at the head of the **Suam Gorge**.

There are also circular day walks from the Mount Elgon Forest Exploration Centre, ranging from 3 km to 11 km. The first is a circular walk via some of the falls, a cave and viewpoint, which takes about three hours. Two shorter walks of about 30 minutes are also available. A fourth trail leads to the enormous Tutum Cave, 14 km away (see below).

Caves

There are numerous caves on Elgon and one of the most interesting and readily accessible is situated within the spur on which Bulago Camp stands. Its impressive entrance is some 9 m wide and 3 m tall, and in wet weather it is partially hidden in spray from a small waterfall, which drops down banks of ferns that almost block the mouth. Just inside the main chamber are flat ledges cut into the rock, that are believed to have been used as sleeping berths by Bugisu people hiding from their enemies. The size of the main chamber is approximately 18 m by 45 m in depth, with a height of over 4.5 m.

According to native legend, the tunnel at the far end of the cave to the left leads to another much larger cavern. This is supposed to be full of deep water. Whether this is true or not is unknown, but water can certainly be seen trickling from the tunnel.

The main cavern has no stalactites or stalagmites, nor any rock paintings. There are instead a number of garnet-like stones, embedded in a nest of a fine scintillating material resembling spiders' webs. The floor of the cave is flat and soft and littered with bat droppings. Looking out towards the entrance of the cave, especially when the sun is shining through the waterfall, giving off rainbows, is a lovely sight.

Numagabwe Cave, about 8 km from Budadiri, is a shrine where local people perform rituals during the year of circumcision (see box, page 102). The entrance to the cave is very narrow and leads into a large chamber inhabited by bats and small birds. Guided walks can be arranged at **Rose's Last Chance** in Budadiri (see page 104). **Tutum Cave** can be reached on a 14-km hike with guides from the Mount Elgon Forest Exploration Centre at Kapkwai.

There is a well-known cave opposite **Sipi Camp**, but it is not comparable either in size or interest with the one described above.

Mount Elgon listings

For Sleeping and Eating price codes and other relevant information, see Essentials pages 21-23.

Sleeping

B-E There is a small, under-used campsite with 4 *bandas*. Camping US$8pp. Simple basic food is available at **Bamboo Grove Canteen**. Guests can use the cooking facilities. There are long-drop toilets and bucket showers.

Activities and tours

Rock climbing with 7 bolted routes is available at Nagudi Rock, located roughly halfway between Mbale and Budadiri, and costs US$2. Climbers must bring their own equipment. Directions are available from the Mt Elgon National Park Office in Mbale (see page 99) or Budadiri (see page 103).

Sipi Falls → *Altitude: 1750 m. Colour map 1, C5.*

Ins and outs

Getting there From Mbale follow the Kumi road for 6 km, then turn right on to the road to Moroto. Turn right at the fork in the road towards Kapchorwa (after 25 km). This is all clearly signposted.

On the lower slopes of Mount Elgon close to the village of Sipi, the Sipi Falls are 60 km and 1½ to two hours' drive from Mbale on the Kapchorwa–Suam recently resurfaced road. From the falls are stunning views of the Mount Elgon and the plains of eastern and northern Uganda. The falls themselves are described as perhaps the most romantic in Africa. There are a large number of falls, not just the one featured in most of the promotional pictures. These are accessible via a network of well-maintained local trails, but the walking is not easy and a reasonable level of fitness is required. The waterfall and the surrounding area are very pretty and it is a pleasant place to spend a few days unwinding.

Sipi Falls listings

For Sleeping and Eating price codes and other relevant information, see Essentials pages 21-23.

Sleeping

L-AL Sipi River Lodge Kapchorwa, 2 km past Sipi village beside the middle waterfall, T075-179 6109, info@sipiriverlodge.com. Chepkui Cottage accommodates 5. There are also 2 double *bandas* and a dormitory for up to 5. Price includes full board. The main house has comfy sofas, a dining room with an open fire in the evenings and a good library. The Sipi river passes through the well-tended lightly wooded grounds. Internet access for laptop owners. Activities include walks, fly-fishing, half-day coffee tours (harvest Sep) for US$15 plus US$10 for non-residents. No credit cards, only cash US$, £, euros and USh.

AL-A Lacam Lodge, 50 m past the police post, 150 m from the road beside the main Sipi Falls, T075-229 2554, www.lacamlodge. co.uk. Comfortable log cabins with 2 double beds, en suite bathrooms, thatched roofs and verandas or camping US$18 (own tent needed). Seasonal rates vary. Price includes full board, with excellent food.

A Sipi Falls Resort, T075-252 9040, sipiresort@yahoo.com. Previously run by **Volcanoes Tours** in a prime position overlooking the main falls and the plains. Originally a 2-room holiday home for the governor and officials during the colonial period. Now expanded with 5 en suite *bandas*.

D-F The Crow's Nest, T077-268 7924 (mob), thecrowsnets@yahoo.com (messages checked once a week only; 'nets' is the correct spelling). Built in 1990s by Peace Corps volunteers, this popular budget choice has spectacular views across to the main falls, as well as views of 2 smaller falls, and a laid-back, quiet atmosphere. Simple log cabins, 4-bed dorm US$12pp and camping US$3pp. Reasonable and very cheap food. **The Crow's Nest** is signposted with left just before Sipi Trading Centre; the gate is about 200 m from the main road.

Eating

There are few eating houses in Sipi village.

Transport

Getting back to **Mbale** can be something of a challenge as *matatus* are infrequent. Generally people hitch on the back of a truck down to the main road near Kamu market for US$0.50, and then catch a *matatu* from there, US$2. This is a well-established practice and no hassle at all.

Contents

Kidepo, Murchison & the north

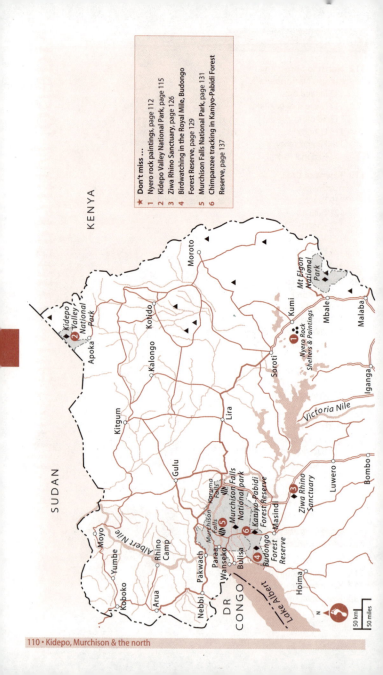

KENYA

SUDAN

DR CONGO

Moroto

Kotido

Apoka

Kidepo Valley National Park

Kalongo

Kitgum

Gulu

Lira

Kumi

Soroti

Nyero Rock Shelters & Paintings

Mbale

Mt Elgon National Park

Malaba

Iganga

Victoria Nile

Luwero

Bombo

Hoima

Masindi

Ziwa Rhino Sanctuary

Kaniyo-Pabidi Forest Reserve

Budongo Forest Reserve

Murchison Falls National Park

Karuma Falls

Murchison Falls

Paraa

Wanseko

Bulisa

Pakwach

Rhino Camp

Moyo

Yumbe

Koboko

Arua

Nebbi

Albert Nile

Lake Albert

50 km
50 miles

N

Northern Uganda contains two of Uganda's jewels: Kidepo Valley National Park in the northeast and Murchison Falls National Park in the northwest. These areas have suffered from civil unrest from the Lords Resistance Army in the north and from the Karamajong's internecine warfare in the northeast along the Kenyan border, with cattle-rustling raids, both inter-clan and with their Kenyan neighbours, the Turkana.

The main towns in the northeast are Moroto, Kotido and Kaabong, and in the far northeast abutting the border with Sudan is Kidepo Valley National Park, an area of outstanding arid wilderness beauty, nestling between two mountain ranges. The scenery ranges from mountains to vast arid savannah plains, in marked contrast to the south of the country. It has one of the greatest diversities of wildlife in Uganda, with 82 species of mammals recorded, but receives the fewest visitors as a result of its remoteness and the previous unrest. Most visitors fly to it. The area is sparsely populated, inhabited by the tough, proud and warlike hunter/pastoralist Karamajong cluster of tribes: Dadinga, Dodoth, Jie, Karamajong, Suk and Sepei. This region was formerly known as Karamoja. Although the name has officially been replaced by the administrative districts of Moroto and Kotido since 1976, the use of the name Karamoja persists, causing confusion as it is no longer recorded on Ugandan maps.

The north includes Soroti, Lira, Gulu and Kitgum. Many of these towns are home to aid workers from various NGOs dealing with the post-conflict problems. The northwest covers what is known as West Nile; anything beyond Murchison Falls and Lake Albert including Pakwach, Nebbi, Arua and Moyo.

The vast Murchison Falls National Park is the main attraction for most travellers. The game viewing is pretty good although it is mainly restricted to north of the river around Paraa. Many consider the boat trip up to the falls almost as good as a game drive because many animals including elephants come down to the river. The Nile crocodiles and pods of hippos are also very impressive.

North to Soroti and Kidepo National Park

A main feature of travel into the north is not so much the beauty of its scenery, which is breathtaking at times, but more that it gives you a glimpse of Uganda's history, from the Arab slave traders of centuries ago, through the colonial era, and the last two decades of civil unrest.

Ins and outs

Safety

Between 1986 and 2006 Kitgum District was terrorized by rebels from the Lords Resistance Army and most of the population were forced to move into internally displaced people's camps for security. In 2006 the rebels were driven out of the country and over the last four years much reconstruction progress has been made.

The Ugandan authorities started a programme to disarm the Karamajong in December 2001 to improve security, and a welcome spin-off has been an increase in wildlife numbers, estimated to be just 5% of what they were in the 1960s.

Nyero rock paintings → *Colour map 1, C5.*

ⓘ *US$4.50. If you don't have your own transport, rent a motorbike taxi from Kumi. It's possible to walk here although the intense heat discourages it.*

Located in dry, rocky attractive scenery in the Kumi district on the Kumi–Ngora road in Nyero village, these rock paintings are regarded as being amongst the best in Eastern Africa. The Nyero rock paintings consist of three painted shelters close to each other. Believed to be between 300 and 1000 years old, the paintings are in red and white pigment and are mainly of geometric shapes.

Nyero site No 1 is a small shelter formed by an overhanging rock. The white-pigmented drawings are of concentric circles, plus some elongated shapes, sometimes described as acacia pods. The main site, Nyero 2, has a vertical rock face with an overhang that has helped to preserve the paintings from the elements and the concentric circles dominate in varying shades of red pigment. Linear motifs, again thought to resemble acacia pods or possibly a boat containing a couple of people, can also be identified. At the top of the rock face are some very weathered marks, said to resemble zebras. Nyero 3 is a short distance away behind the other sites. It contains the painting that has been described as looking like an enormous star or a sunburst, best viewed by lying down underneath it. This white-pigmented painting is a series of concentric circles with lines drawn at right angles to the external circle. This pattern is repeated nearby with red pigment but it is much fainter.

The surrounding area is covered with smooth boulders, many adorned by sunbathing monkeys. Occasionally, reptiles can also be seen basking on the rocks, mostly during the afternoon. Paving stones form a path between the sites, but become very slippery in wet weather. It is possible to climb some of the surrounding rocks for lovely views of low-lying hills to the west past Ngora. The cool breeze is pleasant and tall trees offer welcome shade. The local people water their animals nearby and also fetch water from the rock pools.

Tank Rock

Nine kilometres west of the Nyero rock paintings, near the town of Ngora, is another rock painting known as Tank Rock. A few groups of concentric circles in red pigment can be seen. However, this site was vandalized in the 1960s with red paint. Other attractions in the area include the possibility of viewing and climbing Moru Apeso Rock, and seeing the river Awoja, where there is a campsite.

Nyero rock paintings listings

For Sleeping and Eating price codes and other relevant information, see Essentials pages 21-23.

The small town of Kumi, 8 km from Nyero on the Mbale–Soroti road, offers the closest accommodation to the rock paintings.

Sleeping

C Kumi Hotel, T077-243 4380, T077-249 0659 (mob). It's more expensive than its rival, the Green Top hotel. There is a small restaurant.
E Green Top, Soroti Rd, T077-240 8304 (mob). This roadside inn has 20 rooms, including singles and en suite doubles, with fans, nets, a laundry service and a fairly reliable lighting system. It's less noisy than other nearby hotels. Rooms on the north side have hot water showers.

Soroti → *Phone code: 0454. Colour map 1, C4.*

Although not that far north (293 km or five hours' drive from Kampala), there is something about Soroti that gives it a northerly feeling. It is a hot, airless town with a frontier atmosphere, the site of the Soroti Flying School, set up to train pilots for the whole East African region. The town is situated north of Lake Kyoga on virtually flat plains, with a few rocky outcrops visible. The most spectacular of these is Soroti Rock, a volcanic plug resembling the one at Tororo (see page 97).

The town's architecture reflects its multicultural history. The Asian influence is most apparent along the main streets, the mosques decorated with crenellated projections and delicate minarets. There are also some rather run-down English-style houses, which were built during the colonial period. Central Soroti has a Market Place, where the ingenuity of the local people at refashioning scrap metal to make cooking pots and other household items from the remains of cars and metal drums is to be much admired.

⦿ Soroti listings

For Sleeping and Eating price codes and other relevant information, see Essentials pages 21-23.

Sleeping

C Soroti Hotel, Serere Rd, T0454-561269. Recently renovated, offers clean, good value accommodation. Quiet location 1 km from the town centre and 3 km from the airport.
D Golden Ark Hotel, Mbale–Soroti Rd, T0454-561341, T077-223 5038 (mob). Built in 2006, 20 rooms, restaurant and bar. DSTV and internet.

Bars and clubs

Jose Martin's sports bar. Offers solace to football-deprived travellers.
Trends, 1 km from Soroti along the Moroto–Soroti Rd. Wed-Sat night, US$1.35.

Transport

It is 128 km from Lira, 113 km from Mbale and 177 km from Moroto. The murram road to Moroto becomes very muddy during the rainy season, so getting stuck is commonplace.

Bus

The Post Bus has a daily service to **Kampala**, US$5.25; with **Gateway** and Trust Coaches several times daily, US$6.50.

Directory

Banks Stanbic, Post Bank and Centenary Rural Development Bank have branches here. **Internet** This is available in several small hotels like Garden G/H, Golden Ark and Jose Martin's Inn. Price doubles when the mains electricity is off.

Soroti to Moroto

The drive from Soroti to Moroto is mainly through acacia thorn bush. Every so often you will see a herd of scrawny goats being looked after by a couple of young boys, or perhaps some cattle with some Karamajong guarding them. Most of the time it is very hot and dusty but at certain times of the year there are the most fantastic thunderstorms. On this road, as you pass Soroti District, previously known as Teso, into Karamoja, you go between two hills called Akisim and Napak, 2537 m high in the Kamalinga Hills. They are quite impressive and can be seen for some miles around standing up above the plains. They mark the boundary of the administrative districts of Moroto and Kotido, which combined were known as Karamoja prior to 1976. The use of 'Karamoja' to describe this region persists but confusingly it is no longer referred to on maps.

Moroto → Colour map 1, B6.

In the northeast of the country lie vast open spaces of arid savannah and acacia country, with stands of borassus palms marking the route of Arab traders. Here, rocky mountains interrupt the plains, making it a land of great scenic beauty. Mount Moroto, which reaches a height of 3400 m above sea level, offers challenging climbing. It is the traditional area of the pastoralist Karamajong people (see box, opposite).

Kampala to Moroto is 480 km, a journey that can be done in a day, but not for the faint hearted. There are two routes, either via a good road to Soroti, then across the Bokora Game Reserve. The alternative eastern route is Mbale to Moroto via Chepsikunya that requires a 4WD. The bus from Moroto to Mbale/Kampala or Tororo leaves at about 0900 daily. If you want to stay in Moroto, there is Mount Moroto (**B**), on the edge of town, offering clean, basic accommodation. There are frequent water shortages.

Many beautifully fashioned quartz tools bearing a resemblance to tools of the Stillbay Stone Age Culture of Somaliland have been found close to Moroto. Named after a local waterhole, the small stone age tools are thought to date from between 7000-5000 years ago.

Labwor and Nangeya hills to the northwest of Moroto are noted for their giant inselbergs, volcanic plugs that have remained after the erosion of the cones. Matheniko, Pian Upe and Bokora are all designated game reserves in the area around Moroto, stretching from north of Mount Elgon up to Kotido. However, the description 'game reserve' is inappropriate, as little game remains. This is the result of widespread local firearm availability after Amin's retreating army left the Moroto Armoury open in 1979 as they fled from the Tanzanian troops. Birds survived the carnage better, with over 225 species identified in the area.

The Karamajong

The Karamajong (also spelt Karamojong and Karimojong) are one of the tribes inhabiting the more southerly part of the old district of Karamoja in northeast Uganda.

The marriage system is polygamous, the number of wives being limited solely by financial circumstances. No boy is allowed to marry until he has been admitted by the elders to the status of manhood. Up to this time a boy must pluck out all his pubic hair. When the time comes (usually as one of a group) his father gives him a bull, which the boy kills sharing it with his male relatives. Smearing himself with the dung from the entrails, he gives his mother the head, neck, hump, stomach and ribs. His hair is cut by an adult male friend, leaving a tuft at the back to which a short string is attached. Traditionally when the hair grows back he moulds it into two buns, one on top of the head and one at the back, with coloured clay.

On attaining manhood, he may seek a wife. It is usual that he will already have at least one lover and, if his father approves, his lover may be taken as his wife.

When someone dies the body is wrapped up in a hide and buried in a goat enclosure. If the person is a pauper without friends the body is simply thrown outside the kraal and left to the wild animals. When a husband dies the widow passes into the possession of his principal brother. He will bring a sheep to her door, which he will then kill, and they will smear themselves with dung from its entrails. From this time onwards she belongs to him. If there is no brother then she will pass to the son of a co-wife.

The Karamajong language, Nga Karamojong, is one of the Nilotic languages and is complicated and subtle. You might find these phrases useful:

Formal greeting	*Imaata*!
General greeting	*Ejoka*
Response	*Ejok* or *Ejok Noo*
Did you sleep well?	*Iperi ejok a*?
Yes	*Aye*
	(pronounced Eeh)
No	*Mam*
Please and thank you	*Alakara*
Where is the office?	*Aye ayai apis*

Kidepo Valley National Park

Ins and outs

Getting there Driving here is anything from 571 km to 792 km from Kampala depending on the route chosen. Since the disarmament of the Karamojong, the route up the eastern border, through Mbale and Soroti is considerably less dangerous than before. However, it is still inadvisable, especially during Ugandan school holidays, when cattle rustling and car jacking are at their peak. The Gulu route is a much safer option and the drive to Kidepo from Kampala will take around 10 hours: Kampala–Gulu five hours (sealed road), Gulu–Kitgum two hours (reasonable murram road) and Kitgum–Kidepo three hours (poor murram road). The route to Kidepo from Soroti is along a rough murram road, particularly hair-raising during the rainy season. Before embarking on the trip get up-to-date information from **UWA** ⓘ *T041-435 5000, T031-2355 5000, info@ugandawildlife.org*, or the **Apoka Safari Lodge** (see page 118). ▸▸ *See also Transport, page 118.*

Entry fees US$30 per person for 24 hours.

The park

Kidepo is one of the most spectacular national parks in Uganda but, being the most isolated, it is also one of the hardest to visit. It's located in the far northeast of Uganda on the Sudanese border and close to the Kenyan border (see map, page 25).

Offering the best range of large mammals in any of Uganda's national parks, it is also one of the few remaining places in the world where you get a real feeling of wilderness. Kidepo is also an ornithologist's delight, with over 460 bird species, including the ostrich and kori bustard. It covers an area of about 1334 sq km. The area adjacent to the national park is inhabited by the Ik people, hunters and farmers, who are described unflatteringly in Colin Turnbull's 1972 book *The Mountain People*.

Its altitude ranges from 1350 m to 2750 m. The Napore Nangeya mountain range is located to the west of the camp and the Natera hills to the east. In the distance to the north you will be able to see the peak of Mount Lotukei (2797 m) in the Sudan. The vegetation is typical savannah with some acacia woodland, home to many tsetse flies, with occasional stands of borassus palms. Sand rivers necessitate the use of 4WDs especially in the east of the national park.

Game viewing

One problem that Kidepo Valley National Park suffers from more than the other national parks in Uganda is that of water shortages although the plants and animals of the area have adapted. Low rainfall and a long and severe dry season of almost six months are characteristic of this region as a whole. The effects of this are best appreciated between October and March when the national park is progressively baked, bleached and burnt

Kidepo Valley National Park

Sleeping
Apoka Hostel 1
Apoka Lodge 2
Nga'Moru Wilderness Camp 3

Karamajong cattle

In Karamoja it is considered desirable to mutilate the horns of favoured cows so that they are twisted downwards. At first it may seem to be a natural malformation, but in fact it is deliberately brought about. Exactly how it is achieved and whether it hurts the animal in any way is unclear. The particular attributes of these short-horned, small to medium-size cattle, with cervico-thoracic humps, are believed to result from the interbreeding of zebu and Hamitic long-horn and/or short-horn strains. Over the years zebu cattle have developed some resistance to rinderpest and have survived outbreaks of the disease.

The Karamajong people are known for cattle rustling, frequently carried out to pay a bride price or to replace cattle dying of sickness or lost in other ways. These raids are now less common since the disarmament of the Karamajong.

by sun and often by fire. Every scrap of moisture, except that which manages to survive in a few waterholes and dams, turns to dust under the scorching breath of the tireless northeast wind. Unattractive as this sounds, it is in fact the best time to visit as it creates conditions that are good for game viewing. Animals are more tied to the available water sources, and there tends to be a concentration of animals around Apoka, the site of both high-end Apoka Safari Lodge and the UWA campsite, at the height of the dry season. The animals leave Kidepo Valley, which dries out very rapidly once the rains have ceased, and head for the comparatively lush savannahs and woodlands of Narus valley where there is enough water to see them through until the rain falls again in March or April. Once the rains begin the animals drift back to the Kidepo Valley, and from April to October, when the grass is shorter, this is probably the best viewing area.

Game in Kidepo suffered badly during the period of turmoil and lawlessness, but recovery is well underway. The animals include lion, buffalo, ostrich, elephant, zebra, cheetah, leopard, giraffe, bushbaby and a wide range of antelope including kudu and dik-dik. The programme to disarm the Karamajong people has seen an increase of elephant numbers from an estimated 150-200 in 1994 to over 500 recently.

Other sights

The **Kanangarok Hot Springs** that cross the Kidepo River are worth a visit. The Kidepo River is a sand river, which only flows visibly for a few days of the year. However, below the sand, at depths that vary from a few centimetres to a few metres, there is water; the depth depends on how far into the dry season it is. The animals of the park dig holes to reach the water. This also explains why on the banks of an apparently dry river the vegetation is often more green and lush than elsewhere in the park.

The national park has a small **museum**. There are some pieces of skeletons as well as some insect specimens. There are also photographs of some rangers involved in earlier efforts at conservation.

Idi Amin had a lodge, the now-derelict **Grand Katurum Lodge**, built on the edge of a precipitous cliff in Kidepo Valley. Abandoned 30 years ago these ruins with magnificent views south into the valleys of Acholi have been designated by UWA as a potential site for redevelopment.

Kidepo Valley National Park listings

For Sleeping and Eating price codes and other relevant information, see Essentials pages 21-23.

Sleeping *map p116*

LL Apoka Safari Lodge, T0414-251182, T077-527 7587 (mob), www.wildplacesafrica.com. Overlooking the Narus river valley this luxurious lodge has 10 large en suite rooms built of wood, canvas and thatch, solar-heated power showers, verandas and an external bath accommodating 3 people carved into the rockface. The thatched main lodge houses the restaurant and bar. A pool is set in a rocky outcrop. Apart from the manager and partner and the chef, all the staff are local Karimajong. The price is all inclusive.
LL Nga'Moru Wilderness Camp, T075-450 0555 (mob), afrimax.holdings@gmail.com. Run by Lyn Jordaan and Patrick Devy who also manage **Fugly's Hotel** in Kitgum. New camp just outside the park boundary. 5 safari thatched tents with en suite bathroom and toilet and 2 en suite cabanas. Currently only has cold water but rustic 'Hot Bush' showers are available. Price is for full board but excludes park entry fees. The camp is self drive (4WD needed) as they are awaiting game viewing vehicles. However, there is a game viewing truck rented out at US$135 per day for 15-20 people.
B-D Apoka Hostel, near Apoka Safari Lodge, T077-271 0488 (mob), kvnp@ugandawildlife.org. This modest UWA campsite, previously called **Apoka Rest Camp**, has double *bandas*, en suite or with shared bathrooms. Camping also available. Self-catering or pre-arranged meals can be ordered at reasonable prices. Meals are taken on the veranda with beautiful views of park. Aside from the friendly, though elusive staff, you'll probably meet another camp resident: Bulbul, a large male elephant, who has become very fond of the grounds, often cruising in and out of *bandas* checking out the new intake. When Bulbul is otherwise engaged during your stay, there are plenty of cheeky primates, including the red colobus monkeys sneaking around the camp looking for scraps. Drinks can be bought onsite.

Camping

Other than the UWA camp grounds at **Apoka Hostel** (see above), there is another campsite in the park. It's extremely remote with few facilities and is not for the faint hearted! Book at Apoka Hostel.

Transport
Road

Although there are regular buses and *matatus* that can take passengers from Gulu to Kitgum, there are no public transport links from Kitgum to the park. If you want to rent a 4WD in Kitgum, contact the UWA office (see page 115) to point you in right direction (approx US$110 per day including driver and petrol). Alternatively, you could try your luck hitching a ride with one of the UWA vehicles, which usually leave from Kitgum every couple of days delivering supplies to the park.

Towns of the northwest

Based in many towns in the northwest like Gulu and Kitgum are NGO aid workers, deployed for post-conflict projects. The towns are popular with visitors to the Murchison Falls and Kidepo national parks.

The areas surrounding Gulu and Kitgum have had an outbreak of yellow fever in 2010 with 174 confirmed cases and 45 deaths. See also page 36.

Lira → *Phone code: 4734. Colour map 1, B4.*

Situated in the north, 368 km from Kampala, the town of Lira has a park with fine trees and a bandstand. Lira Spinning Mill, once the main source of income in the town, has fallen into disrepair, and was used as a food warehouse during the civil unrest period. The town is safe, even at night and it is hard to tell that it was in conflict only a few years ago. The road into Lira has just been resurfaced and is almost finished now – just in time for the election!

Lira listings

For Sleeping and Eating price codes and other relevant information, see Essentials pages 21-23.

Sleeping

B Lillian Towers Hotel, 14-18 Inomo Rd, T04734-20954, T077-419 2310, lilliantowers@lilliantowers.co.ug. 18 rooms, mosquito nets, 5 rooms have a/c. 2 computers in the lobby with good internet connection; mobile Orange internet is used so you can borrow this and use in your laptop. Clean hotel, good service, small 10 m pool. Noisy at night as it's near the nightclub 24/7. Offers a shuttle service to Kampala. Very good restaurant (†), with pleasant outside dining area, serving local dishes, steak, pastas and pizzas. Good breakfast.

C-D Gracious Palace Hotel, 5A Akalo Rd, T0392-941392, T077-532 9338 (mob), www.graciouspalacehotel.com. Clean hotel with good service and pleasant garden area. Some rooms have a balcony. Mosquito nets and windows with mesh. DSTV. Free Wi-Fi. Restaurant (†) serves generous portions.

C-D Lira Hotel, 8-10 Erute Rd, T04734-20024, T077-259 4184 (mob), www.st-lirahotel.com. 42 rooms. Recently upgraded with more works planned to build a health club, sauna and gym by 2013,

renovated rooms advised. Rather noisy and draughty due to air vents between rooms. Museveni stays here when he's in town. No a/c, but fans available. DSTV. Guests can rent the mobile internet for US$0.50 for 20 mins or US$7.75 per day. The restaurant is overpriced. The hotel is located opposite a poorly maintained golf course; if you ring the administrator they can arrange for the grass to be cut if you want to play a round.

D 291 Suites, Kampala Rd, Odokomit, T078-701 1362 (mob). About 3 km east of Lira so very quiet. Newly built hotel so currently in good condition. All rooms have a/c and DSTV. No internet access.

D Pan Afric Hotel, 25 Kyoga Rd, Ireda area, 1.5 km from town, T078-236 9140 (mob), ogemaj@gmail.com. 8 en suite rooms with DSTV offering more than football! No a/c. Shuttle service to town and a coach service from Kampala. Good restaurant (†) and pleasant place to sit out in the grounds.

Eating

† The Modern Car Wash Restaurant, 8 Kwania Rd, T04736-60377. Open 0800-2200. Serves a good variety of reasonably priced Indian dishes, local food, pork and chips and alcohol.

Sankofas, opposite mayor's garden on top floor of a tall yellow building, T077-271 2198, sankofacafé@gmail.com. Open 0900 until 2300. Restaurant and internet café serving burgers, pizza, local foods, cakes and biscuits for special occasions plus beers. Great relaxed environment with comfy chairs, good views from the balcony and a lovely breeze as it's on the top floor. DSTV and Wi-Fi.

Whiskers Park, 431 Independent Rd, T077-241 8588 (mob). Open 0800 to midnight. Upcoming place with outside and indoor eating areas, good for evening drinks or afternoon or evening meals. Serves excellent pork and cassava chips, tasty grilled fish, whole roast chicken and a variety of Indian dishes.

Bars and clubs

24/7 Nightclub, Kitgum Rd. Entry price US$0.90; dance floor tariff US$1.10 extra. Theme nights like Club Suiz. Normally very busy on a Fri and Sat night. Beers are reasonably priced at US$1.10.

Club Suiz, Juba Rd near Santa Solo guesthouse. Variety of evening entertainment: Wed ladies' night, Thu 'oldies night', Fri-Sun karaoke.

Shopping
Books

There is a very limited range of bookshops in Lira. Most just sell stationery and school textbooks but no maps or travel guides. **Star Book Shop**, Obote Ave, T077-283 1047 (mob), and **Caravan Bookshop**, Maruzi Rd, T077-416 4822, both open 0730-1800 and sell a limited range of novels.

Crafts

Otino Waa Tower, 18 km before Lira on road from Kampala. Open 0800-1800. Craft shop with a variety of locally made gifts and honey. Training is funded from the proceeds of a café that serves pizzas, hamburgers and range of snacks and ice cream. Transport costs US$1.50-1.75 from town on bicycle *boda-boda*. Contact Bob T077-243 4022 (mob) or Carole T077-286 8920 (mob).

Supermarkets

Pari, Main St opposite market, and **Go Global**, top of town in former Centenary Bank building, 21/23 Kwania Rd; both well stocked and under the same ownership.

Transport
Bus and taxi

Almost all the road to Gulu and Soroti is sealed, in good condition, and bus journeys take about 2 hrs. To **Gulu**, with **Gateway** (1200) or **Kakise** (1500), US$3.50. Shared taxis leave when full, US$4.50pp. Bus to **Soroti**, US$3.50, 0530 (**Gateway** or **Kakise**), 0600 (**Hero**), 0930 (**Gateway**), 1000 (**Kakise**). Shared taxis leave when full, US$4.50pp. To **Kampala**, US$8.75pp, at 0530 (**Otada**), 0700 (**Felister**) and 0830 (**Acanadiro**). Night buses are operated by **White coach**, **Mwenzi** or **Otada**. Mwenzi has the best safety record. There is no Post Bus from Lira.

Directory

Bank Stanbic, Barclays, Obote Ave; Crane Bank and Post Bank have branches in Lira, with foreign currency exchange. Mon-Fri 0800-1700, Sat 0900-1300. Several banks have ATMs but none exchange TCs. **Internet** Smile Internet Café, Too Pe Yero House, Baala Rd, T070-033 3555 (mob). Open 0800-2000. Provident Internet Café, Main St/Obote Ave, T077-652 9881 (mob). Open 0700-2200. US$0.70 per hr.

Gulu → *Phone code: 4714. Colour map 1, B3.*

Gulu, the largest town in northern Uganda, is located to the northeast of Murchison Falls National Park. Between 1986 and 2006 Gulu District was terrorized by rebels from the Lords Resistance Army and almost the entire population outside Gulu town was forced to move into internally displaced people's camps for security. In 2006 the rebels were driven out of the country and talks have brought peace. Over the last four years the population have moved back to their villages and much progress has been made in reconstructing schools, health centres, roads, water and sanitation facilities. The area is thriving and people feel secure once more. Many businesses are moving into Gulu and new hotels, supermarkets, etc are proliferating. The handicrafts made in the area around Gulu range from baskets to earthenware, as well as ironwork.

Ins and outs
Getting there   Gulu is 328 km from Kampala and is accessible via Lira from the east and Masindi from the west. The road from Kampala via Karuma is sealed and in good condition and the journey can be done in four hours. ▶▶ *See Transport, page 122.*

Security   There have been no rebel incursions in recent years and security is good. Visitors are advised not to walk in the town after dark to avoid opportunistic theft. The lack of streetlights or lights on bicycles also make walking at night hazardous.

Sights
Bakers Fort is located at Patiko, about 30 km north of Gulu. This was formerly used as a base by slave traders but was taken over as a fort by Sir Samuel Baker in 1872 when, as Governor of Equatoria Province, he drove the traders out and used it as a base from which to crush the slave trade. It was later occupied by Gordon and Emin Pasha. There are said to be rock paintings at Samuel Baker's camp.

   Aruu Falls are situated off the road between Gulu and Kitgum. After passing through Cwero and Gerlyek and crossing the river Achwa, turn right just before the next trading centre and follow the track.

Gulu listings

For Sleeping and Eating price codes and other relevant information, see Essentials pages 21-23.

Sleeping
AL-A The Bomah Hotel, Eden Rd, T077-994 5063 (mob), bomahhotelltd@yahoo.com. Sited on the northern side of town in the quarter where NGOs have their offices. An upgrade was in progress at the time of writing, including the construction of a pool. En suite single, double and twin rooms. DSTV and mini-fridge. The hotel is set in pleasant gardens and has a comfortable bar and dining area. The menu is varied and reasonable but service can be slow. Sauna, massage, steam room and salon.
A-B Acholi Inn, Queen Elizabeth Rd, T04714-32880, acholiinn@yahoo.com. Also on the northern side of town. Single, double rooms and suites with a/c, DSTV and mini-fridge. Pleasant gardens, pool (US$3 for non-residents), sauna and gym.
B Churchill Courts Hotel, Churchill Dr, T04714-32245, gcchotel@gmail.com. Range of rooms, all en suite, from singles, doubles and twin, executive double, with balcony and view of the garden, to VIP with DSTV and Wi-Fi. Pool, gym and sauna completed in early 2011. The restaurant (♥) has a varied menu of Western or local food.

C-D Hotel Pearl Afrique, Paul Odongo Rd, T04714-32055, pearlafriquehotel@yahoo. com. Off Acholi Rd which leaves Kampala Rd between Caltex petrol station and Stanbic Bank. Singles, doubles, executives and family rooms all with fans and en suite, baths with shower attachments. Pleasant terrace restaurant/bar. DSTV and Wi-Fi. Price includes breakfast. The Pearl Afrique band provides light entertainment Sat and Sun 1900-2200.
F Acholi Ber, Market St, just below the market, T0372-280387, acholibercountry hotel@gmail.com. The best value in town for clean, basic B&B accommodation. All rooms are self contained and beds have nets. Double rooms have TV (DSTV available shortly). Executive double is a bigger room with a balcony. Restaurant has Italian and Indian food.

Eating
ᵗ **The Abyssinian Restaurant**, near Pece Stadium, T077-318 9606 (mob). Good Ethiopian and Italian food at reasonable prices. Pre-booking advisable.
ᵗ **Prince Restaurant**, Plot 6, Acholi Rd, T071-838 6424. Good Indian cuisine.

Cafés
All those listed below offer Wi-Fi.
Café Larem, Market St. Cappuccino and ice cream. Also sells some handicrafts and has a book exchange.
The Coffee Shop, opposite the bus and taxi park exit in town centre. Pricier than other cafés but good for cappuccino and snacks.
Sankofa Café, Cemetery Rd, behind Stanbic and Barclays banks. Their pizzas, samosas and milkshakes are recommended.

Bars and clubs
BJs Club (formerly Bambu Restaurant), Churchill Dr. The current favourite NGO workers' bar and dance venue. Pleasant, relaxed surroundings, pool table, reasonable bar meals with a barbecue and dancing later in the evenings.

Entertainment
Traditional dance
Luo Talent Centre, 1.5 km from the town centre on Kampala Highway, T0392-879950. Visitors are welcome to attend the rehearsals of local traditional dancers on Sat and Sun 1000-1400.

Shopping
Craft shops
There are 2 local craft shops on Jomo Kenyatta Rd, close to the market.
TAKS Art Centre, 3-5 Upper Churchill Dr, behind **Acholi Inn**, www.takscentre.org. Sells a variety of handicrafts made by local groups.
Watoto Kacel Cooperative, at Comboni Samaritans Centre, about 2 km from the town centre. Produces weaving, tie and dye, embroidery, beads and greetings cards.

Activities and tours
Tour operators
Safaris to Murchison Falls National Park can be arranged through **Hotel Binen**, T077-240 5038 (mob).
EJK and Sons Tour and Travel Service, T077-775 5347 (mob), ejkandsons@gmail.com.

Transport
Most of the road to **Lira** and **Soroti** is surfaced. North of Gulu the roads quickly deteriorates and 4WD is advisable as there is evening rain for much of the year.

Bus
The daily Post Bus leaves Kampala at 0800 and Gulu for **Kampala** at 0700, US$7. Cheaper than commercial services (US$8.75) it's also more reliable. Commercial buses to Kampala do not run to a clear schedule; they depart when full. To **Masindi** take the Kampala bus and change at Kigumba. The **Juba** bus passes through Gulu between 0400-0600, stopping at the Total petrol station. To **Busia**, via **Lira**, **Soroti** and **Mbale**, about 0730. To **Moyo**, about 1100 and to **Kitgum**, 1300-1400. Minibus taxis run to **Lira** (infrequent, US$5.25), **Pakwach** and **Kitgum**.

Kitgum → *Colour map 1, A4.*

Located 110 km northeast of Gulu and 435 km from Kampala. The old Acholi District was subdivided in the 1970s by Idi Amin. East Acholi District, which borders Sudan, became Kitgum and West Acholi later became Gulu, west of the seasonal Aswa River. Southern Sudan also has a large population of Acholi-speaking people, separated by the colonial division of Uganda and Sudan at Independence.

Kitgum is generally flat, savannah woodland, with the Lamwo and Agoro mountain ranges to the northeast. There are gentle hills by the Aswa river valley. Kitgum gets few tourists, apart from those en route to Kidepo Valley National Park 140 km further northeast. Badly affected by the two decades of LRA civil war, it has a large population of NGOs as this district had several internally displaced people's camps. Most people have left the camps and returned to their villages. Luo and Acholi are the main languages.

Kitgum listings

For Sleeping and Eating price codes and other relevant information, see Essentials pages 21-23.

Sleeping
B Bomah Hotel, 60-62 Uhuru Dr, T0471-439399. Somewhat deprived sister of the Gulu hotel of the same name. Restaurant and pool.
B Fugly's Hotel, T075-450 0555, afrimax. holdings@gmail.com. Run by South Africans Lyn Jordaan and Patrick Devy. Popular hotel in well-maintained grounds with a small pool. Has 4 en suite rooms with hot water or a dorm house with 5 rooms (all with nets) and communal bathrooms. No a/c, TV or internet but conversations with other travellers offer excellent entertainment. The restaurant and bar is open to non-residents too, serving good food in generous quantities.

Also operates the **Nga'Moru Wilderness Camp** at Kidepo Valley National Park (see page 118).

Eating
Fugly's Bar & Restaurant, Fugly's Hotel, see above.

Directory
Banks Stanbick Bank.

Moyo and Adjumani → *Colour map 1, A2.*

This is one of the northernmost administrative centres in Uganda, on the Sudanese border. It is the headquarters of West Moyo, East Moyo and Obongi, 7 km to the border and is one of the major crossing points between the two countries. However, the FCO and the US State Department advise people to avoid unnecessary travel into Sudan, as civil unrest is expected to follow the 2010 referendum about the separation of southern Sudan from northern Sudan. This is a beautiful part of Uganda and the mountains of southern Sudan can be seen in the distance standing out against the rather flat landscape all around. Deforestation was rife in these parts as it has been host to waves of refugees from Uganda and southern Sudan since the 1960s. You can see for miles and at night the deep inky blackness of the landscape with bright stars above is lovely.

Moyo town itself looks much like all the other towns in the north. Before Independence much of this area was devoted to the cultivation of cotton, with good roads, a reasonable telephone and electricity system and thriving trade centres. The area has suffered terribly from Uganda and Sudan's troubled history.

Ins and outs

Getting there The best route is to go via Gulu continuing 120 km north to Adjumani, and on to Moyo. This route takes you through Pakele and Dzaipi, both small towns with nothing of interest to look at, but useful places to stop for a soda or roasted meat. There is petrol in Pakele. An alternative is via Pakwach if visiting the Murchison Falls National Park then to Arua. There are good public transport links to Arua and Adjumani.

Adjumani listings

For Sleeping and Eating price codes and other relevant information, see Essentials pages 21-23.

Sleeping
Take plenty of insect repellent, as mosquitoes are prevalent in the area.
A Arra Fishing Lodge, near Adjumani, T077-237 4560, www.nileperch.org.

5 en suite double tents on the banks of the Albert Nile, with the bar, restaurant, lounge and pool at the nearby lodge. 30-min drive from the small airfield at Adjumani, this upmarket, German-run facility is for serious fishermen.

Directory
Banks Stanbic Bank has a branch here.

Pakwach → *Colour map 1, B2.*

Pakwach is a tiny town on the western edge of the Murchison Falls National Park. It is little more than one street, with several small restaurants, but has everything a traveller is likely to need. Despite its primitive conditions, it's a very pleasant place to stay. Being on the edge of the river, its environment is green and fertile. The main reasons for being here are either to visit the park or to stop by the Nile. Pakwach is only a few kilometres from the border and is mostly used by local people to cross into DR Congo at the northern tip of Lake Albert. However, the FCO and the US State Department advise against all travel to northeastern DR Congo due to insecurity and lawlessness (issued in January 2011), so avoid this border crossing.

Pakwach listings

For Sleeping and Eating price codes and other relevant information, see Essentials pages 21-23.

Sleeping
There are a number of indistinguishable small hotels.
LL River Camp, north of Pakwach, close to Olobodagi, a small town west of the Nile, T070-199 8444 (mob), www.bahr-el-jebel-safaris.com. The upmarket Bahr El Jebel

specializes in 'winged safaris', packages that include internal flights to Arua and the use of high-speed swamp boats, developed in Florida's Everglades, to negotiate the river both upstream to Murchison's Falls NP and downstream as far as Nimule NP in Sudan. 10 en suite safari tents.
E Global Village Guesthouse, 1 km west of town towards Nebbi. Basic accommodation and internet connection.

Arua → *Colour map 1, B1.*

This small town in the northwest is located close to the border with DR Congo, about 476 km from Kampala. However, crossing this border is not advised (see under Pakwach above). Since the end of the LRA war in Northern Uganda Arua has become a major centre for NGOs working on Ugandan, DR Congolese and Southern Sudanese projects. Arua's other claim to fame is that the despot Idi Amin came from this remote town.

Arua listing

For Sleeping and Eating price codes and other relevant information, see Essentials pages 21-23.

Sleeping
B White Castle Hotel, 4 km out of town at Euwata on the Arua–Nebbi–Pakwach road, T077-288 0830 (mob), T0372-260033, www. whitecastlehotel.com. Detached smart hotel, 30 rooms, mostly 4 unit cottages in a 3 ha garden with pool. DSTV, fans and nets. Bar, restaurant and business centre.
D Heritage Park, 38 Weatherhead Park Lane, T077-245 1689 (mob). The best of 4 in this hotel group, with 12 rooms, a terrace bar and restaurant set in the garden.

Eating
The Grid. A good-value restaurant and bar frequented by aid workers, so called because it is exactly on 3° latitude north and 31° longitude east.

Transport
Bus
The road from Kampala is fully sealed. *Matatus* and **Nile Coach** buses from Bombo Rd in **Kampala** take 6-8 hrs, US$9. Leave at 0300 to avoid travelling in the heat.

Directory
Banks Stanbic, Barclays, Post Bank and **Centenary Bank** have branches here.

Northwest to Murchison Falls National Park

The fast road from Kampala to Masindi means that Murchison Falls National Park is a popular weekend destination for inhabitants of the capital. The park is bisected by the Victoria Nile, and the falls – where the river is squeezed through a gap only 7 m wide – are truly spectacular. Murchison has some of Uganda's best game-viewing and it is one of the few places in the country where giraffes can be seen. South is the Kaniyo-Pabidi Forest Reserve with chimpanzee tracking, and it is a pleasant drive down the east bank of Lake Albert and up the side of the Rift Valley to Hoima, which is about halfway between Murchison Falls and Fort Portal. There are some great views across the lake to the Blue Mountains, which are in the DR Congo, on the far shore.

Although it is not visible from the road there is a big lake system just to the north of Luwero as the Victoria Nile flows first through Lake Kyoga and then Lake Kwania before reaching first the Karuma Falls and then the Murchison Falls before eventually flowing into Lake Albert. The countryside for miles around is low-lying and rather swampy.

Kampala to Masindi

Luwero Triangle
The road to Masindi leaves Kampala heading north starting at the Wandegeya roundabout near Makerere University passing through Bombo and Luwero, before swinging westwards, taking about three hours. About 30 km out of Kampala you cross into the Luwero district and reach the army town of **Bombo** with row upon row of barracks. In the early 20th century the Sudanese Volunteers in the King's African Rifles, known as the Nubians, were based here. Known as the **Luwero Triangle**, the area was severely affected during the Obote II regime when army atrocities resulted in the killing of many thousands of people, their houses looted and burnt and destruction of the surrounding *shambas*. Little evidence remains apart from a couple of burnt-out tanks left to rust on the roadside.

Ziwa Rhino Sanctuary

Ins and outs
Getting there All buses from Kampala going to Masindi or Gula pass close by. Ask to be let off at Nakitoma, from where it is a short *boda-boda* ride to the sanctuary's main gate. The sanctuary is 176 km north of Kampala in the Nakasongola District, 8 km off the Kampala–Masindi road and 7 km south of the Kafu Bridge–Masindi junction.

Visitor information **Uganda Rhino Fund** ① *T077-271 3410, www.rhinofund.org.* UWA park visitation fee US$20 per day. Facilities include a guesthouse with pleasant 1- and 2-bed rooms (C); a restaurant serving generous portions (†); camping US$12pp; tour guides US$15 per group. Future projects include a pool when funds allow. Given rhinos' preference for swampy conditions waterproof footwear is advised.

The sanctuary
The private, non-profit sanctuary is a joint enterprise between UWA, the Uganda Rhino Fund and Ziwa Ranchers Ltd, who reintroduced rhinos to Uganda in 2005, thereby making up the Big Five. Rhinos became extinct in Uganda in 1982 due to poaching and the

internal armed conflict. Initially the reintroduced rhinoceros have been six Southern White (*Ceratotherium simum*), but it's hoped in time to expand the programme to include the Black Rhinoceros (*Diceros bicornis*). Both are endemic to Uganda. To date three calves have been born but plans to further expand the programme depend on funding.

The 7000-ha sanctuary is enclosed by a 60-km-long by 2-m-high solar-powered electrified fence, designed to keep out human predators and protect the rhino, and built by local people, giving much-needed employment. The rhinos have transmitters in their horns and are closely guarded by armed rangers 24 hours a day. Guides can bring visitors up very close to these habituated megafaunas, tracked partly by vehicle and on foot. Other animals found within the enclosure include monkeys, oribi, bushbuck, leopard, hippo, crocodiles and numerous birds. You can enjoy a sundowner around the fire pit, although insect repellent is needed as the mosquitoes are prolific.

Masindi Port

The road from Kampala has no towns of any size after Luwero until it reaches Masindi Port. Easily confused with Masindi, it lies about 40 km to the east, on the Victoria Nile at the western end of Lake Kyoga, which extends across much of central Uganda. When steamers on the Nile were an important mode of transport, the two sets of falls in the Murchison Falls National Park were major obstacles to travelling upriver. Coming from Lake Victoria, the steamers travelled the Victoria Nile and into Lake Kyoga. Passengers and goods then disembarked at Masindi Port and travelled overland to Butiaba on Lake Albert. From here they continued their boat journey north. Masindi Port has since declined in importance and is now mainly a market town.

The tarmac road carries on to Karuma where it crosses the Nile allowing access to Gulu, Pakwach, where it again crosses the river, Arua and, eventually, the DR Congo. To travel to Paraa, the best route is through Masindi. Watch out for the turning just after the Kafu river crossing at Kibangya.

Masindi → *Phone code: 4654. Colour map 1, B3.C2*

Masindi is en route to the Murchison Falls National Park. It is a pleasant town with lots of flowers and greenery, although the main street, Masindi Port Road, is typical of the area, being rather dry and dusty. Masindi has a lively market, located just behind the main street.

Ins and outs
Tourist office **UWA's Murchison Falls Conservation Area Tourist Office** ⓘ *T0465-420428*, is signposted north from the main road, opposite the town council buildings, 50 m west of the post office. The staff are extremely helpful and can also give you information about Budongo Forest.

Around Masindi
Two kilometres from town on Kihande Hill is **Kihande Palace**, the palace of the King or Omukama of Bunyoro, Solomon Gafabusa Iguru. The Bunyoro Kingdom and kingship were abolished in 1967 during the Obote I regime. President Museveni restored the kingdoms returning their ceremonial powers in 1993. Although Omukama Solomon normally resides in his palace in Hoima, there are plans to renovate this old palace. However, since the discovery of oil in this region, Bunyoro has become a hotbed of land

conflicts, with people settling, building houses and enclosing gardens on royal sites including the Kihande Palace.

Kigaju Forest is a small privately owned finger of forest, 5 km west of Masindi, past the Kinyara Sugarcane Plantation Office. Surrounded by sugar cane plantations, it's home to a group of unhabituated chimpanzees. The chimps are best seen either in the early morning at 0600 or late afternoon 1700. Given the chimps frequently raid the sugarcanes bordering the forest, they are easy to view from the road as they are not hidden in tree canopy. Baboon, black and white colobus monkeys and red-tailed monkeys can also be seen here, plus a diverse bird population and many butterflies. A small eco-tourism project aims to protect the forest from the encroaching sugarcane. As the UWA is not involved in this private forest, chimp tracking is exceptionally cheap at US$20 per person for a guided walk. Other **nature walks** ① *T077-255 1484 (mob), you must pre-book and meet the guide in Masindi*, through the forest and cultural tours of the nearby villages have been developed. There is a small campsite and plans to build *bandas* and a restaurant.

Excursions to **Lake Albert** can be made from Masindi. Head for the town of Butiaba Port on Lake Albert, a distance of 70 km. The drive on the escarpment to the Rift Valley is an experience in itself. Once you get to Butiaba ask the local fishermen and you should be able to hire a boat for the day.

Masindi listings

For Sleeping and Eating price codes and other relevant information, see Essentials pages 21-23.

Sleeping
B Masindi Hotel, PO Box 11, 22-34 Butiaba Rd, 1 km out of town past the police post on the road to Hoima, T077-242 0130 (mob) preferred, T04654-20023, www.masindihotel.com. This is a wonderful place to break the journey from Kampala to Murchison Falls. Built in 1923 by the East African Railways and Harbours Company, this is Uganda's oldest colonial hotel, which has preserved a charming, stylish exterior. Many famous people have stayed here, including Humphrey Bogart and Katherine Hepburn whilst filming *The African Queen* at Masindi Port, and Ernest Hemingway, who recuperated here after surviving 2 plane crashes in a week in 1954 at Murchison Falls and at Butiaba airstrip. Now in private ownership it has undergone a major restoration since 2005. Pleasant, spacious en suite tiled rooms. A restaurant serves Indian, Western and local food and there's a bar. Quiet library and internet facilities. Well-maintained campsite and gardens behind the hotel.

C New Court View Hotel, 200 m from Masindi post office, T04654-20461, Nyanga Rd, www.newcourtviewhotel.com. Set in a garden are 15 comfortable small, round, very clean cottages with solar-heated hot water. The restaurant serves excellent food and there's a bar. The gift shop sells a range of locally produced crafts at reasonable prices. Tours arranged. Friendly and fast service.
D Kopling House, Ntuha Rd, T077-246 3203 (mob). Quiet, clean church-run guesthouse, with a small restaurant, located a bit out of town.

Eating
Court View Hotel and **Masindi Hotel** both offer an international menu.
Traveller's Corner Bar & Restaurant, on main road next to the post office. Popular with expats. Attractive wooden veranda, bar and cosy restaurant. Good food, friendly and helpful staff. A good place to stop before tackling the 2-hr drive to Paraa.

Entertainment
Football
There is a sports stadium in Masindi and matches are held there on a regular basis.

Shopping

There are 2 small supermarkets, **Lucky 7** and **Wat General Agencies**, on Commercial St, which offer a few basics. Fresh fruit and vegetables are available in Masindi market.

Activities and tours

Tour operators

Local agents who can arrange excursions into Murchison Falls National Park are: **Yebo Tours**, T077-263 7493 (mob), yebotours2002@yahoo.com; **New Court View Hotel**, T077-279 9969 (mob), www.newcourtviewhotel.com; **Traveller's Corner**, same contact details as the Courtview Hotel; and **Masindi Hotel**, see Sleeping above.

Transport

Bus

Bus to **Kampala** at 0600, 5 hrs, US$4. Post Bus to Kampala from the post office at 0700, 5 hrs, US$4. Regular *matatus* to Kampala, 4 hrs, US$5. Frequent *matatus* travel to **Hoima** along murram road, 1 hr, US$2.

Directory

Banks Barclays Bank, Masindi Port Rd. Stanbic Bank, Kijumburu Rd. ATM and foreign currency exchange (not TCs). **Internet** Masindi Hotel (see Sleeping) and Traveller's Corner Bar (see Eating) offer internet services.

Budongo Forest Reserve → *Colour map 1, C2.*

ⓘ *The proposed entry fee for Budongo is US$20 per 24 hrs, currently US$15 payable at Busingiro, see below.*

The 825 sq km reserve of grassland and forest near Lake Albert, with 482 sq km of the reserve semi-deciduous, tropical forest, is the largest area of unexploited mahogany forest in East Africa, with huge trees growing up to 60 m high. It has exceptional biodiversity with 465 tree species identified. There are spectacular views from Butiaba over Lake Albert and the Blue Mountains of DR Congo on the western shore of the lake. As in all rainforests, conditions are often very wet, so suitable clothing is needed.

About 700 chimpanzees live in the forest. Chimpanzee tracking in Busingiro was discontinued because after habituation the chimps lost their fear of humans and started raiding nearby crops. They remain in the forest and can be spotted especially at dawn and dusk. Other primates are black and white colobus, red-tailed monkeys, blue monkeys, potto, baboons and vervet monkeys. Birdlife is excellent with 366 species recorded, along with 289 butterfly species and 130 species of large moths.

On offer are nature trails and special interest walks. The **Royal Mile**, so called because it was a favourite location of King Kabalega (see page 189), is a wide avenue of trees between the Nyabyere Forestry College and the Research Station, with abundant birds. This is Uganda's best forest birding site and contains a number of endemic species not seen elsewhere. It's 15 km away from the Busingiro eco-centre and is only accessible with private transport.

At the forest edge is Lake Kanyege, with water birds and clouds of butterflies. A historic Polish church stands nearby, built by wartime refugees who were fleeing the Nazis. A small Polish community settled in Uganda although none now remain. Still in use, the church is in the most beautiful setting with the Blue Mountains visible in the background.

Busingiro → *Colour map 1, C2.*

ⓘ *US$15 a day and guides US$10 for foreign tourists, charges in Ugandan shillings, with reduced charges for Ugandans and residents. Matatus from Masindi heading for Butiaba (on Lake Albert) and Wanseko (at the entry of the Nile into Lake Albert) pass by the site, 1 hr, US$3. The entrance is* clearly signposted on the left-hand side of the road, a few kilometres beyond the turning for the Nyabyeya Forestry College. Or take a private hire or a boda-boda is from Masindi. It's very difficult to get transport from Busingero towards Bulisa and Wanseko in the afternoon.

Busingiro is 42 km from Masindi on the road west to Butiaba, lying between Masindi and Lake Albert. This is an eco-tourism site within the rainforest, with a visitor centre that offers information, snacks and drinks and an education centre for schools. It's outside the Murchison Falls Protected Area so is cheaper to visit than Kaniyo-Pabidi. There are two rather run-down *bandas* (US$6 per person), and a basic campsite (US$4 per person with own tent). The *bandas* are a better option because, as in all rainforests, conditions are often very wet, but they are often out of use due to the damp conditions. Cooking shelter and firewood available, but you need to supply all your own food. An upgrade of facilities is planned. Check with **Uganda Lodges** ⓘ *T0414-267153, T077-242 6368 (mob), www.ugandalodges.com/lodges/budongo.*

Murchison Falls Protected Area

Ins and outs
Getting there   From Masindi, it's a two-hour drive of 88 km to Murchison Falls, Paraa and the ferry. This is the direct road that enters the park through the Wairingo Gate, close to Sambiya River Lodge. Take the right turn after the Court View Hotel in Masindi. There is a large barracks on the hill. After 7 km take the left turn to the park at Kyema. Shortly after the road goes through an avenue of termite mounds before reaching Kaniyo-Pabidi (see below). A 4WD is advisable for this stretch during the rainy season. Staff at the Murchison Falls Protected Area may be able to arrange a lift as there is no public transport directly into the national park. Or take a *matutu* from Masindi to Wanseko and Bulisa, but onward travel from these small settlements is limited to *boda-boda* or bicycle. It is recommended that you negotiate the motorbike hire from Wanseko (see page 138) rather than from Bulisa. It's a longer route but allows for a visit to the Budongo Forest Reserve and is a more attractive drive. The road from Bulisa to Paraa enters the park at Bugungu Gate. It is only 30 minutes from here to the ferry.

Murchison Falls National Park

The Murchison Falls National Park is the largest national park in Uganda, covering an area of nearly 4000 sq km. The even larger Murchison Falls Protected Area (MFPA), which includes the adjoining Karuma and Bugungu wildlife reserves, is 5072 sq km. With some of the most spectacular scenery in the country, it offers game viewing, safaris and fishing. It incorporates the Kaniyo-Pabidi Forest Reserve, part of Budongo Forest but within the protected area, which offers excellent chimpanzee tracking.

The park was briefly known as Kabalega Falls National Park in the early 1970s, having been renamed by President Amin after the King of Bunyoro, famous for resisting attempts to colonize his kingdom. Until about 40 years ago, the waters of the Nile were forced through a narrow gap in the rocks to fall through a series of foaming, roaring cascades down a drop of about 50 m, creating one of the world's most spectacular waterfalls. However, in 1961, a year of particularly heavy rains and floods in Uganda, the waterfall broke through another gap in the rocks and there are now two breaches.

Ins and outs

Getting there

Driving Coming overland From Kampala, it takes about four to five hours (two hours on tarmac and 2½ to three hours on murram road) to Paraa in the park, via Masindi. From Masindi an 88-km well-maintained dirt road takes you directly to Paraa in two hours. This is the direct road that enters the park through the Wairingo Gate, close to Sambiya River Lodge. Take the right turn after the Court View Hotel in Masindi. There is a large barracks on the hill. After 7 km take the left turn to the park at Kyema. Shortly after the road goes through an avenue of termite mounds before reaching Kaniyo-Pabidi (see below). A 4WD is recommended in the rainy season.

The more beautiful route is the road via Bulisa. From Masindi you take the Butiaba road through the Budongo Forest Reserve. Before reaching Butiaba, on the shores of Lake Albert, you head north. This is a very attractive drive looking across the Rift Valley towards Lake Albert and across to the DR Congo on the other side. When you reach the village of Bulisa it is 18 km to the gate and 23 km to the Paraa ferry (about 45 minutes' drive). The first part of this road is very good murram; in the latter part are more potholes. A 4WD is recommended during the rainy season, or if you want to go for a game drive on the north side of the park. From Hoima you can take a straight route towards Butiaba and Bulisa. An alternative route is to take the left turning to the Kinyara Sugar Works off the main road from Hoima to Masindi. You will pass through the sugar plantations after which this road meets up with the Masindi–Butiaba road. The road passes through the Budongo Forest Reserve, outside the Murchison Falls National Park. Chobe Lodge is accessed 2 km north of the Karuma bridge, off the main Kampala–Gulu fully sealed road, then along 14 km of murram road in the national park. The journey time is about 3½ hours.

Public transport There is no direct public transport into Murchison, although Chobe Lodge is only 14 km away from the Kampala–Gulu road. You can travel by public transport to Masindi and from there arrange a trip with one of the tour operators (see page 129). Alternatively, head to Bulisa or Wanseko by public transport and stay the night in the small town of Bulisa (see page 138). From Bulisa, either try to hitch (tricky) or hire a bicycle

(2-2½ hours) (US$8) from the Bulisa Corner Guest House (see page 138). It is 23 km to Paraa and it is mostly flat, apart from a steep descent shortly after the park entrance gate. Start early if visiting the park as the ferry runs at two-hourly intervals starting at 0700. Another option is hiring a *boda-boda*. You can do this in Bulisa, but it's often possible to negotiate a better price (about US$20 one way) in Wanseko. Also, if a motorbike taxi from Bulisa needs filling up with petrol they will have to go over to Wanseko anyway to do this!

Park information
The park visitation fee is US$30. The park office is in Masindi, see page 127.

Background

The area around Chobe in the eastern part of the Murchison Falls National Park has been a popular human habitat from early times for a number of reasons. It has good animal and vegetable resources, with agricultural potential, and iron ore suitable for primitive smelting technology was found in the area. The earliest artefacts found in the Chobe

Murchison Falls National Park

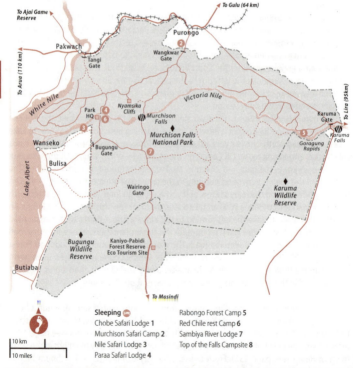

Sleeping	
Chobe Safari Lodge 1	Rabongo Forest Camp 5
Murchison Safari Camp 2	Red Chile rest Camp 6
Nile Safari Lodge 3	Sambiya River Lodge 7
Paraa Safari Lodge 4	Top of the Falls Campsite 8

10 km
10 miles

Hemingway at Murchison

Ernest Hemingway made a couple of visits to Africa. The first was to Tanzania in 1933, when Hemingway, then 34, and his second wife Pauline spent a couple of months hunting and fishing in Tanzania. It was another 20 years before Hemingway would visit Africa again, and this was to be an altogether more eventful trip. By now he was with his fourth wife, Mary. In 1953 they stayed on the Percival farm (Percival was one of the foremost white hunters). On safari, where Ernest shot a big, black-maned lion, zebra and gerenuk.

Ernest began getting into the spirit of Africa with some gusto. He shaved his head, dyed his suede jacket and two shirts with Masai red ochre and went leopard hunting with a spear. He took a liking to an Akamba girl, Debba, and brought her and some friends back to the camp where the celebrations became so enthusiastic that they broke one of the beds. Some months later Ernest observed that he should now be a father in Africa.

In 1954 Ernest and Mary flew from Nairobi, piloted by Roy Marsh. They stopped at Fig Tree camp then headed for Mwanza where they refuelled, before staying over at Costermanville (now Bukavu). As they circled the glassy waters, dotted with islands and hemmed in by green hills, Mary thought Kivu was the most beautiful lake she had ever seen. They put down at Entebbe. The following day, circling Murchison Falls, the plane hit a telegraph wire and made an emergency landing. The three lit a fire and slept under coats. Next day a boat visiting the falls gave them a lift to Butiaba. They engaged a plane and a pilot to fly them from Butiaba airstrip to Entebbe, but taking off from the bumpy runway, the plane suddenly stopped, and burst into flames. Roy Marsh kicked out a window and managed to drag Mary through. Ernest butted the jammed door open and struggled out. A policeman drove them to Masindi, and they stayed at the Railway Hotel before reaching Entebbe and Lake Victoria Hotel. A few days later they flew to Nairobi.

In the meantime, a civilian airliner had reported the plane wreck; the world thought Hemingway had died and newspapers published obituaries. Though alive, he was in poor shape with concussion, ruptured liver, spleen and kidney, a crushed vertebra and burns.

In 1956 there were plans to make a third trip, but poor health meant that it never materialized. Hemingway's experiences on safari provided the material for many short stories, a fine collection of which are in *The Green Hills of Africa*.

area date from the Middle Stone Age, when the banks of the Nile were peopled by small groups of hunters and gatherers, who may also have fished. Rough pebble tools, large flakes, some picks and a hand axe all have been found dating from this period, when the Nile was believed to flow at a higher level than at present.

Throughout the Middle and Late Stone Age, agriculture and the domestication of animals were not known to the riverbank dwellers; they continued to eke out an existence based on hunting and gathering. However, the manufacture of stone tools slowly became more sophisticated with new types of tool appearing. The abundance of flakes and chippings in places along the eroded banks of the river suggests that these may have been places where tools were made, rather than actual settlements. Pottery fragments, ironware and iron slag have been collected along the banks dating back up to 2000 years. Most of the finds, however, are much more recent, dating from the last 200 years.

The settlers who are thought to have first introduced iron technology to this part of Africa left behind a very distinctive type of pottery known as dimple-based ware, characterized by bevelled rims and incised cross-hatched or grooved decoration, and found over much of the Lake Victoria basin. Related pottery types occur over most of the subcontinent; but the most northerly occurrence of this archaeological complex so far is at Chobe. Most of the pottery fragments found in recent years carry decorative motifs identical to those used by the people who live in the area around the national park today. They consist of concentric circles, raised bosses and zigzag chevrons all applied to the wet clay with a carved wooden roulette or a knotted cord.

Flora and fauna

The park is worth visiting as much for the variation in its scenery as for its wildlife, although mammal numbers have greatly increased over the past decade. The further north you travel, the more savannah-like the terrain becomes. The south of the park is green and lush with many small settlements and banana or matoke cultivation everywhere. The further north you travel the drier and hotter it becomes, with infrequent human settlements. Some parts are quite extraordinary, with long, wide alleys of date palm trees and other exotics stretching from left to right to the horizon, planted by Arab slave traders centuries ago, to mark their route in and out of inland black Africa.

Many animals and birds live in the park including Ugandan kobs, buffaloes, hippos, baboons, crocodiles, lions, elephants and antelope.

To reduce the conflict caused by crop-raiding animals, UWA have agreed to construct suitable park boundaries like deep ditches or elephant fences, protecting the communities living in *shambas* abutting the park.

Game viewing

For the best game viewing you have to go to the north of the park; there are very few animals on the south bank apart from small herds of Ugandan kob. If you are south of the river, getting to the north bank necessitates crossing the river by **ferry** ⓘ *0700, 0900, 1100, 1200, 1400, 1600 and 1800; safari vehicles US$13, foot passengers US$2.* Early mornings are unquestionably the best time to see and photograph animals. The Nile valley is one of the hottest places in Uganda and animals tend to look for shade and rest towards 1100. Many animals such as lion, leopard, hyena, buffalo and most of the smaller mammals such as civet cats are most active at night. It is always advisable to take food and water with you on a game drive. Getting stuck in the mud is part of the adventure so travel in a 4WD is recommended, with a ranger guide (US$20 a day).

The best route for viewing animals is the **Buligi Circuit**, which includes the Buligi, Victoria Nile, Queens and Albert Nile tracks. Depending on the time available, there are numerous ways to explore this area. It is recommended that at least four to five hours are set aside for a thorough safari; expect to cover 120-170 km. During the game drive you can spot Rothschilds giraffe, lion, leopard, hyena, elephant, buffalo, Jackson's hartebeest, oribi, Uganda kob and a huge variety of bird species. The amazing shoebill stork resides in the park but you will probably be lucky to glimpse it.

The falls

Launch trip

This trip is recommended and is operated by UWA from Paraa, south of the river, to the falls themselves. If you happen to be on the north side of the river, a small boat can take you over. The cost is US$150 for a minimum of 10 people (with a proposed increase to US$25 per person in 2011). Additional passengers will also pay US$25. There is also the US$30 visitation fee on top of this. During the boat ride you are guaranteed to see hippos, with reportedly 4000 in this stretch of the river, and some huge Nile crocodiles. There is a good chance of viewing elephants, red-tailed monkeys and black and white colobus monkeys, as well as some magnificent birdlife at close quarters. Other game found along the river bank includes buffalo, giraffe and a range of antelopes. The launch trip usually runs twice daily from Paraa, at 0800 and 1400. The round trip takes about three hours. Boat trips to the falls are also offered by other companies. **G&C Tours** ① *T077-389 7275, T070-215 2928, murchison@wildfrontiers.co.ug*, cost US$25 per person, and **Marasa** ① *operators of the Paraa Safari Lodge (see page 136)*, charge from US$18 per person in their 11-seater boats.

Top of the falls

It is possible to stop at the base of the falls from one of the boats to walk up the steep footpath to the top. Alternatively, the drive from Paraa takes about 45 minutes and is roughly 30 km. A visit here should form an integral part of any trip to the park. It is a unique and breathtaking natural spectacle, the most powerful rush of water anywhere in the world. There is a small campsite and ranger post at the falls, the starting point for a short walk downhill to the water's edge. Here it is possible to get within a few metres of the fenced-off falls. The narrow gap and the volume of water that rages through it, vibrating the ancient rocks, can only truly be appreciated from this vantage point. Care is required as the surrounding area can be slippery underfoot. Although there are two breaches, you can in fact only see the original falls. There used to be a concrete bridge spanning the 7-m gap but this was washed away in the 1961-1962 floods. Try to be here at sunset, when hundreds of bats fly over the falls chased by birds of prey.

Murchison Falls Museum/Education Centre

① *Open 0900-1700. No entry fee but a donation is welcomed.*

This recently opened museum/gallery has been developed by **Softpower Education** in conjunction with the UWA and other governmental agencies. They are mounting a major exhibition that will initially be displayed in Kampala from April 2011, before moving to the education centre in around July/August 2011. The exhibition highlights social, historical and cultural attributes that impact upon current conservation issues.

In the interim there is an exhibition displaying amazing paintings of Totems (animals and plants sacred to various Ugandan tribes) by the local artist Taga. Any monies generated are used for Softpower's community conservation outreach programme. See also www.softpowereducation.com.

For Sleeping and Eating price codes and other relevant information, see Essentials pages 21-23.

Sleeping *map p132*

In 1995 the Madhvani Group signed a 30-year monopoly agreement to provide 5-star lodges within an Exclusion Zone Agreement (EZA) in Murchison Falls NP (MFNP) and QENP. Under the terms of the agreement no other investor would set up a lodge within a radius of 40 km. Madhvani run the **Paraa Safari Lodge** and **Chobe Safari Lodge** in MFNP, and the **Mweya Safari Lodge** in QENP. However, in Aug 2010 UWA announced it had unilaterally withdrawn from this EZA as it wished to open the parks to other investors. This action is illegal and not surprisingly led to protests from Madhvani Group, and was later overruled by the president. During peak season there is a 40% room shortage, and the high prices exclude most Ugandans from visiting. UWA is keen to encourage mid-range alternative accommodation to be built but it may be some time before this issue is settled.

Murchison Safari Camp, Wangkwar Gate, in north of the national park, run by **Backpackers Hostel**, Kampala, T077-243 0587 (mob), www.backpackers.co.ug, is due to open soon.

LL Nile Safari Lodge, T0414-258273, T0312-260758, www.geolodgesafrica.com. Situated outside the national park, 11 km off the main road coming from Bulisa to Paraa along an extremely rough track, 5 km downstream from the ferry, therefore not ideal for early morning game drives on the north bank of the river. 5 safari tents with permanent bathrooms, and 5 en suite wooden chalets with balconies on wooden stilt frames. Offers wonderful views of the Nile and for watching the herds of elephants frequently seen on the opposite bank. Restaurant positioned on a communal deck offers a varied menu. Pool, also with Nile views.

LL-L Chobe Safari Lodge, central booking T0312-260260, T0414-255992, www.chobelodgeuganda.com. Reopened in late 2010 after 30 years. The original lodge was destroyed during the 1970s conflict when it was a rebel base. Prior to that it had been famous as a fishing lodge with record-breaking catches of Nile perch. 36 luxurious en suite rooms, 9 with a/c and Nile-facing balconies and terraces, 21 safari tents, 4 suites, a presidential cottage and a health club. The Nile is also visible from the 3-tiered pool and from the bar, and 5-star restaurant. There is a controversial proposal to build a golf course nearby within the park boundary. A weekend air package in partnership with Kampala Aero Club flies a minimum of 2 visitors to Chobe costing US$765pp for 3 days/2 nights full board, including park entry fees, 1 game trip, 1 boat trip and a trip to the top of the falls.

LL-L Paraa Safari Lodge, central booking T0312-260260, T0414-255992, mweyaparaa@africaonline.co.ug. Sited on a small hill on the north river bank, facing the launch jetty, is this luxurious lodge with a colonial theme displaying lots of pictures of the early explorers and other memorabilia. 54 bedrooms, 2 with disabled facilities, 2 suites, own balconies all with a splendid view overlooking the Nile. Outdoor pool with bar. Excellent food. Wildlife is frequently seen around the lodge. A weekend air package in partnership with Kampala Aero Club flies a minimum of 2 visitors to Paraa costing US$765pp for 3 days/2 nights full board, including park entry fees, 1 game trip, 1 boat trip and a trip to the top of the falls.

L-AL Sambiya River Lodge, on the south bank, only 20 mins' drive from the top of the falls, about 40 km north of Kichumbanyobo Gate, T04654-23174 (unreliable if it rains), T0414-233596 (Kampala), T077-623 3596, www.sambiyariverlodge.com. This open-fronted lodge with a pool has 20 thatched cottages with private bathroom and a veranda. Most cottages have 1 bedroom, some have 2. Budget accommodation

East African wildlife

Introduction

A large proportion of people who visit East Africa do so to see its spectacular wildlife. This colour section is a quick photographic guide to some of the more fascinating mammals you may encounter. We give you pictures and information about habitat, habits and characteristic appearance to help you when you are on safari. It is by no means a comprehensive survey and some of the animals listed may not be found throughout the whole region. For information about Uganda's mountain gorillas, see box on page 223, and for details of the ubiquitous kob (not pictured here) see page 157.

The Big Nine

It is fortunate that many of the large and spectacular animals of Africa are also, on the whole, fairly common. They are often known as the 'Big Five'. This term was originally coined by hunters who wanted to take home trophies of their safari. Thus it was, that, in hunting parlance, the Big Five were elephant, black rhino, buffalo, lion and leopard. Nowadays the hippopotamus is usually considered one of the Big Five for those who shoot with their cameras, whereas the buffalo is far less of a 'trophy'. Equally photogenic and worthy of being included are the zebra, giraffe and cheetah. But whether they are the Big Five or the Big Nine, these are the animals that most people come to Africa to see and, with the possible exception of the leopard and the black rhino, you have an excellent chance of seeing them all.

■ **Hippopotamus** *Hippopotamus amphibius*. Prefers shallow water, grazes on land over a wide area at night, so can be found quite a distance from water, and has a strong sense of territory, which it protects aggressively. Lives in large family groups known as 'schools'.

■ **Black rhinoceros** *Diceros bicornis*. Long, hooked upper lip distinguishes it from white rhino rather than colour. Prefers dry bush and thorn scrub habitat and in the past was found in mountain uplands. Males usually solitary. Females seen in small groups with their calves (very rarely more than four), sometimes with two generations. Mother always walks in front of offspring, unlike the white rhino, where the mother walks behind, guiding calf with her horn. Their distribution was massively reduced by poaching in the late 20th century, and now there are conservation efforts in place to protect black and white rhino and numbers are increasing. You might be lucky and see the black rhino in Ngorongoro Crater and in the Selous.

■ **White rhinoceros** *Diceros simus*. Square muzzle and bulkier than the black rhino, it is a grazer rather than a browser, hence the different lip. Found in open grassland, it is more sociable and can be seen in groups of five or more. Probably extinct in much of its former range in East Africa, it still flourishes in some places.

Opposite page:
Leopard with a kill.
Above left:
Black rhinoceros.
Above right:
White rhinoceros.
Right:
Hippopotamus.

iii

■ **Common/Masai giraffe** *Giraffa camelopardis*. Yellowish-buff with patchwork of brownish marks and jagged edges, usually two different horns, sometimes three. Found throughout Africa, several differing subspecies.

■ **Common/Burchell's zebra** *Equus burchelli*. Generally has broad stripes (some with lighter shadow stripes next to the dark ones) that cross the top of the hind leg in unbroken lines. The true species is probably extinct but there are many varying subspecies found in different locations across Africa.

■ **Leopard** *Panthera pardus*. Found in varied habitats ranging from forest to open savannah. It is generally nocturnal, hunting at night or before the sun comes up to avoid the heat. Sometimes seen resting during the day in the lower branches of trees.

■ **Cheetah** *Acinonyx jubatus*. Often seen in family groups walking across plains or resting in the shade. The black 'tear' mark is usually obvious through binoculars. Can reach speeds of 90 kph over short distances. Found in open, semi-arid savannah, never in forested country. Endangered in some parts of Africa. More commonly seen than the leopard.

■ **Elephant** *Loxodonta africana*. Commonly seen, even on short safaris, elephants have suffered from the activities of ivory poachers in East Africa. Tarangire is famous for its elephant population, with as many as 4000 at certain times of the year. Elephants are also prevalent in all other parks in Tanzania.

■ **Buffalo** *Syncerus caffer*. Were considered by hunters to be the most dangerous of the big game and the most difficult to track and, therefore, the biggest trophy. Generally found on open plains but also at home in dense forest, they are fairly common in most African national parks. They need a large area to roam in, so are not usually found in the smaller parks.

■ **Lion** *Panthera leo* (see page i). The largest of the big cats in Africa and also the most common, they are found on open savannah. They are often not disturbed at all by the presence of humans and so it possible to get quite close to them. They are sociable animals living in prides or permanent family groups of up to around 30 animals and are the only felid to do so. The females do most of the hunting.

Left: Common giraffe.
Above: Common zebra.
Opposite page top: Elephant.
Opposite page middle: Cheetah.
Opposite page bottom: Buffalo.

Top: Chimpanzee. Bottom left: Chacma baboon. Bottom right: Vervet monkey.

■ **Vervet monkey** *Chlorocebus pygerythrus*, 39-43 cm. A smallish primate and one of the most recognized monkeys in Africa. Brown bodies with a white underbelly and black face ringed by white fur, and males have blue abdominal regions. Spends the day foraging on the ground and sleeps at night in trees.

■ **Chimpanzee** *Pan troglodytes*, 0.6-1.2 m tall. A primate that is the closest living relative to a human being, with black/brown fur, and human-like fingers and toes. Uses tools, has a complex structure of communicating and displays emotions, including laughing out loud.

■ **Chacma baboon** *Papio ursinus*. An adult male baboon is slender and weighs about 40 kg. Their general colour is a brownish grey, with lighter undersides. Usually seen in trees, but rocks can also provide sufficient protection, they occur in large family troops and have a reputation for being aggressive where they have become used to the presence of humans.

Larger antelopes

■ **Beisa oryx** *Oryx beisa*, 122 cm. Also known as the East African oryx, there are two sub-species; the **common Beisa oryx** is found in semi-desert areas north of the Tana River, while the **fringe-eared oryx** is found south of the Tana River and in Tanzania. Both look similar with grey coats, white underbellies, short chestnut-coloured mane, and both sexes have long straight ringed horns. They gather in herds of up to 40.

■ **Common waterbuck** *Kobus ellipsiprymnus* and **Defassa waterbuck** *Kobus defassa*, 122-137 cm. Very similar with shaggy coats and white markings on buttocks: on the common variety, this is a clear half ring on the rump and around the tail; on the Defassa, the ring is a filled-in solid area. Both species occur in small herds in grassy areas, often near water.

Top: Beisa oryx. Bottom left: Defassa waterbuck. Bottom right: Common waterbuck.

■ **Sable antelope** *Hippotragus niger*, 140-145 cm, and **Roan antelope** *Hippotragus equinus* 127-137 cm. Both are similar in shape, with ringed horns curving backwards (both sexes), longer in the sable. Female sables are reddish brown and can be mistaken for the roan. Males are very dark with a white underbelly. The roan has distinct tufts of hair at the tips of its long ears. The sable prefers wooded areas and the roan is generally only seen near water. Both species live in herds.

■ **Greater kudu** *Tragelaphus strepsiceros*, 140-153 cm. Colour varies from greyish to fawn with several vertical white stripes down the sides of the body. Horns long and spreading, with two or three twists (male only). Distinctive thick fringe of hair running from the chin down the neck. Found in fairly thick bush, sometimes in quite dry areas. Usually lives in family groups of up to six, but occasionally in larger herds of up to about 30.

■ **Topi** *Damaliscus korrigum*, 122-127 cm. Very rich dark rufous, with dark patches on the tops of the legs and more ordinary looking, lyre-shaped horns.

Top: Greater kudu. **Middle:** Sable antelope. **Bottom:** Topi.

■ **Hartebeest** The horns arise from a bony protuberance on the top of the head and curve outwards and backwards. There are two sub-species: **Coke's hartebeest** *Alcephalus buselaphus*, 122 cm, is a drab pale brown with a paler rump; **Lichtenstein's hartebeest** *Alcephalus lichtensteinii*, 127-132 cm, is also fawn in colour, with a rufous wash over the back and dark marks on the front of the legs and often a dark patch near the shoulder. All are found in herds, sometimes they mix with other plains dwellers such as zebra.

Top: White-bearded wildebeest. Middle: Coke's hartebeest. Bottom: Eland.

■ **White-bearded wildebeest** *Connochaetes taurinus*, 132 cm. Distinguished by its white beard and smooth cow-like horns, often seen grazing with zebra. Gathers in large herds, following the rains.
■ **Eland** *Taurotragus oryx*, 175-183 cm. The largest of the antelope, it has a noticeable dewlap and shortish spiral horns (both sexes). Greyish to fawn, sometimes with rufous tinge and narrow white stripes down side of body. Occurs in groups of up to 30 in grassy habitats.

Smaller antelope

■ **Bushbuck** *Tragelaphus scriptus*, 76-92 cm. Shaggy coat with white spots and stripes on the side and back and two white, crescent-shaped marks on neck. Short horns (male only), slightly spiral. High rump gives characteristic crouch. White underside of tail is noticeable when running. Occurs in thick bush, often near water, in pairs or singly.

■ **Kirk's dikdik** *Rhynchotragus kirkii*, 36-41 cm. So small it cannot be mistaken, it is greyish brown, often washed with rufous. Legs are thin and stick-like. Slightly elongated snout and a conspicuous tuft of hair on the top of the head. Straight, small horns (male only). Found in bush country, singly or in pairs.

■ **Steenbok** *Raphicerus campestris*, 58 cm. An even, rufous brown with clean white underside and white ring around eye. Small dark patch at the tip of the nose and long broad ears. The horns (male only) are slightly longer than the ears: they are sharp, smooth and curve slightly forward. Generally seen alone, prefers open plains and more arid regions. A slight creature that usually runs off very quickly on being spotted.

■ **Bohor reedbuck** *Redunca redunca*, 71-76 cm. Horns (males only) sharply hooked forwards at the tip, distinguishing them from the oribi (see page xiii). It is reddish fawn with white underparts and has a short bushy tail. It usually lives in pairs or in small family groups. Often seen with oribi, in bushed grassland and always near water.

■ **Grant's gazelle** *Gazella granti*, 81-99 cm, and **Thomson's gazelle** *Gazella thomsonii*, 64-69 cm (see page xii). Colour varies from a bright rufous to a sandy rufous. Grant's is the larger of the two and has longer horns. In both species the curved horns are carried by both sexes.

■ **Common (Grimm's) duiker** *Sylvicapra grimmia*, 58 cm (see page xii). Grey-fawn colour with darker rump and pale colour on the underside. Its dark muzzle and prominent ears are divided by straight, upright, narrow pointed horns. This particular species is the only duiker found in open grasslands. Usually the duiker is associated with a forested environment. It is difficult to see because it is shy and will quickly disappear into the bush.

■ **Oribi** *Ourebia ourebi*, 61 cm (see page xiii). Slender and delicate looking with a longish neck and a sandy to brownish-fawn coat. It has oval-shaped ears and short, straight horns with a few rings at their base (male only). Like the reedbuck, it has a patch of bare skin just below each ear. Lives in small groups or as a pair and is never far from water.

Above: Bushbuck.

■ **Suni** *Nesotragus moschatus*, 37 cm (see page xiii). Dark chestnut to grey-fawn in colour with slight speckles along the back, its head and neck are slightly paler and the throat is white. It has a distinctive bushy tail with a white tip. Its longish horns (male only) are thick, ribbed and slope backwards. They live alone and prefer dense bush cover and reed beds.

Top: Kirk's dikdik. **Bottom left**: Bohor reedbuck. **Bottom right**: Steenbok.

■ **Impala** *Aepyceros melampus*, 92-107 cm. One of the largest of the smaller antelope, the impala is a bright rufous colour on its back and has a white abdomen, a white 'eyebrow' and chin and white hair inside its ears. From behind, the white rump with black stripes on each side is characteristic and makes it easy to identify. It has long lyre-shaped horns (male only). Above the heels of the hind legs is a tuft of thick black bristles (unique to impala), which are easy to see when the animal runs. There is also a black mark on the side of abdomen, just in front of the back leg. Found in herds of 15 to 20, it likes open grassland or sometimes the cover of partially wooded areas and is usually close to water.

Top: Thomson's gazelle. **Bottom:** Common duiker.

Top left: Oribi. **Top right:** Suni. **Bottom:** Impala.

Other mammals

There are many other fascinating mammals worth keeping an eye out for. This is a selection of some of the more interesting or particularly common ones.

■ **African wild dog** or **hunting dog** *Lycacon pictus*. Easy to identify since they have all the features of a large mongrel dog: a large head and slender body. Their coat is a mixed pattern of dark shapes and white and yellow patches and no two dogs are quite alike. They are very rarely seen and are seriously threatened with extinction (there may be as few as 6000 left). Found on the open plains around dead animals, they are not in fact scavengers but effective pack hunters.

■ **Spotted hyena** *Crocuta crocuta*. High shoulders and low back give the hyena its characteristic appearance and reputedly it has the strongest jaws in the animal kingdom. The spotted variety, larger and brownish with dark spots, has a large head and rounded ears. The **striped hyena**, slightly smaller, has pointed ears and several distinctive black vertical stripes around its torso and is more solitary. Although sometimes shy animals, they have been known to wander around campsites stealing food from humans.

Top: African wild dog.
Middle: Spotted hyena.
Bottom: Black-backed jackal.

■ **Black-backed jackal** *Canis mesomelas*, 30-40 cm tall. Also known as the silver-back jackal, a carnivore with dog-like features, a long muzzle, bushy tail and pointed ears. So-called for the strip of black hair that runs from the back of the neck to the tail.

■ **Warthog** *Phacochoerus aethiopicus*. The warthog is almost hairless and grey with a very large head, tusks and wart-like growths on its face. It frequently occurs in family parties and when startled will run away at speed with its tail held straight up in the air. They are often seen near water caking themselves in thick mud, which helps to keep them both cool and free of ticks and flies.

■ **Rock hyrax** *Procavia capensis*. The nocturnal rock hyrax lives in colonies amongst boulders and on rocky hillsides, protecting themselves from predators like eagles, caracals and leopards by darting into rock crevices.

■ **Caracal** *Felis caracal*. Also known as the African lynx, it is twice the weight of a domestic cat, with reddish sandy-coloured fur and paler underparts. Distinctive black stripe from eye to nose and tufts on ears. Generally nocturnal and with similar habits to the leopard. They are not commonly seen, but are found in hilly country.

Top: Warthog. **Middle:** Rock hyrax. **Bottom:** Caracal.

in small *bandas*. Quiet and relaxing atmosphere with an attractive bar and good homely cooking. The surrounding savannah plain and riverine forest is ideal for birdwatching and fishing.

C-F Red Chilli Rest Camp, T0414-223903, T0312-202903, T077-250 9150 (mob), www.redchillihideaway.com. Previously the Paraa Rest Camp south of the river, close to the ferry. 7 standard twin *bandas*, another 3 en suite, and 2 family *bandas* containing 2 2-bed rooms with fans, a living room, bathroom and veranda. There are 12 large twin safari tents and 2 communal bathroom blocks. Across the road is a separate campsite for overlanders and people with their own tents, with a bathroom block and barbecue food preparation area. Spacious restaurant opens from 0630 to midnight, last orders at 2100, and a well-stocked bar beneath a thatched roof. Power generated until around midnight and there are plans for solar power. Pre-booking at the Kampala office is advisable. Bargain 3-day safari tour from Kampala to MFNP, US$240; for an extra US$45 you can visit Ziwa Rhino Sanctuary (see page 126) en route.

E-F Rabongo Forest Camp, bookings via UWA, T0414-680793, mfnp@ugandawildlife.

org. In the southeast of the park, 1½ hrs' drive from Paraa, in an area of riverine forest surrounded by savannah grassland supporting large herbivores such as elephants and buffaloes. It is an important forest for biodiversity. Accommodation at Forest Cottages Hostel, a wooden cabin with 2 bedrooms, or camp at **Waringo River Camp**. Meals are not available. The Rabongo Forest Ecotourism Centre staff can arrange guided walks through the forest where several primate species live, including black and white colobus monkeys, red-tailed monkeys, baboons and, if you're lucky, chimpanzees.

Camping

There are basic **UWA** campsites at the top of Murchison Falls, 1 hr from Paraa by 4WD and Rabongo Forest. Toilets/pit latrines and showers or bathing shelters are provided. Alternatively, a group of fully self-sufficient 12 or more adults can sleep at the **Wilderness Campsite**, a UWA Category A site, at US$210 per night, accompanied by an armed ranger who may stay in your vehicle to keep it secure. Advanced booking is required at the park office in Masindi (see page 127). A cheaper option is staying at the basic Category B public campsite.

Kaniyo-Pabidi Forest Reserve → *Colour map 1, B2.*

Kaniyo-Pabidi Forest Reserve is incorporated into the Murchison Falls National Park. Highlights of the park include the mighty mahogany and ironwood trees. Occasionally lions, leopards and buffalo can be seen and Pabidi Hill offers views over Murchison Falls Park, Lake Albert and DR Congo. The River Waiga runs through the site and there are many salt licks to attract wild animals, as well as a birdwatching trail and chimpanzee tracking. It's best in the early morning, so an overnight stay is a good idea, but be prepared for the nocturnal blood-curdling screams of the hyrax.

Ins and outs

Getting there Like Busingiro (see page 129), Kaniyo-Pabidi is accessed from Masindi, 29 km away, via the road north to Paraa. There's no public transport, but it may be possible to hire a vehicle in Masindi or take a *boda-boda* for about US$9 (or more if the rangers make the driver pay park entry fees).

Park information US$30 entry fee, chimpanzee tracking fee US$40 per person, birdwatching fee US$10/15 for three/eight hours, 90-minute guided forest walks US$10, four-hour climb up Pabidi Hill US$15. There's an eco-tourism site with a visitor centre, accommodation and restaurant serving good meals. Chimpanzee habituation sessions lasting five to 10 hours accompanying the field researchers are available for up to two adults per day (not July-September), US$100 per person.

Kaniyo-Pabidi Forest Reserve listings

For Sleeping and Eating price codes and other relevant information, see Essentials pages 21-23.

Sleeping

AL-A Cabins and dorms, bookings through Uganda Lodges Ltd, T04142-67153, T077-242 6368 (mob), www.ugandalodges.com/lodges/budongo. Hidden in the forest are 5 well-appointed en suite solar-powered cabins sleeping 1-3. 4 spacious 4-bed dorms with shared bathrooms. Prices for cabins and dorms includes either breakfast or half board. Pre-booking is advised; US$5 surcharge if you pay on site.

Bugungu Game Reserve

Bugungu Game Reserve is located in the Masindi District, immediately south of Murchison Falls National Park, separated from Lake Albert to the west by a narrow strip of land gazetted as a Controlled Hunting Area. Budongo Forest Reserve lies to the south and east. The reserve encompasses the escarpment of the western arm of the Rift Valley. The density of the woodland decreases as it descends to the foot of the escarpment, and by Lake Albert there is bushland. The reserve contains similar animal and bird species as the park, but is also believed to be one of few remaining places where the endangered red-flanked duiker *Cephalophus rufilatus* survives. There are no tourist facilities.

Bulisa → *Colour map 1, B2.*

There are many tsetse flies in the area and little to recommend a stay. From the small village of Bulisa it is 18 km to the park gate, and 23 km to the Paraa ferry.

There is a simple lodge, **Bulisa Corner Guest House (F-G)**, with very basic facilities and friendly staff. A US$30 visitation fee for Murchison Falls National Park is payable at the gate. See page 131, for details of transport to Murchison Falls National Park.

Wanseko → *Colour map 1, B2.*

This small town lies on the shore of Lake Albert close to the Nile estuary about 6 km northwest of Bulisa. It is extremely hot and plagued with huge numbers of mosquitoes at night. The sight of women drying thousands of small fish on the sandy shore against the backdrop of the Blue Mountains in DR Congo beyond Lake Albert, and its small fishing boats, is magnificent. Wanseko has few facilities, but there is a wide variety of birdlife living in the reed beds near the estuary. See page 131, for details of transport to Murchison Falls National Park.

For Sleeping and Eating price codes and other relevant information, see Essentials pages 21-23.

Sleeping
F New Blue Room Lodge, located on a side road. Of a similar standard to **Paramount Pub and Lodge**, but probably the better option, because the *matatus* don't park in the yard, with the accompanying noise in the early morning.

F-G Paramount Pub and Lodge, along the main road. Very cheap and basic. The metal roof means that the rooms are horrifyingly hot with little respite at night.

Transport
The bus to **Masindi** stops overnight here, leaving very early in the morning.

Contents

Footprint features

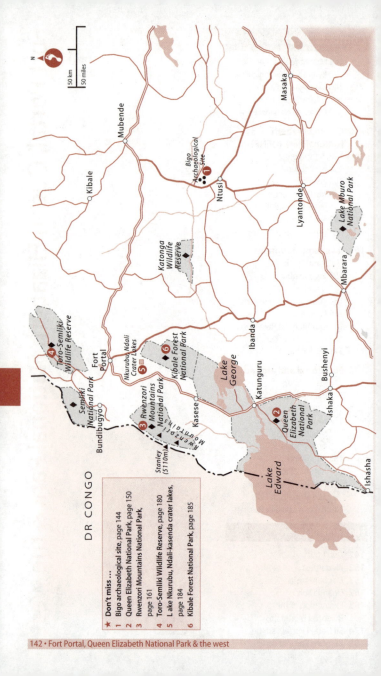

Don't miss...

★

1 Bigo archaeological site, page 144
2 Queen Elizabeth National Park, page 150
3 Rwenzori Mountains National Park, page 161
4 Toro-Semliki Wildlife Reserve, page 180
5 Lake Nkurubu, Ndali-kasenda crater lakes, page 184
6 Kibale Forest National Park, page 185

Most travellers to Fort Portal will go on the main road via Mubende. It allows for a visit to the Bwera archaeological sites with the impressive but rarely visited earthworks at Bigo or the Katonga Wildlife Reserve.

The Mbarara–Kasese road passes through the huge Queen Elizabeth National Park; when crossing the Kazinga Channel it neatly bisects Lake Edward and Lake George. The park allows a good chance of seeing a lot of game including lion and elephants. Many take a cruise along the Kazinga Channel to see pods of hippos and some brilliant birdlife, or visit the chimpanzees in the Kyambura River Gorge.

Kasese is the gateway to the Rwenzori Mountains, the fabled 'Mountains of the Moon'. The border between Uganda and DR Congo runs along the mountain peaks, demonstrating a huge change in vegetation as you climb to the icefields of Mount Stanley, the third highest peak in Africa at 5110 m.

Fort Portal, splendidly located in tea country in the west of Uganda, gives easy access to the Toro-Semliki Wildlife Reserve at the southern end of Lake Albert, Uganda's other royal lake. Hop over the northern spur of the Rwenzori mountains and you can experience the huge Central African rainforest which stretches for thousands of miles to the west in the Semliki National Park proper with its hot springs at Sempaya.

Other attractions around Fort Portal are chimp tracking in the Kibale Forest National Park. This may not be anything like as exciting as gorilla tracking but it does give you a chance to experience chimpanzees in the wild and many more types of monkeys in the dense forest. Consider too cycling around the extraordinary Ndali-Kasenda crater lakes, an ideal place to stop and relax for a couple of days as there are lovely trails connecting the lakes.

Mubende and the Bwera archaeological sites

→ Phone code: 04644. Colour map 2, B3.

From Kampala to Mubende the road is sealed, with major upgrading works in progress on the Kampala–Mityana section. It passes through swampy areas with graceful papyrus beds and woodlands scattered with acacia trees. **Mubende** is a small town, halfway between Kampala and Fort Portal, and vehicles tend to stop here for snacks and drinks; the barbecued chicken on wooden skewers is particularly good. You may wish to stay a night if you are visiting the Nakayima shrine or the archaeological sites at Bigo and Ntusi. Mubende's best hotel is the good-value **Town View Hotel (E-F)**, with no view but a restaurant, sited up the hill opposite Stanbic bank. The Bigo site is difficult to access, 13 km from the main road, and a 4WD is required, or a lift on a *boda-boda* . The Ntusi site is easier to visit, being closer to the road, but is rather less interesting.

Nakayima Shrine

Sited on top of Mubende Hill about 4 km out of town, this is variously spelt Nyakaima, Nakaima or Nyakahuma, an ancient 'witch tree', the base of which has large root buttresses forming nooks and fissures. The 213-m hill, with a flat tabletop where an ancient palace once stood, provides an excellent vista of Mubende town and the surrounding area. The shrine is visited by people paying homage to the matriarch Nakayima of the Bacwezi, a dynasty said to have supernatural powers, which have passed into legend as demi-gods. Nakayima died in 1907. At the tree you can make a wish by giving a coffee bean and a small donation that is placed into the nooks formed by the tree's roots; a local woman explains the shrine. Local people with important wishes may offer chickens, sheep, goats and, reportedly, even cows.

Bigo archaeological site

ⓘ *There are 3 possible approaches to the Bigo site, all about 13 km from the main road. They can be negotiated by 4WD vehicles or motorcycle for most of the way, with a hike of about 3 km for the final approach. It is a good idea to engage a local person as guide when leaving the main road. Coming from Mubende, the first turn-off is at Makole where it is possible to strike east along a track towards the Katonga River and then to the Bigo site. Further along the road from Mubende to Masaka is Ntusi, with a track leading north from just opposite the District Offices, the route following the Bigaga River and passing 2 dams. Finally at Bukiroga, about 8 km beyond Ntusi, is a track to the north, which follows the Kakinga River. Again 2 dams are passed on the way. These descriptions of the Bigo earthworks (and Ntusi, later) are based on Ntusi and Bigo by John Sutton in Azania, 1998, where more detailed accounts can be found.*

This site in the Bwera region appears to have been a significant late Iron Age settlement. Radiocarbon dating suggests that it flourished at some time between AD 1300 and AD 1500, and was then abandoned in the latter half of the 16th century. There are very extensive earthworks, with substantial ditches clearly visible although overgrown with vegetation in places. Excavations

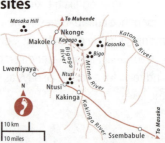

Bwera archaeological sites

at the site have yielded iron blades (most probably used for harvesting grain), pottery with simple decoration, cattle dung and post holes for fencing. The inner ditches were probably developed first and, with strategic mounds, provided a fortified central site for the community. The large area contained by the outer ditches suggests it was extended to provide a secure area for cattle and possibly cultivation of grain such as millet. The nearby Katonga River would have supplied water for the community and its cattle. The northern side is protected by swamps and the Katonga River. The southern outer perimeter comprises about 5 km of ditches and these fortifications enclose more than 4 sq km.

A sophisticated social structure would have been required, first to establish such a settlement, comprising as it did extensive ditches, embankments, fences and gates, and then to man and maintain it for more than 200 years. There is little indication of the identity of the group ruling at Bigo, but it is likely that they were Hima cattle herders in some sort of alliance with Iru cultivators.

In colonial times the site became known as Bigo Bya Mugenyi, which means 'Fort of Mugenyi'. This suggests a dynasty established by Mugenyi, with a royal residence in the inner area surrounded by a huge cattle kraal. Mugenyi would be from the Bacwezi, a people about whom little is known, but who have passed into legend as demi-gods. Some scholars have argued that association of the site with Mugenyi is a recent invention.

What precipitated the decline of Bigo is not known; its demise coincided with the rise of the cattle herding Bunyoro to the north, the Ankole to the south, and the banana-cultivating Buganda to the east. The longer a dynasty endures, the greater the likelihood of it being destroyed by internal conflicts and disputes over inheritance. Expansion of herds and the population would tend to deplete grazing and wood supplies for fuel, and these were probably contributing factors. Today visitors are left to marvel at the sheer scale of the settlement, the outer ditches, ramparts, fences and gateways stretching 3 km from east to west, enclosing cattle and cultivation, and topped by a central compound 500 m wide with impressive thatched dwellings for the ruler and his entourage.

The remains of two forts of considerably smaller dimensions can be found at **Kasonko**, 5 km northeast of Bigo and at **Kagago**, 3 km northwest. They consist of a rampart and a ditch sunk into the slopes of small hills and do not have inner fortifications. It is believed that the constructors of Bigo also built these as part of an all-round defensive system.

Ntusi archaeological settlement

Ntusi appears to have been the site of a substantial settlement of both cattle herders and cultivators. Evidence from radiocarbon dating of fragments found at the site suggests it existed between the

Ntusi archaeological sites

To Bigo

North Hill

Bwogero

To Mubende

Ntusi 'Male' Mound

Ntusi 'Female' Mound

Shops & Stalls

To Masaka

Ntusi Administrative Offices

N

Mounds

400 metres

400 yards

11th and 13th centuries. Near to the present-day Ntusi settlement are two substantial mounds, 4 m high, known as Ntusi 'Male' and Ntusi 'Female', surrounded by many smaller mounds. Excavations have yielded pottery, cattle bones and odd items such as ivory carvings, ostrich eggshell beads, glass beads and copper items. Archaeological interpretation is that these mounds were domestic rubbish heaps, and charred fragments suggest they were periodically burnt off to dispose of rotting material. To the north of the large mounds are a series of depressions, known as *bwogero*, which are thought to have been excavated to provide shallow ponds for watering cattle in dry periods.

Further to the north again is a hill on which signs of dwellings have been found. The dwellings appear to have been of timber frame and thatched roof construction, haphazardly grouped, with no signs of regular streets that would indicate a town. The pottery fragments have roulette decoration made by pressing a piece of toothed wood, or knotted fibre, into the clay. Kaolin (used as a type of plaster for walls) and slip (thinned clay for sealing and decorating) have also been found. The Ntusi Cylinder is an unusual clay object covered with protuberances and several holes, about 14 cm long and 8 cm in diameter. It was discovered at Ntusi in 1944, and is now housed in the Uganda Museum (see page 57). The function of the cylinder is not certain; holes at either end may have allowed wooden handles to be inserted, and the cylinder used as a roller for crushing or flattening.

Ntusi does not have defences like Bigo, leading to speculation that it may have been a satellite community ruled from Bigo, with Ntusi inhabitants retreating behind the Bigo battlements when under attack.

Katonga Wildlife Reserve → *Colour map 2, B2.*

The 207-sq-km Katonga Wildlife Reserve was gazetted in 1964 as a game reserve. It was a corridor for migrating wildlife in search of water prior to the civil unrest of the 1970-1980s, and now much of the land is utilized by the nomadic hamites – Bahima – who graze their large herds of long-horned Ankole cattle. The area is mixed savannah with acacia woodlands, and a few pockets of tropical and riverine forest. A large proportion of the reserve is wetlands, either permanent or seasonal.

Ins and outs

Getting there The most direct route is via the Kampala–Mubende–Fort Portal road. At 48 km past Mubende, at the small town of Kyegegwa, take the left turn in a southerly direction. This unmade road takes you through the villages of Mpara and Karwenyi before reaching the reserve headquarters close to the Katonga River. Katonga is 42 km from Kyegegwa. A 4WD is needed during the rainy season. The journey time from Kampala is about three hours. By public transport there are frequent *matatus* and buses to Kyegegwa. From here *matatus* run south, depending on road and weather conditions, as far as Karwenyi. From here walking is possible or hire a bicycle taxi. There is one taxi that will go direct to Katonga on request through Kyegegwa from Kampala's new taxi park.

An alternative route is to take the Kampala–Mbarara road. Shortly after Lyantonde, take the road north at Nakaiita to Kazo, passing through several small settlements (including Nyakashashara, Nsikisi, Rwensunga and Rushere) until you reach Kenshunga. Here, take the road north to Kazo and then follow the road northeast to Kabagole. From Kabagole it is just a short canoe trip across the Katonga River to the reserve. There is a bus service from Mbarara to Kabagole, or *matatus* via Lyantonde. Kabagole can also be accessed from the Fort Portal–Mbarara road at Ruhoko, which is a short distance to Ibanda. From here, take the road east to Kazo via the small towns of Rwomuhoro, Kanoni and Kitongore. From Kazo take the road north to Kabagole.

Park information Entry fee US$20. The reserve is rarely visited. UWA discourages tour groups coming here and is currently handing management over to a private company. Contact UWA before coming, T04143-455000, info@ugandawildlife.org. Overnight trips into the undeveloped interior can be organized, but not during the rainy season. This is really only an option for the very fit as there are no facilities and you have to take everything with you. Accommodation is limited to camping, at US$9 per night (plus the reserve entry fee). The campsite is located on a hill overlooking the river valley. It has a small canteen, or you can order meals through a local women's group. Another option is to cross the Katonga River by canoe and stay in the small town of Kabagole, south of the railway.

Wildlife

Katonga is one of the few places in Africa to have a large population of the extremely shy and reclusive sitatunga antelope, whose favoured habitat is papyrus swamps. Other mammals include elephant, hippo, black and white colobus monkeys, olive baboon, Uganda kob, waterbuck, duiker and reedbuck. The wetlands support a population of river otter, along with various reptiles and amphibians. In addition there are over 150 species of birds recorded. The reserve has no roads at present, but three trails have been developed to allow visitors the opportunity to see the various ecosystems within Katonga. The early morning walk along the **Sitatunga Trail** offers the best opportunity to spot the timid antelope. Other mammals are frequently seen as you walk through the savannah and later alongside the Katonga river. The **Kyeibale Trail** is a circular trek through the scrubland into the remnants of the forests, passing interesting rock formations and caves used for shelter by the animals. The **Kisharara Trail** traverses the savannah to the wetland canal, follows the Katonga River and continues up one of the tributaries through a variety of ecosystems, offering the visitor an opportunity to see the sitatunga antelope and various primates as well as other mammals and birdlife. Uniquely, it is also possible to explore the reserve by canal. The **Wetlands Canal Trail** is a 2-km ride through the reed and papyrus swamp, guided by a local boat operator and accompanied by a ranger, allowing the best opportunity to spot wetland mammals such as the otter, and an abundance of birds including kingfishers and storks.

Mbarara to Queen Elizabeth National Park → *Colour map 2, B1/2.*

Bushenyi is accessed on the road to the southwest via Mbarara, which forks north to Queen Elizabeth National Park, Kasese and Fort Portal shortly after Mbarara. Bushenyi is the district centre and there is a hospital and a few small shops selling basic household merchandise. There are several hotels, a couple of cheap guesthouses, restaurants serving local food, a pub and two petrol stations. Bushenyi also has a bank and post office.

The road from Bushenyi to **Ishaka**, a larger town 6 km west of Bushenyi, and then on to Kasese is tarmac and in excellent condition. There are very good pineapples for sale on the road opposite Ishaka's Seventh Day Adventist Hospital, with the most surly salesmen in East Africa. If you are visiting the southern sector of the Queen Elizabeth National Park (see page 159), a much shorter alternative if coming from Kampala is to go via Ishaka to Rukungiri. It is not a well-signposted route; Ishaka is on the main Kasese–Bushenyi–

Mbarara road, 6 km west of Bushenyi. From Ishaka take the road south to Rwashamaire and then west to Rukungiri. If you are travelling independently there are *matatus* from Ishaka to Rukungiri. From Rukungiri head for Ishasha village and a few kilometres before you reach it the road joins the main road from Katunguru. Turn up this road and follow it for 7 km to the entrance gate. If you do not have your own vehicle you will have to get off at this junction and walk it or try to hitch a lift to the entrance gate. Once at the gate it is another 7 km to the camp.

Kalinzu Central Forest Reserve

ⓘ *US$15, guides cost US$15 for day treks, night treks US$20, chimpanzee tracking US$50, camping US$9pp, reservations T077-245 8389 (mob). The eco-tourism site contains a campsite within the forest with basic facilities, but you need to be self sufficient. Basic supplies can be bought at Butare Trading Centre, 9 km from the campsite on the Mbarara–Kasese road.* Kalinzu Central Forest Reserve is situated 10 km northwest of Ishaka on the main Mbarara–Kasese road. Sited on top of an escarpment on the eastern edge of the Albertine Rift Valley, it is adjacent to but outside Queen Elizabeth National Park (QENP) and Maramagambo Forest. It is a cheaper option than visiting Maramagambo Forest as entry fees are half the national park fees and it can easily be reached using public transport.

Over 400 species of trees and shrubs have been identified including *Ficus*, *Prunus Africana* and *Stroboia*. There is a fine example of a flame tree, a dragon tree and a viagra tree. There are many fig trees that provide bark-cloth, widely used in the local craft industry. The forest is rich in birdlife with over 370 varieties identified. There are nine primate species here, including chimpanzees, blue monkeys, black and white colobus and vervet monkeys. Two groups of about 70 chimpanzees have been habituated enabling them to be tracked by visitors, currently restricted to four a day. These chimpanzees have been observed ant dipping nests of driver ants, later confirmed by faecal analysis. The forest is also rich in butterflies, moths and reptiles and gets occasional visitors from QENP including leopards, wild pigs and duikers.

Guided and unguided walks along several trails following the contours of the scenic Rift Valley escarpment are available. Four forest trails have been developed. The 2.5-km circular **River Trail** takes an hour and follows the course of the Kajojo (Elephant) River, named after a historically favoured bathing place. There is also a 5-km **Palm Trail** taking two hours, a 3.5-km **Valley Trail** and a **Waterfall Trail** taking four to five hours to complete, covering hilly terrain to the Kilyantama Waterfall, known locally as the 'sheep eater'. Night treks to see nocturnal wildlife like pottos or owls are enhanced by the eerie shrieks of the hyrax.

Kasyoha Kitomi Forest Reserve

This forest is about 35 km north of Ishaka. Set between two crater lakes the forest overlooks the Albertine Rift Valley. Kasyoha Kitomi Forest supports a large biodiversity of forest flora and fauna. The forest is home to many chimpanzees. Within the reserve are Chemo and Mweru crater lakes and further in is Lake Kamunzuku, the 'transparent' lake. The **Ndekye Women's Development Association** hope to develop eco-tourism facilities shortly.

Bushenyi to Queen Elizabeth National Park

From Bushenyi to Kasese the landscape is very hilly and at first the road goes up and down through forested hills, before it reaches the escarpment down to the Rift Valley. Just before descending the escarpment you pass the trading centre of Kichwamba, where a signpost on the eastern side of the road directs you to the Maramagambo Forest (see page 157), part of the Queen Elizabeth National Park, with a campsite and the **Jacana Safari Lodge**. From the cooler heights you descend into the hotter, dustier floor of the Rift Valley that is crossed by the road, passing through the Queen Elizabeth National Park. The vegetation around is mainly acacia bush and the grass is sprinkled with occasional ant hills. On the floor of the valley, just 2 km further to the north, the track to **Kyambura Gorge** (sometimes spelt Chambura), see page 157, is signposted to the right as 'Fig Tree Camp, 2 km'. This is again part of the Queen Elizabeth National Park. The tarmac road continues atop a causeway, which crosses the Kazinga Channel at Katuguru, a natural channel that connects Lake George to Lake Edward.

Here you can turn left and enter the main part of the Queen Elizabeth National Park. The northernmost part of the park is the area of the crater lakes, with fresh or alkaline water.

A bit further along on the road to Kasese you cross from the southern to the northern hemisphere; on each side of the road there is a large round wheel marking the **equator**. Note in reality the equator actually lies 500 m north of this spot, just at the start of the Equator road going to DR Congo. This is unlikely to have any effect on the putative coriolis force effect on water drainage. Nearby is the **Queen's Pavilion**, containing the new **UWA information centre** ⓘ *by the northern park border and park entrance, at the beginning of the Crater Drive road, on the eastern side of the main road, T077-423 0938, T077-262 5125 (both mob), daily 0900-1730*. The Queen's Pavilion was first built in 1959 to mark the visit of Queen Elizabeth II to Uganda and renovated in 2007 for the visit of Prince Philip, to include an internet café, coffee shop and nearby craft shops. The nearest village is Kikorongo. At this park boundary the main Kasese–Ishaka road divides, with a westwards branch going towards Mpondwe, Bwera and the border with DR Congo.

The countryside around is mixed bush with cultivation, including cotton, for many years Uganda's most important cash crop.

Queen Elizabeth National Park (QENP)

→ *Colour map 2, B1.*

The QENP lies across the equator in the southwest of Uganda. It is bordered to the southwest by Lake Edward and to the northeast by Lake George. The two lakes are joined together by the 33-km-long Kazinga Channel. The park covers an area of 1978 sq km, with mainly flat and gently undulating terrain that rises from the lakes to 1390 m above sea level at the crater area to the north of the Kazinga Channel. To the northeast are the Rwenzori mountains, often known as the 'Mountains of the Moon', which rise to over 5000 m. On a clear day it is possible to see the Rwenzoris from the park.

Ins and outs

Getting there

There are two bases for touring the park: **Mweya Safari Lodge** in the north (see page 154) and its environs is the main one, and the more remote **Ishasha River Camp** (see page 159) in the southwest.

Visitor information

The main park booking office is the recently built **Mweya Visitor Information Centre** ① *100 m from the gate at Mweya Safari Lodge (see page 154).* It has information on game drive routes and accommodation and sells maps and postcards. It has a topographic model of the park and lots of informative exhibits describing the park within its Rift Valley setting. There is an outdoor decking area where visitors can sip a drink and enjoy the fantastic views of Katwe Bay, Lake Edward and the Rwenzori Mountains 45 km away.

Park information is also available at the Queen's Pavilion, see page 149.´

There are simple **sub-headquarters** in the southern section of the park, which receives relatively few visitors, at UWA's Ishasha Camp, on the east bank of the Ishasha River, set back about 500 m from the river on the southern (road) circuit.

Background

Prehistory

In the early 1930s Sir Vivian Fuchs discovered fossils from the Early Pleistocene Period along the Kazinga Channel, but it was not until some years later that prehistoric material was found. Fossils of water snails and other molluscs, crocodiles, hippos (including the pygmy variety), members of the pig family and various fish including Nile perch have all been found.

No tools belonging to the Early Pleistocene have been found in the fossiliferous ironstone bands, which are readily seen outcropping along the Kazinga Channel. Elsewhere in Africa this was an important period in human evolution, and in East Africa ape men of the Australopithecine family were beginning to make recognizable stone tools and become effective hunters rather than scavengers. Over a large area of the park, and possibly as far north as Murchison Falls, transient lakes existed in the comparatively shallow trough of the Rift Valley. It seems that the early palaeolithic hunters lived around these lakes, hunting their prey; the bones of that prey are now often found in the ironstone bands.

Following the faulting in the Middle Pleistocene, the Rift Valley became more pronounced and the lakes more permanent. Stone tools found in the deposits from the period have been hand axes of quartz and quartzite, and pebble tools, which are water-worn pebbles flaked to give a sharp cutting edge.

At Mweya, on the peninsula of land leading to the present lodge, stone tools dating from a slightly later period have been found in gravels. The material found in a 1958 excavation consisted of all the types of tools of a fully developed Acheulean hand axe culture: hand axes, cleavers, round stone balls and waste flakes. Similar tools have also been found on the south bank of the Kazinga Channel.

Queen Elizabeth National Park

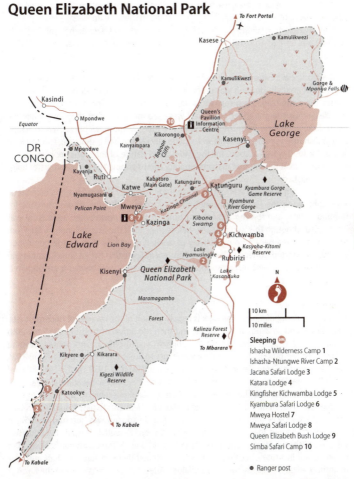

Sleeping
Ishasha Wilderness Camp **1**
Ishasha-Ntungwe River Camp **2**
Jacana Safari Lodge **3**
Katara Lodge **4**
Kingfisher Kichwamba Lodge **5**
Kyambura Safari Lodge **6**
Mweya Hostel **7**
Mweya Safari Lodge **8**
Queen Elizabeth Bush Lodge **9**
Simba Safari Camp **10**

● Ranger post

Rinderpest

The first recorded outbreak of rinderpest in East Africa occurred in 1889 in what was then Somaliland. It is generally believed that the disease followed the introduction of cattle from India and Aden for use by the Italian army during the first expedition to Abyssinia. Once established, rinderpest spread like wildfire over the whole of East Africa, reaching Lake Tanzania by 1890.

The devastation resulting from the disease was terrible. The explorer Sir Frederick Lugard tells of the misery and suffering that the pastoral tribes, such as the Masai and the Bahima, endured as a result of this disease. Many were made destitute with cattle mortality rates generally over 90%. In some areas, not a single animal survived. It is believed that many people also perished along with their animals, often of malnutrition. Many species of game were almost exterminated; buffalo, eland, warthog and wild pig were particularly badly affected.

The stone balls were thought to be wrapped in skin, attached to thongs and used to throw at animals. Hunting was probably conducted by making drives using wooden spears. The stone-bladed hand axe was a standard tool, an all-purpose cutting implement. The cleaver (or straight-edged hand axe) was used for skinning or chopping, while the waste flakes, resulting from the making of the tools, would have been used to scrape skin and sharpen spears. The tools were made quickly and had a short life. The constant search for food would account for the widespread nature of the stone tools as well as their profusion; it is likely that many temporary camps around the lakes and water holes were established.

Judging from the large amount of waste flakes of quartz dating from the Late Stone Age, right along the Kazinga Channel, the park continued to be an area suitable for hunting, fishing and fowling until recent times. It is not known when agriculture was introduced, although this was probably before the end of the first millennium AD. From this time the area became progressively pastoral. It is unlikely that a large population was ever supported. Surface collections of pottery indicate that the Kazinga Channel and lakeshore regions, where fishing supplemented agriculture, were always more populous than the drier plains.

Modern history

The present depopulation of the park is largely a result of the ravages of rinderpest (see box, above) and smallpox in the 1890s, and then the arrival of tsetse in the early 20th century. In 1910 the seriousness of the animal trypanosomiasis and human sleeping sickness led the officials to move the inhabitants to areas free of the tsetse fly. In 1925 the Lake George Game Reserve was established, followed in 1930 by the Lake Edward Game Reserve. These were later enlarged to include the crater areas and the area south of the Kazinga Channel. The Kibale Forest Corridor Game Reserve, to the north of Lake George, was also established, to provide a corridor for elephants to pass to and from Kibale Forest. The park was renamed the Kazinga National Park and was gazetted in 1952. In 1954 it was renamed again following the visit by Queen Elizabeth II. The park headquarters were established in Mweya, and in 1960 the Nuffield Unit of Tropical Animal Ecology, later renamed the Institute of Ecology, was also developed there. In June 2010 an outbreak of anthrax killed 82 hippos and nine buffaloes. Affected were areas close to the Kazinga

Elephant tusks

In the 1930s large herds of elephants were common in Uganda, and most of the adult pachyderms had tusks. Large tusks were believed to have evolved over the years as evidence of reproductive excellence, and were used by dominant bulls to fight competitors for a mate. Elephants that failed to grow tusks were considered to be a rare mutation, affecting less than 1% of the total number.

Elephants use tusks to dig for water and roots in the dry season, and to scrape for salt, as in the caves of Mount Elgon. Elephants have a dominant tusk, just as humans have a preferred hand, which can usually be identified as it is more worn and rounded at the tip. Nowadays, an elephant with large tusks is likely to be a relatively placid, older female that has avoided having her tusks broken during fights.

Over the last few decades poachers have decimated the elephant numbers in the Queen Elizabeth National Park, reducing them from an estimated 3500 in the early 1960s to around 200, 30 years later. In the last 10 years elephant numbers have risen again, but it is rare to find any with large tusks. An estimated 33% of elephants are now tuskless.

A mutation no longer seen nowadays is an elephant with three – or, even rarer, four – tusks. One photograph of an elephant with three perfectly formed tusks, each weighing an average 23 kg, dates back to the 1950s. It was taken by an American client, accompanied by the professional hunter John Northcote in the Kigezi region, close to the Uganda/DR Congo border. Several other sightings of elephants with three or four tusks were reported at the time.

Channel and Lakes Edward and George. In 2004 over 300 hippos succumbed to anthrax and an outbreak also occurred in 1994.

Ecology

The park lies in the area of Africa where two types of vegetation meet: the rainforest which stretches out to the west for thousands of kilometres to the shores of the Atlantic, and the Eastern and Southern Africa grassland. The park, like much of Uganda, gets two rainy seasons each year, from March to May and from September to November. However, there is often rain during the rest of the year and prolonged droughts are unusual. The temperature varies from a minimum of 18°C to a maximum of 28°C.

Animals found in the park include hippos, lions including tree-climbers, elephants, buffalo, Uganda kob, waterbuck, bushbuck and topi. Smaller animals that occur but not easily seen include warthog, hyenas, mongoose, red-tailed monkey, black and white colobus monkey, baboon, vervet monkey, and chimpanzees. Giant forest hogs live in the park, too, especially on the escarpment on the way up to Mweya, just outside the Maramagambo Forest. They look rather like large shaggy warthogs for which they can be easily mistaken. The park is famous for its wide range of birdlife; an estimated 540 species have been recorded. In marshy and waterside areas larger species such as cormorants, goliath herons, egrets, spoonbills and sacred ibis can be seen. Others include fish eagles and pied kingfishers.

Wildlife reserves

QENP incorporates or lies adjacent to several wildlife reserves. In the northeast, east of the Kyambura River Gorge, is the Kyambura Wildlife Reserve within QENP. Immediately south of it is the Kasyoha Kitomi Forest Reserve (see page 148), outside the QENP boundary on the eastern side of the Kasese–Bushenyi–Mbarara road. Continuing southwest, on the western side of this road is the Kalinzu Central Forest Reserve (see page 148), also outside the QENP boundary. Kalinzu Forest Reserve abuts the Maramagambo Forest (see page 157) that lies within QENP. Southwest of Maramagambo Forest, also within QENP, is the Kigezi Wildlife Reserve (see page 159), which extends southwest to Ishasha along the eastern side of the road that runs south from Kikirara to Ishasha.

Northern sector (Mweya Safari Lodge)

This is the most frequently visited part of the park, with better access from Kampala and a wider choice of accommodation.

Ins and outs

Getting there It is 435 km from Kampala, via Mbarara, a journey that takes about six hours. The Kazinga Channel is crossed on an iron bridge and then the road carries on to the small village of Katunguru. From Katunguru there are two different routes. You can either continue on the main road towards Kasese, turning left after 5 km and then a further 15 km to the main gate at Kabatoro, passing Lake Nyamunuka. From the main gate it is 8 km to the lodge. Alternatively, you can turn left immediately after Katunguru and follow the road to the Katunguru Gate from where it is 20 km to the lodge along the Channel Track. The road from Fort Portal and Kasese in the north is sealed. The western route north from Mgahinga and Bwindi parks is gravel and some sandy sections can be difficult when wet.

From Kasese take a *matatu* going in the direction of Katwe on the north shore of Lake Edward; they go daily in the morning. Ask to be dropped off on the main road at the turning for the park entrance, which is 100 m down a track. From the gate it is about 6 km to **Mweya Lodge**; you can either try to hitch, which is not difficult, or take a special hire taxi from Katunguru, US$15.

Launch trip on the Kazinga Channel

The journey takes about two hours and you can expect to see plenty of hippos and a wide range of birdlife. For information ask at the UWA information centre (see page 149) or the desk at **Mweya Safari Lodge** (see page 158). The UWA launch goes four times a day and costs US$15 per person for 20 people. The minimum charge per cruise is US$300. The best chance of getting a group of 20 people together is at the weekend. The luxury launch trip on the 11-seater *Sunbird* costs US$18 each and the super-luxury 14-seater *Kingfisher* costs US$28 each and includes a drink and canapés. You can also organize game drives through **Mweya Safari Lodge** if you don't have your own transport, or rent a special hire in Katunguru or Kasese. A good local tour operator is Mustafa from **Kazinga Channel Tours** ① *T077-260 8614 or T070-107 3159 (both mob), kcsafari@yahoo.com*, based in Katunguru. He can arrange trips in the park and transport at very reasonable rates.

Channel track and north of the Kazinga Channel

This area is perhaps the most popular for game drives and there is a network of roads to choose the length of drive that suits you. If you plan your route well there's no need to double back on yourself. Generally, roads are passable, although after heavy rain patches of thick sticky mud may make some routes difficult. Hippo trails cross the road every so often; it has been observed that individual hippos tend to use the same route every night when they go inland to feed. If you do come across any hippos on land be sure to give them a wide berth and do not come between them and the water. There are hyenas, buffaloes, Uganda kob, and down by the Kazinga Channel are Nile monitor lizards. That most elusive of animals, the leopard, lives in this area, but is extremely difficult to spot.

Crater area

There are seven crater lakes in this area, although only four of these are accessible on the existing roads: Katwe, Kikorongo, Munyanyange and Nyamunuka. They are all alkaline although to differing degrees. The name Nyamunuka means 'animal smell' and the lake is so named because of the strong smell of sulphur that is emitted from the water. Lake Katwe is known throughout Uganda as being an area of salt production and has been producing high-quality salt for many years.

Take the track opposite the main gate at Kabatoro to the **Baboon Cliffs** and follow it through the rolling grasslands. The road is generally good although after rain there may be some muddy patches suitable only for 4WDs. The grasslands are torched regularly as the dominant plants are all species whose growth is encouraged by regular burnings. There is no permanent fresh water in this area so, apart from the rainy season (March-June) when there are often herds of buffalo and elephant, you're unlikely to see many animals. There are always plenty of birds (particularly grassland birds) and the area is especially popular with ornithologists.

The track to Baboon Cliffs is worth taking for the views alone. The road continues upwards, and thorn trees (*Acacia gerrardii*) become more common. About 12 km from Kabatoro the track ends at Baboon Cliffs, with a splendid view of the park and surrounding countryside. The crater of Kyemango is below and in the distance Lake George can be seen. To the north are the Rwenzoris and on a clear day you can see the snow caps.

Lake George and Lake Kikorongo

To follow this route travelling west, take the right turning just after the main gate at Kabatoro and drive towards and then across the main Kasese road. The track continues towards Lake George and the fishing village of Kasenyi through open grassland. About 10 km from the main road look to your left and you should be able to see a Uganda kob *lek*; see box, page 157.

Kasenyi village on the western shores of Lake George is a small fishing village due east of the open savannah area that is the Ugandan kobs' main mating and breeding grounds and thus the best area to spot lions. Kasenyi is best visited in the early morning. Access to this area has been simplified by the opening of the new Kasenyi Gate from where two tracks are seen, one runs east to Lake George and the other south towards the Channel. The Kasenyi Gate is on the eastern side of the Kasese–Ishaka road, located almost opposite the road that goes to Katwe and the main gate and therefore lies within the park boundary. Just before you reach Kasenyi village you will see the small crater lake of **Bunyampaka**, which is also used for salt panning on a small scale. You can take the track around the rim of the crater lake from Kasenyi, which will also lead you to the channel, or continue east towards Kasenyi village. Here you will see poorly clothed children running around. The villages eke a living from salt panning and fishing and live in small semi-permanent huts on the sandy lakeside soil. Hippos can be seen nearby. Alternatively, you can return along the main track and turn right after 6 km. This leads you to the village of Hamukungu; turn left and you will pass through a large swamp and then pass the crater lake of Kikorongo before reaching the main Kasese road. On this latter route you may see elephants. In the swamp there is the possibility of sighting the shoebill, while there are sometimes flamingoes in Lake Kikorongo.

Mpanga Gorge and Falls

Obscured by riparian forest, these 45-m falls are located just inside the eastern boundary of the park, in the northeast corner of Lake George. This rarely visited area, with no facilities, is of great interest to botanists as it has the world's largest collection of cycad species. These slow-growing coniferous plants are sometimes described as living fossils. *Encephalartos whitelockii* is only found in this gorge. Sadly, despite the rarity of these cycads, an American-based company called South Asia Energy Management Systems is bulldozing the cycads to construct an 18-megawatt hydroelectric dam. The ecology of the whole area is likely to be destroyed by the dam and access roads. Visits for the hardy can be made from Fort Portal or Kibale Forest with **Karibuni Safaris** ⓘ *T075-170 7287 (mob), contacts@karibusafari.co.ug.*

Lake Katwe and Pelican Point → *Colour map 2, B1.*

Pelican Point is difficult to access by car, but there is a pleasant picnic spot by a former ranger's station, overlooking the Nyamagasani Delta. To get to Lake Katwe take the left turning just after the main gate and head for the now-abandoned village of Kabatoro. About 5 km from this is Katwe town and on your right are the crater lakes of Katwe and Munyanyange. These provide Katwe inhabitants with their main sources of income: salt panning and fishing. The salt industry at Katwe is 750 years old and over many centuries has provided the local inhabitants with an important source of income. The crater lakes are outside the park boundaries so it is possible to leave your car. You are able to visit the salt works at Lake Katwe on payment of a small fee. Get a guide to show you around and explain the methods by which salt is evaporated and purified. As **Lake Munyanyange** is an alkaline lake it is sometimes the home of lesser flamingos in varying numbers. It is possible to walk around the rim of the lake.

The tiny run-down town of **Katwe**, located just outside the park boundary, receives few visitors. Local children follow you everywhere within this strangely interesting place. Travellers on a tight budget might like to come here as there is no need to pay the daily park entrance fees as at Mbeya. There is an inexpensive place to stay (**E-F**) outside the park near the Kabatoro gate on the main road coming from the national park. Simple local meals can be found at the typical small hotels elsewhere. Hitching along the road through QENP is not difficult even in low season, as long as you're patient, and it's much cheaper than a private hire taxi from Katunguru.

The road beyond Katwe is not in very good condition and, if there has been recent rain, it's advisable to avoid this route unless you have a 4WD. From the track you will be able to see the Nyamagasani Delta and the Kihabule Forest before you reach Pelican Point.

Uganda kob

This is probably the most prevalent mammal in the Queen Elizabeth National Park with an estimated population of about 17,000. It prefers low-lying, open country without too much bush. Female kob and their young form loose herds of about 50. During the dry season they join up with males and with other groups to form herds of up to 1000 in areas where green grass is still available.

Male Uganda kobs mate with females in permanent grounds known as *leks*. Within a *lek* there is a cluster of small, usually roughly circular, breeding territories. For a few days the males will defend their territory by ritualized displays and by fighting when necessary. The females range freely within the *leks* and appear to favour males that hold territories in the centre of the *leks*. For this reason, most activity takes place within the central area, with these males constantly being challenged by other males.

The *leks* can be recognized by the flattened grass that is the result of being trampled on over many years. They are usually located in open grassland near water. During a prolonged dry season *leks* are usually abandoned and the herds join together in search of food and water.

South of Kazinga Channel

Take the main road and cross the Kazinga Channel. About 5 km south of the crossing turn right along the Ishasha road and follow it south. This route is mainly through grasslands, and about 8 km after the turning there is a kob *lek* on your left (see box, above).

Lake Nyamusingiri and the Maramagambo Forest

This is one of the longer trips, taking a full day and requiring a 4WD. Go back to the main Kasese road and turn east towards the Kichwamba escarpment. Cross the Katunguru bridge and continue along the road for about 12 km before turning right and starting to climb up the escarpment. The road takes you through both grasslands and acacia woodland. To your right you should be able to see the Kibona swamp, while ahead of you is the Maramagambo Forest.

Lake Kasanduka and the start of the Maramagambo Forest are reached about 9 km along this track, and a further 3 km on is Lake Nyamusingiri. There are trails into the forest although you are advised to take a ranger who knows it. Chimpanzees live in the forest but are not habituated so you are unlikely to see them. Other primates that you may see are black and white colobus and red-tailed monkeys.

Kyambura River Gorge → *Colour map 2, B2.*

ⓘ *Chimpanzee tracking is organized by UWA; book in advance at Myewa Visitor Information Centre (see page 150) or at UWA in Kampala (see page 46). It's not possible to buy a ticket at Kyambura Gorge. Walks start at 0730, US$50. Mweya Safari Lodge (see page 158) can organize a trip to Kyambura River Gorge for a group.*

The Kyambura Gorge (pronounced and sometimes spelt Chambura) and the former Chambura Game Reserve have been incorporated into QENP. The gorge was formed by a river that flows off the Kichwamba escarpment and into the Kazinga Channel at Katunguru. The gorge is 10 km long and supports dense forest, which is home to many different forest-living species, including chimpanzees. However, there is concern that the chimpanzees are over visited, affecting their fertility, reproduction rates and increasingly frequent displays of aggression towards humans.

On each side of the gorge is savannah, and the view from the edge is spectacular. Walking along the top of the gorge and looking down on to the forest gives a wonderful view of the tops of the trees and any birds or animals that may be feeding off them.

The easiest way to get to the gorge is to take a park ranger with you, who will be able to advise you on up-to-date conditions locally. One possible route is to take the road from Katunguru for about 8 km towards the escarpment. There is a turning off to the left shortly before the road begins to climb the escarpment and from here it is about 2 km to the edge of the gorge. Once you get to the gorge it is possible to climb down the 200 m into it. This is a bit of a scramble as it is fairly steep. You pass from dry grasslands at the top to thick forest and the river at the bottom.

Northern sector listings

For Sleeping and Eating price codes and other relevant information, see Essentials pages 21-23.

Sleeping *map p151*
Due to open in 2011, **Kyambura Safari Lodge** (T0414-346464/5, www.volcano essessafaris.com) is the latest upmarket lodge of Volcanoes Safaris, with 8 solar powered thatched *bandas*, close to Kichwamba village adjacent to the gorge.

LL Jacana Safari Lodge, 11 km from the main road on an all-weather road, on the south side of Kazinga Channel, run by GeoLodges Uganda, T0414-258273, www.geolodgesafrica.com. On the edge of Maramagambo Forest is this upmarket camp, with 10 cottages attractively arranged around Lake Nyamusingiri. It's a glorious location but facilities are jaded. The restaurant and bar are positioned high over the lake. The view is spectacular especially after rain at sunset. There is a pool and campfire area.

LL Katara Lodge, T077-301 1648 or T071-281 2560 (both mob), www.kataralodge.com. New upmarket addition of 5 thatched cottages on the Kichwamba escarpment overlooking the plains of QENP and the distant Rwenzoris. Cottages are generous family sized with glorious views. A pool is under construction. Food and service are excellent. The access road is very bumpy.

LL Mweya Safari Lodge, T0312-260260, www.mweyalodge.com. Managed by Marasa section of the Madhvani Group. Located on the Mweya Peninsula on a bluff overlooking Katwe Bay, the original lodge was built in the mid-1950s but has been luxuriously rebuilt. It has well-appointed accommodation, reminiscent of a luxury Kampala hotel, in cottages, suites or rooms overlooking the Kazinga Channel, plus a pool and health club. The bar is superbly located. The restaurant has a strong Indian influence and non-residents can eat there. Lunch and evening buffet US$25. DSTV, shop and foreign exchange facility. Weekend air package US$765pp (minimum 2 people) in partnership with Kampala Aero Club for Kampala–Mweya flights, 3 days/2 nights full board accommodation, park entrance fees, game drive and boat trip.

AL Kingfisher Kichwamba Lodge, Kichwamba, T077-415 9579 or T075-336 7980 (both mob), www.kingfisher-uganda.net. Outside the park, opened in 2006, 18 rooms. Price includes half board. Pool. German operated, popular with families. Sister to the Kingfisher Safari Resort in Jinja. The kitchen needs improving.

A-B Queen Elizabeth Bush Lodge, T0312-294894, T077-463 6410 (mob), www.naturelodges.biz. 6 safari tents overlooking the seasonal Kamera River and Kazinga Channel. It's just outside the park so no visitation fee is payable. At sunset the animals can be seen making their way up from the channel. It's located just off the main Kasese–Mbarara road, 500 m after the

bridge over the Kazinga Channel if heading south. Look out for the signpost and take the murram road a further 2 km to the camp. **B Simba Safari Camp**, on the Equator road, just outside the camp going towards Kasese, T077-242 6368 (mob), www.safari-uganda. com. Run by **Great Lakes Safaris**. Decent accommodation at a reasonable cost.
C-D Mweya Hostel, T078-280 2650 or T077-260 9969 (both mob). Also known as the **Albertine Rift Safari Hostel** or the Institute of Ecology. Cheap, very popular, basic hostel close to **Mweya Safari Lodge**. It's advisable to book. 12 rooms with shared bathrooms or 2 guesthouses are available for family accommodation. There's a small restaurant.

Camping
There are a number of campsites (**F**) near **Mweya Safari Lodge**. The most convenient if you want to use some of the lodge's facilities is the one on the south side of the peninsula overlooking the Kazinga Channel, 4 km from the lodge. It has running water and toilet facilities, but do not attempt to use them at night since you may encounter wild animals.

Eating
♉ **Tembo Canteen**. An excellent budget alternative to **Mweya Safari Lodge**. Cheap decent food and drinks served in a pleasant garden overlooking the Kazingo Channel, and an entertaining mongoose running around.

Southern sector (Ishasha River Camp) → Colour map 2, C1.

Made up of open partly wooded grasslands and forests, heavily populated with animals, the southern and larger part of the park is beautiful. It is less accessible than the northern part and so receives substantially fewer visitors. South of Maramagambo Forest is the **Kigezi Wildlife Reserve** which acts as a buffer zone between Maramagamba Forest and the very densely populated areas south of QENP. It consists of forest to the north supporting varied primates, chimpanzees and colobus monkeys and more open grasslands further south. The forested areas are used by elephants migrating south from Maramagambo Forest and east from DR Congo at the start of the rainy season. There are no visitor facilities at present although UWA advertised in 2010 for private investors to manage the reserve.

   Ishasha River Camp, in the far southwestern corner of the park, is close to the DR Congo border. There is both upmarket and simple accommodation available (see Sleeping, below). The park sub-headquarters are here, some 120 km south of Mweya (see page 150). The 'tree-climbing' lions of Ishasha, which allegedly perch on savannah fig trees, are not easily spotted. However, the birdlife is excellent. Two main game-viewing routes run out of Ishasha. Using a guide will greatly improve your chance of spotting wildlife.

Ins and outs
Getting there From **Mweya Lodge** take the main Kasese–Mbarara road south and turn off right at Katunguru. This route is used by commercial traffic including heavy trucks bound for DR Congo, Rwanda and Burundi, and has benefited from recent, much-needed maintenance. About 100 km after joining the road at Katunguru you will see a turning to the right with a sign to the Katookye Gate. For the direct route from Kampala via Ishaka, see page 147.

South Kigezi route
This route covers a distance of about 16 km and begins at the *bandas* at the Ishasha campsites (see Sleeping, below). Close to Campsite Two of the Ishasha campsite is a large hippo wallow, which is also a watering point for various antelope and buffalo. The birdlife here is also fairly extensive, with herons, storks and ibises.

The tree-climbing lions live in the woodland in this southern area. They are rarer now and it has been suggested that their habit of climbing trees is less common. You may also see topi around here. These are splendid animals with beautiful coats, also found in Lake Mburo National Park (see page 207), and in a few national parks in Kenya and Tanzania.

North Kigezi route
There are plans to renovate the roads in this rarely visited part of the park. It is an area of grassland with patches of woodland. The elephants in this area are the ones that move between Uganda and DR Congo, and they are very reclusive. The northern route is reputed to be the best section of the national park for viewing lions.

Southern sector listings

For Sleeping and Eating price codes and other relevant information, see Essentials pages 21-23.

Sleeping *map p151*
The 3 Ishasha campsites built during the colonial period are currently closed due to security reasons. They are set among trees with their frontage on to the Ishasha river, the border with DR Congo, and are shown on many maps. They are still a wonderful place to view hippos and antelopes coming to drink and they can still be visited on a picnic.
LL Ishasha Wilderness Camp, T0414-321479, T077-250 2155 (mob), www. ugandaexclusivecamps.com. Opened in 2005, with 10 large well-appointed en suite tents situated in glades by the Ntungwe River. Good food. Outdoor log fires in the evenings.
LL-L Ishasha-Ntungwe River Camp, T077-260 02205, ishashantungwe@gmail. com. Sited on the west bank of the Ntungwe River, outside QENP, 3 km from the Ishasha Gate, this tented eco-friendly resort offers a cheaper alternative to the **Wilderness Camp**.
E-F Ishasha Campsite, on the Southern circuit near the park sub-headquarters. A new campsite with 2 twin-bed rooms and 2 *bandas* or you can pitch your own tent. Non-potable water only and firewood and available. Bring all food and cooking utensils.

Rwenzori Mountains National Park

→ *Colour map 2, B1.*

The Rwenzoris (Ruwenzoris) lie along the border of Uganda and DR Congo, rising to a height of about 5100 m above sea level. The range is about 100 km in length and about 50 km wide. It was formed from a block that was tilted and thrust up during the development of the Rift Valley. These beautiful, often mist-shrouded mountains are non-volcanic and offer mountaineers and walkers superb country and wonderful views. Also known as the 'Mountains of the Moon', they were first described as such by Ptolemy because they were believed to be the Lunae Montes predicted by the ancient Greeks to be the source of the Nile. The explorer DW Freshfield said in 1906 that "you may be familiar with the Alps and the Caucasus, the Himalayas and the Rockies, but if you have not explored Rwenzori, you still have something wonderful to see."

Ins and outs

Getting there

Chartered flights go to Kasese from where you can complete the journey by road (see page 171). Ibanda, in the Mubuki Valley, can be reached from Kampala via Mbarara and Kasese from where it is a further 18 km. Alternatively, go from Kampala to Fort Portal and then another 75 km on the Fort Portal–Kasese road before turning off for Ibanda. Coming from Kasese, about 10 km along the main Kasese–Fort Portal road, there is a turning off to Ibanda. Take this for about 12 km; it's a fairly good gravel road.

Best time to visit

The Rwenzoris have a justified reputation for being wet. The best times to visit are from late December to February and from mid-June to mid-August. The rest of the year there is often a lot of rain and, apart from making the walk or climb slippery, it also means that the views are not so good with mist sometimes shrouding the mountains and peaks.

Tour operators

The Rwenzoris can be climbed from Kyanjuki Village, Kilembe, with Rwenzori Trekking Services (RTS), or from Ibanda in Mubuku Valley with Rwenzori Mountaineering Service (RMS), both official tour operators. **Rwenzori Mountaineering Services (RMS)** ① *New Saad Hotel, Rwenzori Rd, T04834-44936, T075-259 8461 (mob), www. rwenzorimountaineeringservices.com*, organizes all treks from Nyakalengija on the Central Circuit in Rwenzori Mountains National Park, see page 166.

    Rwenzori Trekking Services (RTS) ① *Kilembe Office, T077-611 4442 (mob), or the Kampala Office, T077-411 4499, www.rwenzoritrekking.com*, is an Australian enterprise operating in conjunction with Backpackers in Kampala. In mid-2009 it was granted a licence to operate an alternative mountaineering service to RMS. Despite supporting local communities RMS have long had negative feedback from users of their services. RTS offer a different southern route to the summit from RMS's Central Circuit. The office and starting point for the RTS climbs is at **Trekkers Hostel** in Kyanjuki Village, Kilembe, 12 km from Kasese, see page 170. Their trails begin at Kilembe and go via Nyamugasani, Kamusoni and Nyamwamba river valleys. Overall this is a longer route so reaching the higher peaks requires an additional one to two days. Trekkers place a premium on safety and all staff have undertaken the Wilderness First Aid course organized by the Norwegian expert Anders Bahr.

Equipment

Most gear that you need can be hired from RMS or RTS. RTS have the newest equipment. Take all the food you'll need; supplies can be bought in Kasese. Take a camp stove as open fires are forbidden in the park. It is wet for much of the year and cold at night,

Rwenzori Mountains National Park Treks

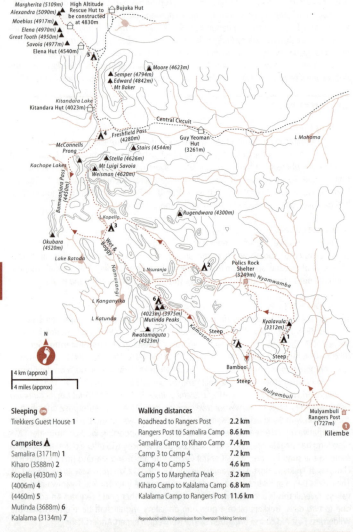

Sleeping 🛏️
Trekkers Guest House **1**

Campsites ⛺
Samalira (3171m) **1**
Kiharo (3588m) **2**
Kopella (4030m) **3**
(4006m) **4**
(4460m) **5**
Mutinda (3688m) **6**
Kalalama (3134m) **7**

Walking distances

Roadhead to Rangers Post	2.2 km
Rangers Post to Samalira Camp	8.6 km
Samalira Camp to Kiharo Camp	7.4 km
Camp 3 to Camp 4	7.2 km
Camp 4 to Camp 5	4.6 km
Camp 5 to Margherita Peak	3.2 km
Kiharo Camp to Kalalama Camp	6.8 km
Kalalama Camp to Rangers Post	11.6 km

Reproduced with kind permission from Rwenzori Trekking Services

Exploration of the Rwenzori Mountains

It is now generally accepted that Ptolemy (c AD 150), when writing of the 'Mountains of the Moon', the legendary source of the Nile, was referring to the Rwenzori massif. Interestingly, Speke, discovering the Virunga volcanoes in 1861, associated them with Ptolemy's description.

In the 19th century, Samuel Baker observed the Rwenzoris (and called them the 'Blue Mountains') but failed to appreciate the importance of this natural feature. Sir Henry Stanley was the first to proclaim the existence of the Rwenzoris as Snow Mountains. In *Darkest Africa* he claims to have made the discovery himself, but in fact two members of his expedition, Surgeon Parke and Mountenoy-Jephson, had seen the snows a month before him, on 20 April 1888. The following year another member of the expedition, Lieutenant Stairs, ascended the mountains to a height of over 3050 m.

It is to Stanley that we owe the name Rwenzori (often spelt Ruwenzori). The word means 'the place from where the rain comes'. No name appears to have been given to the mountains by the local residents; their custom was to name the rivers running off the mountains rather than the actual peaks.

In the summer of 1891 Emin Pasha's companion Dr F Stuhlmann climbed up the Butagu Valley to a height of 4062 m and had the first close glimpse of the snow. A few years later naturalist GF Scott Elliott also made a number of expeditions, which were of significant botanical importance. In 1900 an expedition by CS Moore proved the presence of glaciers, and shortly afterwards Sir Harry Johnston reached the Mobuku glacier at a height of 4520 m. The first purely non-scientific climb, and the first by a woman, was in 1903 by the Reverend A B and Mrs Fisher.

The twin peaks of Mount Stanley, Alexandra and Margherita, were climbed for the first time in June 1906 by an expedition led by the Duke of Abruzzi. This expedition produced important scientific results, and an excellent topographical survey of the range was completed with information on the areas of the glaciers. It was this expedition that named most of the main peaks. The duke chose to name the lowest, Luigi di Savoia, after himself.

so come well prepared, with waterproofs and plenty of warm clothing. Some people bring wellies, which are useful for the many boggy areas. Walking sticks are the most important equipment for the trip, along with waterproof boots. Pack everything inside your rucksack in plastic bags.

Porters and guides

It is obligatory to take porters and a guide. Porters from RMS (see above) carry loads of 22 kg excluding their own blankets and supplies. The headman does not carry a load although he is expected to relieve a tired member of the party. Guides are also necessary. Before departure, it is important to clarify what the charges are going to be, depending on the number of days and the stages covered. More serious climbers who intend to tackle the glacial peaks should ensure that their guide is experienced. You should take all the food that you will need and a portable stove.

Books

The best guide is *Osmaston and Pasteur's Guide to the Rwenzoris*, updated in 2006, from **Stanfords Map and Travel Bookshop** ⓘ *12-14 Long Acre, Covent Garden, London WC2E 9LP, T020-783 61321, www.stanfords.co.uk*. The other good guide with a detailed map is *Wielochowski's Rwenzori Map and Guide*, also available from Stanfords or from **West Col Productions** ⓘ *Goring, Reading RG8 9AA, www.mapsworldwide.com*, or from **Geolodges** ⓘ *T0414-258273*, in Uganda.

Insurance

Anyone climbing over 4000 m must ensure that they have a comprehensive adventure and mountaineering insurance policy to cover all medical and rescue costs.

Geology

The Rwenzoris are relatively young mountains, at less than 10 million years old. Until that time, the area was part of a huge plain that extended to the Atlantic coast to the west and rivers flowed to the west. A series of movements of the earth's crust resulted in major rifting and, in the Rwenzori area, an uplifting of the underlying rock. The Rwenzoris are made up of quartzite and gneiss.

Although not the highest, the Rwenzori range is certainly the largest and most important group of snow mountains in Africa. Mount Kilimanjaro (5968 m) and Mount Kenya (5225 m) are both higher, but are single volcanic peaks. The Rwenzori, whose highest point is the Margherita Peak of Mount Stanley (5110 m), is a massif composed of six separate mountains, all of which carry permanent snow and glaciers. A number of the mountain peaks are named after early explorers to Uganda (see box, page 163). Apart from Stanley, there are Speke (4889 m), Baker (4843 m), Gessi (4797 m), Emin (4791 m) and Luigi di Savoia (4626 m). The other summit on Mount Stanley is Alexandra (5044 m). There is some dispute about the actual heights of these peaks and some sources mark them as being significantly higher. The general axis of the range is north–south and the snow peaks, divided by lower snow-free passes, lie roughly along this axis in the middle of the range. Unlike the other great mountains of Central Africa, Rwenzori is not of volcanic origin but is the result of an upthrust associated with the formation of the Western Rift Valley, in which it stands.

There are six separated glaciated groups and the glaciers are the equatorial type. That is, they are more truly ice caps than ice rivers; movement is very slight as can be seen from the clearness of the streams and the absence of large moraines (accumulations of debris carried down by the glaciers). There have been times of much greater glaciation in earlier eras on the Rwenzoris, reaching thousands of metres below the current levels, and many of the valleys are characteristically shaped by ice erosion. The existing glaciers are in retreat.

Vegetation and wildlife

One of the most delightful aspects of the Rwenzoris is the diversity of plants and trees. Cultivation rarely extends above about 2000 m around the base of the mountain, and in many places it is considerably lower. In the foothills most of the vegetation is elephant grass, up to about 1800 m. Next comes the montane or true forest, a mixture of trees, bracken and tree ferns. In this zone, which extends to about 2500 m, it is possible to see orchids. Higher still is the bamboo zone, which continues up to about 3000 m. The vegetation here also includes tree heather and, in moister patches, giant lobelias. The next fairly extensive zone is the heather forest, which extends from 3000 m up to 3800 m. The humid climate at this altitude causes vigorous development of mosses and lichens, which cover the ground and the trunks of living and fallen trees. At this level, on the better-drained slopes, tree groundsels and shrubby trees flourish, while the wetter parts are distinctly boggy. This zone also has brambles, orchids and ferns, all of which form a tangle that makes passage difficult. The highest vegetative zone, extending from about 3800 m to the snowline, is alpine. From here most of the common herbaceous plants disappear, leaving tree heaths, giant lobelias and senecios. Reeds grow in the marshes and shrubby bushes with everlasting flowers (*Belichrysums*) are abundant. The rocks are covered with a loosely adhering carpet of moss. Above 3000 m there is little sign of life except hyrax and other small rodents. Birds are also fairly sparse.

People

Living on the Rwenzoris are the Bakonjo, a Bantu tribe who speak Lukonjo, believed to be one of the earliest forms of Bantu speech. They are a short and sturdy people and frequently find work as guides and porters as many are excellent climbers. Apart from when they are acting as guides and porters, they rarely actually go high up into the mountain range, believing that a god called Kitasamba lives in the upper reaches of the mountains. On your ascent you may see small grass huts containing offerings to Kitasamba.

Climbing the Rwenzoris

The Rwenzoris are suitable for almost all climbers and walkers who are reasonably fit. There are hiking routes in the foothills for those with no climbing experience; all you need is a little stamina and waterproof clothing. Both RMS and RTS, see page 161, offer short hikes lasting one to two days up to the first hut or camp in the Rwenzori Mountains to give travellers an opportunity to experience the mountain and its impressive vegetation. More demanding is the ascent of Mount Speke, which is a simple glacier requiring mountain experience. Most difficult are some of the routes on mounts Stanley and Baker; only those with experience in rock, snow and ice climbing should attempt these.

The Northern Spur of the Rwenzoris can also be trekked starting at Kazingo Village, see page 180. The main focus is trekking the spectacular Karangora Peak, 3014 m. It is also possible to take short guided one to two day trips around the foothills. For example, you can trek from Kazingo to Bundibugyo town or Semliki National Park in one day.

The Kilembe Trail

Trekking essentials RTS offer a different southern route to the summit from RMS's Central Circuit. Their trails begin at Kilembe and go via Nyamugasani, Kamusoni and Nyamwamba river valleys. Overall this route is longer so allow an additional one to two days to reach the higher peaks. The descriptions of the RTS treks are most easily followed with the help of the RTS map, see page 162.

RTS use six- to eight-person permanent tents until new mountain huts are built. The rates for RTS's treks vary according to the number in the party, from US$100 cheaper per person if there are six or more in the group. The 10-day trek to **Margherita Peak** (5109 m) costs US$1080-980 plus the gate entrance fee payable to UWA of US$270 each, paid separately in cash; the nine-day trek to the highest point of the **Stanley Glacier** (4910

m) costs US$960-880 plus the UWA fee of US$240. The eight-day trek to **Mount Baker** (4842 m) costs US$840-790 plus UWA fee of US$210. The six-day trek to **Weismann's Peak** (4620 m) costs US$630-570 plus UWA fee of US$150. RTS also offer shorter one- to five-day treks through the montane forests, bamboo forests and up to the giant heathers and lobelias at a lower cost.

Charges include all current fees, camping and meals, and one porter per person, as well as porters for food. Additional porters for personal luggage above 15 kg are charged at US$12 per day. Climbing ropes, harnesses with carabinas and crampons are supplied free of charge but trekkers can bring their own if preferred. Items for hire include climbing boots US$20, ice axe US$10, warm jacket/sweater US$10, rubber boots US$5, garters US$5, gloves US$5 and sleeping bag US$2 per day. Prices are per trek with the exception of the sleeping bag.

Treks The 10-day trek to Margherita Peak covers the full extent of the Kilembe Trail, ascending through diverse vegetation culminating in splendid views of DR Congo and the whole Rwenzori range. The final ascent requires some climbing skills.

The nine-day trek to the highest point of the Stanley Glacier, just below the Alexandra Peak, gives a fine panorama dominated by the Margherita Peak. The trek has the advantage that it can be undertaken by anyone with a reasonable level of fitness, and does not require special climbing skills.

The eight-day trek to Mount Baker provides excellent vistas of the major peaks, and is a relatively easy ascent.

The six-day trek to Weissman's Peak has great views of the glacier lakes, and in from September to October and April to May there can be heavy snowfalls.

The five-day trek passes through Kiharo Camp and then takes the left fork of the trail to Mutinda Camp and includes an overnight at Kalalama en route for Kilembe. The scenery is splendid and passes the waterfall overlooking the Mutinda peaks.

The four-day trek has nights at Samalira Camp, and the cliff-ringed Kiharo Camp before returning to overnight at Kalalama Camp. There are grand views of Lake George.

The three-day trek has overnight stays at Samalira Camp and Kalalama Camp, hiking through rainforest, encounters with many smaller primates and bamboo afforestation, culminating in a panorama featuring Kasese in the distance.

The two-day trek heads for Samalira Camp with the option the next day of an ascent to nearby Kyalavula, before descending to Kilembe.

The one-day trek takes the left fork in the trail leaving Kilembe, following the Mulyamabuli River (the name evoking memories of Sam the Sham and the Pharaohs), passing through the forest with lunch at Musenge, before returning. There are excellent opportunities to observe birds and the smaller primates.

Central Circuit

RMS, see page 161, hold the concession to provide accommodation, porters, guides and rescue services for the Central Circuit. A trek for six days in seven stages within the park costs US$780, which includes entrance fees, guides, huts, porters and food for the porters. There is an optional additional charge for food of US$140; a cook costs US$70.

If you want to climb the peaks you need to budget for four to five additional days and costs at US$120 per day. Also, if you have a lot of gear you will have to pay for extra porters at US$70 each. Ascent of the peaks is now categorized a technical climb requiring peak physical fitness and specialist mountaineering knowledge and equipment. RMS's equipment hire costs US$25 each for rope, crampons, harnesses, ice axe, sleeping bag or climbing boots; US$7 rubber boots; US$5 for a cap, trousers, jacket/sweater, garters or gloves; and US$50 for a gas cooker and fuel per group of three or less.

If taking the RMS option you should allow about six to seven days for the trek along the Circuit route. This is obviously just one possibility; you can break the route up with more frequent stops. For example, Day 1 to Nyabitaba; Day 2 to Nyamiliju; Day 3 to Bigo; Day 4 to Lake Bujuku; Day 5 to Kitandara; Day 6 to Guy Yeoman and Day 7 back to Nyakalengija.

Day 1 Begin by heading for Nyakalengija (1600 m), see page 171, 5 km from Ibanda and 22 km from Kasese, where the trail begins and from there take the path to the Nyabitaba Hut (2651 m), about 10 km. If you have made arrangements through the RMS they should be able to arrange transport to their office at Nyakalengija where you will pay your fees, etc. You can also park vehicles here fairly safely, and camp if you want to start the walk early the next day. From Nyakalengija head through a coffee plantation and a field and on into some elephant grass. The path gradually deteriorates as you enter the bush and the cultivation disappears and is replaced by elephant grass and nettles. The Mubuku River on your right contains trout that were introduced by the British. You descend to the edge of the river and then climb up and into the forest. Cross two streams and continue for several kilometres before crossing the Mahoma River. The final ascent is up a moraine ridge to Nyabitaba (2651 m); before you get to the hut itself there is a small rock shelter. There is a larger rock shelter a little beyond the hut, used by many people in preference to the hut. Alternatively, you can camp in the clearing by the hut. The two-roomed Nyabitaba hut, built in 1987, sleeps up to 12 people. There is a water supply at the hut.

Day 2 This is the most difficult day of the Circuit, and will take you at least seven hours from Nyabitaba to John Matte Hut (3505 m). You follow the ridge through the forest and

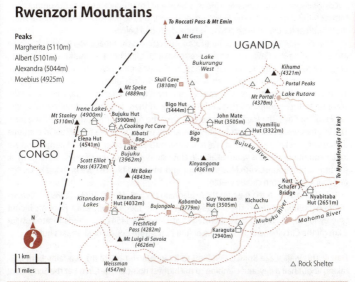

Rwenzori Mountains

Peaks
Margherita (5110m)
Albert (5101m)
Alexandra (5044m)
Moebius (4925m)

To Roccati Pass & Mt Emin
Mt Gessi

UGANDA

Lake Bukurungu West

Skull Cave (3810m)

Kihuma (4321m)

Mt Speke (4889m)

Portal Peaks
Lake Rutara

Mt Portal (4370m)

Bigo Hut (3444m)

John Mate Hut (3505m)

Nyamiliju Hut (3322m)

Irene Lakes
Mt Stanley (5110m)
Mt Irene (4900m)
Bujuku Hut (3900m)
Cooking Pot Cave
Kibatsi Bog
Elena Hut (4541m)
Lake Bujuku (3962m)

Bigo Bog

Bujuku River

DR CONGO

Scott Elliot Pass (4372m)
Mt Baker (4843m)

Kinyangoma (4361m)

Kurt Schafer Bridge

Nyabitaba Hut (2651m)

Kitandara Lakes
Kitandara Hut (4032m)
Bujongolo
Kabamba
Guy Yeoman Hut (3505m)
Kichuchu

Mubuku River

Mahoma River

To Nyakalengija (10 km)

N

Freshfield Pass (4282m)
Mt Luigi di Savoia (4626m)

Karaguta (2940m)

1 km
1 miles

Weissman (4547m)

△ Rock Shelter

then fork down steeply to the left to the Mubuku River. This you cross using the Kurt Schafer Bridge which was built in 1989 after the old one collapsed. From here you climb up again on the other side – the path gradually gets harder, becoming a slippery scramble – and continue on to the bamboo forest. The walk through the bamboo forest is relatively easy but, before reaching Nyamiliju, there is a long hard climb upwards. It is here that you will start to go through the heather and groundsel towards Nyamiliju; in fact, Nyamiliju actually means 'place of beards', a name that refers to the moss and lichen that hang from the trees. The old hut at Nyamiliju (3322 m) is a round uniport with a wooden floor. It is not used much any longer as most people prefer to push on to John Matte Hut. But if you wish to go slower, it has a good water supply. There is also a nearby rock shelter, which some people prefer to use but which has no room for tents. If it is a clear day you should be able to see Mount Stanley and Mount Speke as well as the glaciers, and Nyamiliju can make a good lunchtime stop. From here it is a further two hours to John Matte Hut (3505 m), climbing up through the giant heather and groundsel forest. The trail is much less clear; start by crossing the stream just below the rock shelter and carry on towards the river, but don't actually cross it. Continue from the heather forest until it opens out a bit, and up two fairly steep moraines before you reach the camp. The hut is in good condition and close to the Bujuku River, where you can collect water.

Day 3 On the third day, from John Matte Hut (3505 m) to Lake Bujuku (3962 m), you go through the muddy bog of Bigo, past the Bigo Hut and on to the Bujuku Hut. Begin by crossing the river and then head for the left-hand edge of the valley, skirting around the bog. You will find it almost impossible to avoid getting muddy. Bigo Hut (3444 m) sleeps 12 and is in fairly good condition and there is flowing water nearby. There is also a rock shelter here, which the porters tend to use.

From Bigo Hut you can choose a number of different routes. You can go north to Roccati Pass, which runs between Mounts Gessi and Emin; or northeast to Bukurungu Pass between Gessi and the Portal Peaks; or southwest to Lake Bujuku. The latter route is the most popular for Circuit users and is the one described below.

From Bigo (3444 m) to Lake Bujuku (3962 m) you cross the Kibatsi Bog to what is known as the Cooking Pot Cave and from there to Lake Bujuku Hut, in beautiful surroundings. Begin by following the route that swings southwestwards with Mount Stanley on your right (west) and Baker on your left (east). The path starts off rather steep but levels off as you round the southern spur. You will shortly reach the Kibatsi bog, which will take you two to three hours to cross and from the bog there is another steep climb. At the Cooking Pot Cave, the track splits into two. Take the right (northwest) route to the huts. The left fork leads to the Scott Elliot Pass and you will return here tomorrow to continue the Circuit. The Lake Bujuku Hut is actually two huts which sleep up to 14 people and are in fair condition. There is water available close by. It is one of the loveliest settings of all the huts on the routes, with Mount Stanley and an incredible ice cave in the Peke Glacier on Mount Speke both clearly visible.

Lake Bujuku Hut is the base for those planning to climb Mount Speke (4889 m). Serious climbers hoping to reach the highest point on the range, Margherita Peak on Mount Stanley (5110 m), should base themselves at Elena Hut (4541 m). This is located about 2 km off the Circuit and is about three or four hours from Bujuku or Kitandara huts.

Day 4 This walk, Lake Bujuku (3962 m) to Kitandara Hut (4032 m), is a fairly light one, taking about half a day, and climbing to the highest point on the Circuit at the Scott Elliot

Pass. Begin by returning to the Cooking Pot Cave and from there take the southerly path that leads to the Scott Elliot Pass (4372 m). The track takes you through groundsel to a scree slope. At the head of this is a rock buttress and the pass is to the right. There is a cleft in the rocks to the left and from here the descent continues with the vertical cliffs of Mount Baker on your side. Before reaching Lake Kitandara the path rises then descends again. The two huts at Lake Kitandara are also in a wonderful setting, next to one of the two lakes and close to the foot of Elena glacier.

Day 5 This walk goes from Lake Kitandara Hut (4032 m) to the Kamamba rock shelter (3779 m) or to Guy Yeoman Hut. If you go on to the Guy Yeoman Hut, it's a walk of about five hours. The day begins with a steep climb to the Freshfield Pass (4282 m), followed by a descent to a rock overhang called Bujongolo. This is where the first expedition to explore the mountains in 1906 based itself. A little further on is a second, larger rock shelter called Kabamba located close to a waterfall, where you can spend the night. Alternatively you can continue on to the Guy Yeoman Hut (3505 m), one of the newer sites.

Day 6 Guy Yeoman (3505 m) to Nyabitaba Hut (2651 m), or on to Nyakalengija (1600 m). Continue your descent via Kichuchu where there is another rock shelter. From Kichuchu the descent continues through bog and bamboo forest and then across the Mubuku River. Having forded the river, follow the path along a ridge and down to the Nyabitaba Hut (2651 m). Alternatively, you can go via Lake Mahoma where there is a hut, if you want to spend an extra night. From Nyabitaba Hut you then have to retrace your steps back to Nyakalengija, about another three-hour hike.

Kasese and Kilembe → *Phone code: 4834. Colour map 2, B1.*

Kasese is the main base for expeditions into the Rwenzori Mountains (see above) as it is close to the gateways into the park at Kilembe or Ibanda. It is an industrial town that was once infamous for its dusty Wild West-style roads and is still an unpleasant place, because it is extremely hot and the mosquitoes are most troublesome at night. Factories, including a cotton ginnery, line the main road as it bypasses the town centre. Trains from the East African Railways used to stop here, coming all the way from Mombasa, but the passenger train services between Kampala and Kasese stopped in 1997.

Kilembe Copper Mines have closed and **Kilembe** town, 14 km west of Kasese, has lost its former glory. These mines were once an important source of foreign exchange for Uganda. In Kasese an Australian-financed foundry is now extracting considerable amounts of high-grade cobalt from the residual sludge of the copper mines. The plant is along the Kasese–Queen Elizabeth National Park road, a few kilometres out of Kasese. Many people confuse the old copper mines with the newly opened cobalt processing plant.

Kasese and Kilembe listings

For Sleeping and Eating price codes and other relevant information, see Essentials pages 21-23.

Sleeping *map p170*
AL-A Margherita Hotel, Kilembe Rd, near Kasese, T04834-44015. This former

government hotel has a lovely setting but is overpriced. It's 3 km down the road to Kilembe, west of town and so inaccessible without your own transport. There is a restaurant.
D New Saad Hotel, Rwenzori Rd, Kasese, T04834-46296, info@newsaadhotel. com. Recently renovated popular budget

hotel. There's a restaurant but no alcohol is permitted. **Rwenzori Mountaineering Services (RMS)** is based here, see page 161. **D Rwenzori International Hotel**, 1 Mbogo Rd, in the residential suburb of Kawaiba 3 km south of Kasese, T04834-44148, T078-228 2008 (mob), rihlkasese@yahoo.com. This 36-room place offers excellent value and has DSTV, sauna, gym, tennis court and grass badminton court. It's close to the Kasese–Mbarara road and the airstrip. **E Trekkers Hostel**, (aka Rwenzori Backpackers Hostel), Kyanjuki Village, Kilembe, T077-611 4442 or T077-419 9022 (both mob). Located 12 km from Kasese by the Nyamwamba River just outside the park.

Situated 500 m above Kasese it is pleasantly cooler. En suite rooms, double rooms, dorms or camping areas for a range of budgets. Restaurant, bar plus pleasant area on veranda. The office and main stores for RTS, see page 161, are based here. **E White House Hotel**, off Kilembe Rd, T04834-44706. Central location and the recommended best budget option. Also used by RTS, see page 161. Bar, restaurant, DSTV and internet facilities.

Eating

There's little to choose between places to eat. The food at **Margherita Hotel** is reasonable but uninspiring.

Kasese

To **2** (2.5km), Kilembe (11km), **5**, Golf Club & Thirties Club (Kilembe) & Kyanjuki Village (12km)

Rukidi III Rd
Rwenzori Rd
Titi's Supermarket
Kilembe Rd
6
Emin
Alexandria St
Speke St
Shell
Reroc
Portal Rd
Lion of Judah Supermarket
Margherita St
@TTL
Stanbic **S**
1
Stanley St
3 Rwenzori Mountain Service
Barclays **S**
Total
Taxis
Clothes
Bus Park
Kitabikibi St

To Fort Portal & Airport

Fort Portal: Mpondwe Rd (A109)

To **4** (2km, signposted), Queen Elizabeth National Park & Mbarara

N

200 metres
200 yards

Sleeping
Ataco Holiday Inn 1
Margherita 2

New Saad 3
Rwenzori International 4
Trekkers Hostel 5

White House 6

Shopping

There are several shops in Kasese, close to the market where you can buy food suitable for hiking, such as dried soups imported from Kenya.

Titi, Rwenzori Rd, close to the post office, Kasese. The best supermarket.

Transport

Air

Charter flights go to Kasese airport although, as they are usually taking wealthy tourists, they are more likely to go direct to the Mweya Safari Lodge landing site in QENP or Toro-Semliki Game Reserve. Plans have been mooted to make Kasese an international airport, which is possibly a long-term dream.

Road

Kasese is 418 km from Kampala via Mubende and Fort Portal. The more common route is via Mbarara because the road is sealed all the way. At 0630 you can get the Post Bus to **Kampala** from the post office, 8 hrs, US$8. Buses leave from the bus park, next to the taxi park. To Kampala, 7 hrs, US$8. If travelling by *matatu* to Kampala, change in Mbarara. To **Mbarara**, US$3. To **Kabale**, 6 hrs, US$6. To **Fort Portal**, 2 hrs, US$2. There is a daily bus service from Fort Portal, via Kasese and Mbarara, to Kabale, departing at 0600 from Fort Portal. To **Kilembe**, a special hire taxi costs US$8.75 or a *boda-boda* US$1.50-US$2.00.

Directory

Banks Barclays Bank, 68 Rwenzori Rd. ATM. **Stanbic Bank**, corner of Rwenzori Rd and Stanley Rd. Changes TCs. **Internet** Reroc Internet, Rwenzori Rd, near junction with Margherita Rd. **White House Hotel**, off Kilembe Rd.

Nyakalengija → *Colour map 2, B1.*

This is a small village on the fringe of the Rwenzoris, 22 km northwest of Kasese, and is the starting point of the Central Circuit route (see page 166). There is an RMS office here, used as the assembly point where people meet to start RMS treks.

This is an agricultural area whose inhabitants also depend on income from guides and porters. *Matatu* from Kasese to Ibanda, 5 km from Nyakalengija, US$1.50. Walking to Nyakalengija from Ibanda takes about an hour. If driving to Nyakalengija from Kasese, take the Fort Portal road 10 km north, turning westwards at Mubuku, from where it's another 12 km to reach Ibanda along a fairly good gravel road. Nyakalengija is a further 4 km.

Nyakalengija listings

For Sleeping and Eating price codes and other relevant information, see Essentials pages 21-23.

Sleeping

AL RMS Safari Lodge, T04834-44830. Built in 2008 on the park boundary. Cottages with private bathrooms.
E-F Ruboni Backpackers campsite, just opposite the RMS office, T077-419 5859 (mob), rubonibackpackers@gmail.com. Near the park entrance, offering a community experience in the foothills of the Rwenzori Mountains. En suite *bandas*, safari tents and camping with restaurant services. **Ruboni** organizes guided village walks, hill climbing, dance performances and farm experiences. It's ideal if you want to have a feel of local life. It is outside the park so no visitation fees are payable.

Fort Portal and around

→ *Phone code: 4834. Colour map 2, B2.*

Heading to Fort Portal from Kasese is another beautiful drive. The road climbs out of the dry plain and gradually enters the hilly greenness that surrounds Fort Portal. Located a little over 300 km west of Kampala and 80 km north of Kasese at 1600 m above sea level, Fort Portal is situated in the foothills of the Rwenzoris and from the town is a beautiful view of the snow-capped mountains, although cloud often obscures the peaks. Some visitors base themselves at Fort Portal while organizing a trek up the mountains but, although not so pleasant, Kasese is more convenient. Small, quiet and refreshing, Fort Portal is one of Uganda's most agreeable towns. It is now the district headquarters for the Kabarole district and is the centre of the Toro Kingdom. The River Mpanga meanders through the municipality, its source being the tributaries from the Rwenzoris. This river is the main water source for the town.

Ins and outs

Getting there

Most travellers to Fort Portal will take the sealed road via Mityana and Mubende. It takes 3½ to four hours by private transport. There are frequent *matatus* to and from Kasese and the nearest airport.

Best time to visit

Fort Portal has an excellent climate, almost temperate in nature, with moderate sunshine and heavy downpours during the rainy season. The main rains are March to May and from September to November, although there is no real dry season. The annual temperatures are 25-28°C. The climate is mainly influenced by the surrounding environment, particularly by the hills and mountains but nocturnal temperatures can drop, requiring a fleece/sweater.

Background

Fort Portal was founded in 1893 under the name of Fort Gerry, and later renamed Fort Portal after the diplomat Sir Gerald Portal. He never set foot in the town but contributed decisively to convincing the British government of the benefits of explorer Sir Frederick Lugard's plan that this area should become part of the British Empire, and was instrumental in the signing of agreements with the leaders of the kingdoms of Uganda that led to the formalizing of protectorate status for the country.

Fort Portal is in the centre of the Toro Kingdom and the town was a base from which British colonial power protected the then Omukama (or King) of Toro. In 1876 Toro was captured by the Banyoro King Kabalega, but the British expelled him in 1891 and replaced him with a new Toro King, Kasagama. In later years Catholic and Protestant missionaries followed the colonial administration in order to establish churches, schools and hospitals. By 1900 the town was expanding rapidly, its development helped by the booming trade in food and cash produce. In the 1930s Europeans and Indians came to set up large tea estates, and shops and residential premises were built. The growth of the town was also helped by the establishment in 1952 of the railway line from Mombasa as far as Kasese, for the transportation of copper from the mines at Kilembe. A cement factory was set up at Hima along the Fort Portal–Kasese road. As with the other kingdoms in Uganda, Toro was abolished in 1966 during Obote's first term of office. However, it was restored by Museveni in 1993.

Fort Portal centre

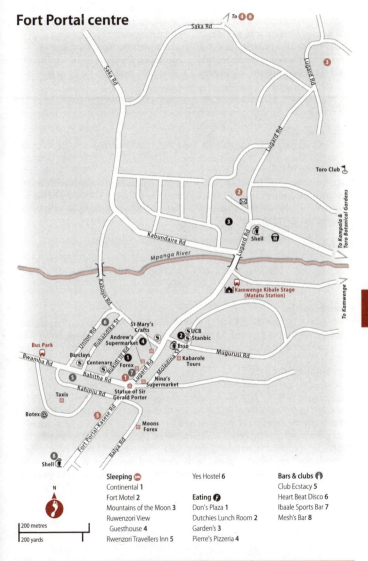

Sleeping
Continental 1
Fort Motel 2
Mountains of the Moon 3
Ruwenzori View
  Guesthouse 4
Rwenzori Travellers Inn 5

Yes Hostel 6

Eating
Don's Plaza 1
Dutchies Lunch Room 2
Garden's 3
Pierre's Pizzeria 4

Bars & clubs
Club Ecstacy 5
Heart Beat Disco 6
Ibaale Sports Bar 7
Mesh's Bar 8

Sir Gerald Portal's statue

The statue of Sir Gerald Portal, British Special Commissioner to Uganda after whom the town is named, was moved from the centre of the roundabout when the Kasese-Fort Portal road was re-built. It was dumped in a municipal yard and left to ruin. However, in December 2010 Tony Duckworth, with the help of other British nationals, retrieved the statue and erected it in front of his hotel, Rwenzori Travellers's Inn, approximately 200 m from its original position. Now the municipal authorities want it back, claiming that visitors looking at the statue are destroying the grassy area around it and propose to move it to the Boma ground.

Sights

Toro Palace ruins

Fort Portal's highest point, Kabarole Hill, is the site of the former round palace of the King of Toro (Omukama). The original palace was built in the 1960s for the then Omukama, Rukidi III (son of Kasagama), but was looted during Amin's time (1979). Thanks to the support of Colonel Gaddafi of Libya, a new round palace has been erected overlooking the Rwenzoris. The present Omukama, King Oyo, was crowned king in 1995, when he was only three years old, after the sudden death of his father (Omukama Kaboyo). He recently took over office on his 18th birthday.

Old Fort ruins

The fort after which the town is named is now the site of the town's golf course (see page 176), and is little more than a collection of rocks. It is said that one of these rocks contains the footprints of Sir Gerald Portal's men.

Karambi tombs

Located about 5 km out of Fort Portal on the main Fort Portal–Kasese road, on the right-hand side, these are the burial grounds for the Toro royal family, where Kasagama, Rukidi III and Kaboyo are buried. On display are personal artefacts of the kings, including drums and spears.

Toro Botanical Gardens

ⓘ *Between the golf club and the Mountains of the Moon Hotel, 1.5 km out of town on the Kampala Road, T078-267 3188, www.toorobotanicalgardens.org. Guided walks US$2.25.*
Established by retired Professor Rugumayo, the rationale for this 40-ha garden is to collect and conserve the local flora of the Albertine Rift region as well as raising local awareness. Among the plants growing here is sweet wormwood (*Artemisia annua*), an aromatic herb that produces artemisinin, containing anti-malarial properties. Self funded and employing 32 people there are medicinal plants, herbs, spices and vegetables, as well as trees and flowers. The workers' salaries are funded by sales of their produce that are packaged on site.

Fort Portal listings

For Sleeping and Eating price codes and other relevant information, see Essentials pages 21-23.

Sleeping *maps p173 and p178*

There are some excellent lodges and campsites in the surrounding area.

LL Kyaninga Lodge, about 10 km from Fort Portal, T077-299 9750, www.kyaningalodge.com. Opened in 2010 having taken 6 years to build, this high-end Anglo-Ugandan project has 8 log cabins and a lodge built on the rim of an ancient volcanic crater lake with magnificent views, a pool, tennis and badminton courts, croquet, guided nature walks, boating and Wi-Fi. Much of the excellent food is locally grown. Reforestation of the local area has begun. To get here, turn north (left) at the Mpanga Bridge, 2 km outside Fort Portal on the Kampala road. Follow this road for 1.8 km, and turn left at the Kyaninga Lodge sign. Follow this road for a further 6 km till you reach the lodge.

AL Mountains of the Moon Hotel, 4 Nyaika Ave, about 1.5 km from the town centre next to the Toro Botanical Gardens, T08434-23200, T077-555 7840 (mob), www.mountainsofthemoon.co.ug. This is a lovely renovated old colonial hotel, with generous-sized rooms, set in 6 ha of beautiful grounds. The garden is an ideal place for an afternoon drink. A restaurant, bar, pool, gym and sauna are available but they are allegedly short on hairdryers. Pleasant staff. The business centre has a good internet connection.

A Fort Motel, 2 Lugard Rd, T08434-422052, T077-250 1731 (mob), www.fortmotel.com. Stylishly restored old colonial house, adjacent to the golf course with 10 en suite double rooms, a small pool, a sauna and a steam cabin

A Kluges Guest Farm, near Kabahango, 15 km south of Fort Portal, T077-244 0099 (mob), www.klugesguestfarm.com. A German-Ugandan enterprise, this is a working farm, set in lovely countryside with the Rwenzoris as a backdrop. It offers 8 spacious cottages with private bathrooms, a guesthouse with 2 rooms and a kitchen, large enough for a family, and camping facilities, with your own tent or a hired one. Good food and pool. If travelling from Fort Portal, after 11 km branch off eastwards (signposted) at the **Kasusu Trading Centre** and continue for another 4 km. Pick-up from Fort Portal can be arranged.

B RuwenZori View Guest House, 15 Lower Kakiiza Rd, T04834-22102, T077-272 2102 (mob), www.ruwenzoriview.com. Well signposted in Boma, a lush suburb about 500 m before the **Mountains of the Moon Hotel**. Excellent hotel, 7 en suite rooms with private verandas, way above usual standards. Outstanding food served for dinner. Hosted by Ineke Jongerius and Maurice Barnes, a Dutch/English couple. The lounge has a display of locally made crafts for sale.

C Rwenzori Travellers Inn, 16 Kyebambe Rd, T04834-22075, T077-529 9591, www.rwenzoritravellersinn.com. Central, comfortable hotel but noise from the popular bar and restaurant on the top floor may disturb your sleep.

E Continental, T077-248 4842 (mob). The most budget popular hotel if you want to stay in the town centre. There's an additional charge for TV in the en suite rooms. Rooms without a TV and with shared bathrooms are much cheaper.

F YES Hostel (Youth Encouragement Services), Kakiza Rd, Boma, yesuganda@gmail.com. A 50-bed hostel with cheap dorms. Set up by an NGO that supports orphans. Use of kitchen. Has lovely views to the rear overlooking the pastures and the Rwenzoris. Located close to the **RuwenZori View Guest House**.

Eating *map p173*

In addition to the places listed below, there is a variety of places where you can eat local food like *matooke*.

♥♥ Mountains of the Moon Hotel, see Sleeping above. Offers more classy meals. It's a bit out of town, but in an attractive setting and varied international menu. Good for Sun lunch in the garden.

♥ **Dutchies Lunchroom**, Mugurusi Rd, just behind Stanbic Bank. Serves espressos, smoothies, ice creams and light lunches. These 2 dynamic Dutch entrepreneurs are also opening a small cheese factory next to the **Lunchroom**.

♥ **Garden's Restaurant**, opposite the market. Good-value Ugandan buffet, very popular with travellers. Other dishes like pepper steak and chips available. Attractive outside bar, busy in the evenings. Artists regularly perform, look out for the banners.

♥ **Pierre's Pizzeria**, off Kaboyo Rd, in town centre close to Stanbic roundabout, T077-928 0292. Opened in 2009 by an Italian émigré, it has added variety to local meals with a restaurant serving Italian pizzas and grills. They also offer a home delivery service.

♥ **Rwenzori Travellers Inn**, see Sleeping above. Serves tasty grills, as does **The Snack Bar** next door, with speedy service.

Bars and clubs *map p173*

Club Ecstacy, in a small alleyway opposite Barclays bank. Open Wed, Sat and Sun. Popular club.

Don's Plaza, on the main street opposite Andrew's Supermarket. Open at weekends until the last guest leaves. A popular bar that serves some food.

Heartbeat Discotheque, Nightclub and Pub, Rumandika Rd, near **Cornerstone Hotel**. Mostly open at weekends.

Ibaale, round the corner from **Don's Plaza**. A newly opened bar and grill where you can watch the Premier League on a big screen whilst eating spicy chips with steak or drinking a beer.

Mesh's Bar, behind the Shell station on Kasese Rd. Another good bar to hang out in.

Shopping
Markets

Cloth market, close to the post office. Worth a visit.

Mugusu Market, 11 km from Fort Portal town on the road to Kasese. Wed morning.

This market sells everything, including a large selection of second-hand Western clothes.

Supermarkets

Andrew's Supermarket, Lugard Rd. Well-stocked. Also here is **Mary's Craft Shop**, with locally made crafts and cards.

Activities and tours
Golf

Toro Club, on the site of the remains of the Old Fort (see page 174), a 20-min walk up Lugard Rd past the post office. A 9-hole golf course, open to members and those from affiliated clubs. Temporary membership is also available.

Tour operators

Kabarole Tours, Moledina St, behind the Caltex station, T04834-251156, T077-405 7390 (mob), www.kabaroletours.com. A long-established company with friendly, helpful staff and excellent tour guides. Day trips to Lake Nkuruba, Rwenzori Mountains, Kihingmi Wetlands and Mpanga Waterfalls, US$30-70. There are also local cycling tours visiting crater lakes, waterfalls and caves, and countrywide tours on short safaris. Bicycle maintainance is poor, so check them over before paying for local tours or hiring them. They are active in promoting eco-tourism in this part of Uganda. You can visit local communities and learn about their cultural traditions and farming practices.

Transport
Air

The nearest airport is Kasese.

Road

Fort Portal is accessible by road, by 2 alternative routes from Kampala. The quiet sealed road via Mityana and Mubende is about 300 km but due to ongoing major roadworks this journey currently takes about 5 hrs. When the roadworks are completed it will reduce travelling time to 4 hrs. The other road runs through Masaka, Mbarara, Bushenyi and Kasese and is 430 km. By bus the journey takes about 4-5 hrs and goes through exceptionally beautiful countryside.

To **Kampala** a bus leaves hourly, 4-5 hrs, US$8. **Kalita** and **Link** operate this route, the latter having the better maintained buses, but both companies are known for speeding. The Post Bus no longer runs to Fort Portal. However, many more buses now travel from Kampala via Fort Portal to Kasese, and some of them even continue to the border with DR Congo at Bwera, north of Lake Edward.

Matatus run to **Kasese** frequently, 2 hrs, US$2. Very few *matatus* now do the whole route between Kampala and Fort Portal.

Matatus to **Masindi/Hoima** (changing in Kagadi), 7 hrs, US$10. A weekly bus goes directly to Hoima on Sat, leaving at 0630 from Bwamba Rd. If it has rained recently, be prepared to get off the bus on uphill stretches and help push (rnale passengers only). Bus to **Kabale**, 7-8 hrs, US$9. To **Mbarara**, 4-5 hrs, US$4.50.

Directory

Banks You may get up to 25% worse exchange rate than in Kampala. Changing TCs is difficult, but **Barclays** and **Stanbic** banks have ATMs. **Internet** There are several cyber cafés. **Mugasa Internet Café**, part of the best stationery shop in town just across the road from Rwenzori Travellers Inn. Very helpful staff. **Armsat Internet Café**, in the Voice of Toro FM Radio Building, opposite the Continental Hotel, Lugard Rd. **Rwenzori Travellers Inn**, see Sleeping above. **Libraries** The public library has an excellent selection of books. **Places of worship** Most major religions are represented at Fort Portal.

Around Fort Portal

The countryside surrounding Fort Portal is famous for its tea, which remains an important export commodity for Uganda. During the colonial period many **tea plantations** were run by Europeans on land leased from the government (and rarely owned). Now the land is mostly owned by a few large companies, but smallholdings are encouraged. Labour is largely imported from southwest Uganda and this causes some social problems. Many of the original tea plantations had fallen into disrepair when the infrastructure of the country collapsed between 1972 and 1986. Since then a massive rehabilitation programme has been successful in restoring them to their former glory. If you leave Fort Portal early to go chimp tracking in the Kibale Forest, you will notice lots of 'squads' getting ready to head out to work in the fields.

Fort Portal is a base for trips to Kibale Forest, Magombe Swamp, Bigodi, Ndali-Kasenda Crater Lake Fields, Semliki National Park and Sempaya Hot Springs, Toro-Semliki Wildlife Reserve, hikes in the foothills of the Rwenzoris and Amabere Caves and Waterfall. You might also stop over here on the way to the Murchison Falls National Park (although it is a long day's travel to the north, along a notoriously bad road).

Lake Saka → *Colour map 2, B2.*

Amabere Caves and **Waterfall** and three crater lakes lie west of Fort Portal off the Bundibugyo Road. After 8 km you branch off towards Nyakasura school, and follow the signs towards Amabere Caves and Waterfall; it's another 2 km till you get there. Don't expect anything too spectacular; the caves are small, just shallow overhangs of rock, and moss-covered pillars half conceal the entrance. The first cave is dominated by the waterfall. There are stalagmites and stalactites (in the shape of a woman's breast, which is what the name Amabere means). The caves are dark, so bring a torch.

The local guide can tell interesting stories about the traditional history. The area around the caves is attractive and the walk to the nearby crater lakes is worthwhile. Guides from the Amabere Caves will be happy to show you the way. After a short steep climb there is a spectacular view over three crater lakes: Kigere, Nyabikere and Saka. Nyabikere means 'place of frogs', and amphibians are plentiful here. Kigere means 'footprint' in the local language. According to legend a footprint of a man was found in the stones of the caves after a volcanic eruption. The print has since disappeared but the lake and legend remain. You can walk from Fort Portal over the Saka Road towards Lake Saka, but it is not possible to swim in this lake unless you have the permission of the Catholic Seminary,

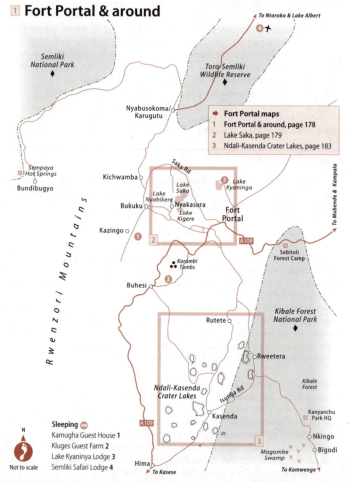

1 Fort Portal & around

To Ntoroko & Lake Albert

Semliki National Park

Toro-Semliki Wildlife Reserve

Nyabusokoma/ Karugutu

➡ **Fort Portal maps**
1 Fort Portal & around, page 178
2 Lake Saka, page 179
3 Ndali-Kasenda Crater Lakes, page 183

Sempaya Hot Springs

Bundibugyo

Kichwamba

Saka Rd

Lake Saka

Lake Kyaninga

Lake Nyabikere

Bukuku

Nyakasura

Fort Portal

Lake Kigere

Kazingo

To Mubende & Kampala

A109

Sebitoli Forest Camp

Karambi Tombs

Buhesi

Rwenzori Mountains

Kibale Forest National Park

Rutete

Rweetera

Kibale Forest

Ndali-Kasenda Crater Lakes

Isunga Rd

Kasenda

Kanyanchu Park HQ

A109

Nkingo

Hima

Magombe Swamp

Bigodi

To Kasese

To Kamwenge

N

Sleeping 🛏
Kamugha Guest House 1
Kluges Guest Farm 2
Lake Kyaninya Lodge 3
Semliki Safari Lodge 4

Not to scale

whose grounds include the lakeside. Another local lake, Lake Kaitabarogo, meaning 'killer of witches', is where so-called 'bewitched' people were thrown. You cannot visit this lake because it is situated within the area of the army barracks.

Lake Saka listings

For Sleeping and Eating price codes and other relevant information, see Essentials pages 21-23.

Sleeping *map p178*

F Amabere Caves Campsite, near the caves, about 1 km from the crater lakes. Pit latrines and shower enclosures. Tent hire also available for US$10. A self-contained lodge (**B**) with 2 rooms, each sleeping 2 costs US$90. Beers and sodas and simple meals are available.

Transport

If you don't have your own transport, you can walk to the caves, hire a *boda-boda*, get a special hire taxi, or take a *matatu* and get off at Nyakasura stage. **Kabarole Tours** (see page 176) organizes bicycle safaris to this area, on bikes similar to those used for bicycle taxis, but without the seat on the back, and a roughly drawn map. Feedback about the quality of these bikes is negative, so check the bikes before booking.

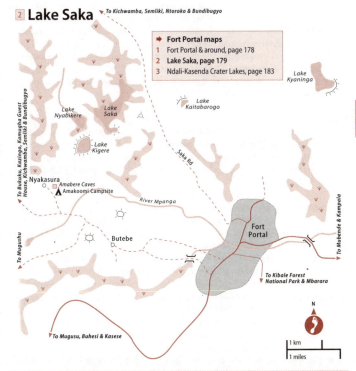

2 Lake Saka

To Kichwamba, Semliki, Ntoroko & Bundibugyo

→ **Fort Portal maps**
1 Fort Portal & around, page 178
2 Lake Saka, page 179
3 Ndali-Kasenda Crater Lakes, page 183

To Bukuku, Kazingo, Kamugha Guest House, Kichwamba, Semliki & Bundibugyo

Lake Nyabikere
Lake Saka
Lake Kigere
Lake Kaitabarogo
Lake Kyaninga

Nyakasura
Amabere Caves
Amakoomi Campsite

River Mpanga

Saka Rd

Fort Portal

To Mugushu

Butebe

To Mugusu, Buhesi & Kasese

To Kibale Forest National Park & Mbarara

To Mubende & Kampala

N

1 km
1 miles

The northern spur of the Rwenzori Mountains → *Colour map 2, B1.*

The road northwest from Fort Portal to Bundibugyo offers many spectacular views. It skirts the northern spur of the Rwenzori Mountains and in clear weather provides good views of the Kijura Escarpment and Lake Albert to the north, and the Semliki River Valley to the northwest. As the road descends into the Rift Valley, it is astonishing to find that the scarp is heavily cultivated; incredibly narrow terracing on a 60-degree slope contains a patchwork of fields – a green quilt, laced with black soil and dimpled by the cassava plants. At Nyabusokoma/Karugutu a road branches off to the fishing village of Ntoroko on the southern shore of Lake Albert, passing through the Toro-Semliki Wildlife Reserve (see below).

Kazingo Trading Centre is in the foothills of the Rwenzori Mountains, about 12.5 km from Fort Portal, and is a base for treks into the northern sector of the mountains. To get to Kazingo, take the Bundibugyo road and after 8 km branch off to the left at Bukuku for Kazingo. You can get a *matatu* up to Bukuku, and walk the remaining 3.5 km to Kazingo. Alternatively, you can hire a private taxi car.

Kamugha Guest House (**F**), T077-262 1397, is a 10-minute walk from Kazingo (see map page 177) and offers simple accommodation and local food. It also offers camping (**E-F**) in an enclosed compound.

From Kazingo Trading Centre there are several treks in the northern Rwenzoris ranging from a day trek to the peak of **Mount Karangora** (3014 m) within the park; hiking via the Bwamba Pass to Bundibugyo or Semliki National Park; or shorter hikes to do some birdwatching, follow the waterfall trail and identify medicinal plants or visit local communities to observe customs, culture and environment. This area has two distinct tribes: the Batoro of the lowlands and the Bakonzo of the mountains. **Abanya Rwenzori Mountaineering Association** ⓘ *based in Kazingo, T077-262 1397 (mob), http://sites. google.com/site/abanyarwenzori*, or **Kabarole Tours** (see page 176) can arrange trips through the northern Rwenzoris.

Itwara Forest

Located 25 km northeast of Fort Portal, this forest has a large number of small mammals as well as a great range of birdlife. Primates found include chimpanzees, black and white colobus, blue monkey, red-tailed monkey and red colobus. Also found are the African palm civet, the giant forest squirrel and the scaly-tailed flying squirrel. Tourist facilities have not been developed.

Toro-Semliki Wildlife Reserve → *Colour map 2, A2.*

ⓘ *US$20 per 24 hrs. Take the road from Fort Portal to Bundibugyo. At Nyabusokoma/ Karugutu (also spelt Karogoto) a road branches off to the fishing village of Ntoroko on the southern shore of Lake Albert and passes through the reserve. A 4WD is preferable as the road is poor and rocky 20 km after leaving Fort Portal. There are daily matatus from Fort Portal going to Semliki and Bundibugyo. There are many matatus plying the Fort Portal to Bundibugyo route serving the Semliki park. Alternatively, the Kalita executive direct bus route on the Kampala–Bundibugyo route leaves Fort Portal around 1500, taking 1¾-2¼ hrs to reach Bundibugyo, US$2.50. For Toro-Semliki change at Nyabusokoma/Karugutu. Toro-Semliki gets less public transport but there are frequent trucks transporting fish, travelling along the Fort Portal–Ntoroko route. Alternatively, take a matatu to Nyabusokoma/Karugutu, and complete the journey in a fish-carrying lorry/pick-up truck.*

It is very easy to get confused over Semliki. There are two different parks: the Toro-Semliki

Wildlife Reserve, home to the upmarket **Semliki Safari Lodge**. The Semliki National Park, see page 181, is over the spur of the Rwenzori Mountains.

The oldest protected area in Uganda, Toro-Semliki Wildlife Reserve was previously known as the Toro Game Reserve. It is unique, gifted with geographic barriers that have formed a natural haven for wildlife. It is an area containing riverine forest, woodland and savannah, previously famous for its very high densities of wildlife including massive maned lions, buffalo, Jackson's hartebeest and forest elephants, known to the hunting fraternity as 'Semliki rats' and reputed to be very aggressive. Leopard, hippo, crocodiles and giant forest hogs were also common and the reserve had an estimated 10,000 Uganda kob (see box, page 157). Chimpanzees and black and white colobus monkeys were frequently seen and there was also prolific birdlife. Apparently, as game was so plentiful in the Semliki Valley in the late 1960s, and the habitat was similar to that in India, a proposal was mooted to breed tigers in the valley, in the hope that, in 10 years or so, the numbers would have multiplied sufficiently to allow tiger hunts to be offered in Africa!

Most of the savannah game was decimated during the period of Amin and Obote's leadership, while the forest species were better equipped to survive the effects of the civil unrest and poachers. However, in the past few years Museveni has very successfully implemented measures to reduce the activities in this area of the rebels who terrorized the villagers and poached much of the wildlife. The lions and buffalo have returned and the number of Uganda kobs has multiplied and is now estimated to be over 8000. Poaching and rebel activity are no longer major issues and game numbers are recovering. Toro-Semliki is the only place in Uganda where you can go on night drives with a good chance of seeing leopard.

The original Semliki Lodge, designed by the Kampala architect Benito Larco, was destroyed by fire, but an upmarket camp has been built nearby. You can take guided walks to observe the wildlife, go birdwatching or track chimpanzees, some of which are being habituated for research. Birdlife is still plentiful, with over 400 species recorded. This is the best place in Uganda to see the rare shoebill stork, most easily viewed from a hired boat on Lake Albert. Sport fishing for Nile perch, tiger fish and tilapia is excellent.

Toro-Semliki Wildlife Reserve listings

For Sleeping and Eating price codes and other relevant information, see Essentials pages 21-23.

Sleeping

Plans are underway to upgrade the UWA campsite near Ntoroko, at the northern tip of the Toro-Semliki Wildlife Reserve on the southern shore of Lake Albert. This joint venture with a private company is expected to offer a range of budget accommodation.

LL Semliki Safari Lodge, T077-248 9497 (mob), www.wildplacesafrica.com. A luxury facility with 8 well-equipped tents, a dining and relaxation area plus a pool. Activities include swimming, birding, hiking and game drives (including night drives). The food is simple but well prepared and very tasty: try the aubergine chips as a snack. The guides are very knowledgeable.

Semliki National Park → *Colour map 2, A1.*

ⓘ *The park headquarters are beside the campsite at Ntandi Gate, 5 km onwards from the Sempaya gate, on the road from Fort Portal to Bundibugyo, situated just outside the park boundaries. Visitation fees are US$20 per 24 hrs. The road has been upgraded from Fort Portal making the journey possible in under 2 hrs. This road becomes treacherous after* heavy rains, requiring a 4WD. Kalita Executive bus service operates daily from Fort Portal at 1500, US$2.50, returning from Bundibuygo at 0700 but suffers from the usual overcrowded conditions. Matatus from Fort Portal stop at the park, US$3, if you're willing to spend the night in Bundibugyo. Journey time is 1¾-2¼ hrs. If wet the journey will take an additional 45 mins. The Chinese are rebuilding this road (as it also leads to Uganda's newly discovered oil reserves). So these journey times are likely to improve over the next couple of years.

The road from Fort Portal heads north to cross the northern tail of the Rwenzori range and then doubles back through Ntandi, Bundibugyo and Sempaya. This road is undergoing major rebuilding by the Chinese. Taking the main road from Nyabusokoma/Karagutu to Bundibugyo, the road loops around the northern edge of the Rwenzori Mountains and descends from 1200 m to 720 m in a series of spectacular hairpin bends. At the bottom of the escarpment are the **Sempaya Hot Springs**, located inside the Semliki National Park.

Semliki (sometimes written Semuliki) National Park lies 52 km northwest of Fort Portal, located in the Bundibugyo District, on the far side of the northern tail of the Rwenzori Mountain range. On old maps it was known as Bwamba Forest. The name is now mostly associated with the virus responsible for a cold-like viral infection transmitted by mosquitoes that is often mistaken for malaria. There are few facilities here as this area was until recently home to thousands of internally displaced persons, living in makeshift tents, fleeing from unrest in DR Congo.

It is mainly very dense tropical lowland forest, effectively an extension of the Congo's Ituri rain forest, but with some grassland, wetland and bamboo forest. The terrain is quite flat, and the Rwenzori range forms a backdrop to the east. It rains a lot, and visitors should come prepared with waterproofs. The Semliki River defines the border with DR Congo, and several tributaries run through the park, providing watering places and good spots to observe animals. There are also some hot springs, and these attract birds and animals using the salt licks. The various habitats attract a wide variety of wildlife, including elephants, buffaloes, leopards, civets, scaly-tailed flying squirrels and bush babies. Primates are well represented, with eight species reported, and more than 400 bird species and 300 butterfly species have been observed. A trail round the park takes in the hot springs, and excursions to other areas can be arranged through the park headquarters.

Semliki National Park listings

For Sleeping and Eating price codes and other relevant information, see Essentials pages 21-23.

There is currently no accommodation within the park.

Sleeping
F-G Rainbow Inn, Bundibugyo, T077-252 6600 (mob). Along with **Vanilla Hotel**, this is one of the better places to stay.

F-G Tour Guardian Guest House, Bugomba, near Bundibugyo, T078-305 7864 (mob). Recently opened with shared facilities in a former church.
F-G Vanilla Hotel, Bundibugyo, T077-266 9941 (mob).

Camping
2 campsites, one near Ntandi and one at Sempaya, offer basic self-catering facilities. Insect repellents is advisable. Both campsites are being developed (slowly) by UWA in conjunction with private organizations.

The **Bunyaruguru Volcanic Fields** are an area with extensive cones and craters, located about 30 km south of Fort Portal between the main Fort Portal–Kasese road and Kibale Forest National Park. Crater lakes are formed by vulcanicity, with a violent eruption causing the top of a volcano to be blown off, leaving a crater. There are several lakes of varying size and character, and many have well-developed tourist facilities. Interesting features include a fascinating natural lava formation making a bridge under which water flows. Although reputed to be bilharzia-free the crater lakes are not, with the exception of

3 **Ndali-Kasenda Crater Lakes Crater Lakes**

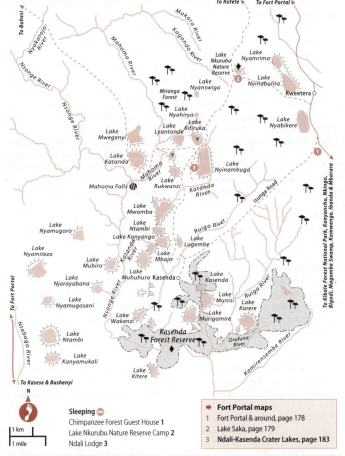

Sleeping
Chimpanzee Forest Guest House 1
Lake Nkurubu Nature Reserve Camp 2
Ndali Lodge 3

Fort Portal maps
1 Fort Portal & around, page 178
2 Lake Saka, page 179
3 Ndali-Kasenda Crater Lakes, page 183

Lake Nkurubu. They are therefore unsafe for swimming and there are leeches. However, they offer good fishing and the opportunity to do some serious birdwatching, with an estimated 300-400 species.

Ins and outs

Getting there There is little traffic on the roads to the crater lakes but *matatus* go from Fort Portal to Rwaihamba, more frequently on the market days of Monday and Thursday. For Lake Nkuruba take the *matatu* to Rwaihamba, 40 minutes from Fort Portal, US$2. Lake Nkuruba is 2 km from Rwaihamba. *Boda-bodas* can be hired in Rwaihamba to go to the crater lakes. A 'special hire' (private taxi) from Fort Portal to Lake Nkuruba takes about 45 minutes, costing US$9-11 for three people per car.

A shared taxi would take six people plus baggage for US$1.50 per person.

By car, take the Kibale road from Fort Portal for 17 km and take the right fork, from where it is another 8 km to Lake Nkuruba.

Lake Nkurubu

This beautiful small crater lake is the only crater lake remaining unspoilt by deforestation. It offers reputedly bilharzia-free safe swimming, because it is the only lake clear of the freshwater snails that carry the fluke. There are frequent sightings of black and white colobus monkeys, plus an occasional visit from Henrietta, a solitary nomadic hippo who travels between Lake Nkuruba and Lake Nyabikere. From here you can walk in the surroundings or hire a bicycle (with gears) for a trip around some of the nearby crater lakes or to the Mahoma Falls. Maps are available for different trips and walks.

Lake Nkuruba Nature Reserve ⓘ *T077-326 6067 (mob), www.traveluganda.co.ug/ lake-nkuruba. Day visit charge US$2.25*, is a community conservation project that funds local education. The tranquil settings provide an ideal base for budget travellers to explore the crater lakes with good walks to the 'Top of the World', to neighbouring lakes, the Mahoma Falls and the explosion crater. Accommodation is available (see Sleeping, below).

Lake Nyinambuga

South of Lake Nkuruba, this blue-green lake offers the only luxurious facilities in the crater lake field (see Sleeping below).

Lake Nyabikere

Meaning 'lake of frogs', Lake Nyabikere is only 13 km or 30 minutes' drive from Fort Portal on the Kamwenge road, and just 100 m off the main road at the edge of Kibale Forest National Park. It is 10 km from the centre of Kibale Forest. It is possible to walk from Lake Nyabikere to Lake Nkuruba via Lake Nynabulita and Lake Nyamirima. The route is shown on the map and part of it can be done by car.

Other lakes

Most other lakes are difficult to reach or to enter. You can arrange a visit to Mahoma Falls in Kabata village, near Ndali Lodge (see Sleeping below), or hire a bike with directions at Lake Nkuruba. **Kabarole Tours** (see page 176) in Fort Portal can also arrange crater lake tours.

Ndali-Kasenda Crater Lakes listings

For Sleeping and Eating price codes and other relevant information, see Essentials pages 21-23.

Sleeping *map p183*

LL Ndali Lodge, Lake Nyinambuga, T077-222 1309, www.ndalilodge.com. This well-appointed lodge is set on a narrow ridge overlooking the lake 100 m below. There are stunning 360° views of the mountains to the west, the Rift Valley lakes to the south and the crater lakes to the east and north. Originally a tea planter's house, the lodge has 8 cottages set on the hillside in a well-kept garden. There is no electricity but plenty of hot water heated by Tanganyika ovens. Service is impeccable and simple but beautifully cooked meals are served. There is a pool, sauna and yoga platform. Boat trips can also be arranged by the lodge.

C Chimpanzee Forest Guest House, Lake Nyabikere, 23 km south of Port Fortal on the Kamwenge road, T077-248 6415, chimpgueste@yahoo.com. With Lake Nyabikere views, this place offers B&B accommodation in the house, *bandas* or camping in wonderful grounds,
including gardens, indigenous forest and tea plantations. Built in the 1950s, it was previously the home of the British District Commissioner.

E Lake Nkuruba Nature Reserve, T077-326 6067 (mob), www.traveluganda.co.ug/lake-nkuruba. Accommodation ranges from campsites and a *banda* (US$8pp) to the romantic lakeside house. There are lots of black and white (and red) colobus monkeys in the trees above the house. Camping costs US$3pp and tent hire US$1. Delicious evening meals made with locally grown vegetables cost US$3.50. Vegetarian food is available and chapattis are baked fresh to order and served at the lakeshore. Be aware that a rival campsite with a similar name, **Nkuruba Enfuzi**, has opened for business next door, and the owner or 'pastor' employs shady practices to divert custom to his campsite. This includes paying the taxi drivers in Fort Portal to bypass the LNNR entrance gate and take travellers to his campsite. There is only one entrance to LNNR via a blue and yellow gate with an MTN sign, visible from the left side of the taxi. Alternatively, call LNNR staff Adeline or Patrick to arrange transport.

Kibale Forest National Park → *Altitude: 1230 m. Colour map 2, B2.*

About 35 km south of Fort Portal, Kibale Forest provides a rich and unique habitat for more than 250 species of animal and over 300 types of bird. The animal species include 11 primates, including chimpanzees, black and white colobus monkeys, red colobus monkeys, blue monkeys and baboons, the highest concentration of primate species in East Africa. Monkeys can often be spotted from the road to the forest and the viewing of chimpanzees in their natural environment is the main attraction. The forest's emblem is a black and white colobus monkey designed by Lysa Leland, a researcher and photographer who, with her husband Tom Struhsaker, worked in Kibale for many years, long before it became popular.

Kibale Forest National Park covers an area of about 760 sq km and is divided into seven zones for management purposes: research, natural reserve, civic-cultural, recreation, harvest, community and protection. There is an emphasis on conservation, sustainable utilization and non-consumptive use of the forest. Nature trails into the forest have been created and, quite apart from the chimps, the walks are wonderful.

Ins and outs

Getting there The two access points for the park are Kanyanchu and Sebitoli. The park is located off the Fort Portal–Kamwenge–Mbarara road. Take a *matatu* from Fort Portal from the Kamwenge stage, just near the bridge over Mpanga River, opposite the market on Kibale Road, but not early in the morning to reach Kibale in time to track the chimpanzees. The road to Kibale Forest is gravel, but in good condition, scheduled to be upgraded shortly. *Matatus* to Kibale Forest/Bigodi leave throughout the day, but are more frequent in the afternoons, 1½ hours, US$3. If you want to track chimpanzees at 0800 you'll have to arrange your own transport or stay the night in or near Kibale Forest (see Sleeping, below). Alternatively, hire a *boda-boda* from Fort Portal.

Park fees   The park fee is US$30 for 24 hours, plus US$90 per person chimpanzee tracking fee. Guided walks cost US$15/10 for full/half day in addition to the park fee. No fee is charged for driving through the park on the Fort Portal–Kamwenge road or for visiting the Bigodi Wetland Sanctuary (see page 187).

Chimpanzee tracking

Tracking the habituated chimp troops is conducted by trained guides who will also be able to tell you about the forest generally. The group of chimps in the Kanyanchu community is probably the largest in Kibale Forest, numbering about 45. Other animals found in the forest include elephants, buffaloes, bush pigs and duikers. However, many of these are very reclusive and you will be lucky to see them. There is also a huge range of birdlife and an estimated 140 species of butterfly.

There are organized trips to track the chimps twice daily, leaving from Kanyanchu at 0800 and 1500. A maximum of three groups of six people can track the chimpanzees in a morning or afternoon. The morning walk is reported to offer a better opportunity to see the primates, usually to be found in the fig trees. Visitors are not allowed to walk in the forest unaccompanied and the guide's knowledge will also enhance your enjoyment of the walk.

Sebitoli Tourist Centre

A northern entrance to Kibale National Park called Sebitoli Tourist Centre, and is on the main road from Fort Portal to Kampala, 1.5 km from Fort Portal. Designed to take pressure off the Kanyanchu section this site offers nature walks, birding activities, but no chimpanzee tracking available as none have been habituated in this part of the forest. Simple food and drink are usually available..

Kibale Forest National Park listings

For Sleeping and Eating price codes and other relevant information, see Essentials pages 21-23.

Sleeping

LL-A Primate Lodge, Kibale, T0414-267153, T077-242 6368 (mob), www.ugandalodges. com. Run by Great Lakes Safaris, 8 safari tents, cottages, camping or a short walk away, the Sky Tree House. Sited very close to the trailhead for tracking chimpanzees.
AL-A Chimp's Nest, T077-466 9107, www.chimpsnest.com. Dutch enterprise near Nyabubale village between Nkingo and Bigodi, offering cottages, a 6-m-high treehouse within the forest, backpacker rooms or camping. Sited 15 mins' drive from the start point for chimpanzee tracking and even closer for the Bigodi Swamp Walk. Very positive feedback.
AL-A Kibale Forest Camp, T077-982 0695 (mob), www.naturelodges.biz. Has 7 en suite safari tents or treehouse (single bed). Sited close to Bigodi Wetlands (see below). Friendly staff and tasty food, especially the Indian dishes.

E Sebitoli Camp, Sebitoli Tourist Centre. 3 *bandas* and camping within the park.

Transport

To **Fort Portal** there are regular *matatus*, but don't leave it too late. On Tue there is a market at Rukunyu, a village between Bigodi and Kamwenge, so there is more traffic on the road.

Bigodi Wetland Sanctuary and Magombe Swamp

ⓘ *Bigodi and Kibale Forest NP are located off the Fort Portal–Kamwenge–Mbarara road. For transport details, see page 185. Entry US$15 includes a guide.*

Managed by KAFRED (Kibale Association for Rural Development), the sanctuary is a community-based organization that supports eco-tourism initiatives and funds local projects like a school, health centre and library. It is situated 3 km past the Kibale Forest towards Bigodi. In the morning and late afternoon you can take a guided swamp walk along a trail with occasionally muddy boardwalks. The swamp is rich with a variety of vegetation. The most common tree species are wild palms, polita figs and wild rubber trees. In addition there are ferns, water lilies, flowers such as those of the Ipomea species, fire lilies, wetland grasses, sedges and reeds. The dominant vegetation is the papyrus. Primates such as the red colobus, black and white colobus and red-tailed monkey live in the swamp, along with over 138 bird species, including the great blue turaco, and a large number of butterflies. The guides are excellent at identifying the birds, more visible during the morning excursions. Make sure that you take precautions against red ants ascending your legs by wearing closed shoes or boots, avoiding open-toed sandals and tucking trousers into socks.

Beside the visitor's centre for the swamp walk is the **Tinka-Homestay (E)**, where you can be a guest in a Ugandan home and enjoy home-grown, freshly harvested traditional food. Cultural activities like storytelling and dance take place.

Fort Portal to Hoima and Murchison Falls

Heading for Hoima and Masindi from Fort Portal, the first 50 km, to Kyenjojo, is sealed. Take a left turn here for the road to Hoima. This road has a bad reputation of sometimes being impassable but has been considerably improved recently. However, during heavy rains it can be very slippery. When you reach the halfway mark, at Kagadi, you have negotiated the worst part. If you have the time and a good 4WD you will be rewarded by a trip through one of the most lovely parts of Uganda. For the first part of the journey the landscape is one of low cultivated hills, but as you proceed north it becomes mountainous and partly forested. Every so often the road reaches a spot where you can see for miles. It really is fantastically beautiful. The forest is interspersed with patches of cultivation but, being so cut off, this is one of the poorer parts of Uganda.

Hoima → *Phone code: 4654. Colour map 2, A3.*

The most direct route to Hoima from Kampala is on a sealed road via Kiboga, which is an interesting journey through the bush. The landscape is hilly with a scattering of huge boulders amongst the farmland. The rather shabby and run-down town of **Kiboga** is about 120 km from Kampala and is strung out along the road.

Soon after leaving Kiboga the road begins a gradual descent into the plain beyond which Hoima, the capital of Bunyoro, is located. The plain is punctuated by the occasional

Bunyoro Coronation

As part of the programme to restore traditional structures, as with the Buganda (see box, page 195), the monarchy was restored with the coronation of the 42-year-old, British-educated Solomon Iguru in 1994.

The previous king, Sir Tito Winyi IV, had been crowned in 1924, but deposed in 1967 when Obote abolished the monarchies (see page 239). It is the tradition that the king nominates his successor from among his heirs. There was a wide choice as King Winyi had several wives and 104 children. His choice of Solomon was disputed by another son, John, who claimed that, as the eldest son of the only wife to have been married in a Christian ceremony, he was the legitimate heir. The High Court of Uganda, however, decided in favour of Solomon.

The coronation took place on 11 June at Hoima where the king has a palace, a large, strong construction with two wings and a blue tiled roof, where the Rukerato, the Bunyoro parliament, is located. The ceremony was attended by President Museveni, the King and Queen of Toro

and a representative of the Kabaka of Uganda. As the previous coronation had been 70 years before, the procedures were uncertain. In the event it began with representatives of various religious denominations giving their blessing. A number of ceremonial objects were presented to the king: slippers to help him travel; a spear to kill anyone despising his people; a dagger for protection; a *kaliruga*, a club to beat anyone vexing him; a *kujunju*, a staff to punish offenders; an *empese*, a hoe symbolizing fathership of the people; a bow and quiver for fighting enemies; a leopard skin bag to assist in trading; a bamboo whistle to sound the war alarm; a *kasisi*, a vessel to ensure peace; and a second hoe to ensure good harvests.

The ceremony also included the presentation of 20th-century 'slippers' in the form of a Land Cruiser from President Museveni, and some centenary pottery from Leeds, where the new king had studied. Events were concluded with traditional music, drumming and dancing.

JJ Pearlman

---

bare hill, and Hoima itself is spread across two such hills. Hoima can be seen from quite a distance, surrounded by eucalyptus trees that were planted as an anti-malarial measure during the colonial era. On entering the town you pass through the instantly recognizable old colonial part of town: bungalows with wide verandas, set in large gardens, and fading government offices. The town centre sits overlooking a deep valley with a number of buildings, including one of the town's churches, on the opposite side.

Access to Kabwoya Wildlife Reserve (see page 189) is via Hoima. The discovery of oil reserves in the nearby Kaiso area of Lake Albert have given a huge boost to the development of local infrastructure like roads, and if sensitively managed could transform the lives of this poor remote area.

Around Hoima

Katasiha Fort is located 3 km along the Butiaba road, which leads north out of town towards Lake Albert. The fort was established in 1894 by Colonel Colville when he was trying to subdue Kabalega, the King (known locally as the Omukama) of Bunyoro. All that survives of the fort are a rampart and a ditch.

The **Mparo Tombs**, 3.5 km from Hoima on the road to Masindi, are the burial places of the two most influential Bunyoro kings of modern times. Cwa II Kabalega was born in 1850. When his father King Kamasuri died, in 1869, there was a succession struggle. In 1870, at the battle of Buziba, Kabalega defeated his brother Kabigumire, forcing him to flee and giving himself the opportunity to bury his father and claim the throne. Establishing his palace at Mparo, Kabalega strengthened and consolidated his kingdom, and established a formidable military capability. In 1872 Sir Samuel Baker, Governor of Equatoria in southern Sudan, formally annexed Bunyoro. Kabalega began a hopeless struggle against the British, which culminated in his capture in 1899. Kabalega was exiled to the Seychelles, baptised as a Christian and, at the age of 49, taught to read and write. Six counties were transferred from Bunyoro as a punishment. In Kabalega's absence, the British installed his 12-year-old son, Prince Kitehimbwa, who ruled under the guidance of a series of regents. In 1902 Kitehimbwa was replaced by another of Kabalega's sons, Duhaga. In 1923 Duhaga requested that the British allow his father to return. Kabalega sailed back the next year, and was provided with a residence at Jinja, where he died two months later. He was buried at Mparo, having requested that only traditional roofing materials should be used to cover his tomb. In 1973 Murchison Falls National Park was renamed Kabalega Falls by Amin (though it has now reverted to its original name).

Duhaga died the next year, and he was succeeded by Tito Winyi, yet another son of Kabalega, who had been educated at King's College, Budo. By cooperating with the British, Tito Winyi achieved considerable progress in the kingdom. He was knighted in 1934 and in 1964 negotiated the return of the six counties after a referendum. In 1967, Milton Obote abolished the traditional kingdoms and Sir Tito Winyi IV retired to Masindi. He died in 1971, and is buried at Mparo. In 1994, the kingdom was restored, and Tito Winyi's son Solomon Iguru was crowned at Hoima (see box, above).

As well as the two monarchs, several other members of the royal family are buried at Mparo. In keeping with his wishes, Kabalega's tomb has a thatched roof supported by a circular stone wall. Inside, the tomb is covered with a stretched cow hide and surrounded by a collection of the king's traditional personal belongings. Sir Tito Winyi's tomb is similar. The site is surrounded by bark-cloth trees and a reed fence. Outside the compound is a memorial to Kabelaga and Emin Pasha.

Kabwoya Wildlife Reserve → Colour map 2, A3.

ⓘ *Entry fee US$10 per 24 hrs.*

The Kabwoya Wildlife Reserve was gazetted in 2002. A tripartite agreement between UWA, the Hoima District Local Government and Lake Albert Safaris has resulted in the development of this new reserve, opened in 2006, located between Lake Albert and the Escarpment of the Albertine Rift Valley. The reserve is mostly savannah and riverine forest that was decimated of wildlife during Uganda's troubles or used by pasturalists for grazing domestic livestock. However, numbers and varieties of wildlife are now rapidly rising, including hippos, buffalo, kob, bushbuck, oribi, duiker, warthogs, elephants, chimpanzees, black and white colobus monkeys and olive baboons, along with the occasional leopard and lion. Birdlife is prolific with over 450 varieties. Re-introduced species, courtesy of an USAID PRIME/West programme, are 20 Jackson's hartebeest and 20 waterbuck from Murchison Falls National Park. Ironically, given the sterling work undertaken to increase wildlife, this reserve is one of the few in Uganda where controlled quotas of game are permitted to be hunted as sport trophies.

Kabwoya Wildlife Reserve listings

For Sleeping and Eating price codes and other relevant information, see Essentials pages 21-23.

Sleeping

L Lake Albert Safari Lodge, T077-222 1003, www.lakealbert.com. The main lodge and *bandas* are set on cliffs that overlook Lake Albert with wonderful views westwards of the Blue Mountains in DR Congo. 12 thatched cottages with private bathroom, or camping US$17pp. Good food and a well-stocked bar. Small pool is shared by guests and the occasional wildlife. Activities include guided walking including night walks, birding, horseback safaris, fossil hunting, fishing on Lake Albert and hunting. The lodge is 70 km due west of Hoima near Kaiso. Drive 5 km along the Hoima–Butiaba road, then take the 2nd left at the signpost for Karongo or the **Eco-Gardens Tourist Hotel**. The road passes through Biseruka Trading Centre then heads south to Kabaale. Continuing south for another 8 km you reach Kaseeta, then turn right (west) and the escarpment is a further 8 km. The lodge and lake lie another 15 km west. If lost at this point ask for directions to the fishing village of Kyehoro.

C Kon Tiki Hotel, 2 km out of town on the Kampala approach road, T077-277 5005 or T077-330 4752 (both mob), www.hoimakontiki.com. Has a good restaurant and lovely gardens. Thatched cottages and an attractive restaurant/bar make this a popular choice.

D Kopling Society Guesthouse, T04654-40167. Clean, pleasant church-run guesthouse with friendly staff, set in a well-kept garden with smallish rooms. Private facilities, good mosquito nets and a great restaurant, serving local and international dishes.

F Nsamo Hotel, close to taxi park on Buhangura Rd. Has a pleasant inner courtyard with flowers, cool running water and reasonably intact mosquito nets. En suite rooms or, at half the price, rooms with shared bathrooms.

Eating

The best food is found at the above hotels but there are many cheaper local alternatives.

Transport

Kampala is about 200 km away, via Kiboga, a drive of 2½ hrs on a sealed road. Or go via Masindi, about 60 km away, making a total of about 260 km from Kampala, or from Fort Portal. Taking the latter route on public transport you will probably have to change at least once, usually at Kagadi. Post Bus to **Kampala** via Masindi leaves Hoima post office at 0630, US$5.50. Regular *matatus* go to **Masindi** US$2.50. Bus to **Fort Portal** leaves early morning Mon, Wed and Fri, 6 hrs in good weather, US$5. Regular *matatus* leave for **Kagadi**, change for a *matatu* to Fort Portal, US$4.

Directory

Banks Barclays, 56 Main St. Stanbic bank. ATM. **Internet** Net, down an unmade road by the mobile phone mast, past the Nsamo Hotel.

Contents

Footprint features

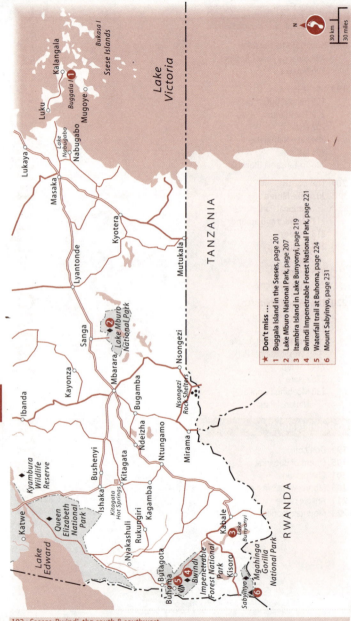

N

30 km
30 miles

Lake Victoria

TANZANIA

RWANDA

Kalangala
Luku
Buggala I
Mugoye
Bukasa I
Ssese Islands

Lukaya
Lake Nabugabo
Nabugabo

Masaka
Kyotera
Lyantonde

Sanga
Mbarara
Lake Mburo National Park
Nsongezi
Mutukala

Ibanda
Kayonza
Bugamba
Ndeizha
Ntungamo
Mirama
Nsongezi Rock Shelters

Kyambura Wildlife Reserve
Bushenyi
Kitagata
Katwe
Queen Elizabeth National Park
Ishaka
Kitagata Hot Springs
Nyakashuli
Rukungiri
Kagamba

Lake Edward
Butagota
Buhoma
Bwindi Impenetrable Forest National Park
Kabale
Lake Bunyonyi
Kisoro
Lake Sabyinyo
Mgahinga Gorilla National Park

If your time is limited then the south and southwest could well be for you. The 84 lush, tropical Ssese Islands are a major tourist attraction. Many of the islands are heavily forested with waterfalls, the wildlife includes many monkeys and the islands teem with birds including kingfishers, grey parrots and fish eagles. There are empty beaches, friendly islanders and trekking and fishing are popular activities.

From Masaka, the stepping off point for attractive Lake Nabugabo, an excellent road takes you southwest. Lake Mburo National Park offers walking safaris in tranquil surroundings of rolling hills and lush grass-covered valleys. Beyond Mbarara, the road forks southwest to Kabale and nearby picturesque Lake Bunyonyi.

The far southwest has the dramatic Virunga volcanoes that straddle Uganda, Rwanda and DR Congo. Here is spectacular tropical rainforest scenery of mountain peaks and steep valleys with enormous trees and dense undergrowth, home of the threatened mountain gorillas, which can be tracked at either Bwindi Impenetrable Forest or Mgahinga Gorilla national parks.

Kampala to Masaka

The road out of Kampala can be hectic, especially in the mornings as it passes through Natete, with its endless trade stores and matatu stops. The road is very fast and exciting as matatus swerve around the matoke bikes, which men push for miles to market. Some 10 km out of Kampala, King's College, Budo is reached. Nearby is a flower growing operation at the Dutch-owned Nsimbe Estate. Swamps and small patches of forest alternate with fertile, well-watered fields.

About 40 km out of Kampala is Mpigi and, if you are hoping to buy any traditional musical instruments (particularly drums), this is the place to do so. There are drum-makers and their stalls on the side of the road. Mpigi is also the closest place to buy provisions for the nearby Mpanga Forest Reserve. Unlike the Mabira Forest on the Jinja road, only a very small patch of the Mpanga Forest Reserve is visible so watch out for the signs carefully. The reserve is an excellent day trip from Kampala. Further on is Masaka, a major hub for traffic to Tanzania and the Ssese Islands if travelling from the west.

Mpanga Forest Reserve → Colour map 2, B4.

Mpanga is a 450-ha lowland forest reserve about an hour's drive and 36 km from the capital. This remnant of the Guineo-Congolian rainforest, dating from the Pleistocene period 15,000 years ago, was gazetted for protection in 1951, when research plots were delineated within the forest to establish the productivity of indigenous forest trees. The main attractions are the mighty trees with their knotted roots, as well as monkeys, birds and over 180 varieties of butterflies. The most easily viewed mammals are the red-tailed monkeys, flying squirrels and the bush pig. Over 180 birds have been recorded here including the African pied hornbill, the great blue turaco and the black and white casqued hornbill. The forest is contiguous with a papyrus swamp where the rare shoebill stork can be spotted (see box, page 74). Snakes can also be seen. The forest provides five types of timber used in drum making. The Royal Drum-Makers are in the nearby village of Mpambire.

Ins and outs

Getting there The main Kampala–Masaka road bisects the forest. It is well signposted, and there is a murram track from the highway to the reception centre. Public transport from the new taxi park in Kampala to Mpigi is US$1.40, then take a boda-boda to the reserve, US$0.70. A matatu from Kampala for Masaka will drop you off at Mpanga, US$3.

Park information The entry fee for foreigners is listed as US$15 per day, with guided walks at US$15 per person, night walks to see the bush babies US$5, guide fees US$1.50. Despite this listed tariff, when this book went to press foreign visitors were being charged US$5 entrance fee and another US$5 guided forest walk fee. However, these charges will escalate if the new NFA tariffs are implemented (see box, page 26). At the reception centre are trail maps, guides, a craft shop and secure parking.

Trails

Three trails have been marked. The **Base Line Trail** traverses the forest to a papyrus swamp 3 km away on the west side. The trail crosses a couple of streams with drifts of butterflies to be seen in the clearings. The **Butterfly Loop** takes less than 30 minutes and involves some scrambling over fallen trees and struggling through thick vegetation. Tracks of both

Drums of Buganda

There is a saying in Luganda that goes *Tezirawa ngumba* which means 'They are not beaten without a reason'. In modern times you are most likely to hear drums being played at traditional weddings, funerals, and particularly in rural areas. Drums are often played on occasions of celebration, too, such as the Kabaka's coronation (see box, page 188).

Although drums are frequently thought of as being merely musical instruments, they in fact have a wide range of uses. In the past there were literally hundreds of different beats for the drums and each rhythm was known and had a definite meaning; for example, a certain dance taking place, a call to war, a fire alarm or the news that a certain chief was passing. As a person heard the drum it was their duty to repeat the message so that within a few minutes the message could pass over many miles.

Traditionally, the drums belonged to the Kabaka and when he presented a chief with a position of office he bestowed upon him a drum. This is why the playing of the drums was an important part of the ceremonies involved in the crowning of the Kabaka – once he had 'tuned' the drums no one else was allowed to play them.

Kiganda (as Buganda culture is known) has drums of two kinds – the first is made of a hollowed block of wood, tapering towards the base, with skins stretched over the head and base. The skins are laced with thongs of hide. They are named according to their size and use, and the important ones are also given names individually. The other type, seen more rarely nowadays, is known as *ngalabi* and exists in various sizes. Also made of hollowed-out wood, it is long and slender, tapering gradually and then widening out again to form the base on which the drum stands. The top is covered with a skin – usually that of a

type of water lizard – which is pegged on. The bottom of the drum is left open. These drums are particularly attractive and large ones may be as much as 140 cm high.

In the past the ceremonies of the Baganda court were closely tied to the use of a large number of drums belonging to the Kabaka. Each drum or group of drums was named and men were specifically appointed to take up residence at the Lubiri (the Baganda palace) for the sole purpose of beating drums.

The range of drums used in the past was enormous – each was made slightly differently of varying sizes with different decorations. Each type served a distinct purpose and was played in a slightly different way, often by a specific clan. Examples of names include Nakawanguzu, which means the 'Conqueror'. This drum was played when the Kabaka had been successful in his attacks on surrounding tribes. The Kyejo was used when the Kabaka executed troublemakers as a warning to others. The Makumbi warned people to cultivate their banana gardens or risk having their hands cut off. The Va-mu-lugudo, meaning 'get out of the way', was used when the wives of the Kabaka were out walking; no one was allowed to be on the road in front of them, so the drummer went ahead to warn people to stand aside.

Drums are also associated with chieftainships, with each chief having his drum bestowed with his office by the Kabaka. The various clans of Baganda also had their own drums and particular drum beats. Selected clans were responsible for the making, beating, maintenance and safekeeping of the drums – different clans for each particular drum type.

There is a splendid collection of drums at the Uganda Museum in Kampala (see page 57). Drum-making can be seen in the Mpanga Forest Reserve (see opposite).

bush-babies and leopards are reported but, alas, the mammals themselves are rarely seen. The **Hornbill Trail** follows a 5-km loop taking about three hours along streams with exotic fungi, butterflies, birds and monkeys all on view.

Mpanga Forest Reserve listings

For Sleeping and Eating price codes and other relevant information, see Essentials pages 21-23.

Sleeping and eating

There are camping and picnic areas, and some simple accommodation. An eco-tourism centre was established in 1999 offering accommodation and guided forest walks. The camping, barbecue, picnic and latrine facilities are near the reception centre, and another picnic site is in a forest glade about 100 m from the start of the Base Line Trail. Water and firewood are available. Food is available if pre-ordered or bring your own food and tents. Purchase provisions can in nearby Mpigi.

C-F Bamboo House, a cottage on stilts. There are also *banda* rooms, dorms US$4.50pp, camping US$2.25pp.

To Masaka

The roadside along this section is marshy, due to its proximity to Lake Victoria. As you approach Lukaya, you will see roadside stands selling fresh and smoked fish. About 75 km from Kampala just after Buwama you cross the **equator**, which is marked by a large concrete circle. Shops sell papyrus mats, trays and baskets. The Katonga River, which links Lake Victoria and Lake George, is also crossed. There are also large termite mounds on either side of Masaka Road, some 2 m tall and 1.5 m in diameter at the base. There is a weighbridge for heavy vehicles at Luyaka. Taxis and *matatus* are weighed, and as a result there are lots of street vendors milling around. Some of the good eats are half a roast chicken (*nkokko*) on a stick for US$0.90, roasted Gonjja bananas (*matooke*) for US$0.25, water and soft drinks US$0.70.

From here onwards Ankole cattle with their long horns, goats and sheep are seen grazing along the roadside. The vegetation also changes, from papyrus grass in the swamps, to plantations of banana (*matooke*), coffee, cassava, mango and papaya. Masaka is 30 minutes past Lukaya.

Masaka → *Phone code: 4814. Colour map 2, B3.*

Masaka is a pretty town, built on the side of a hill, but the extensive damage done during the Tanzanian invasion of 1979 is still visible. A huge radio mast dominates the skyline. It is a stopping-off point for the Ssese Islands.

Ins and outs

Getting there Normally, the 128-km trip from Kampala to Masaka takes two hours, but with current roadworks it is now closer to three hours. There are frequent *matatus* and Coaster buses from Kampala; most leave soon after daybreak, US$3. If continuing to the Ssese Islands in the same day, make sure you get a Coaster bus from Kampala, getting to Masaka by lunchtime, which means getting to the capital's taxi park by 0800 to allow time for the bus to fill up and make the journey. *Matatus* continue later in the day.
➤➤ *See Transport, page 198.*

Nyabajuzzi Valley and Wetland Swamps
ⓘ T0414-540719, nature@natureuganda.org, US$1.

This is home to some of the rarest species in Uganda after gorillas, with over 200 bird species identified including the shoebill stork (see box, page 74) and crowned cranes. It also has the sitatunga, an aquatic antelope. The Sitatunga Corner Observation Tower, complete with a telescope but rather shaky stairs, has been constructed by nearby communities. The tower is positioned right off the bypass road leaving Masaka for Mbarara, next to the sewage treatment plant.

Masaka

To Bukakata (39 km), for Ferry to Ssese Islands

Sleeping
Brovad 1
Golf Lane 2
Zebra 3

Eating
Aid's Child Ten Tables 1
Café Frikadellen 2

200 metres
200 yards

N

Masaka listings

For Sleeping and Eating price codes and other relevant information, see Essentials pages 21-23.

Sleeping *map p197*
AL-A Golf Lane Hotel, Kizungu Hill, Katwe, T0392-200 669/70, www.golflanehotel.com. 3-star hotel, opened in 2008, on the highest point overlooking Masaka. In the former mansion of ex-Vice-President Muwanga, this business hotel has a Western-style atmosphere. 78 well-appointed en suite rooms and 7 suites, DSTV, with great balcony views. There's a bar, restaurant, health club and pool.

A-B Hotel Brovad, 6 Circular Rd, T077-242 5666 (mob), www.hotelbrovad.com. Functional rather than charming, this hotel has 125 en suite rooms, DSTV, a bar and a restaurant. Conference facilities and a business centre.

C-B Hotel Zebra, Baines Terr, T4814-20936, T078-286 3725 (mob), www.hotelzebra.net. Quieter than its competitors, this new hotel is located uphill, on a crescent off the Kampala–Mbarara road behind **Stanbic Bank**. 50 en suite rooms with cable TV. Pleasant terrace and garden overlooking Nyabajuzzi Valley. The bar and restaurant has a varied menu. Internet is available for residents.

E-F Masaka Backpackers' Cottage and Campsite, 4 km from Masaka, on the Bukoba–Kyotera road, Nyendo, T04814-21288, T078-267 7201 (mob), masakabackpackers@yahoo.com. Well positioned for travellers going to the Ssese Islands. Semi-rural hilly site overlooking banana plantations with en suite rooms or dorm. Cooking facilities or food prepared to order. Book exchange service. Taxi/minicab shuttle to Kirimya, disembark at Kasanvu and follow the signs.

Eating map p197

The big hotels offer a good standard but even better are the following.

¥ **AidChild's Ten Tables**, Plot 6A Victoria Rd, close to the Masaka Lions Children Centre, T078-270 0591 (mob). This restaurant set up by an American NGO serves truly delicious Western and local food in lovely surroundings, with artwork on the walls and tables covered in crisp white linen. Offers a 2-course lunch for US$2.25 or the 4-course dinner menu for US$5.25, all beautifully presented. Upstairs has a lounge with DSTV showing football, a balcony where drinks are served, a private dining room seating up to 12, and a home cinema showing films at 2000, US$2.25. All income generated helps support a local hospice and palliative care centre for children suffering from AIDS.

¥ **Café Frikadellen**, 1 Mutuba Gardens, in the same compound as Uganda Childcare. Run by a Danish couple, this café serves Western dishes only. Shaded outdoor or indoor seating and high-speed Wi-Fi. The profits go to support local schools.

Bars and clubs

Ambiance Disco, Ddiba St, off Kampala Rd, and **Tendo Disco Sounds** further down the Kampala Rd in Nyendo are the current choices for nightlife.

Transport

Matatus go to **Bukakata**, 40 km away, for the Ssese Islands. *Matatus* leave frequently to Nyendo stage, 2.5 km east of Masaka, 20-30 mins, US$1. At this clearly signposted junction, traffic for Lake Nabugabo and the Ssese Islands branches off the main Kampala road. *Matatu* traffic beyond Nyendo eastwards is infrequent and you may need to take a shared taxi to the ferry. However, there is usually 1 *matatu*, US$4, connecting Nyendo for each ferry departure, except for the last boat of the day. There is a public bus service from the main bus station in Masaka at around 1400, to connect with the 1600 ferry, to **Kalangala** (the main town on Buggala Island), US$6.

To get to **Mutukala** on the border with **Tanzania**, 88 km from Masaka, take one of the frequent *matatus* in the morning to Kyotera, 1 hr, US$2. (Kyotera is a small town about halfway between Masaka and the Tanzanian border.) Then take another matatu to Mutukula to the border, 1-1½ hrs, US$2.50 (more sporadic service). Visitors need to get to the border crossing at Mutukula by about 1500 to allow time for the administrative procedures to be completed as the customs post closes at 1700. See also page 206.

Directory

Banks Barclays, Broadway Rd, near the police station. **Stanbic Bank**, Birch Ave, close to the post office. Cashes Amex TCs. **Internet** Café Frikadellen, see above. Offers a reliable service with their own back-up generator. **Masaka Internet Services**, Lastonet Building, Broadway Rd, T04814-20065. Open 0800-2030. Offers a good connection; all profits support children's education.

Ssese Islands

→ *Phone code: 4814. Colour map 2, B/C4.*

This collection of islands (sometimes spelt Sese or Ssesse) is situated in the northwestern part of Lake Victoria and is an increasingly popular tourist destination. There are 84 attractive islands in the group. All the islands are hilly and the smaller islands remain fringed with dense rainforest, containing 240 bird species, several species of monkey and the occasional large snake. The islands are also suited to those keen on walking or sport fishing. Being quite remote, they have retained an easy-going atmosphere. Buggala Island's Lukoboka Bay is where most tourist hotels are found, along the white sandy beaches. Few visitors travel beyond Buggala Island to visit the smaller islands.

Early in the 20th century the Ssese Islands were depopulated following a widespread outbreak of sleeping sickness. After 15 years some people began to drift back again, but there were few settlers until the period of civil unrest during the 1980s, when the remoteness of the islands offered safety against the insurgents. As a result of the low population numbers the islands were not marred by development. Regrettably deforestation now scars great tracts of land with an estimated 40% of forests felled on Buggala Island. Cash crops like palm oil plantations have been planted and industrial vessels over-fishing Lake Victoria for the past 15 years have created a crisis for local fishermen.

Ins and outs

Getting there
There are several ways of reaching the Sseses. The best option at the time of writing was to go on the *MV Kalangala* ferry service from Nakiwogo port, on the western side of the

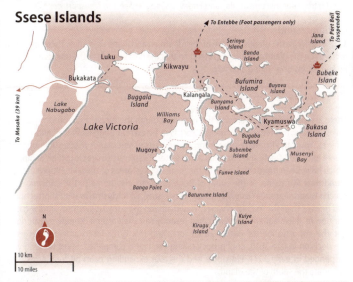

Entebbe peninsula. To get there, turn off the Kampala–Entebbe road at Wilson Street, also known as Nsamizi Road, on to Nakiwogo Road for 3 km. Daily departure time 1400, 3½ hours. There is also a free Bukakata–Buggala Ferry from Bukakata on the mainland, departing Monday-Saturday at 0800, 1130, 1330 and 1600, 50 minutes, to Luku on Buggala Island. (For transport to Bukakata, see page 204) It's possible to take a car if you're willing to squeeze it on, but remember the bus has priority. Adherence to this timetable is fluid. On Sundays there are no morning ferries in either direction.

There's a bus from Masaka at 1400 to Kalangala, via Bukakata, the ferry and Luku, arriving in Kalangala around 1900, US$6. The 34-km stretch of road between Luku and Kalangala takes a long time as goods are offloaded at every stop. A faster option is to take a *matatu* from Masaka or Nyendo, US$7. This will bring you right down the beach. Nyendo to Bukakata takes an hour, then you have to wait for the ferry to arrive and turn around (less than 30 minutes). At Luku the same *matatu* will take 1½ hours. Be prepared to be jammed in tightly in the *matatu*. If you're staying at the **Ssese Habitat Resort** (see page 202), you can be collected from the ferry, US$35.50.

The Entebbe–Kalangala ferry service was suspended for over six months following an accident in July 2010. It is inadvisable to travel to the islands during stormy weather, as the record of accidents involving Ugandan lake vessels is very poor.

Motorized lake-taxis (dug-out canoes), with a poor safety record and rarely equipped with life-jackets, offer a service to most islands other than Buggala Monday to Saturday leaving from Kasenyi (see page 155), close to Entebbe. (The motorized lake taxis also go to Buggala Island; however, the ferries are safer.) Despite a nominal timetable, rarely adhered to, users are advised to seek out 'Mama Grace' of Kasenyi Takeaway for help. The canoes are moored 20 m offshore through bilharzia-infested viscous mud, and passengers are carried there on the shoulders of porters, who will often try to extract more money by claiming the tourists are too heavy. Boats to Banda Island take three to four hours, leaving at 1200 from Kasenyi on Tuesday and Friday, US$4.50. ▸▸ *See also Transport, page 203.*

Getting around

To get between the islands ask one of the fishermen and agree on a price. There are a few *matatus* on the island of Buggala. Other than that the best way to see the islands is on foot, by *boda-boda* or by hiring a bicycle.

The islands

There are beautiful walks around the islands, through the forest, and you can visit the caves of bats, the remains of Speke's Fort (see below) on Buggala Island, and fishing villages. You can also make a boat trip to see parts of the islands inaccessible on foot, where birds nest freely and otters roll in the water. It's still rare to see crocodiles or hippos, which have been frightened away to the more isolated areas of the lake. Hippos are still found near Mulabana, at the south of Buggala Island, also home to the endemic sub-species island sitatunga (*Tragelaphus spekei sylvestris*), which is smaller with shorter horns and hooves than the mainland variety found among the papyrus swamps. Trophy game hunting of these aquatic antelopes had recently restarted after a 30-year moratorium, but the conservationists' outcry about including this CITES-listed antelope reversed the decision in late 2010, until a stock-taking exercise is completed. Sport hunting was suspended in early 2011. Pineapple and the ever-expanding palm oil tree farms now dominate the south of the island.

Chameleons

Anyone spending some time in East Africa is likely to see a chameleon. In Uganda, the Baganda call them *nawolovu* and most of them are terrified of these creatures and will not touch them.

The best-known characteristic of the chameleon is its ability to change colour depending on its surroundings. It also has a long and worm-like tongue that can be suddenly extended for a distance greater than the length of its own body. Insects, particularly flies, which adhere to the sticky club-shaped tip of the chameleon's tongue, are then drawn into its mouth. The eyes are set on prominent cones, which are covered with skin except for the little pupil openings at the end. Each eye moves independently so that while one eye is seeing where the next foothold is, the other is looking around for food. Its movements are slow and deliberate, perhaps to help in the concealment that is attained by the change of colour to match the surroundings.

The eggs of the chameleon are laid in a hole in the ground. The female digs the hole during the day. She uses her front feet to collect up the earth, which is then pushed under her body towards the back limbs. When a small pile has collected under the middle of the animal the rear feet push the earth as far back as they can reach. This process is continued until the hole reaches about 18 cm deep, a process that takes about seven hours. The actual laying of eggs usually takes place at night and the hole is then covered up again.

One of the myths that surround the chameleon is that the female dies soon after giving birth. Another popular myth is that if you place a chameleon on a red surface it will burst; both these are in fact untrue.

The islands are hilly with an undulating terrain and, in the uncultivated parts, are still forested with 240 bird species, the ubiquitous vervet monkey and the occasional large snake. The most important crops are cassava, banana, sweet potato and coffee. It can be difficult to resist swimming in Lake Victoria on a sunny day, but in many places, there is a risk of bilharzia, although many resorts claim otherwise. Recently, Nile crocodiles seeking to redress the shortage of fish in Lake Victoria have attacked humans. The HIV/AIDS infection rate is very high in these islands, especially in the fishing villages.

The power supply on the island is sporadic, only available in the resorts that have a generator, with power usually switched on from 1900 to 2200. There are electronics recharging stations that run off generator power for phone and camera batteries in Kalangala town, Buggala Island.

Buggala Island

About 34 km long, Buggala Island (sometimes spelt Bugala) is the biggest and has about 50 km of road on it. The best way to explore is on foot or by bicycle, available for hire from most beach resorts. Its main towns are Kalangala – also the name of the district or spelt Kalengala – and Luku, which are linked by bus and *matatus*. All around are wonderful views of the lake and of the other islands, some forested, cultivated or a mixture of both. The forests have some wildlife, but nothing spectacular. There are various species of monkey and a profusion of birdlife plus millions of lake flies. Malaria is common. Mutambala Beach, off the Kalangala–Luku road, is popular.

Speke's Fort ① *1.5 km north of Kalangala town on the eastern headland overlooking Lutoboka Bay*, consist of the little-visited remains of a fort built by John Hannington Speke in 1861-1862. He stayed on Buggala Island for a short period whilst his emissaries sought permission from Mwanga Mutesa to search for the source of the Nile. Now lost to the jungle, the ruined fort consists only of moss-covered stone walls, interspersed with mature trees and vines. It's inaccessible and difficult to visit.

Other islands

Most visitors stick to Buggala Island, but provided you are flexible you can explore the other islands too. The second largest island, **Bukasa**, is particularly attractive, as it has a smaller population, is more forested and has a wider range of wildlife. There are two beautiful beaches on the island as well as a waterfall. **Bufumira Island** can be easily visited from Kalangala for the day, as can many of the uninhabited islands. The verdant **Banda Island** is a remote, beautiful, small island in the north of the archipelago, a long-established backpacker resort. Its visitor numbers have gone down as Buggala Island has developed over the past decade.

👁 Ssese Islands listings

For Sleeping and Eating price codes and other relevant information, see Essentials pages 21-23.

🛏 Sleeping

Buggala Island

The following are all in Kalangala.

AL-A Islands Club, next to Ssese Islands Beach Hotel, T0414-250757, T077-250 4027 (mob), sseseclub@yahoo.com. Well-maintained resort and gardens, with a clean, white sandy beach. Several superbly decorated luxury wooden chalets for 2-3 people, with fully tiled showers in the bathrooms, and 1 family unit. The excellent meals are also served to non-residents. Sport fishing trips can be arranged. Conference facilities available. Visitors are collected from the ferry.

A Ssese Palm Beach Resort, T0414-254435, T077-275 0331 (mob), www.islandssese. com. Managed by former air hostess Mrs Nina Muayanda Mutebi, wife of the representative of the Buganda King for the Ssese Islands. Situated at the top end of the island at Lutoboka Point. More remote and private than other resorts, this resort has well-maintained gardens and a stretch of white sandy beach. There are 13 *bandas* with private balconies overlooking the beach with DSTV, plus restaurant and bar.

Conference facilities. Camping with your own tent is US$5pp.

A-B Ssese Habitat Resort, T0312-278318, T077-269 2269, ssesehab@gmail.com. A 2008 development, currently the best facility on this island, located some distance from the main Lutoboka Beach and uphill, giving an incredible view. It has 4 lake-facing properties, 3 with 5 en suite rooms and 1 with 4 en suite rooms, which are modern, well-equipped with fully tiled bathrooms, some with bathtubs. Communal areas have sofas, DSTV, VCR, DVD player and dining table. There's an open-air bar and restaurant, a children's play area, bicycle rental and sauna and steam rooms. Camping with your own tent is US$6.50pp. Monkeys play in the forest between the resort rooms up the top and the beach. You can walk to the beach through the forest, or along the road, or the private transport van will take you. Private transport pick-up from Luku, US$35.50. Private high-speed boat to Entebbe for US$750. Free transfers to the Kalanagala Bay pier. There are discounts for the under 15s.

B Mirembe Resort Beach, T0392-772703, T078-252 8651 (mob), www.miremberesort. com. Located at Lutoboko Bay at the secluded, tree-fringed, northern end of the beach, next to Islands' Club. Cottages, en suite rooms or tents. DSTV and internet.

Camping with your own tent is US$10pp. The restaurant offers a varied à la carte menu. Activities include boat rides to local islands, fishing, volleyball and walks to see birds and butterflies. Conference facilities.

B Pearl Gardens Beach, T077-237 2164 (mob), www.pearlgardensbeach.com. A 2.43-ha site with a narrow beach strip, sited between **Hornbill Campsite** and the fishing village at the eastern end of Lutoboka Bay. This is the party resort with very loud music and a DJ at night on the beach, drawing a crowd from the other resorts, so is best for young adults. It has 9 wooden *bandas*, a 32-room hostel and 14 rooms. Camping (full board) single US$15.50, double US$33.50. The restaurant offers a large local and Western menu, but several items are 'unavailable'. The beach bar sells beer and sodas. Offers a 4-hr guided forest trek, US$4.50. Conference facilities.

D Panorama Cottages, near the jetty in lower Kalangala, uphill from the beachfront resorts, T077-301 5574, arnoldinislands@gmail.com. A peaceful place with lots of vervet monkeys around. 18 cottages with bathrooms and solar lighting; the larger ones have a TV. Electricity (generator) 1900-2230, and hot water on request. Camping, tents provided, US$4.50pp. Run by a former military man who lives on the property with his wife, and keeps everything running to exacting standards. Prices include breakfast. Food is good but takes a while to come. Drinks are available and there is a small shop near the jetty.

Camping

E-F Hornbill Campsite, T077-588 0200, T075-380 3121 (both mob). Run by a friendly German couple but located 500 m down a steep track, near the lake with a private 'beach', in a remnant forest clump. There's a couple of very basic huts, a good camping area and a bar. The beach area is deep and sandy, but the water's edge is murky and uninviting. Cooking food takes a long time. Tents for rent, US$4.25pp.

Bukasa Island

B Bukasa Island Guesthouse, formerly Agnes' Guest House, contact **Just Travel Uganda**, www.justtraveluganda.com. An old colonial house that was once a grand affair set in attractive gardens in a beautiful location on a hilltop, north facing, overlooking the lake. It has now undergone extensive renovations by a local MP and is a significantly more expensive option.

E-F Father Christopher's Guesthouse, 30 mins from the landing point. Friendly, chatty priest offers small basic rooms or camping beside an old Russian Orthodox church. It's the only budget option at present.

Banda Island

B-E Banda Island Resort, T077-222 2777 (mob), www.traveluganda.co.ug/banda-island. Run by a sociable retired British-Kenyan engineer, with a good fund of stories. Full board *bandas*, dorms or tents. The food is excellent and plentiful. It's important to text/SMS ahead as the mobile reception is variable. The low-key activities include exploring the island and sunbathing.

⊖ Transport

Bus

If you want to go to one of the places down at the lakeside in Kalangala, you need to arrange a *boda-boda* or a special hire. From Luku to Kalangala a *boda-boda* is US$7.

Ferry

In 2010 a contract to build 2 new privately run ferries to service the islands had been agreed, scheduled for completion by mid-2011. It was planned that the ferries would replace the current (free) government Bukakata–Buggala ferry (see below). In Aug 2010 MV Kalangala, the Entebbe–Buggala Island ferry, sank just outside Entebbe. In Jan 2011 the government announced that it would take back the previously privatized operation. The service restarted in Feb 2011 just before the presidential and parliamentary elections. All schedules are subject to change, so check ahead of time.

From Lutoboka port site in Kalangala district, the MV Kalangala ferry service leaves at 0800, arriving at **Entebbe** at 1130. Foot passenger 1st class US$7, 2nd class US$5 one way. Vehicle rates are determined by their length, US$25-30 one way.

A private high-speed boat to Entebbe costs US$750; contact **Ssese Habitat Resort** (see page 202).

From Luku, on the northwest side of Buggala Island and 1½ hrs by road from Kalangala, to **Bukakata**, the free Bukakata–Buggala Ferry departs Mon-Sat at 0900, 1230, 1430 and 1700, 50 minutes.

Alternative route crossings are tough, even by African standards. Residents of Bukasa tend to sail directly to **Kasenyi** (see page 155), near Entebbe, rather than travel to the mainland via the other islands and you may find it cheaper to travel this route from Kalangala (to Bukasa Island and then Kasenyi), at US$5 per leg of the journey. The Kasenyi–Ssese Islands route is usually done in open boats operated by local fishermen called lake-taxis, which are canoes with outriggers and outboard motors, with a poor safety record, and are rarely fitted with lifejackets. 5 hrs is a typical journey time, and it can be especially miserable in heavy rain and after dark. Getting out of the boats at Kasenyi is quite an experience. The shoreline has 20 m of mud. Local men on shore will carry people on their shoulders to and from the boats. Competition among the men can be fierce and the experience intimidating on the return journey, when the boat is suddenly surrounded by men all shouting and trying to pull your bags out of the boat. The best advice is to sit on your bags and clearly indicate your choice of porter.

To get to the smaller islands from Buggala Island you will need to pick up the motorised lake-taxis from Myeena, as they travel between the islands, US$5 per leg or negotiate directly with one of the fishermen. A special hire boat from Buggala Island to **Banda Island** will cost about US$45 one way. A special hire boat from Buggala Island to **Bukasa Island** and back the following day will cost about US$70 return from Myeena, with the fisherman staying overnight returning you the following day.

ⓘ Directory

Buggala Island
Banks Stanbic Bank, Kalangala. No ATM.
Internet Kalangala Information Centre, Lutoboka Rd, Kalangala.

Lake Nabugabo → *Colour map 2, B4.*

Ins and outs
Getting there Lake Nabugabo is 16 km from Masaka, 6 km off the Masaka–Bukakata road. The easiest way to get there is from Masaka on the Bukakata bus that goes to the Ssese Islands. It leaves at about 1400 from the main Masaka bus station, and goes past the turning to Lake Nabugabo which is clearly signposted, from where you have to walk the last 6 km. Alternatively, if travelling from Kampala on the main road to Masaka, you can get off the bus 2 km before Masaka (or 2 km past Masaka if you are coming from Mbarara) at the Total petrol station near Nyendo town. From the petrol station it is 1 km to the Nyendo market where you can get a *matatu* to Bukakata, or you can take a special hire up to Lake Nabugabo for US$10, to save you walking the last 6 km.

The lake
An easy detour from Masaka, Lake Nabugabo is a small shallow, oval, freshwater lake, 8.2 km by 5 km, separated from the western shore of Lake Victoria 3 km distant, by an arm of the

Lwamunda swamp and a sandbar. It's estimated to have developed about 3700 years ago, since when the cichlid fish have undergone speciation. The northern shore is forested and there are sandy beaches on the eastern edge. Because of the mineral content of the lake, it is claimed that bilharzia does not occur here and this has made it popular for swimming.

It's a very peaceful place to relax and to watch birds, either along the shores of the lake or from a small fishing boat. In 2004 Lake Nabugabo was declared a Ramsar wetland site, where almost 300 plant species have been identified and over 180 bird species confirmed, including the shoebill stork (see box, page 74), kingfishers and crested cranes, along with important migratory birds like the blue swallow.

It was always popular with expats during the colonial period. One reason was the supposed absence of crocodiles. One report of a crocodile seen in 1932 was dismissed, but when a dog was snatched while swimming in the lake in 1946, a meticulous search was made. So much for no crocodiles: in a period of three months a total of 10 crocodiles were seen and shot in the lake. These included a particularly large male that was 4.5 m long and thought to be around 30 years old. The lake was cleared of crocodiles with the aim of making it safe for swimmers. However, after exceptionally heavy rains later that year flooded the land between the lake and Lake Victoria, crocodiles reappeared. It is doubtful whether there are currently crocodiles in Lake Nabugabo, but you might want to check with local residents before you dive in.

◉ Lake Nabugabo listings

For Sleeping and Eating price codes and other relevant information, see Essentials pages 21-23.

Sleeping and eating
D-F Nabugabo Holiday Centre, T077-243 3332 (mob), www.nabugabo. com. Previously the **Church of Uganda Guesthouse**, built in 1926 as a holiday resort and conference centre for the missionaries of the Church of Uganda, who also run **Namirembe Guesthouse**, Kampala (see page 61). It offers executive cottages (full board option available; food is reasonably priced) and camping US$4.50-6.50pp, tent hire US$4.50-9. Enjoy boat trips, birdwatching, nature walks, monkey watching or fishing. It also hosts conferences and meetings. You can have a picnic for a modest entry fee of US$0.25-0.50 each. It's an alcohol-free resort.

E Sand Beach Resort, 1 km from the **Nabugabo Holiday Centre**, T077-241 6047 (mob). The place to be if you want a lively atmosphere. Although not a lot of sand is found on the lakeshores, it's a good place to swim, especially for children, because the water has a shallow gradient. There are

8 en suite smallish doubles, with flushing toilets and hot showers. It's popular at weekends and holidays. Camping, US$2.25, is permitted but bring your own equipment. Food is available in the restaurant if pre-ordered, but no alcohol is served. However, you can buy plenty of beer next door, as indicated on the signboard of the **Green View Site on the Lake**, a campsite with no facilities worth mentioning, apart from its well-stocked bar.

E Terrace View Beach, PO Box 70, Masaka T078-532367, www.lake-nabugabo.net. New development offering 2-bed en suite *bandas*, warm water available. Tents for rental. Snacks, beers and sodas for sale. Restaurant and bar planned. Electricity generator operates 1900-2200.

Transport
You can arrange transport back (US$5) to the Masaka–Bukakata road, from where you can continue to the Ssese Islands or Masaka. Either ask around in the resorts to see if anyone else is doing the trip when you want to leave, or pick up a *boda boda* on its return leg.

To Tanzania (Bukoba)

From Masaka you can head for Tanzania (see Transport, page 198); the only current option is road travel. You can take a large bus from Tawfiq in Kampala all the way to Bukoba, or go in shorter *matatu* hops. The road is now good, with tarmac all the way to Bukoba.

Heading south from Masaka town will take you to Tanzania via Kalisizo and Kyotera. **Kalisizo** town is a small town 30 minutes south of Masaka with several attractions including a model village with innovative methods and crops suitable for small farmers. A guesthouse (**E-F**) offers full board.

It takes between 30 minutes and two hours to get through the Ugandan-Tanzanian bureaucracy at the border and if you are driving your own vehicle, you need a letter from the government in Kampala confirming that the vehicle you are using is yours and not for sale, as well as a vehicle registration document, third party insurance papers and a carnet de passage en douane from your home motoring organization. A temporary import licence (TSh20,000) for one month can be purchased at the border. There is also a one-off fuel levy of TSh5000. If you get to the border shortly before dark you may want to stay at the small, highly recommended **Mutukula Safari Lodge** (**E-F**) on the Uganda side of the border, which is clean, excellent value, and has meals available for US$2 per person. Otherwise there is nothing on the Tanzania side until you get to Bukoba.

The southwest

Heading west of Masaka the countryside gradually gets drier and more hilly and the population more sparse as you move into Ankole, home to pastoralists. Lake Mburo National Park lies south of the main road, four hours' drive from Kampala, where animals can be observed on foot, horseback or by quad bike. North of Lake Mburo is Ntusi, an archaeological site, and west of it is Katonga Wildlife Reserve, where animals and birds can spotted from a canoe. Mbarara, the heart of the former Ankole Kingdom and the next major town, has few tourist attractions. The road divides after Mbarara with one branch travelling northwest leading to Queen Elizabeth National Park via Ishaka, while the road southwest passes through Ntungamo. The far southwest of Uganda is very beautiful with many lakes, crops grown on terraced hillsides and dramatic volcanic mountains where gorillas can be tracked along steep sided ravines. Kabale, the largest town in this region, has some fine colonial-era buildings. Close by is charming Lake Bunyonyi, one of Uganda's most popular tourist destinations. From Kabale the road divides, one branching south to Rwanda via Gatuna (Katuna) and another looping westwards to Kisoro and Bwindi Impenetrable Forest National Park.

Lake Mburo National Park → *Colour map 2, C2.*

Ins and outs
Getting there The park can be reached from the main Kampala–Mbarara road. From Kampala it is 230 km, and it takes about four hours. From Mbarara it is 47 km, a journey

Lake Mburo National Park

Sleeping
Arcadia Cottages **1**
Lake Mburo Camp **2**
Mihingo Lodge **3**
Rwonyo Rest Camp **4**

Campsites Λ
Lakeside Campsite No 2 **1**

Mburo: what's in a name?

It is said that the two brothers Kigarama and Mburo once lived in the Ruizi (sometimes spelt Rwizi) River Valley. One night Kigarama dreamed that they were in great danger, and urged his younger brother to take refuge with him up in the hills, but Mburo ignored the advice. The Ruizi flooded the valley, and Mburo was drowned. The lake is named after the drowned brother, while the hills bear the name of the brother who was saved.

The cassine tree is found in the area and is called mboro in the Ankole language. The tree is said to have aphrodisiac powers (coincidentally, the word mboro in Swahili is a vulgar term for penis). A cassine tree can be seen at the crossroads at the start of the Kigambira trail in the park; it shows signs of bark and branch loss, so it seems the local people believe in its powers.

takes of less than one hour. There are two entrances: Nshara Gate and Sanga Gate. Coming from Kampala, the Nshara Gate turn-off is the left, 10 km past the Lyantonde trading centre. It is signposted. The park gate is 8 km along an unsealed track. The Sanga Gate, coming from Kampala, is down a left turn at the Sanga trading centre, about 33 km before Mbarara. There is a large blue and white sign with 'Lake Mburo NP'. The park gate is 13 km from the main road on a poor, unsealed track that is particularly difficult September-January during the rains, when a 4WD is essential. Travelling by *matatu* from Kampala, ask to be set down at Lyantonde trading centre. From Mbarara, ask to get off at Sanga trading centre and then hire a taxi for US$18, or a *boda-boda* for US$7, to take you to the park gate.

Park information   The entry fee is US$30 per 24 hours.

The park

Lake Mburo National Park is one of the newest of Uganda's national parks. A great attraction is that it is possible to walk around the park, with an armed ranger, rather than having to tour in a vehicle, so it's quite possible to get close to zebra, warthogs and impala. However, independent exploration is proscribed as a pride of lions has returned after several years' absence, with recent sightings of a lioness with two cubs in April 2010.

The landscape is of open plains, acacia grasslands and marshes. Around the lake itself is thicker riverine woodland while much of the rest of the park is acacia woodland. Within the park boundary are five lakes, which are best viewed from the Kazuma lookout point. For many years there has been a dispute over its use, which began during the colonial period when the area which was declared to be a hunting ground for the Ankole royalty. After Independence it became a game reserve and in the early 1980s was finally gazetted as a national park. However, to establish the park it was necessary to resettle large numbers of people and their herds of cattle, and this remains a controversial issue.

Fauna

Animals found here include impalas, zebras, topis, oribis, elands, klispringers, buffaloes, waterbucks, reedbucks, warthogs, hyenas and jackals but no elephants. The shy sitatunga, a swamp-dwelling antelope, with its elongated hooves and flexible toe joints, is well adapted for living in the papyrus swamp. Baboons and vervets are commonly seen and the lake contains hippos and crocodiles, while buffaloes can often be found in the marshes. Lions, leopards and roan antelopes are present but are rarely seen. Interesting birds include the shoebill stork (see box, page 74), crested crane (Uganda's national emblem), saddlebill storks and Abyssinian ground hornbills. There are also a wide range of water birds. A salt lick attracts many animals and can be viewed from a wooden hide.

Lake Mburo National Park listings

For Sleeping and Eating price codes and other relevant information, see Essentials pages 21-23.

Sleeping map p207

LL Arcadia Cottages, T077-298 1155 (mob), www.arcadiacottages.net. Related to the Lake Bunyonyi cottages of the same name (see page 219). Well positioned for park activities like walking safaris and boat trips, 7 en suite comfortably furnished stone *bandas* set in acacia woodlands within an enclosed area with parking. The reception and open-sided bar and restaurant, serving meals with a distinctive African input and open, are a short distance away. It's the cheapest option out of the 3 places listed here.

LL Lake Mburo Camp, 3.5 km north of Rwonyo, www.lakemburocamp.com. A luxury tented camp run by Kimbla-Mantana, sited on a hilltop overlooking the lake, within the park offering the full bush experience. Has 9 solar-powered, spacious, en suite safari tents on raised wooden platforms, with verandas set upon a lightly wooded ridge. The bar and dining room serving international fare are also on a raised platform. At sundown enjoy a drink by the large pit fire just uphill from the dining room. Access is via the Sanga Entrance Gate; follow the Impala Track for 7 km then take the signposted left turning eastwards for 500 m.

LL Mihingo Lodge, T075-241 0509 (mob), www.mihingolodge.com. Upmarket, well-run facility, opened in 2007, located adjacent to but outside the park on its eastern flank. 10 solar-powered, large, tented en suite rooms on stilts under a thatched roof with verandas in varied settings, some in riverine forest, others with a lake view and 4 wonderfully positioned on top of a *kopje* (small hill). The thatched dining room, serving excellent meals, is west facing with

panoramic views over the park, especially stunning at sunset. There's a spacious pool and horseback safaris (see below). Access is via the Nshara gate, 9 km from the main road. Follow the Zebra Track for 5 km then turn a sharp left along the Ruroko Track and the lodge is signposted from here.

Camping

There are 3 campsites, US$7pp. **Campsite 1** or **Rwonyo Rest Camp** (see below) is right beside the park headquarters. The best is **Lakeside Camp 2**, sited 1.5 km away from Rwonyo, in a wonderful position to view the wildlife. The outlying **Kingfisher Campsite 3** requires your own transport.

E Rwonyo Rest Camp. Run by UWA and located beside the park headquarters with friendly and helpful staff. Double and single *bandas* and a 4-bed family *banda* are basic (US$8pp). Showers are shared, with hot water mornings and evenings. Meals are cheap and simple or you can self cater.

Eating

Rwonyo Rest Camp does not keep food supplies within the park. Visitors must come with everything they need or use the **Lakeside Restaurant** (see below). Rwonyo Rest Camp staff can arrange for your own food to be cooked for a small fee, or you can use barbecues. Non-residents can eat at Arcadia Cottages.

¶ Lakeside Restaurant. This has reasonable food but horrendous waiting times and the bar offers an excellent hippo-viewing area. As you're not allowed to walk unescorted from the park headquarters to the restaurant you have to take the *boda-boda* service, US$2.25.

Activities and tours

For night game drives and night walks described below, bring along your own high-powered torch, as the UWA spotlights only function briefly.

Boat trips
It's possible to hire a boat for US$10pp, or a minimum of US$40 per boat (for up to 8). This motorboat trip leaves from the jetty by the **Lakeside Restaurant** at the main campsite, 1 km away from Rwonyo Campsite, offering good views of fish eagles, hippos, buffalo and the odd crocodile. It's a 2-hr trip leaving every 2 hrs from 0800. There are 2 boats, one seating 8 and the other 14. Pre-book at the park headquarters at Rwonyo, T0392-711346.

Fishing
Permits are obtainable from UWA (www.uwa.or.ug/tariffs.htm) for 1 day US$15; 2 days US$25; or 3 days US$35.

Game drives
Game drives during the day in the 4WD park vehicle can be arranged at US$20 per guide, but they are often unavailable at short notice. **Kimbla-Mantana**, www.kimbla-mantanauganda.com, have a 4WD landcruiser that can be hired with driver. Night game drives must be pre-booked. They start from the park headquarters at Rwonyo, T0392-711346, usually between 1900-2000 and take 2-3 hrs, US$15pp.

Horseback safaris
Mihingo Lodge, see page 209. A new way to explore the area's fauna and birdlife from an equine vantage point both around Mihingo Lodge and within the eastern section of the park. Catering for a range of horse riding abilities, US$38 (1 hr) to US$757 (3 days).

Quad bike safaris
African ATV Safaris, T077-237 7185 (mob), www.africanatvsafaris.com. This is a New Zealand enterprise, with another outlet at Bujagali Falls near Jinja (see page 96). Quad bikes are probably best suited to

this terrain, which is boggy in places. They tour the park in small groups up to 5, accompanied by a guide and park ranger. 2-hr Eland Track US$75; 3-hr Ankole Trail US$95; 4-hr Ruroko Track US$115. 2 safaris daily usually at 0830 and 1400; some flexibility available. Price includes free introductory training, plus helmets, overalls, goggles and refreshments. Wear enclosed shoes. Under 15s must go as passengers with the guide/ranger/guardian, US$20 per child. There are no credit card facilities in the park but they will accept all major currencies plus Ugandan or Kenyan shillings.

Walking
Guided **day nature walks** must be pre-booked and start from the same place as night game drives. Accompanied by an armed ranger, cost US$10pp for up to 4 hrs. From 4 hrs to a maximum of 6 hrs it's US$15pp. The ranger is invaluable in locating wildlife, and a precaution in case you run into a leopard, lion or a water buffalo. Early morning and evening are best.

The **night nature walks** must be pre-booked and start at the same place as the night game drives. Usually start between 1900-2000 and take 2 hrs, US$25pp.

Rubanga Forest Walks must be pre-booked at the park headquarters, see under night game drives above. This 2-hr walk through a remnant of closed canopied tropical forest that supports a large and diverse bird population is accompanied by an armed ranger. It starts from the western side of the lake, past the fishing village, to Rubanga Forest. A sitatunga lookout platform is being built to aid sightings of this aquatic antelope that lives in the papyrus swamp.

Transport
Car hire
The nearest place to rent a vehicle is Mbarara. Try **Crested Crane** on Main St or ask in **Mbarara Coffee Shop**. A 1-day car rental is around US$80, and a 4WD US$100.

Ankole cattle

These very large cattle, with their horns, are famous throughout the country. Large horns are considered to be very beautiful and are highly prized. Some cattle have horns that are so large that they are unable to raise their heads, or their heads are constantly leaning to one side.

Mbarara and around → *Phone code: 4854. Colour map 2, B2.*

The countryside becomes flatter towards Mbarara with more banana plantations as the acacia shrubs recede. There are lots of Ankole cattle grazing (see box, above). Mbarara is a busy town that has greatly expanded in recent years. Since the Masaka bypass was built it is now the first major town you come to when travelling southwest from Kampala. It is a crossroads for travellers heading towards the Queen Elizabeth National Park, Lake Mburo, Rwenzori Mountains and Kabale in the southwest. There is a wide choice of places to stay and eat.

Ins and outs

Getting there Mbarara is located nearly 300 km from Kampala and about 150 km from Kabale. The road is excellent, one of the best in the country. There are frequent buses to and from Kampala. They leave from the private bus station in the capital from 0600 when they are full, and cost US$5.

Background

Mbarara is the centre of the Kingdom of Ankole that was broken up soon after Independence. The Palace of the Omugabe (King) of Ankole is located in Mbarara on a hill on the outskirts of town. The buildings are used as accommodation for soldiers' wives and families. Although you will probably not be able to walk around the palace (which is in poor repair), you can drive past it. There is one main building and a few secondary ones. To the right of the main structure is the building that used to house the royal drums (see box, page 195). Three and a half kilometres west of Mbarara are the Nkokonjeru Tombs at Kakika, the burial place of the last two Omugabe of Ankole, Kahaya II and Gasyonga II.

Sights

This area is renowned for Ankole cattle, and just before you enter the town centre you will see in the middle of a roundabout a statue of a steer with impressive horns. The huge Coca Cola bottling plant is close by which makes for an interesting cultural juxtaposition. The town is home to one of Uganda's new universities and this, together with the regional offices and the Bank of Uganda regional building, tends to split the town into two. The town centre is in the west, where the central market and taxi and bus parks are located on William Street.

There is not much of architectural interest although the **Library** on Main Street is an old colonial single-storey building, with a well-sheltered courtyard with foliage in front, which has unfortunately been allowed to deteriorate. The **Aga Khan School**, just on the eastern edge of town, is an impressive building combining neoclassical and Indian architectural styles. There are three arches at the front with double mock columns. Portico windows face the building and above the main entrance are crossed flags and the date of construction (1948).

Nearly 5 km to the west and beyond the university is an interesting suburb, the **Old Market area** or Rwizi Arch area, close to the River Rwizi at the junction of the Fort Portal and Kabale roads, and somewhat quieter than the town centre. It has a traditional market, and is lively at night with many eating places and bars.

Around Mbarara

The **Nsongezi Rock Shelters** overlooking the Kagere River are approximately 65 km due south of Mbarara, close to the small town of Kikagati, where tin used to be mined. Nearby on the fast-flowing river that forms the boundary with Tanzania is **Kansyoke Island**. Both are important Stone Age archaeological sites, dated to around 1000 AD, where several artefacts have been discovered including dimple-based ware and Iron Age pottery, which can be seen in the Uganda Museum in Kampala (see page 57). Kansyoke Island has also served as a place of refuge for the rulers of the Nkore Kingdom, Ntare IV and Rwanaga, during times of conflict.

About 40 km west on the Ishaka road are the **Kitagata Hot Springs**. These sulphur-rich springs are used by local people suffering from rheumatism and arthritis.

Mbarara

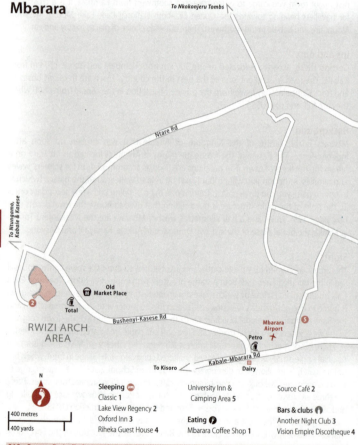

Sleeping
Classic 1
Lake View Regency 2
Oxford Inn 3
Riheka Guest House 4

University Inn &
  Camping Area 5

Eating
Mbarara Coffee Shop 1

Source Café 2

Bars & clubs
Another Night Club 3
Vision Empire Discotheque 4

☉ Mbarara listings

For Sleeping and Eating price codes and other relevant information, see Essentials pages 21-23.

⊖ Sleeping

Mbarara *p211, map p212*

A-B Lake View Resort Hotel, T077-236 7972 (mob), www.lakeviewresorthotel. co.ug. This 70-room hotel is in pleasant surroundings on the western outskirts of town. It has a pool, tennis, gym, sauna,

massage and beauty salon, internet, restaurant, bar and conference facilities. All rooms are en suite and have TV and some have a/c. The lake is said to have belonged to the King of Ankole and on top of a hill nearby you can see his palace. In front of the hotel is an interesting collection of concrete sculptures of traditional figures by S Rwemizhumbi.

B Agip Motel and Campsite, on the Masaka highway from Kampala, on the left-hand side as you approach from the capital, T04854-21615, www.agipmotelmbarara. com. Modern and comfortable. There's a restaurant serving Western and local food, a bar, DSTV, phone and a conference centre. Camping available (see below).

C Hotel Classic, 57 High St, T04854-21131, T077-249 7758 (mob), www.hotelclassic africa.com. Centrally located. All 30 rooms have en suite facilities, DSTV and telephone. Restaurant and bar, secure parking and conference rooms.

C Oxford Inn, 12 Bananuka Dr, next to Pelikan Hotel, T077-254 6538 (mob), kamupat@yahoo.com. Rooms at the front have balconies overlooking the street; ones at the back are darker. All 10 rooms are en suite, with TV and fridge. Price includes breakfast. Located in same street as 2 popular (ie noisy) nightclubs.

D University Inn, 9 Kabale Rd, T04854-20334, T077-248 5148 (mob). Situated close to the university in a pleasant wooded area. 20 simple, comfortable doubles with bathrooms. The water supply is variable but the surroundings make it worth staying here. There's a restaurant and bar. It also has a convenient camping area (see below).

E Riheka Guest House, T04854-21314. Set away from the town centre in quiet surroundings close to the golf course. Rooms are simple and comfortable, with en suite showers. Price includes breakfast.

Camping
Agip Motel, see above. Camping on a large, flat area behind the hotel, securely enclosed by a wall, with a barbecue area and washing and toilet facilities, US$5pp.
University Inn, see above. Camping area often used by overland trucks, US$5pp.

Around Mbarara *p212*
E Uganda Lodge, Ruhanga, 50 km west of Mbarara, T077-476 8090 (mob), www.ugandalodge.com. Built to house volunteers supporting local projects or offering a break for travellers to the southwest. It can accommodate 20 people in rooms or *bandas*. Camping is also available. Restaurant and bar. Local excursions arranged.

Eating

Mbarara *p211, map p212*
Most hotels offer reasonable Western and local dishes.

Bars and clubs

Mbarara *p211, map p212*
Pub Mercury, on the main through road, has a pleasant veranda.

Mbarara has 2 big and very noisy nightclubs, **The Vision Empire** and **Another Life**, both on Banaunka Dr.

Transport

Mbarara *p211, map p212*
Bus
Mbarara is a major crossroads and transport is plentiful. Buses to **Kampala** are frequent, US$5. There are also *matatus* although many people choose to avoid them as they drive particularly fast on this road. It is also very easy to get a bus to **Kabale** from the bus park, or a *matatu* from the taxi park, or the Shell petrol station near the post office, US$4. Buses run to **Kalshaka/Kasese** and **Fort Portal**, 180 km away on a newly improved road.

Directory

Mbarara *p211, map p212*
Banks Stanbic Bank. Changes foreign currency and Amex TCs. **Internet** Jinja Source Café, High St, near the Ankole Steer statue. This excellent café serves great coffee and has a fast internet connection. **Mon Pearl cyber café**, post office building, High St.

Ntungamo → *Phone code: 4854. Colour map 2, C2.*

Travelling on the southwest fork of the road that leaves Mbarara, the first town of any notable size is Ntungamo. The town is about 350 km from Kampala, and is the district headquarters. Lots of shops now line the bypass, and there are several simple lodgings, eating places, and a disco. The town is situated in an undulating landscape with mixed vegetation and cultivated plots. Travelling 25 km southeast to Mirama, just before the borders with Rwanda and Tanzania, there are good views from Mirama Hill over the landscape and across to Rwanda.

About 24 km from Ntungamo is **Lake Nyabihoko**, which offers boating, fishing and swimming (in a lake reputedly free of bilharzia), as well as a chance to see crocodiles, hippos and plenty of birdlife. Proceed north toward Ishaka and Kasese, and after 13 km, just past Kagamba, take the first left. After another 3 km turn left again, and after 8 km you will reach the lake. The road is sound and is possible without a 4WD, even in the rainy season. There are several simple guesthouses (**F**) with basic facilities and a small campsite (US$5 per person).

The road from Mbarara to Kabale is good, passing through pastoral areas, a mix of dry plains and undulating countryside. Some of the views are simply stunning: cattle grazing in hedged fields, with hills denuded of trees in the far distance. Shortly before you reach Kabale the terrain changes and becomes more hilly and greener and increasingly dramatic with steep slopes. Early in the morning the valleys are mist filled. The area around Kabale is ideal for hikers; it's often described as the 'Little Switzerland' of Africa.

Kabale is located in the far southwestern corner of Uganda, an area characterized by great diversity of topography, landscape and vegetation. Parts of this area are densely

Kabale

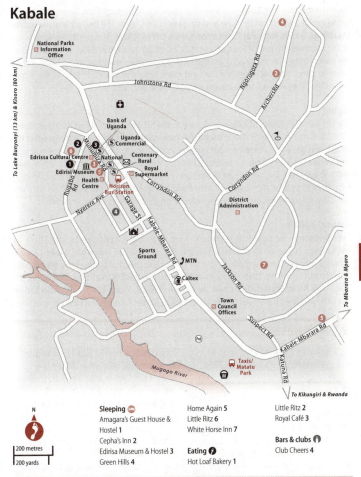

Sleeping 🛏	Home Again **5**	Little Ritz **2**
Amagara's Guest House & Hostel **1**	Little Ritz **6**	Royal Café **3**
Cepha's Inn **2**	White Horse Inn **7**	
Edirisa Museum & Hostel **3**		**Bars & clubs** 🍸
Green Hills **4**	**Eating** 🍴	Club Cheers **4**
	Hot Loaf Bakery **1**	

forested while the rest is extremely heavily populated and intensively cultivated. During the colonial era some hillsides were terraced, to increase the cultivable area.

Ins and outs

Getting there Kabale is about 400 km from Kampala. The Post Bus, the safest service, operates from Kampala Monday to Friday at 0800, US$8. There are direct daily buses, leaving the private bus station in the capital around 0600, eight hours, US$12. After the Post Bus, the next safest service is Horizon; Gateway is best avoided. Or take a *matatu*, which leaves when full. They are a bit cheaper, usually leave about mid-morning and take about an hour less than the buses.

Tourist information Kabale is the town that you will pass through if you are planning a visit to the gorillas, which can be done in Uganda or in DR Congo. The **Bwindi Impenetrable/Mgahinga Gorilla National Parks Information Office (UWA)** ① *near the Highland Hotel, at the northwestern end of town on the right hand side of Kabale–Kisoro road as it leaves the town, T0414-700696, binp@ugandawildlife.org,* provides transport information for the national parks, finds accommodation, and gives details of places to visit in the Kigezi Mountains. They also sell tourist maps, postcards and handicrafts.

Sights

The old part of the town of Kabale is located up the hill. Here you will find the government offices and many buildings dating back to the early colonial period, such as the hospital, the church and the White Horse Inn. That other essential part of colonial life, the golf course, is also on the hill. Everything is spaciously laid out, with well-kept flower beds and mowed lawns in between. The newer part of the town is spread out along the main road, down in what used to be a swampy valley, with the buildings set back from the road. There are some attractive colonnades marked with the years when the buildings were completed.

Around Kabale

Lake Bunyonyi, see page 218, is around 13 km away and is a popular day trip. There are **hot springs** 10 km south of Kabale towards Katuna. You can either hire a bike or walk, although you may need a guide to find them. Many of the local people have traditionally used the hot springs for their ablutions and find the presence of tourists embarrassing. The 27-m-high **Kisiizi Waterfalls** are near the village of Kisiizi, about 30 km north from Kabale. The falls have been harnessed to provide electricity for the hospital and local communities.

◉ Kabale listings

For Sleeping and Eating price codes and other relevant information, see Essentials pages 21-23.

◉ Sleeping

Kabale *p215, map 215*
B White Horse Inn, 25-27 Rwamafa Rd, T04864-23399, www.whitehorseinnkabale. com. Set in 2-ha gardens on a hilltop overlooking the town near the golf course.

This is the best hotel in Kabale but features a brick veranda off a rather soulless dining room. It has 2 suites and 39 en suite rooms in cottages with steep shingle roofs connected by walkways. Camping is also possible. DSTV, Wi-Fi, tennis and a pool table are available. There's a pleasant lounge, a bar and a restaurant. The wonderful log fire is welcome as it is quite cold at night. The access road is only negotiable in the rain with a 4WD.

C-D Cepha's Inn, 7 Archers Rd, opposite **Greenhills**, bordering the golf course, T04864-22097, T077-324 09646 (mob), www.cephasinn.com. 22 rooms with DSTV, pool, sauna, restaurant, internet and conference room.

D Greenhills Hotel, Ngorogoza Rd, on Makanga Hills above town, slightly off-the-beaten path, T04864-24442, T078-460 0381 (mob), www.greenhills-hotel.com. Quiet and beautiful hotel with 24 en suite rooms, pool, sauna, 2 restaurants and 2 bars with DSTV.

E-F Amagara, Muhumuza Rd, adjacent to **Edirisa**, T077-295 9667 (mob). A well-maintained hostel with 4-bed dorms or rent the whole room for US$18. Communal bathrooms. Attached restaurant serves good local food, has a TV but not DSTV. In the back there is table football.

E-F Edirisa Museum Hostel, Kisoro Rd, T075-255 8222 (mob), www.edirisa.org. By far the best budget place to stay in Kabale, just across the road from the **Hot Loaf Bakery**. Cool, modern appearance, with friendly staff. Has en suite rooms and dorms. Very popular, so pre-booking is essential. Restaurant menu includes pizza, burgers and *soup de jour*. There is a gift shop/bar. Movies shown in the evenings. Wi-Fi for guests. It's an excellent place to meet other travellers for a beer and a chat without a noisy bar atmosphere.

E-F Home Again, Kigonge Rd, T04864-22151, T077-495 9757 (mob). Simple, clean place in a central location. 20 rooms with shared hot-water showers, flushing toilets, snacks at the bar.

Camping
White Horse Inn, see above.

Around Kabale *p216*

E Kisiizi Hospital Guest Accommodation, due north of Kabale, about 30 km by road, turning off the road to Mbarara at Muhanga towards Rukungiri, T0392-700806, kisiizihospital@yahoo.com. Kisiizi Hospital run by Church of Uganda has 2 cottages, 1 with a private bathroom, when not required by official hospital visitors. You can't pre-book, but you're encouraged to try this option as any money generated goes towards hospital running costs.

🍴 Eating

Kabale *p215, map 215*
There are few restaurants, but all the hotels provide meals.

🍴 **The White Horse**, see above. The most expensive, but quite reasonable quality.

🍴 **Hot Loaf Bakery**, opposite **Uganda Commercial Bank**. Sells excellent pizzas and pastry, and the best cakes in Uganda.

🍴 **Little Ritz Restaurant**. One of the best budget places to eat in town. The menu includes curries, pizza, pasta and traditional Ugandan food.

🍴 **Royal Café**, just around the corner from **Edirisa**. Run by an Indian man and serves really tasty foods like curry, pizza, steak sandwiches, soups and chips. He sells the best lattes and cappucinos in town.

🍷 Bars and clubs

Kabale *p215, map 215*
Club Cheers, formerly **Earthquake**, Kabale Rd. Bar and pool table, discos on Fri, Sat and Sun. Its sister club the **Pine Health Club**, along with **Match & Mix**, are the best clubs in town. They are open every day, but the best days are Fri to Sun. Match & Mix is also recommended on Wed.

🛍 Shopping

Kabale *p215, map 215*
Books
Book exchange service offered at **Edirisa Museum Hostel**, see Sleeping.

Supermarkets
Royal Supermarket, located close to the Post Office. Sells many items that are hard to get in Uganda like hot sauce, ground meat, cheese, wine, cereals and sweets.

▲ Activities and tours

Kabale *p215, map 215*
Golf
Visitors can have a round of golf at the course to the northwest of town for around US$15.

⊖ Transport

Kabale *p215, map 215*
Bicycle taxi
One of the features of flat Kabale is the bicycle taxi with a padded seat for the passenger behind the saddle, a cheap and quick way to get about town.

Bus
There are daily buses to **Kampala** departing frequently throughout the morning from 0600, 8 hrs, US$12. Or take the Post Bus, which leaves for Kampala at 0645, US$8.

It's possible to get to **Kasese** or **Fort Portal** in a day, but it takes a lot of patience; take the bus to Mbarara and change there. There is 1 daily bus that goes to Fort Portal (292 km away), via Mbarara and Kasese; it's supposed to leave at 0600, but often goes earlier if it's full, 8½-9½ hrs.

For **Bwindi Impenetrable National Park**, ask at the Bwindi Impenetrable/Mgahinga Gorilla National Parks Information Office, see page 216. Travel is best on Fri because there is a market in Buhoma, the gateway to the park, on Sat.

There are 2 possible routes to **Rwanda**. The first is the border post of Gatuna (also known as Katuna), which is the more direct. Alternatively, you can go via Kisoro to Ruhengeri; it is longer – about 3 hrs – but more scenic. **Horizon Express** for Rwanda via Katuna stops at the Kiomesa office, south of town on the Mbarara Rd, at around 1000-1100. Bus to Kisoro, US$7.50. 90-day visas are available at the border, US$60. *Matatus* to Kisoro go occasionally throughout the day. This is a wonderful journey through what some say is the most beautiful part of Uganda.

Pick-up and taxi
To **Bwindi** in a pick-up, 4 hrs, US$10pp. Shared private hire to **Kisoro**, US$5.25-US$7.80 depending on the number of passengers.

Around Kabale *p216*
Bus
To **Kisiizi** daily at noon (return from Kisiizi at 0700). *Matatus* leave Kabala once an hour and take 2 hrs.

⊙ Directory

Kabale *p215, map 215*
Banks Most banks are on the main street close to each other, around the corner from **Edirisa** off Kisoro Rd and down the road from **Match & Mix** club. **Centenary Bank**. ATM but shorter opening hours Mon-Fri 0830-1600, Sat 0830-1330. **Crane Bank**. Mon-Fri 0830-1700, Sat 0900-1400, will exchange TCs, ATM. **Stanbic Bank**. Same opening hours as Crane, also has an ATM. **Internet** Kundle Internet Café, T078-252 9232 (mob). The best in town, with private computers and a printer, US$0.25 per 30 mins. There are also good connections at **Amagara Café** and the **Voice of Kizesi Internet Café**, 50 Mbarara Rd.

Lake Bunyonyi → *Altitude: 1840 m. Colour map 2, C1.*

Reputedly free of bilharzia, Lake Bunyonyi is fine for swimming and makes a popular day trip from Kabale. Meaning 'the place of many little birds', Lake Bunyonyi remains a haven of calm, with villagers paddling their canoes. On its southwest shores there are a number of villages. Most tourist facilities are clustered around the village of Rutinda, on the eastern side of the lake. Pygmies walk over the mountains from Rwanda to sell their produce at the market at Hakekuba on Saturdays. Despite popular belief, the lake is not actually very deep, averaging about 40 m. On the Rwandan side here are a number of sinkholes, which have bubbling cold water welling to the surface. They are reported to be well over 200 m deep.

Ins and outs

Getting there You can get here from Kabale, 13 km away, either on foot (2½ hours) or by hired bike (be prepared for a long hard slog up and a wonderful run down). On the road towards Kisoro and Kisizi there is a turn-off after 1 km, and a signpost to Lake Bunyonyi on the left-hand side. A taxi from Kabale takes about 20 minutes, US$5. Lake Bunyonyi Overland Resort, see Sleeping below, run a twice-daily shuttle from Highland Inn at 0930 and 1630, subject to demand, US$2.25.

Lake Bunyonyi listings

For Sleeping and Eating price codes and other relevant information, see Essentials pages 21-23.

Sleeping

Several campsites and resorts have been developed around the village of Rutinda and on the nearby islands. At the head of the lake is Idi Amin's old villa, still due to be redeveloped. It was leased to a Belgian company in 2009 so things may change.

L Heritage Lodge, Ha' Buharo Island, T0312-265454, T077-235 7424 (mob), www.tangazatours.co.ug. Upmarket Kampala tour operator-owned development has safari tents on raised platforms or cottages on this wooded island. The lounge is enhanced by local artwork. Excellent food and a small pitch and putt golf course. Free motor boat transfer for guests.

A Arcadia Cottages, high on a hillside overlooking the lake, close to Rutinda village, T04864-26231, T077-298 1155 (mob), arcadiacottages@yahoo.com. Family-run business offering 11 cottages with private bathrooms, and a restaurant and bar overlooking the lake.

A Bushara Island Camp, Bushara Island, T04864-26110, T077-246 4584 (mob), www.busharaislandcamp.com. Run by Church of Uganda to fund local community projects and developed with support of Canadian NGOs. Offers en suite tents, cottages and a treehouse. Excellent for birdwatching. Luxury furnished tents (doubles) with wood and stone deck or singles. The full

board price includes motor boat transport, secure car parking, accommodation and hot showers. Pitch your own tent for US$3.

A Nature's Prime Island, formerly Far Out Camp, Akarwa Island, T077-242 3215, T075-262 2009 (both mob), www.naturesprime island.com. On a 1-ha island more or less opposite the Bunyonyi **Overland Camp Resort** (see below). Peaceful resort with Scandinavian log cabins or safari tents on raised platforms. Restaurant and bar. Free boat transfer.

C-E Bunyonyi Overland Resort, on the eastern shoreline of the lake, close to Rutinda village, T04864-26016, T077-240 9510 (mob), www.bunyonyioverland.com. Lively, crowded and noisy camp, popular with overlanders' trucks. 10 safari tents on raised platforms, 12 cottages, 2 family cottages, 4 rooms with shared bathrooms, or camping (US$6-32, tents available for hire). B&B to full board available. Secure parking for US$1 per car per night, hot showers, DSTV, internet, small shop and a fully stocked bar. Restaurant serves locally caught crayfish; pre-book or be prepared for a long wait. Activities include swimming, canoeing, birdwatching, volleyball, biking and fishing. Mountain bike rental US$10 per day, US$5 if staying overnight; canoe rental US$5 per day/US$2.50. Emergency VHF radio contact. Car hire and transport can be arranged.

C-E Byoona Amagara Island Retreat, Itambira Island, T075-265 2788 (mob), www.lakebunyonyi.net. Budget place of choice, this non-profit project supports education, healthcare and sustainable development. Solar-powered geodomes, dorms, wooden cabins, cottages or pitch your own tent. There's a central lodge, a library, a restaurant serving excellent food and a shop with locally made crafts and basic goods. Canoe transfer to the island is free, but the return costs US$1.50, and the motorboat US$7.

D Crater Bay Cottages, Rutinda, close to **Bunyonyi Overland Resort**, T04864-26255, T077-264 3996 (mob), craterbay@yahoo. com. Much quieter and less busy, with 5 en suite brick *bandas*. There's also a restaurant serving excellent pizza, a games area and plenty of activities. Camping US$4pp with your own tent.

The far southwest: gorilla land

For many people, Uganda is synonymous with gorilla tracking. The gorillas are in the corner of the country where Uganda meets Rwanda and the DR Congo, the only three countries in which it is possible to visit mountain gorillas (Gorilla beringei beringei). The route here is mountainous and spectacular, as the road winds from Kabale to Kisoro, cut into the sides of peaks with glorious views of deep valleys, streams and lakes. Slopes are now largely logged out, but there are deep fertile valleys. It comes as a shock to find fir trees growing nearly on the Equator, but much of the time you will be travelling at over 2000 m. There are two ways of seeing the gorillas. The first is to organize transport, permits and camping equipment, etc, yourself. The easier but expensive alternative is to go on an organized tour, arranged in Uganda or before you arrive.

Ins and outs

Permits

Most travellers will book their gorilla tracking permits through tour operators or backpacking hostels. This is quick and convenient as they will take away most of the hassle. However, it is worth knowing about the way these are allocated. It is very strictly controlled by the Uganda Wildlife Authority (UWA), see page 46. The choice of park largely comes down to a question of permit availability. There is not really much point in visiting more than one of the national parks.

Several family groups of gorillas have been habituated in Uganda and the majority are found in Bwindi Impenetrable Forest where five groups (40 permits daily) can currently be tracked. There is also one in Mgahinga Gorilla National Park (see page 230), with eight permits. As gorilla family groups enlarge and subdivide the number of permits increase, but the extra permits are only initially available from UWA offices at Bwindi park headquarters, until there is some certainty that the subdivision is permanent. These gorilla families also move around within the mountains, sometimes over the border into Rwanda and DR Congo. Within Bwindi Impenetrable Forest there are three sectors from where gorilla tracking starts: Buhoma, Ruhija and Nkuringo. The cost at Bwindi is US$500 per permit for both Bwindi and Mgahinga. As changes are sometimes made, check the excellent UWA website www.ugandawildlife.org or www.friendagorilla.org. **Kampala Backpackers** (see page 61), which organize gorilla tracking visits, are also a reliable, up-to-date source of information.

It is not advisable to turn up hoping that someone will drop out due to illness, as this rarely happens. The strict 0800 deadline is not always adhered to and the exclusion of visitors with upper respiratory infections is lax, with people claiming that they are suffering from hayfever.

Porters

If you're not very fit, consider taking a porter, especially if you're on one of the longer trips. Arrange porters through the tour company as they're not available from UWA; they cost US$10-15 per day. Agree an amount for tips (such as USh5000 per head) and then give it to the ranger leading your trek. The ranger will ensure that it is fairly divided between the rangers and guards.

What to take

Good shoes, waterproofs and dirt-resistant clothes are essential as gorilla tracking is very muddy. Make sure you've got lots of water.

Bwindi Impenetrable Forest National Park → *Colour map 2, C1.*

Ins and outs

Getting there All buses and *matatus* stop at Butogota and you will need to arrange alternative transport up to Buhoma, 17 km away and the starting point of the gorilla trips. As you have to start tracking at around 0800 in the morning it is strongly advised that you get to Buhoma the night before. If you're late you lose your booking and do not get any money back.

Two coaches go direct to the nearest village, Butogota, from where it is a 17-km hike to the park headquarters at Buhoma from Kampala: Muhabura (recommended) and Gateway (avoid), leaving around 0600 and taking 11-12 hours, US$14-16. From Kabale it is a journey of five to six hours to the campsite at Buhoma but transport links are difficult.

Getting to the campsite at Buhoma the cheapest alternative is to take a *matatu* as far as possible and then walk the rest of the way. *Matatus* go part of the way, leaving from the Kabale *matatu* stand at about 0800, taking three to four hours to Butagota. A taxi from Butogota to Buhoma costs about US$8.75 or you may be able to hitch a ride from other tourists going to Buhoma in their own vehicles.

If you're relying on public transport and want to be sure not to miss your allocated day to see the gorillas, you should allow at least one spare day. There is plenty to do around the forest itself.

Safety There have been no security problems since the **Bwindi massacre** in 1999, when eight foreign tourists were killed by Rwanda's Interahamwe militia. There is a strong army presence in Bwindi and along the border, although they no longer accompany the tour groups. An armed ranger accompanies the tracking groups as protection against animal attacks.

The park

This park lies along the Uganda-DR Congo border in Kabale and Rukungiri districts, in southwestern Uganda on the edge of the Western Rift Valley. Covering an area of 321 sq km, Bwindi was first gazetted to the status of a forest reserve in 1932, then in 1961 as an animal sanctuary. From 1961 it was under the joint management of the Forest and the Game Departments, until 1991, when it became a national park. The forest has had a number of names in the past including Bwindi and Kayonza. In the local language Bwindi means 'a place of darkness' and the name refers to the region's thick vegetation, also reflected in the park name 'Impenetrable Forest'.

What is most striking when you arrive is the steepness of the valley's sides. It is easy to pick out the huge trees in the forest but they are completely dwarfed. It is very tiring going up and down the valley slopes, so be prepared; take lots of water and don't worry about stopping to rest for a few minutes. Some slopes are so steep that you may well have to crawl for part of the way. If you are going during the rainy season be prepared to get very wet and muddy. Your group is allocated when you book permits in Kampala; it is worth asking where the groups are and picking the easy or hard trek and the nearest accommodation accordingly.

Buhoma Sector

This was the first sector to be developed and is better served by accommodation, transport links, shops and a community hospital. Most importantly, there are more habituated gorilla groups nearby, so finding one of them is almost guaranteed.

There are at least 10 accommodation choices here, an apparent mismatch to the number of available daily permits to track the gorillas. Most lodges or camps are clustered near the park gates. The park gate into Bwindi is manned mainly to stop vehicles entering the park unless on official business. Four lodges are sited inside the gate on the edge of the forest, close to the gate: **SGFC**, **Buhoma Lodge**, **Buhoma Community Rest Camp** and **Bwindi View Camp**. Visitors to these lodges do NOT have to pay the US$30 visitation fee per day, until they want to go into the forest. This can only be done with an official guide to whom you will have to pay the fee.

Ruhija Sector

Ruhija is 50 km from Buhoma in the southeast of the park. Like Nkuringo Sector, there are poorer transport links, far less accommodation and fewer habituated gorilla groups in the environs, compared to Buhoma Sector. The roads are challenging and journey times can be up to two hours between the gates. This high-altitude section of Bwindi is mostly visited by keen birdwatchers and is home to the reclusive forest elephants. Gorilla tracking of the habituated Bitakura group became available from July 2008. Eight permits are available per day.

Nkuringo Sector

Located in the southwest of the park, gorilla tracking started here in 2004 when the Nkuringo group were habituated. In May 2009 the Nsongi group were habituated 17 km away in Rushaga, Kisoro District. In July 2010 the Nsongi group subdivided and the new group is known as the Mishaya group. At present permits to track the Mishaya group are being sold on the day of the trek, unlike the other gorilla tracking permits in Bwindi. The length of the trek depends upon their location, and can be up to 17 km. In October 2010 a new baby was born in the Nsongi group. Rushaga is a two-hour journey from Kisoro so staying overnight locally is advisable.

The gorillas

DNA analysis has confirmed the Bwindi gorillas belong to the Eastern lowland gorilla (*Gorilla beringei beringei*). There are now eight habituated gorilla groups that can be tracked at Bwindi but only six of them are open to visitors. The Mubare and Habinyanja groups live around the Buhoma forest area. The Nkuringo group are found in the area of the same name, in the southwest section of the park. In 2009 the Nsongi (or Nshongi) family of 34 gorillas, including three silverbacks, were declared ready for viewing. They are located in Rushaga, Kisoro district, 17 km from Nkuringo. In mid-2010 the Nsongi group subdivided and the new group is known as the Mishaya group. (Since the split UWA have confirmed that extra

Mountain gorillas

In the far southwest of Uganda are two national parks, Bwindi Impenetrable and Mgahinga Gorilla, where half the world's 820 remaining endangered mountain gorillas are found. The majority of these magnificent primates are located at Bwindi, whereas the gorillas at Mgahinga's habituated groups sometimes move on a seasonal basis across the volcanic Virunga Mountains chain into neighbouring Rwanda (where Dian Fossey established her Study Centre, immortalized in the film *Gorillas in the Mist*) and DR Congo. These heavily forested mountainous regions have steep peaks and valleys covered in dense undergrowth and trekking the gorillas is an arduous, damp but rewarding experience.

Gorillas are vegetarians, spending most of their day eating shoots and leaves, living in family groups led by mature males called 'silverbacks'; easily recognisable by the silver or grey hair on their backs. Silverbacks are immense, growing to between 1.5-1.8 m in height and weighing between 204-227 kg. When angered, the Silverback starts hooting, drums his fists on his chest, rears up, grimaces to reveal two rows of fearsome teeth, screams and charges. By contrast, newborn gorillas are small, weighing about 2.5 kg with a gestation period similar to humans. Infant mortality rates are high with only half the young reaching maturity. Their estimated life span is thought to be about 25-30 years.

Interest by Louis Leakey in the origins of mankind led to the creation of the Dian Fossey project which culminated in humans making close and friendly contact with groups of habituated gorillas in their natural setting, such that visitors can get to observe the family groups from only a few metres away, a breathtaking experience. The development of gorilla tourism, and habituation of the gorillas, is proceeding with great care in order to avoid dangers such as the gorillas catching human diseases.

permits are being issued, but this is not advertised and appears to be on a daily and ad hoc basis.) The Bitukura group are usually found in the Ruhija area. The Rushegura group have moved to DR Congo at present and the Kyagurilo group are only available to researchers. As this information is subject to change, see www.friendagorilla.org for updates.

Flora and other fauna

The forest has been estimated to have at least 120 species of mammal, of which 10 are primates. In addition to the gorillas, there are chimpanzees, black and white colobus, red-tailed monkeys and vervets. Other species include giant forest hogs and bushbucks, although these are both rare and shy animals. A small group of forest elephants have survived in the southeast section of the park, although their population was brought close to extinction. The forest supports a huge range of birdlife, with over 330 species. The plant and insect life is also phenomenal, with 202 butterfly varieties; there are about 150 tree species as well as a wide range of ferns, orchids, mosses and lichens.

Walks

From Buhoma There are several guided walks of the forest available that can be started at any time from 0900-1415 (except the longer Ivi River Walk which has to be started at 0800). The reception at **Buhoma Community Rest Camp (BCRC)**, see Sleeping, page 225, near the park gate takes bookings and organizes the walks and guides (guide uniforms are sponsored by Bwindi Community Hospital). Guided walks are US$15 per person and you can obtain a packed lunch from BCRC for US$10. The **Muyaga River Nature Walk** is a short semi-circular walk that takes less than 30 minutes lying just outside the park boundary but inside the gate. This is free, on the edge of the forest, and no guide is necessary. The **Waterfall Trail** is a return three-hour walk, through the dense forest, leading to a series of three waterfalls and is recommended. The three-hour **Muzabajiro Loop Trail** is through forest to the slopes of the Rukubira Hill, where a wildfire in 1992 created an open view across the forest towards the Virunga volcanoes. The **Rushara Hill Trail** is a three-hour trek to the top of the highest hill in the immediate area of Buhoma. The steep climb, to 1915 m through fields and regenerating forest, can be strenuous, but you're rewarded with views across the Western Rift Valley to the Virungas to the south, and as far north as the Rwenzori Mountains on a very clear day. The **Ivi River Walk** is a six- to eight-hour return walk along a route cleared in 1970 for a never-completed road to Kisoro. The path is an important route for the local people, and leads to the Ivi River at the southwestern boundary of the park. There is also a Buhoma Community Village Walk.

From Ruhija These walks are in the southeast of the park, along the shorter but poorer road from Kabale to Buhoma; contact the International Tropical Forestry Commission (ITFC), see Sleeping below. The **Guesthouse Nature Trail** is a short 30-minute loop through the forest. The **Bamboo Trail** is a winding walk of at least six hours through bamboo to Rwamunyonyi Hill, the highest part of the park, which offers views as far as Lake Bunyonyi. The **Mubwindi Swamp Trail** is a four-hour walk that you need to arrange with the park management or the director the IFTC, which runs a guesthouse at Ruhija (see page 225). This leads to a swamp of about 2 sq km, from which Mubwindi forest is supposed to have got its name (meaning 'a muddy, swampy place of darkness'), home to many animals.

◉Bwindi Impenetrable National Park listings

For Sleeping and Eating price codes and other relevant information, see Essentials pages 21-23.

🛏 Sleeping

Butogota is a pleasant village with wide green verges but quite spread out around the rim of the hill. Butogota has some simple accommodation (try Pineapple Club (**E**), simple but clean, on the main street where the bus stops) and many find that this is the easiest solution to spending an extra night at Buhoma.

Buhoma Sector *p222*
LL Buhoma Lodge, formerly Homestead, T0414-321470, T077-250 2155 (mob), www.ugandaexclusivecamps.com. Renovated in 2008. 8 cottages with private bathrooms and

verandas. The well-appointed restaurant and bar overlook the Munyaga Valley.
LL Gorilla Resort, just outside the park gates, T0312-288667, T077-241 9238 (mob), www.gorillaresort.com. Luxury camp offering cottages or safari tents, with a large roll-top, claw-foot bath in every room. The main lodge has a lounge bar and restaurant.
LL Sanctuary Gorilla Forest Camp (SGFC), T0414-340290, T077-634 0290 (mob), uganda@sanctuaryretreats.com. Positioned just inside the park entrance at Buhoma accessed up a very steep hill. Upmarket camp with 8 large tents and separate bathroom on a wooden deck. The restaurant and bar are tastefully decorated.
LL Silverback Lodge, outside Buhoma village, T0414-258273, T0312-260758, www.geolodgesafrica.com. Opened in 2008, high

up on the hill overlooking the forest, with wonderful views. 7 en suite rooms, a bar and restaurant.

LL Volcanoes Bwindi Lodge, T0414-346464/5, T077-274 1718 (mob), www.volcanoessafaris.com. 8 solar-powered, stone and tile, en suite eco-lodge *bandas* with composting toilets. Pleasant communal areas, large fireplace and veranda overlooking the forest. Very attentive staff and good food. Gorillas occasionally visit the camp.

AL-A Gorilla Conservation Camp, aka Silverback Gorilla Camp, T0414-531389, T077-233 0139 (mob), www.ctph.org. Solar-powered tented camp offers good value. It's a project of Conservation Through Public Health (CTPH), a non-profit organization working to reduce disease transmission between humans and animals.

A-D Buhoma Community Rest Camp (BCRC), T077-238 4965 or T077-252 9081 (both mob), buhomacrc@yahoo.com. A long-established, locally operated budget campsite with clean *bandas* or safari tents, either en suite or with communal bathrooms. The small restaurant serves hearty, basic meals; it's advisable to pre-order. Within easy walking distance to the park gates, with views similar to those on offer nearby at 10 times the cost. It also organizes walks (see Walks, page 223).

Ruhija Sector *p222*

LL Trekkers Tavern, 2 km from the Ruhiji park headquarters, past the trading centre of Ikumba, T0312-111490, T0312-248659, www.accessugandatours.com. Long-established as birding accommodation, this eco-friendly venue on a hilltop overlooking Bwindi has 5 en suite cottages. Friendly service and first-rate food.

D International Tropical Forestry Commission (ITFC), T0392-709753, info@itfc.org. 2 simple guesthouses, with dorms sleeping 8 and 12. Self catering only. As the altitude is over 2000 m, it's cold at night, so it's advisable to bring your sleeping bag (although bedding is provided).

Nkuringo Sector *p222*

LL Clouds Gorilla Lodge, T0414-251182, T077-248 9497 (mob), www.wildplacesafrica.com. Upmarket lodge with 8 spacious and 2 family cottages, each with a lounge, fireplace and luxury bathroom. The lodge has huge timber roof beams. It was built as a partnership between Wild Places Africa, Ugandan Safari Company and Nkuringo Community Development Fund (NCDF), which supports the local community.

LL-C Nkuringo Gorilla Camp and adjoining Hammerkop Bunkhouse, T077-480 5580 or T075-440 8637 (both mob), www.nkuringocampsite.com. There is a choice between 2 new en suite cottages or 5 twin-bed rooms in the old Hammerkop Bunkhouse with communal bathrooms. Or you can camp with your own tent, US$6.50pp (no meals). There is a small restaurant.

D-F Nshongi Camp, Rushaga, 5 mins' walk from the southern gate of Bwindi, close to the UWA hut, http://nshongicamp.altervista.org. This new budget venture offers excellent value with 3 double *bandas*. Full board, B&B or camping in your own tent at very reasonable rates.

Transport

To **Kampala** are daily buses from Butugota. Two set off at 0400 and there is a night bus leaving at 2000 that is not recommended and is known as the *Flying Coffin* for its frequent crashes.

Directory

Buhoma Sector *p222*

Internet Bwindi Community Hospital, Buhoma. The only internet service in the area. **Medical services** Bwindi Community Hospital, Buhoma. With English-speaking non-Ugandan doctors and nurses. The Mother's Waiting Hostel has greatly reduced maternal and infant mortality for the local community.

Kisoro → *Phone code: 4864. Colour map 2, C1.*

Kisoro is in the extreme southwestern corner of Uganda, about 510 km from Kampala, and just over 80 km from Kabale. It's the nearest town to Mgahinga Gorilla National Park (see page 230), 14 km away. The nearby Mufumbiro Mountains on the border of Uganda, DR Congo and Rwanda are also known as the **Virunga Range**. They are made up of three extinct volcanoes: Mount Muhavura, meaning 'the guide' , 4137 m; Mount Gahinga, 'small pile of stones', 3474 m; and Mount Sabyinyo, sometimes spelt Sabinyo, 'old man's teeth', 3674 m. These can be climbed, see page 230. Kisoro has a lively twice-weekly market, incredible hill walking and clean, safe swimming lakes, such as Lake Mutanda and Lake Chahafi nearby.

Ins and outs

Tourist information   **UWA office** ⓘ *Main St, T04864-30098, snp@ugandawildlife.org, open 0800-1700.* Arranges permits for the Mgahinga Gorilla National Park and sells maps.

Around Kisoro

One lovely trip north of Kisoro is a hike to the Mutanda Eco-Community Centre (MECC) on **Lake Mutanda**, about one to two hours' walk over a ridge and down to the water. Innumerable footpaths will take you there, but one of the best is over the hill at the end of Seseme Playing field (then ask for directions) or buy a map 50,000:1 from the national park office (see above). Beer and sodas available on arrival, but if you want food you need to order in advance from the **Golden Monkey Guest House** (see Sleeping, below) in town. The lake water is free of hippos, crocodiles and bilharzia. It might be worth asking around for a taxi number to call from the lake to save you the return journey on foot. Pick-up from MECC to Kisoro costs around US$8.75.

Another attractive walk with a stunning destination, about 9 km southeast from Kisoro close to the Rwandan border, is the route to **Lake Chahafi** campsite. The first half is

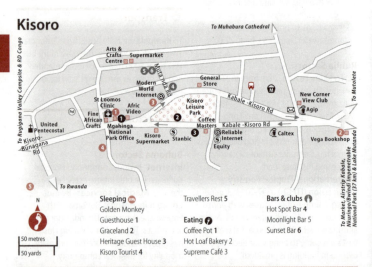

Kisoro

Sleeping
Golden Monkey
Guesthouse **1**
Graceland **2**
Heritage Guest House **3**
Kisoro Tourist **4**

Travellers Rest **5**

Eating
Coffee Pot **1**
Hot Loaf Bakery **2**
Supreme Café **3**

Bars & clubs
Hot Spot Bar **4**
Moonlight Bar **5**
Sunset Bar **6**

along a stretch of paved roads, currently under construction, and the second leg is along beautiful country tracks, with breathtaking views and big skies. When you arrive you will find a charming small half-built campsite sitting on top of the water. The view from the deck is simply jaw-dropping, with the beautiful, sleepy, papyrus-fringed lake scattered with lilypads, home to some truly spectacular birds and a full frontal view of the majestic Muhabura volcano. The 19.2 sq km lake is a bird sanctuary, home to the African jacana, great blue heron, pelican, African fish eagle, pied kingfisher and bronze sunbird, amongst others. Sodas and beers are available, although food must be ordered in advance. You can pitch a tent for US$2.25 and enjoy a night of campfires and fireflies.

If you're interested in getting into the national parks, the **Batwa trail** ① *organized by UWA and the United Organization for Batwa Development in Uganda (UDOBDU), Bunagana Rd, next to the Stanbic Bank, open office hours, US$80 including park entry fees,* is an excellent project developed by and directly benefiting the local displaced Batwa communities. This five-hour tour, led by several Batwa guides, walks you through their ancient habitat, telling stories about their history and way of life in the forests. The walk ends inside of the large Garama Cave where visitors are led through the many chambers to explore the large dark interior with a few acoustic treasures. Bring a good torch.

It's also possible to scale any of the three majestic volcanoes near Kisoro, Mount Muhavura, Mount Gahinga and Mount Sabyinyo; see page 230.

Kisoro listings

For Sleeping and Eating price codes and other relevant information, see Essentials pages 21-23.

Sleeping *map p226*
See page 231 for accommodation at Mgahinga Gorilla National Park.
AL-A Travellers Rest, 100 m from UWA office, T0414-200221, T077-244 5805 (mob), www.gorillatours.com. Old colonial hotel with 12 rooms in a mature garden setting, a haven for birdlife. It's a well-known hotel among gorilla experts for it was once known as the unofficial gorilla headquarters. In the mid-1950s its owner, game warden Walter Baumgartel, was the self-styled 'King of the Gorillas'. He was one of the first people to take an interest in gorillas and their protection. Dian Fossey and George Schaller stayed here and it became a centre for primate experts from around the world. Baumgartel left Uganda in the late 1960s. Renovated a decade ago, apart from the beautiful private gardens and handsome rustic sitting room that sets this hotel apart from the rest, it has an impressive collection of authentic Congolese masks for sale. It has

10 en suite twin rooms and 2 suites with double beds. There's a welcoming log fire, a new management team and the best food in Kisoro. Activities include village walks, volcano climbing, gorilla tracking, bike rides or visits to Lake Mutunda.
A Kisoro Tourist Hotel, Kisoro Rd, opposite the UWA office, turning down a small driveway, T04864-30135, T077-248 0682 (mob). Modern, featureless hotel, en suite rooms with DSTV, showers and sunny balconies. Large garden and safe parking. Internet acess. Restaurant food is mainly Western with good goulashes. The bar has an interesting selection of beers.
D-E Golden Monkey Guest House, opposite Virunga Hotel just behind the UWA office, T077-243 5148 (mob), www.mcdoa.org. Centrally located, this budget option has clean rooms and toilets and fantastically friendly staff. The menu here is varied and tasty, but make sure you order in advance, because, as with many places in town, all dishes are cooked on a charcoal stove and can take up to 2 hrs to prepare! The Mexican wraps are particularly good.

Camping

In addition to those listed below, camping is also available at **Virunga Hotel**, Kisoro.
MECC, Lake Mutanda. Camping in your own tent US$2.70; permanent tents with bed and sheets US$6.50pp or the charming, simple twin-bedded 'Tree House' with exceptional views of the lake and hills US$17.75.
Rugigana Valley Campsite, 1.5 km west out of Kisoro, T077-264 7660 (mob). Tents US$4pp, also lodge accommodation (**E**). Organizes hikes and hill climbing.

Eating *map p226*

Travellers Rest Hotel, see above. Dinner at 1930, US$10.50. The only gourmet restaurant in town with mouthwatering themed buffet dinners, including Lebanese, French and West African. The hotel employs local farmers to grow more exotic salads and vegetables for their tempting dinner menu. After being starved of salads and green vegetables during your travels around the bush, this restaurant is a breath of fresh air. Non-residents need to order by 1400. Lunches, however, are disappointing.
Coffee Masters, at the top of Kisoro Rd a few shops up from **Kisoro Supermarket**. Sitting on the tall bank is this place, with gorgeous views of the Kisoro hills and comfy cushioned chairs. It's good for banana and passion fruit smoothies, but most items on the menu are not available,
The Coffee Pot, next to the UWA office at the top of town. This comfortable, well-furnished café/book exchange is a good stop off for a relaxed lunch, serving great sandwiches, salads, coffees and delicious homemade cakes. Closes at 1800.
Graceland Hotel, on the main street. Open all day. For one of the speediest services in town, and cheap, well-prepared local and Western food. The balcony is the best place to watch the hustle and bustle below, and to view the beautifully colourful market sellers carry their wares on Mon and Thu. But be prepared to hear the buses honking their horns and revving their engines to drum up business for the nightly race to Kampala.
Hot Spot Inn, near the bottom of Mutanda Rd. Open all day. For the best local fare in town. Sweet potato, *matoke*, *posho*, yams, beans, meat stews and fat avocados. The large pint jugs of delicious fresh passion fruit juice for US$0.45 is worth a trip in itself.
Sunset Bar, near the top of Mutanda Rd, next to **Moonlight Bar**. This a good local joint to come to get your hands greasy and enjoy the best of Ugandan fast food. It has exceedingly tasty pork *muchomo*, cold beers and a lively atmosphere. Pork is served after 1900.
Supreme Café, overlooking the high street, a few shops down from **Stanbic Bank**. Open all day until 2200. With an attractive wooden first-floor balcony and a good espresso machine, this is a good place to get a sandwich and coffee and watch the world go by. Serves a Western menu of breakfast, lunch and dinner.

Bars and clubs *map p226*

The most lively place to be in the evenings is Mutanda Rd. Brimming with bars, late-night hair salons and delicious street food like chips and *muchomo*, it's worth just cruising up and down to see who's pumping out the best music.
Countryside 'B', at the bottom of Mutanda Rd. Has an outside terrace and is more chilled than **Moonlight**.
Heritage Guest House, Kabale Rd, the lesser main street in town. If you feel like going somewhere you'll be a little less conspicuous, this place has a bar with a cool and comfortable ambience.
Moonlight, Mutanda Rd. One of the busier late-night hubs, with good beers and reasonably flat pool table.

Shopping
Handicrafts

Fine African Crafts, next to the UWA office at the top of town. Daily 0900-1800. Has a great selection of locally made arts, crafts and jewellery. Also offers a decent choice of English, German and Dutch books to buy or exchange.

Markets

Kisoro market, held on Mon and Thu, is a fantastic and interesting spectacle and well worth a visit. It is very busy and colourful, attracting traders from Uganda, DR Congo and Rwanda. It sells fresh fruit and vegetables, colourful African fabrics, second-hand Western clothes, soap, kerosene lamps, and much more. Be careful with cameras as taking photos is frowned upon, unless money is offered in exchange. The market used to take place on the Congolese-Ugandan border until the tense political situation prompted its move.

Activities and tours
Golden monkey tracking

Contact the UWA office (see page 226) to arrange a visit to see these endangered monkeys (see page 230). Cost US$50 per day, price includes guide fee and park entrance fee.

Transport
Road

A *boda-boda* to **Mgahinga National Park** is a cheap option although you may have to walk over some of the roughest parts of the route. A special hire taxi will cost about US$10, more in the rainy season. A *matatu* to the park is an extortionate US$11.50 'fixed price', which is more than the fare to Kampala, 490 km away. The road is very rough although improved in recent years, and is steep towards the end.

The first 50 km section of the new Kabale–Kisoro road was completed in late 2010 improving journey times. *Matatus* to **Kabale** go occasionally throughout the day. *Matatus* out of Kisoro are few and infrequent, but you can pick up a shared taxi to Kabale, 2½ hrs, US$4.50-US$9, from the taxi park in town, between Kabale and Mutanda roads. Be warned that shared taxis fit 3 passengers, but squeeze in 4, including the driver, in the front, and 4 adults in the back seat. It's very cramped and they speed on the mountain roads, so avoid overcrowded shared taxies on these routes. Buses (see below for more details of companies) depart at 0600 and 1900, 2½ hrs, US$4.50.

To **Kampala** day buses depart around 0600 and night buses depart about 1900, 10 hrs, US$8.75. To **Mbarara**, same departure times, 5 hrs, US$6.50. Day buses tend to be pretty similar in both speed and safety. Bismarken tends to leave most promptly at around 0600 though **Horizon**, **Gateway** and **Muhabura** also run regularly at similar times to Kampala. Night buses tend to be a bit more risky with the odd hijacking and over-tired driver, but are generally 2-3 hrs faster as they avoid traffic and roadworks.

There are *matatus* to the **Rwanda** border to cross to Ruhengeri, taking about 3 hrs, a scenic route through one of the most beautiful parts of Uganda.

Directory

Banks Stanbic Bank. Currently has the only ATM in town, though more ATMs are planned. The worst days to withdraw money are market days, Mon and Thu and the first few days of the month, when civil servants are paid. If you need to take out money on these days, go early in the morning or late in the evening. When changing currency, Stanbic does not accept notes older than 2001, and 2006 preferably. Denominations less than US$50 receive a poorer exchange rate. It does not change TCs. Forex exchanges, like **Africana's** on the corner of Kisoro Rd next to the mosque, offer a slightly better rate with less hassle and queueing. **Internet** Modern World Internet, at the top of Mutanda Rd, 30 m from Golden Monkey Guest House. Open 0800-1900. US$0.60 for 30 mins. **Reliable Internet**, on the high street next to Equity Bank. Open 0800-2000. Good Wi-Fi, US$0.60 for 30 mins.

Mgahinga Gorilla National Park → *Colour map 2, C1.*

This, the smallest national park in Uganda at just 36 sq km, was established in 1991. It is in the far southwest of the country in Kisoro District, 14 km south of Kisoro. It makes up the northeastern part of the Virunga volcano range which extends into DR Congo and Rwanda. The viewing platform near the park headquarters offers the best place to photograph the spectacular volcanoes. Viewing the gorillas in this park is often less busy than the other gorilla sites, and easier to access from cheaper accommodation than the limited choice of mainly high-end lodges in Bwindi.

Ins and outs

Permits These can only be reserved and purchased at the UWA office in Kisoro (see page 226), not more than two weeks before the planned trek, due to the gorillas' past tendency to cross the border into Rwanda or DR Congo. Eight permits are issued per day. You must arrange your own transport to and from the park, at around US$13.50 each way for a taxi, and a packed lunch and water. Gorilla tracking begins at 0800 sharp daily; late arrivals may lose their place.

Porters These are optional at US$15, but are extremely helpful during the more challenging sections of the hike, and strongly recommended for less fit trekkers.

Gorillas

The protection of gorillas on the Ugandan side of the Virunga volcanoes began in the mid-1950s when game warden Walter Baumgartel took an interest in them. Baumgartel left Uganda in the late 1960s and in the years that followed there was much encroachment into the forest, particularly along the lower slopes of Muhavura, Gahinga and Sabinyo volcanoes. Poaching was also a threat and many of the gorillas retreated into better-protected areas in the neighbouring countries. It has been estimated that the gorilla population of the Mgahinga National Park declined by about 50% between 1960 and the early 1980s.

It was not until 1989 that gorillas began to receive some protection under the Gorilla Game Reserve Conservation Project, which began to operate along the Virunga volcanoes on the Uganda side. This became the Mgahinga Gorilla National Park Project in 1991. It is not always possible to see gorillas in Mgahinga as they can move over to DR Congo, but after an absence of several years the Nyakagezi group have consistently been in the Ugandan Section of Mgahinga forest since September 2009.

Other animals

Apart from gorillas, there are a small number of forest elephants, buffaloes, giant forest hogs, the golden monkey and the blue monkey. The endangered golden monkey (*Cercopithecus kandt*) on the IUCN red list is only found in the Virunga mountains in highland forest, especially near bamboo stands, and two other forests in Central Africa. Similar to but separate from the blue monkey (*Cercopithecus mitis*), the golden monkey is no longer thought to be a subspecies of it. The monkey gets its name from the colour of its fur, which unfortunately puts it under threat from poachers.

Climbing

It is possible to climb to the peaks of Gahinga, Sabyinyo and Muhavura, although the pace set by the ranger and armed escort may be exhausting unless you are fit. Climbs of

Gahinga and Sabyinyo start at 0700 at the park gates. Climbs cost US$50, including park entrance fees and ranger guide fees. Porter's fees are an extra US$15 per person. Book at the UWA office in Kisoro, see page 226. Tipping the rangers after the climbs is not compulsory, but appreciated. You need to arrive at the park gates by 0630, to walk the 5 km to the start of the Muhavura climb, led very quickly by armed rangers.

The summit of **Mount Muhavura** is the highest point of the park at 4137 m, and is a long steep climb of four to five hours up and three to four hours down. The top of volcano conceals a small, beautiful crater lake, a great incentive to make it to the top. The view from the summit is frequently obscured by cloud. The vegetation in the park includes montane, alpine and sub-alpine flora at each of the different levels up the volcano, varying with altitude. The lowest vegetation zone of the mountain is mainly bamboo and this is the area where the gorillas are more likely to be found. The alpine zone is dominated by the impressive giant senecios and giant lobelias that are found at an altitude of between 3600 m and 4200 m.

Mount Sabyinyo offers a more varied, exciting and highly recommended climb, and the opportunity of straddling Uganda, Rwanda and DR Congo simultaneously. It is a very different hike from the neighbouring volcanoes but similarly challenging, with an eight- to nine-hour return journey. There are three peaks to climb. Peak one is reached along a ridge on the eastern side. Reaching peak two involves a traverse along the ridge with Rwanda on one side and Uganda on the other. Trekking to peak three involves the use of a series of ladders, some angled, others horizontal, to help cover the terrain to the tri-border apex (Uganda/Rwanda/DR Congo). These ladders to the summit are occasionally out of action, so check before you start the trek.

The **Mount Gahinga** climb includes a pleasant walk through bamboo forest, known locally as *rugano*, before the gradient increases up to the summit. There was a small crater lake at the summit but it has turned into a swamp over time. It can be cloudy on top, but it does offer the opportunity to step into Rwanda. The hike takes around six to eight hours round trip, covering a distance of 12 km.

Garama Cave

① *Organized by UWA and the United Organization for Batwa Development in Uganda (UDOBDU), Bunagana Rd, next to the Stanbic Bank. Open office hours. Cost US$80, including park entry fees.*

Alternative shorter walks include a visit to the enormous Garama Cave, over 340 m in length and 14 m deep. This was where the Batwa (Pygmies) warriors used to live during their long-running conflict with their neighbours, the Bantu, almost 100 years ago. The Bantu were unaware of the existence of the cave and had difficulty locating the Batwa after their periodic raids. The caves are currently occupied by bats. It is recommended to bring a torch.

Mgahinga Gorilla NP listings

For Sleeping and Eating price codes and other relevant information, see Essentials pages 21-23.

Sleeping

LL Mt Gahinga Safari Lodge, T0414-346464/5, T075-274 1718 (mob), www.volcanoessafaris.com. Located high above Kisoro town at the base of the Sabyinyo/Mgahinga park entrances is this comfortable, 100% carbon neutral lodge overlooking the emerald green Lake Mutanda, which is dotted with small islands covered with banana trees and framed by the imposing Virunga mountain range. Has 8 well-equipped stone and tile *bandas*. Price includes food, alcohol, local activities and massages. **Volcanoes** donates US$100 from every safari traveller to local community projects. It's very convenient for tracking of gorillas and golden monkeys, trekking the volcanos, gorge walking and other park activities.

D-E Amajambere Iwacu Community Group (AICG), about 500 m from the park entrance, bookings via the **Golden Monkey Guest House** in Kisoro, see page 227. A considerably cheaper and less luxurious alternative is the neighbouring AICG campsite, with single or twin *bandas*, and dorms. Located in the beautiful foothills of the park and the Gahinga/Sabinyio volcanoes, this project is an income-generating community initiative. The co-op has a gazebo dining area, attractive campsites, running water, bucket showers and a pit toilet. Food and drink is limited, but most basic dishes can be prepared with notice. Staff are helpful and can arrange trips and activities. It's worth staying here if spending more than a day in the park as it saves you the pricey round-trip fare to Kisoro.

Contents

Footprint features

Background

History

Before the arrival of the British there were as many as 30 different ethnic groups in the area that now forms modern Uganda, each with its own language, culture and social organization.

The political organization of these different states ranged from those with a highly developed centralized rule, through small chiefdoms, to areas with no obvious system of government. Buganda, Toro, Bunyoro and Nkore (Ankole in the colonial period) were all of the first type, and all had a highly developed centralized system with a monarch in place. Until 1830 Toro was part of Bunyoro, but broke away when Prince Kaboyo rebelled against his father. For some time Bunyoro was the strongest and most powerful of the four, but from the second half of the 18th century it was overtaken by Buganda. In Nkore the system was rather different as the minority pastoral Bahima ruled over the majority agriculturalist Bairu.

Other areas had no obvious system of government and interpersonal relations were controlled by fear of spirits and the supernatural.

The first foreigners to arrive in the area were Arab traders in the 1840s. From about 1850 the first Europeans began to arrive. John Speke reached Buganda in 1860 and was the first European to identify the source of the Nile (see box, page 86).

The late 19th century was a period of instability in much of Uganda, and there were wars on a surprisingly large scale. In 1888 the British East Africa Company was given a Royal Charter and their control over the area was consolidated by a treaty with the Kabaka of Buganda (the central and most prominent kingdom) in 1891. However, the Company found the administration of the territory too much to manage, and in 1894 the British government took over responsibility and Buganda was declared a protectorate. Similar status was given to Bunyoro, Toro and Ankole in 1896. During the following years the boundaries of the country were finalized, with a section of Uganda being transferred to Kenya as late as 1912.

Buganda Agreement of 1900

The so-called 'Buganda Question' goes back to the signing in 1900 of the Uganda Agreement (at this time, and until about 1906, the British referred to the District of Buganda as Uganda). It proved to be a watershed in the history of Buganda and, indeed, the whole of Uganda. It formalized the association between the British and the Buganda that had been developing since Speke's arrival in 1862.

One of the most important aspects of the agreement was that it secured a remarkably privileged position for Buganda in comparison with its neighbours. The constitutional relationship between the protectorate government and the government of the Kingdom of Buganda was set out at some length, and it emphasized Buganda's political identity while assuring it a greater measure of internal autonomy than the other districts enjoyed. Some of the other districts had their own agreements, but none were as comprehensive or as favourable as that accorded to the Buganda.

The agreement led to important changes in land tenure. It won over the majority of the chiefs by giving them land grants known as *mailo*, and in doing so it recognized that land was a marketable commodity. The land not given to the Kabaka (the ruler of the Baganda) and chiefs became Crown land to be used for the benefit of the kingdom. The agreement thus created a landed class. It also gave, for the first time, recognition to the notion of indirect rule through the chiefs. The colonialists needed local allies to help them administer with the minimum expenditure, and to produce an economic surplus that could pay for the administration. In time the interests of the chiefs and the government became more closely interwoven. The chiefs collected regular salaries and promoted government policies, and in the public's mind they began to be associated with the administration of the protectorate.

The benefit of the agreement added to the natural advantages that Buganda already had, with its fertile soils, regular rainfall, and a location on the shore of Lake Victoria that ensured good transport links. Missionary activity in the area, stimulated by competition between the Protestants and Catholics, led to a greater concentration of hospitals, schools and other educational facilities. Britain encouraged the production of cotton, the major cash crop in the south, while parts of the remaining areas were discouraged from growing cash crops and were instead developed as labour reserves. This served to accentuate further the differences between Buganda and the rest of the Protectorate, with the south producing cash crops and the north providing migrant labour. In keeping with this division, the north also provided soldiers to the army throughout the colonial period. Buganda's farmers benefited greatly from high coffee prices after the war, and in the early 1950s industrial and commercial development were concentrated in the south generally and in particular in Buganda with its locational and educational advantages.

The period of British rule in Uganda saw dramatic changes in the politics and economy of the country. Most of the wars and disputes were brought under control and the peace that grew up became known as Pax Britannica. The country was divided into districts, each headed by a District Commissioner, and the districts into counties (*saza*), sub-counties (*gombolola*), parishes (*miruka*) and sub-parishes (*bukungu* or *batongole*). A system of indirect rule was developed, with local people used at all these levels. In cases where a system of government was already in place the incumbents were used, but where this was absent other Ugandans – usually Baganda – were brought in. This meant that in many parts of Uganda in the early years of British administration, the British controlled large areas of Uganda through appointed Baganda chiefs.

While the south of the country developed into an agriculturally productive area producing mainly cotton and coffee, the north and southwest became labour pools. Migration into the southern and central region became crucial to maintaining the high production in these areas. There was also a great deal of migration from outside Uganda to the central region. This was mainly from what was then known as Ruanda Urundi (later to be Rwanda and Burundi) but was also from Tanganyikya and the Congo. Migration was not just to large-scale government employment, such as the building of the railway and the army, but also to work for individual cotton and coffee farmers in Buganda. There were some big European-owned farms and plantations in Uganda, but they were never as extensive as in Kenya and it was always planned that Uganda should be developed primarily for Africans. During the Depression of the late 1920s and early 1930s, the Uganda colonial government was not prepared to give the Europeans financial support to get them through the difficult times. Many went bust and left the country. A number of the plantations were later bought up by Asians and were developed into the sugar plantations that can be seen on the road from the Kenya border to Kampala.

The Christian missions arrived in Uganda early and their impact was enormous. Islam was also introduced into Uganda but never made the same impact. The first schools and hospitals were all mission run; the Catholics and Protestants tried desperately to win the most converts, and the key was to provide superior education. The two Christian faiths divided the country up between themselves so that, for example, the White Fathers went to Southern Uganda, the

The history of East Africa

Archaeological sites at Olduvai Gorge in Tanzania and at Lower Awash River in Ethiopia suggest that man began to evolve in the Rift Valley more than 3 million years ago, and hunter-gatherer communities were established. The area then experienced an influx of people from West Africa (the Bantu Expansion), beginning around 500 BC. In the Horn it is thought that Cushitic immigrants came from Mesopotamia (now Iraq) around 300 BC. The newcomers were cultivators and pastoralists, and they began to change the pattern of subsistence away from hunting and gathering.

Contact with other areas began as seagoing traders arrived from the north, sailing down the east coast of Africa and coming from as far as India and China. A sprinkling of settlements by Islamic people from Shiraz in Persia were established along the coast from about AD 1000.

European contact began with the arrival of the Portuguese who sailed round the southern tip of Africa and passed up the east coast from 1500 onwards. They set up fortified settlements to consolidate their trading presence, several of which remain, most notably Fort Jesus in Mombasa.

A struggle for dominance of these coastal strips began between Arab groups drawing support from the Persian Gulf and vying with the Portuguese for the trade in gold, ivory and slaves. By the end of the 17th century the Portuguese found themselves stretched to retain their hold in East Africa, and Fort Jesus fell to the Arabs in 1698. For most of the next two centuries Arab rule prevailed at the coast, and they began to penetrate the interior with caravans to capture slaves and ivory. These set out from Bagamoyo and Kilwa on the coast of present-day Tanzania, following routes that stretched over 1000 km to the Great Lakes, Uganda and beyond.

In the interior, meanwhile, pockets of centralized rule and formalized social structures emerged, particularly to the west of Lake Victoria.

European exploration began in the 18th century. A Scot, James Bruce, in 1768-1773 travelled from Suskin on the Red Sea up the Abara River to join the Nile.

The origins of the White Nile (which joins the Blue Nile at Khartoum) began to exercise the imagination in Europe, and the source was eventually traced to Lake Victoria by Burton and Speke in 1860. The two great journeys by David Livingstone in 1858-1864 and 1866-1873

Mill Hill Fathers to Eastern Uganda and the Verona Fathers to the north. The Church Mission Society (CMS) is to be found across most of the country and its influence was significant.

Countries under colonial rule have usually achieved independence when a growing nationalist movement has been successful, both in mobilizing a large section of the population and in extracting concessions from the colonial power. In Uganda however, it has been said that it was not nationalism that produced independence but rather the imminence of independence that produced nationalist parties. It was assumed that independence would be granted at some stage, and the focus was turned to the position and role that Buganda would take in an independent country. The Baganda did not wish for their role to be diminished after Independence. By the same token, the rest of the country had no wish to be dominated by the Baganda.

Uganda's territory was not affected by the hostilities in the First and Second World Wars. However, Ugandan troops served in the Kings African Rifles in both conflicts, and reached Lake Tanganyika and beyond, and were followed by Stanley's expedition in 1874-1877 which crossed the continent from east to west.

The activities of the explorers were followed by missionary activity and a campaign to end the slave trade. Although slavery was made illegal in 1873, it was some time before it was finally eliminated.

The European nations formalized their presence with the British occupying Kenya, Uganda and Zanzibar, and the Germans establishing themselves in what is now mainland Tanzania, Rwanda and Burundi. The Belgians held the eastern DR Congo.

Economic progress had taken place in the interior as iron implements replaced more primitive stone and wooden tools, and cultivators accumulated farming knowledge. However, droughts, locusts, rinderpest and local conflicts contrived to keep populations fairly stable. Progress accelerated with the advent of European occupation. Diseases were controlled, new crops introduced, roads and railways were built. Death rates fell, birth rates remained high and the population began a steady expansion. Living standards improved and significant sections of the population received basic education.

After the First World War the British took over the part of German East Africa that became Tanganyika, and Belgium absorbed Rwanda and Burundi. Settler presence increased, particularly in Kenya, and the Asian communities consolidated their positions in commerce.

Nationalist movements began to emerge as significant political factors after the Second World War. In Kenya, where there was by now a substantial settler population, there was an armed conflict in the 1950s (the Mau Mau uprising) over land grievances and generally in support of self-determination. All three British territories obtained Independence in the early 1960s. The immediate post-Independence period typically saw the establishment of single-party regimes. In Uganda, Rwanda and Burundi, there have been disastrous collapses of peace and security. Economic development was pursued by the adoption of socialist development strategies with heavy reliance on the public sector. A slowdown of economic progress followed. In the 1980s most countries began to reverse their economic policies. Multiparty political systems were introduced in the 1990s, although Uganda has retained a form of non-party rule.

experience abroad, hearing of former colonies that had become independent, was a factor in the movement for self-determination.

Kabaka Crisis of 1953-1955 and Independence

The issue of Baganda separatism came to a head when Sir Andrew Cohen was appointed governor in 1952, and indicated that he was determined to push Uganda as quickly as possible along the road to self-government. A vital principle underlying his policies was that Uganda must develop as a unitary state in which no one part of the country should dominate any other. Thus a strong central government was required, in which all districts, including Buganda, would be represented on an equal footing. This challenged the privileged position that the Buganda had enjoyed since 1900.

The crisis of 1953-55 was sparked off by a chance remark in London by Sir Oliver Lyttleton, the colonial secretary, about the possibility of introducing a federal system in East Africa embracing the three British territories of Kenya, Uganda and Tanganyika. This was very unpopular with all Ugandans as it was feared that the federation would be dominated by the Europeans in Kenya. The Baganda were even more fearful that they would be unable to safeguard their privileged position in a wider union. Cohen responded to Lyttleton's remarks by giving public reassurances in the Legislative Council that there would be no imposition of a federation against public wishes. The Kabaka, Mutesa II, accepted these reassurances but took the opportunity to ask for the affairs of Buganda to be transferred from the Colonial Office to the Foreign Office. This would be a clear indication that Baganda was not just another colony, but had a more privileged position as a protected state whose monarch had invited British protection. Finally, Mutesa asked for a timetable for independence to be drawn up.

The Kabaka then went a step further and rejected the policy of a unitary state and asked for the separation of Buganda from the rest of the country. Cohen demanded assurances in line with the 1900 agreement that the Kabaka would not publicly oppose the government's policies for Uganda's development. However the Kabaka refused, pleading that he first needed to consult the *Lukiko*, the Buganda council of elders. On 30 November 1953 Cohen signed a declaration withdrawing Britain's recognition of Mutesa as Native Ruler in Buganda, deported the Kabaka by air to Britain and declared a State of Emergency. Troops were deployed around Kampala but there was no outbreak of violence.

Following the Kabaka Crisis discussions to attempt to resolve the situation led to the Namirembe Conference of July-September 1954. In October 1955 the Kabaka returned to Uganda and signed the Buganda Agreement that was the outcome of the conference. The agreement declared that Buganda should continue to be an integral part of the Protectorate of Uganda, and recommended that the *Lukiko* should agree to elected Baganda participation in the Legislative Council, a step which, fearful of being submerged, it had consistently rejected. The Kabaka in theory returned as a constitutional monarch stripped of political power, but in reality the crisis had served to unite the various clans of the Baganda firmly behind the Kabaka, and thereby increase his political influence.

The crisis had a number of major effects. First, the question of federation with the rest of East Africa was ruled out. Second, the Buganda continued to have a special position and virtual internal self-government. Third, the Kabaka's personal power and popularity increased. Fourth, a statement was made in the British House of Commons that Uganda would be developed primarily as an African country, with proper safeguards for minorities. Fifth, non-Baganda members of the Legislative Council adopted an increasingly nationalist attitude and began to question the special treatment accorded to the Buganda, sowing the seeds of confrontation. And finally, now that independence in Uganda was clearly just a matter of time, the major question was related to who would hold the power after independence, and to a definition of the future role of the Buganda and the Kabaka.

From the mid-1950s the first political parties were formed. The Democratic Party (DP), led by Benedicto Kiwanuka, had particular support among Catholics. They wanted a unitary state after independence and wanted to limit the powers of the Baganda – so initially they did not find much support in Buganda. The Uganda National Congress (UNC) was more nationally based and wanted greater African control of the economy in a federal independent state. In 1958 a splinter group broke off from the UNC and formed the Uganda People's Congress (UPC), led by Milton Obote. A political party called Kabaka Yekka (KY) – 'The King Alone' – also formed, representing the interests of the Baganda.

In the immediate run-up to independence the Baganda did not co-operate, fearing the loss of their political identity as part of a unitary state and becoming increasingly hostile towards the protectorate government. They refused to proceed with elections for Buganda's legislative councillors until Buganda's role in a future central government and the role of the Kabaka had been determined. On 31 December 1960 the Baganda declared themselves independent but this was a meaningless gesture as they did not have the power to make independence a reality.

In 1961 an inquiry was set up to look into the question of the relationship of the various parts of Uganda with the centre. It recognized that Buganda enjoyed what was virtually a federal relationship with the rest of the protectorate, and recommended that this should continue. Uganda should therefore become a single democratic state with a strong central government, with which Buganda would have a federal relationship.

The first elections were held in 1961 – the two main parties being UPC and DP. The Baganda boycotted the election so that only 3% of the Buganda electorate voted, allowing the DP to make a clean sweep in Buganda. Overall UPC won a majority of votes but DP's success in Buganda gave them the majority of the seats. Obote, as leader of the UPC opposition, and the Kabaka were both anxious to eject the DP from power in the 1962 elections, and so Obote agreed to support Buganda's demands – particularly for indirect elections to the National Assembly – in return for Buganda's return to the centre and acceptance of a single central government. Thus Buganda participated in the Constitutional Conference in London in September 1961.

Obote I

At the 1961 conference the structure of the future government was agreed and the date of full independence was set for 9 October 1962. Buganda obtained virtually everything that it had demanded. There would be a federal relationship with the centre, and the constitution would define all matters concerning the Kingdom of the Kabaka and traditional institutions (three other Kingdoms were recognised: Bunyoro, Ankole and Toro). This opened the way for the Baganda to participate once again in central government, which they did through the Kabaka Yekka party, formed in 1961. They made an alliance with the UPC and the February 1962 elections in Buganda were really a fight between KY and DP; KY won 65 of the 68 seats. The KY victory determined the composition of the new government formed after the national, pre-independence elections, in April 1962. Obote's UPC won a comfortable victory over DP outside Buganda, within it the KY-UPC alliance ensured a majority of seats for the alliance. In May 1962 Obote was sworn in as prime minister of the UPC-KY government and the Kabaka's role was that of constitutional monarch. On 9 October 1962, the day Uganda became an independent nation, Obote spoke of the joy felt by all in Uganda at the achievement of Uganda's independence, particularly as this had been reached in an atmosphere of peace and goodwill. He went on to speak of the need for a unity of purpose, mutual understanding and respect, and a resolve to place country above tribe, party and self.

However, the coalition between UPC and KY was fragile and by 1964 enough KY and DP members had crossed the floor to join the UPC so that the alliance was no longer necessary. Obote dismissed KY from the government.

In February 1966 Obote suspended the constitution, deposed the president and transferred all executive powers to himself. Shortly afterwards an interim constitution was imposed, which the parliament had neither read nor debated, withdrawing regional autonomy, and introducing an executive presidency – assumed by Obote who thus became head of state with absolute power. This became known as the 'pigeon-hole constitution' because MPs were told to vote on it before they were allowed to read it – it was simply placed in their pigeon-holes for them to read afterwards. When the Baganda demanded the restoration of their autonomy, troops led by the second-in-command of the army, Colonel Idi Amin, seized the Kabaka's palace. The Kabaka fled to Britain, where he died of alcohol poisoning in exile in a Bermondsey council flat – an ignominious end for a man who had been a captain in the Grenadier Guards, and once spent much of his time at Cambridge travelling to the engineering works in Derby to supervise the carving of ivory from elephants he had shot to make the switches for the dashboard of his Rolls Royce.

Colonel Idi Amin

The late 1960s saw the beginning of the years of trouble for which Uganda was later to became notorious. Detentions and repression became increasingly common. A 'Move to the Left' was introduced, which redistributed resources by way of nationalization and increased central power. Obote, who had used the army to prop up his own regime, was to be ousted by that same army under the command of Amin. The takeover occurred in January 1971 while Obote was out of the country at a Commonwealth Conference. Amin declared himself the new head of state and promised that there would be a return to civilian government within five years. This, however, was not to be.

It is worth remembering that Amin was initially greeted with widespread support among the Ugandan population, particularly the Baganda, as well as in the Western world. Not long into his regime, however, Amin suspended all political activity and most civil rights. The National Assembly was dissolved and Amin began to rule the country by capricious decree. In August 1972 he announced the expulsion of all non-citizen Asians. The directive was later expanded to all Asians, although under pressure he did backtrack on this. However, in the event the atmosphere that had been established drove all but a handful of the 75,000 Asians to leave the country. Most went to Britain, while many others went to Canada and the United States. Britain cut off diplomatic relations and imposed a trade embargo. By the end of the year most other Western countries had followed suit. The businesses that had been owned by Asians were Africanized, that is, given to various cronies of Amin. The expulsion of Asians and policy of Africanization was popular with the majority of the Ugandan population, many of whom had resented the success of the Asian businesses. However, many businesses collapsed and the sudden and dramatic loss of technical skills brought other enterprises to a standstill. Amin also attempted to gain the popularity of the Baganda by returning the body of the Kabaka for burial in the Kisubi Tombs outside Kampala.

Amin's administration was propped up by military aid from the Soviet Union and Libya, but the infrastructure – water supply, schools, hospitals, roads – collapsed. Many former cash-crop producers returned to subsistence production in an effort to survive. Unexplained disappearances increased, particularly among the Acholi and Langi people. There was conflict within the army.

In 1976 a group from the Popular Front for the Liberation of Palestine hijacked an Air France flight that was bound for Israel and forced it to land at Entebbe. The terrorists were welcomed by Amin. The passengers were transferred to the terminal and released except for the Israelis and Jews. The Air France crew elected to stay with the hostages. The terrorists demanded the release of 53 Palestinians held in Israeli jails and around the world, threatening to kill the hostages. A raid by Israeli commandos, landing under cover of darkness at Entebbe in four transport planes, succeeded in freeing the hostages and destroying 11 Ugandan Mig-17 fighters on the ground. Four hostages lost their lives, as well as the leader of commandos, 46 Ugandan soldiers, and the six terrorists. The episode was a major humiliation for Amin.

In 1978, in an attempt to detract attention from the internal turmoil, Amin launched an attack on Tanzania. The Kagera Salient in southwest Uganda has, since the drawing of international boundaries, been rather a problematic area. Just to the west of Lake Victoria the international boundary is a straight line following the 10° latitude. However, the Kagera River forms a loop to the south of this. There is, therefore, an area of land that is part of Tanzania but, because of the river, has more contact with Uganda. One of the most important agreements that the Organization of African Unity (OAU) reached soon after its formation was that, however unfair or illogical the international boundaries drawn by the colonial powers, they should not be disputed. Amin's claim to the Kagera Salient was clearly in breach of this. Amin's undisciplined troops were no match for the Tanzanian army and the 1979 war led to massive destruction, as the army fled north pillaging and destroying as it went. Amin fled and went into exile, first in Libya, and later in Saudi Arabia.

His Excellency, self-styled Field Marshal and Life President of Uganda, Amin awaited the call to return once the 'misunderstanding' that led to his overthrow was cleared up. At his villa in Jeddah, he remained convinced that his people still loved him. The money he took with him from Uganda was soon gone, but the Saudi government granted him an allowance. He died in Jeddah in 2003.

Following the war, the Tanzanian army remained in Uganda to maintain the peace. Meanwhile, on the political front, the Tanzanians arranged the Moshi Conference in March 1979. At this conference Dr Lule (who had formerly been vice-chancellor of Makerere) was chosen to be the leader of the National Consultative Committee of the Uganda National Liberation Front, which, together with a military commission, undertook the interim rule of Uganda. In April Lule was sworn in as president. However, in June he was voted out of office by the 30-strong National Consultative Committee, and former Attorney General Binaisa was put in his place. His length of office was to be only a year and in May 1980 the UNLF's military commission took over. This was headed by Paul Mwanga and was supported by Museveni as vice-chairman. Elections were set for December 1980 and were contested by four political parties: UPC (headed by Obote) and DP (headed by Paul Ssemogerere), as well as a newer party, the Uganda Patriotic Movement (UPM), headed by Yoweri Museveni, and the Conservative Party, largely a Buganda-based party derived from Kabaka Yekka.

Obote II

This election for which Uganda had such high hopes is widely believed to have been fixed; crowds had gathered in the streets of Kampala as the first results came out and word was that the DP had won. However, Mwanga announced that no further results of the election could be released before they had been approved by him. Needless to say, when the results were finally published – announcing a UPC victory – there was widespread belief that they had been falsified. The truth of the election result will probably never be known but in the end the UPC had a majority of 20 seats, and Obote was proclaimed president with Mwanga as vice-president. The election of the new government did not, however, bring peace and stability to the country. The policies that the UPC put forward were aimed at attracting World Bank and IMF-sponsored economic reconstruction, but rebuilding the country was not to be easy. On the security side the situation in many parts of the country deteriorated still further.

The dissatisfaction that resulted from the doubts over the elections led to a number of groups going into the bush from where they carried on a guerrilla war. These included the National Resistance Army (NRA), led by Yowari Museveni, a political science graduate from the University of Dar es Salaam. The NRA was based largely in the southern part of the country. It was well organized and grew from a small collection of fighters into a powerful army. The atrocities perpetrated by the government in what became known as the Luwero Triangle, an area to the north of Kampala, were an attempt to rid the NRA of civilian supporters. Large numbers of people displaced by these atrocities joined up with the NRA, including children orphaned by the civil war.

Meanwhile there was also trouble within the Uganda National Liberation Army (UNLA), an ethnic division within the army largely made up of Acholi and Langi, which was to lead to another change in leadership in July 1985. This was led by the two Okellos (Tito and Basilio, not related). Obote fled to Kenya and from there to Zambia, to die of kidney failure in a Johannesberg hospital in 2005.

Tito Okello took over as president. The NRA did not join Okello but remained fighting and within a few months had taken over Fort Portal and Kasese in the west of the country. By the end of the year the NRA was within a few miles of Kampala. There were efforts at negotiation at a conference in Nairobi, and in late December a peace treaty was signed. However, just three weeks after the signing, Museveni's troops advanced on Kampala.

Museveni

Okello's troops fled north, Museveni was sworn in as president and formed a broad-based government with ministries being filled by members of all the main political factions. However, fighting continued in the north. By the late 1980s, under an amnesty offered to the rebels, almost 30,000 of them had surrendered.

Museveni, however, has not been without his critics. An Amnesty International report published in late 1991 accused the NRA of torturing and summarily executing prisoners during the operations against the rebels in the north. The criticism most commonly aimed at Museveni, particularly by the Western donors, is his apparent avoidance of democratic elections. When he first came to power political parties were suspended and it was announced that there would be no elections for three years. In October 1989 the NRM extended the government's term of office to a further five years from January 1990, when their mandate was due to run out. Museveni argued that the time was not ready for political parties and that a new constitution had to be drawn up before elections could take place. In March 1990 the ban on political party activities was extended for five years. A new constitution was adopted in 1995, which provided for an assembly with 305 members, 214 elected, the remainder nominated or ex officio.

Museveni was elected president in 1996, and re-elected in 2001. In 2005 a constitutional amendment sanctioned a multi-party system and abolished the limit on the number of terms a president could serve. Museveni was duly re-elected in 2006. In the February 2011 elections Museveni was again returned to power. Opponents accused his party of using state resources to bribe voters. EU observers expressed concern at ruling party candidates' widespread distribution of money and gifts to voters during their electoral campaign.

The Kabaka of Baganda was allowed to return to the country and to be crowned in a highly publicized ceremony in 1993 (see box, page 243). This was obviously immensely popular

The Coronation of the Kabaka

This event eventually took place at the end of July 1993. There had been a number of delays since it was first announced that the son of Edward Muteesa II could return to Uganda and be crowned. An amendment had to be made to the constitution and it was made clear that the new Kabaka would not have any political powers but would be a cultural leader. The occasion also gave rise to much discussion as to the future of the other four kingdoms in Uganda; the people of at least one of these kingdoms (the Ankole) did not want their king to return.

Finally it was declared that the coronation could go ahead and suddenly the Baganda found they had a huge amount to organize before the great day. There were invitations to be sent out, a hill-top to clear, large grass-thatched constructions to be built, a road to be surfaced, not to mention all the traditional rituals that the Sabataka (the one who was to be King) had to perform before he could be pronounced the Kabaka. These included the tuning of the drums and a series of visits to culturally important sites around Buganda.

In the weeks before the coronation day hordes of volunteers gathered at the site at Namugongo near the famous Kings College, Budo, and set about clearing the hill top. Groups of women sat around cleaning and preparing the reeds used for the construction of walls of the buildings. They were dressed in the Ugandan basuti, many made from bark cloth. The atmosphere was one of great anticipation, and they frequently broke into song.

Eventually the great day arrived. Events began at daybreak with a mock cane fight in which the Sabataka had to prove his worthiness to become the Kabaka. Thousands of people began to arrive in traditional dress and gathered on the hill top. It was a wonderful sight, with fine views of Buganda all around and, as the sun rose, the mist gradually cleared.

Foreign dignitaries took their places in the shade of a pavilion. President Museveni and his wife were the last of the guests to arrive and the president was greeted extremely warmly as the Baganda thanked him for returning their king to them. The ceremony was split into two parts: the first being the traditional one under a tree, and the second, in view of many more people, was the religious ceremony when prayers were said. The Sabataka was carried into the enclosure where the coronation was to take place and took his seat on a covered with bark-cloth throne underneath the traditional tree. As part of the ritual he prodded a cow (in the past he would have killed it) and as the ceremony progressed he was dressed in layers of bark-cloth covered by animal skins.

Just after the actual crowning, dark clouds started to gather and the wind suddenly rose. There had been no rain in the area for a few weeks and now it looked as if there was to be a thunderstorm, which would forebode ill. But after just a few spots of rain the clouds cleared and the sun came out – and the Bagandans said: God is being kind to us.

with the Baganda, although his role is purely ceremonial without any political function. The Kingdoms in Bunyoro (see box, page 188), Busoga and Toro have also been restored.

The Asian community have been encouraged to return, and the property they relinquished on their departure has been restored. The Asians have been cautious, but they are once again filling positions in all sectors of the economy.

In 1990 the security situation in outlying parts began to be a matter of concern for the government. There were four areas where there were regular outbreaks of fighting. In the north, the Lord's Resistance Army (LRA), led by Joseph Kony, mounted attacks on communities around Gulu and Kitgum, abducting prisoners, including many children. The LRA was thought to be about 1000 strong. Although the LRA initially had the aim of setting up a Christian state in Uganda, it quickly descended into kidnapping and banditry which became a way of life for its members. It received support from Sudan, and Uganda has retaliated by giving support in southern Sudan to the Sudan People's Liberation Army (SPLA), which was fighting for secession from the Islamic government in the north. In December 1999 Uganda and Sudan reached an agreement whereby each country would not offer refuge or support to the other country's rebels. Uganda followed this up with an offer of an amnesty to the LRA, held open for six months. There was a disappointing response to these initiatives. In March 2002 the LRA attacked a Sudanese garrison meaning that the attitude of the Sudanese government hardened towards their former allies and they allowed the Ugandan army to pursue the LRA inside Sudan. Attacks by the LRA on Sudanese citizens caused the SPLA to contemplate targeting the LRA. This move has embarrassed Uganda as it could hardly co-operate with the SPLA having agreed earlier not to support it. As all parties were by now opposed to the LRA, there was more optimism that they could be hunted down and their ghastly activities terminated.

In the northeast of Uganda there was fighting between clans of the pastoralist Karamajong. During the Amin and Obote II periods firearms were acquired, and they were used to try to settle disputes over cattle thefts. Several hundred people were reported killed, and the government became involved in trying to maintain law and order by implementing a programme to disarm the Karamajong.

There was also rebel activity in the southwest of the country, around Kasese. A series of bomb attacks on buses and two serious assaults on Kasese displaced some 70,000 people. It is thought that the groups forming the Allied Democratic Forces (ADF) were opportunistic rather than idealistic, and number only around 200 activists. Material support is said to come from Libya, Iran and the United Arab Emirates, and the ADF is believed to have a strong Islamic element. While the government has had some military success against the ADF, the nearby mountainous terrain of the Rwenzori Mountains provides a refuge that makes it difficult to imagine that the rebels can be easily defeated by military means.

In addition to the internal worries, Uganda has also become involved in the conflict in DR Congo. Uganda was concerned to prevent incursions by armed groups formed mostly from Hutu displaced by the troubles in Rwanda and Burundi. In March 1999, eight tourists and four rangers were killed by Rwandan Hutu rebels in the Bwindi Impenetrable Forest National Park. Museveni responded by improving security for visitors in the area.

Uganda supported Laurent Kabila in overthrowing the rule of President Mobutu, in the hope that an ally in DR Congo would help in achieving secure borders. However, Uganda rapidly became disenchanted with Kabila, and, with Rwanda, began supporting the Rassemblement Congolais pour la Democratie (RCD) against the DR Congo government. RCD has since split into factions based on Goma (supported by Rwanda) and Kisingani (backed by Uganda). As a result there was fighting between Rwandan and Ugandan troops who were at one time allies. In 1999 there was a peace agreement signed in Lusaka, with the UN committing 500 observers and promising 5000 peace keepers after a ceasefire was established.

East African Integration

The three British territories in East Africa, Kenya, Tanzania and Uganda, were closely linked in the colonial period. The three all used the same currency (the East African shilling), and many services were common to the three territories including customs and internal revenue, the court of appeal, the postal and telecommunications services, railway and higher education (Makerere University). There was free trade between them.

After Independence the three countries began setting up their own currencies and central banks, but the creation of the East African Community (EAC) in 1967 with a Secretariat in Arusha Tanzania, sought to retain the free trade area and run certain services such as the railway, ports, telecommunications and airlines in common. Relations within the community were never easy, however. Tanzania and Uganda argued that the Free Trade area favoured Kenya as they both had trade deficits with their more industrialized partner. Kenya argued that its tourism sector generated most of the income from the airline, and was irked when the EAC industrial policy allocated cement factories and fertiliser plants to Tanzania and Uganda which she felt should be sited in Kenya if efficiency was the criterion.

In the early 1970s the countries began to drift apart ideologically, with Kenya retaining a strong private sector, Tanzania nationalizing everything (including butcher's shops) and Uganda descending into the anarchy of the Amin years. In 1977 Kenya bailed out the railways when Tanzania and Uganda were unable to remit funds to pay salaries, but when the situation occurred again, Kenya announced that they were withdrawing from the community. It is said that they chose a moment when all the EA Airlines planes were in Kenya, and there were teams ready to paint them with the new Kenya Airways logo. Tanzania retaliated by closing the border with Kenya. A dispute over who owned what dragged on and was finally settled by World Bank mediation in 1982.

The border was re-opened and Kenya promptly launched the Nairobi Railway Museum, having previously kept quiet about the historic steam engines it had collected in case Tanzania and Uganda claimed a share of them.

Negotiations began in 1993 to establish the East African Cooperation with a Secretariat again in Arusha, with the objectives of re-establishing free trade between the parties, setting up a regional assembly and a court of justice. The new treaty, signed in 1999 re-established the East African Community, and has the eventual objective of political federation, although progress on this, as with all the other measures, has been very slow.

In early 2002 an East African newspaper carried a story that East Africa would become the Swahili Nation in October, with President Moi as the Supreme Leader, and Idi Amin recalled as Minister for Humanity. The date of the announcement was 1 April.

The assassination of Kabila in January 2001 saw the leadership of DR Congo pass to Joseph Kabila, the former president's son. There were hopes that the new regime would show a more sympathetic approach to an effective peace deal.

In the first months of 2002, an Anglo-French initiative held talks with the presidents of Burundi, DR Congo, Rwanda and Uganda. The plan was to offer increased aid in return for disarmament in the region but no progress was made. Although Rwanda insists that its presence in DR Congo is to prevent incursions by Hutu dissidents, it is thought that a further motive is the desire to continue profiting from mineral extracted in DR Congo. It is estimated that Rwanda earns US$12 million a year from coltan (a mixture of columbite and tantalite). As capacitors use tantalum, and are therefore found in mobile phones and computers, the potential market is vast. With this in mind Britain is proposing that multinationals be prevented from trading in minerals if this trade sustains conflicts.

In April 2002, a deal was struck to form an interim government formed from Kabila's administration and the rebel Movement for Congolese Liberation (MLC). However, the RCD factions are not party to the agreement, nor are several other opportunistic armed groups in the area, and it is unlikely that this initiative will herald the end of the conflicts. A historic peace agreement was signed in July 2002 between Rwanda and DR Congo, with Rwanda withdrawing its troops and DR Congo disarming the Hutu militia, the Interahamwe.

The LRA is now fragmented and in 2005 became established in northeast DR Congo. This led to the US backing an expedition to destroy the LRA bases. Some success was achieved, but Kony has not been captured, and an estimated 200 or so terrorists remain, causing misery quite out of proportion to their numbers, and culminating in extensive massacres in 2009 in DR Congo. Since 2006 when the LRA rebels were driven out of Uganda much reconstruction progress has been made.

Economy

Economic strategy has fluctuated, with Obote initially pledging to pursue a socialist development path, followed by the chaos of the Amin years which included the expulsion of the skilled Asian community. The restored Obote regime relied on market forces, but lack of security prevented any substantial progress. Museveni spent a while considering development options, but has now committed the government to an IMF-supported market-orientated strategy.

Economic structure

The population in mid-2010 was estimated at 32.4 million. The uplands in the east and west form the most densely populated areas, whereas the west has low population densities. The average population density is 138 persons per sq km, and this is about four times the African average. Urban population, at 13% of the total, is low. Turmoil in the past has led many to flee the towns to survive by subsistence production in the countryside. As urban employment opportunities have expanded only slowly, many people have been reluctant to return. The population growth rate at 2.7% a year is high despite the impact of AIDS, and this rate results from a high birth rate, with 6.7 children born, on average, to each woman.

GDP in 1999 was US$15.7 billion (exchange rate conversion) and US$38.2 (purchasing power parity conversion). In terms of economic size it is a medium-sized economy among the East African group. Income estimated by the exchange rate conversion method was US$486 per head, placing Uganda firmly in the low-income category. Estimated by purchasing power of the currency it is rather higher, at US$1200 per head, but again this indicates low-income status.

Agriculture provides 24% of GDP. It is even more important in that it provides the livelihood of around 82% of the population. Industry generates 25% of GDP, but incomes are high in this sector, as it comprises only 5% of total employment. Similarly services contribute 52% of GDP, but make up only 13% of employment.

Most expenditure, as to be expected in a low-income economy, is in private consumption. Investment is slightly higher than the African average and is supported by donor contributions to rehabilitation of infrastructure. Government spending is low, and reflects limited ability to raise revenue and to administer and monitor spending.

Exports make a contribution at 24% of GDP, although this probably underestimates export activity as the main crop, coffee, is easy to smuggle out through neighbouring states, where prices are often higher. Exports are 70% coffee, with gold at 8% and fish at 6%. Imports are 27% of GDP, and this level can only be sustained, in view of the earnings from exports, by aid from the donor community. Imports are mostly machinery and transport equipment (47%) and fuel (21%).

Economic performance

Given the state of the economy following the Amin period and its aftermath, Uganda has made an excellent recovery. GDP growth was around 5.3% a year in 2009 and living standards are rising by 1.6% a year.

It is the resurgence of the industrial and services sectors, boosted by the return of the Asian community, that has spearheaded this performance. In recent years, the inflation rate has varied, and is currently at 13% a year. This is a higher inflation rate than earlier in the decade, and as a result the value of the Ugandan shilling is depreciating at 25% a year.

Aid is very important and comprises 14% of total income. Without this support, the level of imports could not be sustained, essential agricultural inputs of machinery and fuel would fall and economic progress would be impossible to maintain.

Recent economic developments
In May 1987 President Museveni ended the period of indecision over Uganda's economic strategy when agreement was reached on a programme with the IMF on a return to a market-based economic strategy. The Kampala Stock Exchange opened for business in January 1988.

A privatization programme is under way, with 90 enterprises sold or liquidated out of a total of 148. Progress has been slow as it has proved difficult to value assets and confirm trading records to present to potential buyers. Tourism dipped in 2005 to 467,000 arrivals, but had recovered strongly to 843,000 visitors by 2008.

Economic outlook
Future prospects depend on the maintenance of political stability and internal security. The problems in the north, the northeast and the southwest, and the hostile groups operating from DR Congo, have dented Uganda's image. If these problems can be contained and brought under control, confidence will increase and international business will be encouraged to continue to expand investment. As things stand, Uganda can expect to enjoy rising living standards, and this modest pace of improvement will accelerate if mining can be restored to the levels of the 1960s and tourism continues to expand.

Social conditions
Adult literacy is about 67%, and has recovered from the disruption of the Amin years and the aftermath. Life expectancy is 52 years, and has improved dramatically from 42 years just a decade ago.

Uganda introduced a Universal Primary Education Programme in 1997, and in two years the numbers enrolled doubled, and the enrolment rate is now around 97%. Secondary and tertiary provision is less good with enrolments at 22% and 4% respectively.

There is a high participation of women in work outside the home, caused by the heavy reliance on subsistence production and demands on women to contribute to household farm production. The burden on women is increased by large family sizes and low access to contraception.

Culture

People
The largest group in Uganda are the Baganda (Bantu) with 16% of the total. Other main groups are the Soga (Bantu) with 8%; the Nkole (Bantu) with 8%; the Teso (Nilotic) with 8%; the Kiga (Bantu) with 7%; the Lango (Nilotic) with 6%; the Gisu (Bantu) with 5%; the Acholi (Nilotic) with 4% and the Alur (Nilotic) with 4%. The Ik are a small group of remote mountain people who inhabit a chain of volcanic mountains in the northeast of the country between the Timu Forest bordering Kenya and Kidepo Valley National Park. In all, there are 14 groups with more than 1% of the population. Prior to their expulsion by Amin in 1972 the Asians comprised about 2% of the total, and their community numbered 70,000. There were also around 10,000 Europeans.

Ugandan peoples

There are over 30 ethnic groups in Uganda. The peoples of Bantu origin occupy southern Uganda, and in total comprise about half of the population. They are not an ethnic group, but are identified by unique linguistic similarities. They are thought to have migrated from West Africa in several waves over the period AD 1000 to AD 1300.

Of these the Baganda, the largest ethnic group estimated at 16% of the total population, live in central and southern Uganda. In western Uganda several ethnic groups are found including the Bakiga from the far southwest, the Banyankore who lived in the Kingdom of Ankole, centred around Mbarara, the Batoro who came from the Kingdom of Toro in the foothills of the Rwenzori mountains, the Bamba bordering DR Congo in Bundibugyo district and the Bakojo from the Kasese district. Further north the Banyoro peopled the ancient Bunyoro-Kitara Kingdom, and their descendants are found around Kibale and Mubende districts and part of Luwero district. In eastern Uganda, the Basoga occupy the area around Jinja, and to the north the Bagisu inhabit Mbale and the foothills of Mount Elgon.

Many travellers find Bantu languages bewildering because they have an elaborate morphological system of noun and verb prefixing, making several words from a common root. The prefix 'ba' refers to an ethnic group or people; the prefix 'bu' refers to the land that they occupy; the prefix 'lu' refers to their language; the prefix 'mu' refers to an individual; and the prefix 'ki' refers to their customs. For example: the Baganda people live in the traditional Kingdom of Buganda and speak a language called Luganda. The singular form of Baganda is Muganda, and Kiganda refers to their culture and customs. The generic term Ganda is sometimes used for all these terms by non-native scholars.

Nilotic groups migrated from north of present-day Uganda somewhat later than the Bantu, around the 15th to 18th centuries. The Teso, of Nilo-Hamitic origin, (sometimes referred to as the Iteso) are a major group in eastern Uganda mainly living in and around Soroti district. Northeast Uganda is where the hunter/pastoralist Karamajong people are found. Classified as Nilo-Hamitic they are believed to have common origins with the Teso and the Lango, one of the largest ethnic groups, from northwest Uganda. The Acholi, also classified as being of Nilo-Hamitic origin, occupy the area north of the Langi up to the border with Sudan. Two major groups of Sudanic peoples are found in the far northwest Uganda: the Lugbara and the Madi.

Land and environment

Geography

Uganda is a medium-sized landlocked state bordered by Sudan, Kenya, Tanzania, Rwanda and DR Congo (formerly Zaïre). Uganda lies between latitude 4° North to 1° South and longitude 30° West to 33° East. It forms part of the Central African plateau, dropping to the White Nile Basin in the north. Lake Kyoga and Lake Albert lie in the Rift Valley and much of the territory to the south is swampy marsh. To the east is savannah and the western part of the country forms the margins of the Congo forests. Generally speaking, the south is agricultural and the north is pastoral. Over 75% of the land area is suitable for cultivation or grazing, and, despite population growth, there are still extensive uncultivated areas, with only about a quarter of the land suitable for arable agriculture being cultivated.

There are hydroelectric schemes on the Owen Falls Dam. Mineral resources include copper, tin, bismuth, wolfram, colombo-tantalite, phosphates, limestone, gold, the gemstone beryl and the recent discovery of oil deposits close to Lake Albert.

Climate

Temperatures vary little in an equatorial climate but are made cooler and wetter by altitude. Rainfall, greatest in the mountains and the Lake Victoria region, reaches an annual average of up to 200 cm. Elsewhere it averages 125 cm but the dry northeast and parts of the south receive less than 75 cm. The dry season lasts only one month in the centre and west, but three months (June, July and August) in the south. There are two dry seasons in the north and northeast, in October and from December to March, making two harvests possible.

Environment

Economic collapse invariably has an adverse effect on afforestation in low-income countries. There is increased demand for land and wood fuel for cooking, and in Uganda the forested area has been diminishing by about 1% a year.

Freshwater supplies are plentiful with adequate rainfall, resulting from the high altitude and location by Lake Victoria. Low industrial output means annual water usage per head is low, and only 0.3% of renewable freshwater supplies is used.

Further reading

Anthropology

Knappert, J *The Aquarian Guide to African Mythology*, Wellingborough: Aquarian Press, 1990. Entries on the Alur, Ankole, Buganda, Bunyoro, Busoga and Teso.

Thomas, EM *Warrier Herdsmen*, London: Secker & Warburg, 1965. Fascinating account of the day-to-day life of the Dodoth people of northeast Uganda, and the neighbouring cattle-raiding Turkana.

Archaeology

Sutton, J E G *Archaeological Sites of East Africa,* Nairobi: British Institute in East Africa, 1998. Has a scholarly section on the sites at Ntusi and Bigo in Uganda.

Art

Phillips, T (ed) *Africa – the Art of a Continent,* London: Royal Academy of Arts, 1995. Section on East Africa covers the art of the Acholi, Nyoro and the Karamajong in Uganda.

Rychner, R *Contemporary Art in Uganda,* Kampala: Ugandan Artist Promotion Committee, 1996. Biographies and colour photographs of the work of 17 modern Ugandan artists, illustrating how the unique eye and imagination of African sculptors and painters has been extended by the use of modern materials.

Biography

Bierman, J *Dark Safari,* New York: Alfred Knopf, 1990. The life of Henry Morton Stanley, who found David Livingstone at Ujiji and who later made 2 great journeys across Africa from coast to coast, from the east in 1874-1877 and from the west in 1887-1889, passing through Uganda on both occasions.

de Bunsen, B *Adventures in Education,* Kendal: Titus Wilson, 1995. Autobiography of the principal of Makerere when it was the University College of East Africa, running from the colonial period to the early years of Independence, revealing well how Africa gets into your blood.

Herne, B *Uganda Safaris,* Tulsa: Winchester Press, 1979. White hunter's experiences in Uganda from 1956-1976, with excellent observation of the period, peoples, customs and laws.

Manyolo, CS, **Carr-Gomm, R**, **Lion Clan Representative** *Coronation Special Souvenir* Kampala: World of Women Publications, 1993. A charming account of the coronation of Ssaabasajja Labaka Ronald Muwenda Mutebi II, with background on the Buganda people.

Mukasa, H *Uganda's Katikiro in England,* Manchester: Manchester University Press, 1998. An enchanting account (originally in Luganda) of the visit of Sir Apolo Kakwa, chief minister of Buganda, to the 1902 coronation of King Edward VII in London, written by his secretary.

Theroux, P *Sir Vidia's Shadow,* London: Hamish Hamilton, 1998. The story of the travel writer's friendship with Nobel Prizewinner for Literature VS Naipaul, which began at Makerere University in Uganda in 1966 and ended in 1997 in London.

Fiction

Foden, G *The Last King of Scotland,* London: Faber and Faber, 1998. Fictionalized account of a medic serving in Uganda, engaged as Idi Amin's personal doctor. Captures well the mood of Uganda in the 1970s. Made into a film of the same name in 2006.

Theroux, P *Fong and the Indians,* New York: Houghton Mifflin (included in Theroux, P, 1996 *On the edge of the Great Rift Valley*

London: Penguin), 1968. A novel about a Chinese grocer living in Kampala in the 1960s.
Theroux, P *The Collected Short Stories*, New York: Viking, 1977. Includes vignettes of life in Uganda.

Field guides

Blundell, M *Wild Flowers of East Africa*, London: Harper Collins, 1994. Comprehensive, includes maps, glossary and illustrations.
Guggisberg, C *Mammals of East Africa: Ungulates, Carnivores, Primates*, Nairobi: Sapra Studio, 1970. Black and white illustrations and photographs of 275 species in East Africa.
Hosking, D and **Withers, M** *Larger Animals of East Africa*, London: Harper Collins, 1996. Describes 76 common East African species, each photographed with descriptive text.
Kingdon, J *The Kingdon Field Guide to Mammals*, 1997 New York: Academic Press. Written and illustrated by Kingdon. Over 1000 mammals described.
Schaller, G *The Year of the Gorilla*, Chicago: Chicago University Press, 1997. Very readable account of the mountain gorilla in its forest environment.
Stevenson, T, and **Fanshawe, J** *Field Guide to the Birds of East Africa*, New York: Academic Press, 2001. Comprehensive guide to the resident and migratory birds of this region.
Williams, J *Birds of East Africa*, London: Harper Collins, 1995. Describes 1283 species with 660 colour illustrations.

General

Hansen, B and **Twaddle, M** (eds) *Uganda Now*, London: James Currey, 1988. An excellent series of essays on the political, economic and social problems that have plagued Uganda since Independence.

History

Coster, G *Corsairville*, London: Viking, 2000. Splendid account of the flying boat service from Southampton to Durban, touching down on Lake Victoria. Written around a flying boat that turned left by mistake on leaving Port Bell, Kampala, crash landed on the River Dunga in the then Belgian Congo, and was (eventually) successfully repaired and flown out.
Dowden, R *Africa: Altered States, Ordinary Miracles* London: Portobello Books, 2009. Excellent compassionate analysis of this troubled continent's history.
Hill, M F *Permanent Way: The story of the Kenya and Uganda Railway*, Nairobi: East Africa Literature Bureau, 1949. Classic scholarly work delivers exactly what it says in the title, with plenty of reference to the historical, political and anthropological background to the project.
Hills, D *The White Pumpkin*, London: Random House, 1976. An analysis of the politics, government and social conditions during the turbulent times of Idi Amin by the lecturer whose life was threatened by the despot.
Jorgensen, J J *Uganda: A Modern History*, 1981. Particularly strong on the economic history of Uganda.
Miller, C *Lunatic Express*, London: MacMillan, 1971. Weaves the history of East Africa round the story of the building of the Uganda Railway, from Mombasa to Kampala, well researched, engagingly written, and with a fine eye for the bizarre and amusing.
Moorehead, A *The White Nile*, London: Hamish Hamilton, 1960. Highly readable account of exploration to find the source of the Nile.

Natural history

Blundell, M A *Field Guide to the Wild Flowers of East Africa*, London: Collins, 1987.
Dorst, J and **Dandelot, P A** *Field Guide to the Larger Mammals of Africa*, 1970, London: Collins.
Hedges, N R *Reptiles and Amphibians of East Africa*, Narobi: Kenya Literature Bureau, 1983.

Larcassam, R *Handguide to the Butterflies of East Africa*, London: Collins, 1971.
Williams, J and **Arlott, N A** *Field Guide to the Birds of East Africa*, London: Collins, 1980.

Travelogues

Burton, RF *The Lake Regions of Central Africa*, London: Constable and Company, 1995. Reissue of the original 1860 account of the great explorer's travels around Lake Victoria.
Busk, D *The Fountain of the Sun*, London: Max Parrish, 1957. Travels in East Africa which includes expeditions to the Ruwenzori range, and some splendid colour photographs.

Churchill, W *My African Journey*, London: Hodder & Stoughton, 1908. Engaging account by the young politician, which displays an infectious enthusiasm for Uganda and which coined the phrase 'Pearl of Africa'.
Murphy, D *Ukimwi Road*, London: Flamingo, 1994. A trip by bicycle from Kenya to Zambia, taking in Uganda by an intrepid sexagenarian Irish traveller.
Speke, J H and **Grant, J** *Journal of the Discovery of the Source of the Nile*, New York: Dover Publications, 1996. Reissue of the tale of the epic journey which established that the source of the Nile is at Jinja in Uganda.

Contents

Footnotes

Index → *Entries in* **bold** *refer to maps*

Y

yellow fever 36

Z

Ziwa Rhino Sanctuary 126

Notes

Notes

Notes

Acknowledgements

Initial background material came from Grace Carswell and Margaret Carswell who wrote on the flora and fauna of Uganda.

Recognition is due to the large number of people who have contributed to the update of this book. David Cecil and his colleagues David Wasamoyo and Moses Gebrehiwot helped update Kampala. Peter Knight of All Terrain Vehicles and Mark Vine, Operations Manager at NRE were unfailingly helpful about activities at Bujagali. John Hunwick of Rwenzori Trekking Services contributed an excelllent map of their treks. Richard Smith of Red Chilli Hideaway, Shaz Webb, Softpower and Grace Muhindo of Marasa helped update Murchison Falls. Liz Willoughby, Rose Musoke and her VSO colleagues Poppy Krivine of Kisoro, Michaela Much of Kabale, Andy Farrer of Bwindi, Liz & Michael Watson of Gulu and Debs Kay of Lira all helped enormously with the update inputting their local knowledge. Grateful thanks are also due to Ineke Jongerius, Joseph Kirigwajjo, Jayne Wick, Richard (Tony) Powell and Lyn Jordaan, Angie Genade, Mutebi Hassan, Ntambi Africa, Miranda Bekkers, Sheba Hanyurwa, Onzi Muyindo, Michaela Piehl, Steve Williams, Agnes Nakanjako and Felex, of Ruboni Community Camp, who have all helped to provide useful information and deserve recognition.

Credit is also due to the team at Footprint, in particular Jo Williams and Nicola Gibbs who have greatly enhanced the finished result by judicious editing.

Credits

Footprint credits

Project editor: Nicola Gibbs
Text editor: Jo Williams
Layout and production: Emma Bryers
Cover and colour section: Pepi Bluck
Maps: Kevin Feeney
Proofreading: Jo Williams

Managing Director: Andy Riddle
Commercial Director: Patrick Dawson
Publisher: Alan Murphy
Publishing Managers: Felicity Laughton,
Nicola Gibbs
Digital Editors: Jo Williams, Jen Haddington,
Tom Mellors
Marketing and PR: Liz Harper
Sales: Diane McEntee
Advertising: Renu Sibal, Elizabeth Taylor
Finance and administration:
Elizabeth Taylor

Photography credits

Front cover: Lion resting in tree,
Andrew Plumptre / photolibrary.com
Back cover: Karimojong women by
Mount Kadam, McPHOTO / age fotostock

Printed in India by Nutech Print Services

Every effort has been made to ensure that
the facts in this guidebook are accurate.
However, travellers should still obtain advice
from consulates, airlines, etc about travel
and visa requirements before travelling.
The authors and publishers cannot
accept responsibility for any loss, injury
or inconvenience however caused.

Publishing information

Footprint Uganda
3rd edition
© Footprint Handbooks Ltd
May 2011

ISBN: 978 1 907263 41 5
CIP DATA: A catalogue record for this book
is available from the British Library

® Footprint Handbooks and the Footprint
mark are a registered trademark of
Footprint Handbooks Ltd

Published by Footprint
6 Riverside Court
Lower Bristol Road
Bath BA2 3DZ, UK
T +44 (0)1225 469141
F +44 (0)1225 469461
footprinttravelguides.com

Distributed in the USA by Globe Pequot
Press, Guilford, Connecticut

Colour section photography credits

P1: William Gray. P2-3: Martin Zwick / age fotostock. P6-7: Pichugin Dmitry / shutterstock.
P8: Olivier Goujon / Robert Harding World Imagery.

Map symbols

▢ Capital city	▬ Building
○ Other city, town	▪ Sight
International border	♱♰ Cathedral, church
Regional border	♨ Chinese temple
⊖ Customs	Hindu temple
Contours (approx)	Meru
▲ Mountain, volcano	Mosque
Mountain pass	Stupa
Escarpment	✡ Synagogue
Glacier	Tourist office
Salt flat	Museum
Rocks	✉ Post office
Seasonal marshland	Police
Beach, sandbank	Ⓢ Bank
Waterfall	@ Internet
Reef	♪ Telephone
Motorway	Ⓜ Market
Main road	Medical services
Minor road	Ⓟ Parking
Track	Petrol
Footpath	Golf
Railway	Archaeological site
Railway with station	♦ National park,
✈ Airport	wildlife reserve
Bus station	Viewing point
Ⓜ Metro station	▲ Campsite
Cable car	Refuge, lodge
Funicular	Castle, fort
Ferry	Diving
Pedestrianized street	Deciduous, coniferous,
Tunnel	palm trees
One way-street	Mangrove
Steps	Hide
Bridge	Vineyard, winery
Fortified wall	Distillery
Park, garden, stadium	Shipwreck
Sleeping	✕ Historic battlefield
Eating	Related map
Bars & clubs	

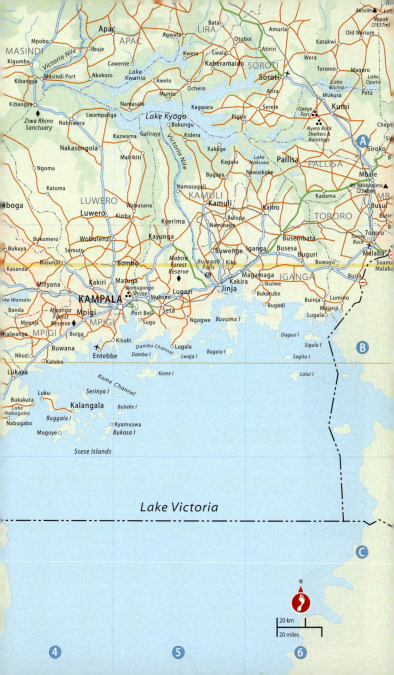

Footprint story

It was 1921

Ireland had just been partitioned, the British miners were striking for more pay and the federation of British industry had an idea. Exports were booming in South America – how about a handbook for businessmen trading in that far away continent? The Anglo-South American Handbook was born that year, written by W Koebel, the most prolific writer on Latin America of his day.

1924

Two editions later the book was 'privatized' and in 1924, in the hands of Royal Mail, the steamship company for South America, it became The South American Handbook, subtitled 'South America in a nutshell'. This annual publication became the 'bible' for generations of travellers to South America and remains so to this day. In the early days travel was by sea and the Handbook gave all the details needed for the long voyage from Europe. What to wear for dinner; how to arrange a cricket match with the Cable & Wireless staff on the Cape Verde Islands and a full account of the journey from Liverpool up the Amazon to Manaus: 5898 miles without changing cabin!

1939

As the continent opened up, the South American Handbook reported the new Pan Am flying boat services, and the fortnightly airship service from Rio to Europe on the Graf Zeppelin. For reasons still unclear but with extraordinary determination, the annual editions continued through the Second World War.

1970s

Many more people discovered South America and the backpacking trail started to develop. All the while the Handbook was gathering fans, including literary vagabonds such as Paul Theroux and Graham Greene (who once sent some updates addressed to "The publishers of the best travel guide in the world, Bath, England").

1990s

During the 1990s the company set about developing a new travel guide series using this legendary title as the flagship. By 1997 there were over a dozen guides in the series and the Footprint imprint was launched.

2000s

The series grew quickly and there were soon Footprint travel guides covering more than 150 countries. In 2004, Footprint launched its first thematic guide: *Surfing Europe*, packed with colour photographs, maps and charts. This was followed by further thematic guides such as *Diving the World*, *Snowboarding the World*, *Body and Soul escapes*, *Travel with Kids* and *European City Breaks*.

2011

Today we continue the traditions of the last 90 years that have served legions of travellers so well. We believe that these help to make Footprint guides different. Our policy is to use authors who are genuine experts who write for independent travellers; people possessing a spirit of adventure, looking to get off the beaten track.

Join us online...

Follow us on **Twitter** and **Facebook** – ask us questions, speak to our authors, swap your stories, and be kept up to date with travel news and exclusive discounts and competitions.

Upload your travel pics to our **Flickr** site – inspire others on where to go next, and have your photos considered for inclusion in Footprint guides.

And don't forget to visit us at footprinttravelguides.com